HOW TO STUDY YOUR BIBLE

Rightly Handling the Word of God

Edward D. Andrews

HOW TO STUDY YOUR BIBLE

Rightly Handling the Word of God

Edward D. Andrews

Christian Publishing House

Cambridge, Ohio

Unless otherwise indicated, Scripture quotations are from the Updated American Standard Version of the Holy Scriptures, 2016 edition (UASV).

HOW TO STUDY YOUR BIBLE: Rightly Handling the Word of God

Authored by Edward D. Andrews

ISBN-13: **978-1-945757-62-4**

ISBN-10: **1-945757-62-0**

Table of Contents

INTRODUCTION Why Have Some Christians Taken to Deeper Bible Studies While Others Have Not?

The Six Major Contributing Factors

There are **SIX major contributing factors** as to why some Christians have taken to deeper studies while others have not.

The **FIRST contributing factor** that contributed to **the wave of interest** in such fields as hermeneutics (Biblical Interpretation), textual criticism of the Old and New testament (TC), Bible translation process and philosophy, church history, apologetics, among many others? Several factors have contributed to the rehabilitated awareness of such important subject areas. The internet has allowed such tools like Facebook groups, Yahoo and Google discussion boards, where scholars and laypersons alike can discuss the science and art of textual criticism and other academic areas. The internet has given the lay person many free websites that offer comprehensive information about these areas of study.

The **SECOND contributing factor** is evangelism, which has created a resurgence of this deeper studies for churchgoers. **Evangelism** is the work of a Christian evangelist, of which all true Christians are obligated to partake to some extent, which seeks to persuade other people to become Christian, especially by sharing the basics of the Gospel, but also the

1

deeper message of biblical truths. Today the Gospel is almost an unknown, so what does the Christian evangelist do? **Preevangelism** is laying a foundation for those who have no knowledge of the Gospel, giving them background information, so that they are able to grasp what they are hearing. The Christian evangelist is preparing their mind and heart so that they will be receptive to the biblical truths. In many ways, this is known as apologetics.

Christian Apologetics [Greek: *apologia*, "verbal defense, speech in defense"] is a field of **Christian theology** which endeavors to offer a reasonable and sensible basis for the **Christian faith**, defending the faith against objections. It is reasoning from the Scriptures, explaining and proving, as one instructs in sound doctrine, many times having to overturn false reasoning before he can plant the seeds of truth. It can also be earnestly contending for the faith and saving one from losing their faith, as they have begun to doubt. Moreover, it can involve rebuking those who contradict the truth. It is being prepared to make a defense to anyone who asks the Christian evangelist for a reason for the hope that is in him or her.–Jude 1.3, 21-23; 1 Pet 3.15; Acts 17:2-3; Titus 1:9.

What do we mean by **obligated** and what we mean by **evangelism** are at the heart of the matter and are indeed related to each other?

EVANGELISM: An evangelist is a proclaimer of the gospel or good news, as well as all biblical truths. There are levels of evangelism, which is pictured in first-century Christianity. All Christians evangelized in the first century, but a select few fit the role of a full-time evangelist (Ephesians 4:8, 11-12), as was true of Philip and Timothy.

Both Philip and Timothy are specifically mentioned as evangelizers. (Ac 21:8; 2 Tim. 4:5) Philip was a full-time evangelist after Pentecost, who was sent to the city of Samaria, having great success. An angel even directed Philip to an Ethiopian Eunuch, to share the good news of Christ with him. Because of the Eunuch's already having knowledge of God by way of the Old Testament, Philip was able to help him understand that the Hebrew Scriptures pointed to Christ as the long-awaited Messiah. In the end, Philip baptized the Eunuch. Thereafter, the Spirit again sent Philip on a mission, this time to Azotus and all the cities on the way to Caesarea. (Ac 8:5, 12, 14, 26-40) Paul evangelized in many lands, setting up one congregation after another. (2 Cor. 10:13-16) Timothy was an evangelizer or missionary, and Paul placed distinct importance on evangelizing when he gave his parting encouragement to Timothy. –2 Timothy 4:5; 1 Timothy 1:3.

The office of apostle and evangelist seem to overlap in some areas, but could be distinguished in that apostles traveled and set up congregations, which took evangelizing skills, but also developed the congregations after they were established. The evangelists were more of a missionary, being stationed in certain areas to grow and develop congregations. In addition, if we look at all of the apostles and the evangelists, plus Paul's more than one hundred traveling companions, it seems very unlikely that they could have had Christianity at over one million by the 125 C.E. This was accomplished because all Christians were obligated to carry out some level of evangelism.

OBLIGATED: In the broadest sense of the term for evangelizer, all Christians are obligated to play some role as an evangelist.

• *Basic Evangelism* is planting seeds of truth and watering any seeds that have been planted. [In the basic sense of this word (euaggelistes), this would involve all Christians.] In some cases, it may be that one Christian planted the seed, which was initially rejected, so he was left in a good way because the planter did not try to force the truth down his throat. However, later he faces something in life that moves him to reconsider those seeds and another Christian waters what had already been planted by the first Christian. This evangelism can be carried out in all of the methods that are available: informal, house-to-house, street, phone, the internet, and the like. What amount of time is invested in the evangelism work is up to each Christian to decide for themselves?

• *Making Disciples* is having any role in the process of getting an unbeliever from his unbelief state to the point of accepting Christ as his Savior and being baptized. Once the unbeliever has become a believer, he is still developed until he has become strong. Any Christian could potentially carry this one person through all of the developmental stages. On the other hand, it may be that several have some part. It is like a person that specializes in a certain aspect of a job, but all are aware of the other aspects, in case they are called on to carry out that phase. Again, each Christian must decide for themselves what role they are to have, and how much of a role, but should be prepared to fill any role if needed.

• *Part-Time or Full-Time Evangelist* is one who sees this as their calling and chooses to be very involved as an evangelist in their local church and community. They may work part-time to supplement their work as an evangelist. They may be married with children, but they realize their gift is in the field of evangelism. If it were the wife, the husband would work toward supporting her work as an evangelist and vice-versa. If it were a single person, he or she would supplement their work by being employed part-time, but also the church would help as well. This person is well trained in every aspect of bringing one to Christ.

• *Congregation Evangelists* should be very involved in evangelizing their communities and helping the church members play their role at the basic levels of evangelism. There is nothing to say that one church could not have many within, who take on part-time or full-time evangelism within the congregation, which would and should be cultivated.

The **THIRD contributing factor** for the renewed interest is the New Atheist, Agnostic, and Skeptic, who seeks to cast doubt on the existence of God and his Word. These new critics of God and the Bible are different from those of say 60-years ago, as they are far more evangelistic than even Christianity. These new critics pen many books, magazine articles, advertise on billboards, news, and radio shows, and publicly debate Bible scholars. They seem to be everywhere and are contributing to the spiritual shipwreck of tens of thousands of Christians.

The adult Christian came on the internet in a burst (1993-2003), ready to share their faith based on decades of studying children's books about the Bible. You know, those booklets about 120 pages long that cover as doctrine or the whole of a Bible book like Romans, written on a 6th-7th-grade level, and some even having cartoon illustrations. This coupled with dumbed-down Bible translations like the GNT, CEV, NLT, even the NIV.

WHAT HAPPENED NEXT? The Christians by the hundreds of thousands were terribly defeated by the atheists and Bible critics who were far more informed. It was an absolute slaughter. Some tucked their tail and ran. A handful stayed and decided the only way to overcome this mountain like obstacle was to take on a personal deeper Bible study program. Apologetic books, textual criticism books, Hermeneutic books, Bible translation books, Bible Difficulty books, began to become best sellers. They developed their own personal Bible study program where they studied for 30-60 minutes each day of the week. They prepared for the Christian meeting by studying what was going to be covered. They commented and participated in meetings that allowed such.

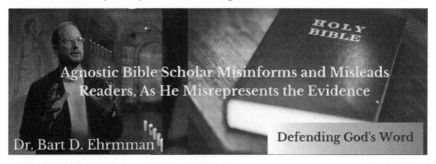

Agnostic Bible Scholar Misinforms and Misleads Readers, As He Misrepresents the Evidence

Dr. Bart D. Ehrmman

Defending God's Word

THEN came Dr. Agnostic Bart. D. Ehrman in 2005 with his New York Times Bestseller *Misquoting Jesus: The Story Behind Who Changed the Bible and Why*

Over the past eleven plus years, it has taken a boatload of scholars just to contain this Michael Jordan of textual criticism. Some were initially mad at him for writing on a popular level, but that was the conduit, which opened the floodwaters. His book and others like them became the bullets in the gun of the atheist who was decimating the average Christian. Then we had Daniel Wallace, Timothy Paul Jones, Randall Price, Craig A. Evans, Darrel Bock, M. James Sawyer, and others trying to deal with this onslaught. All the while, textual scholars were moving from the goal of getting back to the original to the earliest possible text.

EHRMAN has been a blessing and a curse. He has been a blessing because he has woken the Christians to the idea of real Bible study, real in-depth research. He has also stirred some publishers at the thought of taking highly technical subjects and making them available to the average Christian. He has been a curse in that he has unseated the weak faith of so many. Those, whose faith had never been tested, either fought their way back or threw their hands up and became apostate cheerleaders for Ehrman. Of course, he already had the liberal-moderate scholar and student all along.

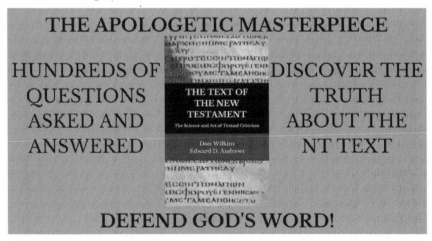

THE APOLOGETIC MASTERPIECE

HUNDREDS OF QUESTIONS ASKED AND ANSWERED

THE TEXT OF THE NEW TESTAMENT
The Science and Art of Textual Criticism
Don Wilkins
Edward D. Andrews

DISCOVER THE TRUTH ABOUT THE NT TEXT

DEFEND GOD'S WORD!

The FOURTH contributor to this renewed interest is scholarly books written for the layperson, which has enabled the churchgoer to enter the conversation. We now have a plethora of books dealing with numerous biblical fields, which enable the Christian to avoid falling into the trap of doubting, that what they have is, in fact, the Word of God, inspired and fully inerrant. There is absolutely no one to be blamed if we end up in repeated conversations that cast doubt on our beliefs and the Word of God, but ourselves.

The FIFTH contributor to this renewed interest is the words of Jesus Christ and the apostle John.

Matthew 7:21-23 Updated American Standard Version (UASV)

[21] "Not everyone who says to me, 'Lord, Lord,' will enter the kingdom of heaven, but **the one who does <u>the will</u> of my Father** who is in heaven. [22] On that day many will say to me, 'Lord, Lord, did we not prophesy in your name, and cast out demons in your name, and do many mighty works in your name?' [23] And then I will declare to them, 'I never knew you; depart from me, you who practice lawlessness.'

What is the first and foremost question we should ask? What is the will of the Father? Jesus brings up those **who wrongly believed** that they were doing the will of the Father in verse 22. "On that day many will say to me, 'Lord, Lord, did we not prophesy in your name, and cast out demons in your name, and do many mighty works in your name?'" However, Jesus has **some very bad news** for these ones in verse 23. "And then I will declare to them, 'I never knew you; depart from me, you who practice lawlessness.'" The apostle John tells us at 1 John 2:17, "The world is passing away, and its lusts; but the one who does the will of God remains forever." Who will live forever? Oh, yeah, "whoever does the will of God." There it is again, the will of the Father. We already noted that the will of the Father is the key. Thus, the second most important question is, what is the only way of knowing the will of the Father? Yes, the only way to know is by a deep study of God's Word.

If the average Christian is going to know the will of the Father truly, it will be by knowing the Word of God. We may think that we know the will of the Father but the apostle Paul has some very important advice for us. If we heed any of the words in this book, it should be these next one in the section that discusses the **SIXTH contributing factor**, which is one of the most important pieces of counsel that Paul ever gave.

2 Corinthians 13:5 Updated American Standard Version (UASV)

[5] **Keep testing** yourselves to see if you are in the faith. **Keep examining** yourselves! Or do you not realize this about yourselves, that Jesus Christ is in you, unless indeed you fail to meet the test?

When was the last time that we truly took a good look at ourselves? How did we feel about what we saw? When we ponder over our personality, what are we actually projecting to others? Most of us are very complex people when it comes to our thoughts, feeling and beliefs so it might be difficult to lock down what kind of personality that we have. As a man, are we faithful like Abraham one moment and then blown back and forth like doubting Thomas the next? As a female, are we submissive like Sarah when we are in public and then like domineering Jezebel in private? As a Christian, are we devoted and energetic for the truth on Christian meeting days and then loving the world like Demas[1] the other days out of the week? As a Christian, have we entirely taken off the old person with its practices and clothed ourselves with the new person? – Colossians 3:9-10; Ephesians 4:20-24.

Some women are known to spend much time every morning, 'putting on their face,' as it is commonly expressed. So much so, it has been commonly joked about, and men know not to interfere until the project is over. However, truth be told, men are very much concerned with how they look when going out into public. Thus, all of us are conscious of whether our hair is out of place, if we have a pimple or a cold sore, or if there is something about us that is unkempt, ruffled, scruffy, or messy. We want to look our best. What we may not have considered is, our personality is always showing as well. The deeper question though is "are we putting on our personality to cover over before we go out in public while our real personality is on display in private?" Is what the public sees, who we really are? Does our real personality bring honor to God?

A man walking the roads of the countryside in a small European country comes to a fork in the road. He is uncertain as to which way he should go. Therefore, he asks several who are passing by for directions, but some told him to take the left fork, and others said to make the right. After receiving contradictory information, he simply did not know what to do, how was he to go on, without knowing for certain which path led to the destination. He was unable to move on until he knew what the right path was. Having doubts about our faith, our walk with God, his Word can influence us similarly. It can actually cause severe emotional turmoil as we go about our Christian life.

There was a similar situation on the first-century Corinthian congregation. Some known as "super-apostles" were actually taking the apostle Paul to task, as to Paul's walk with God, saying, "His letters are

---

[1] A "fellow worker" with Paul at Rome (Col. 4:14; Philem. 24), who eventually, "in love with this present world," forsook the apostle and left for Thessalonica (2 Tim. 4:10). No other particulars are given concerning him. (ISBE, Volume 1, Page 918)

weighty and strong, but his bodily presence is weak, and his speech of no account." (2 Cor. 10:7-12; 11:5-6, ESV) Certainly, we can see how a Christian in that congregation could wonder if they were truly walking with God when the apostle Paul himself was being called into question.

Paul founded the Corinthian congregation in about 50 C.E.[2] on his second missionary journey. "When Silas and Timothy arrived from Macedonia, Paul was occupied with the word, testifying to the Jews that the Christ was Jesus. And the Lord said to Paul one night in a vision, 'Do not be afraid, but go on speaking and do not be silent, for I am with you, and no one will attack you to harm you, for I have many in this city who are my people.' And he stayed a year and six months, teaching the word of God among them." (Acts 18:5-11, ESV) The apostle Paul was deeply interested in the spiritual well-being of the brothers and sisters in Corinth. Moreover, the Corinthian Christians were interested in their spiritual welfare as well, so they wrote Paul for his counsel on certain matters. (1 Cor. 7:1-40) Therefore, Paul, under inspiration offered them inspired counsel in what would be his second letter to them.

"Keep testing yourselves to see if you are in the faith. Keep examining yourselves! Or do you not realize this about yourselves, that Jesus Christ is in you unless indeed you fail to meet the test?" (2 Cor. 13:5) If these brothers in the days of having Paul found their congregation, who spent sixteen months under the guidance of the greatest, inspired Christian, needed to self-examine themselves, how much more should we need to do so, as we are 2,000-years removed? If these brothers followed this advice to examine themselves, it would have offered them direction on how to walk with God and let them know if they were on the right path.

Remember, Jesus warned, "Not everyone who says to me, 'Lord, Lord,' will enter the kingdom of heaven, but **the one who does** the will of my Father who is in heaven." (Matt 7:21, ESV) In other words, not every Christian was going to enter into the kingdom, even though they felt that they were walking with God. Jesus spoke of their mindset in the next verse, "On that day many will say to me, 'Lord, Lord, did we not prophesy in your name, and cast out demons in your name, and do many mighty works in your name?'" (Matt. 7:22, ESV) Yes, these ones, who felt that they were walking with God, on that day they supposed that they were truly Christian, were in for a rude awakening. What is Jesus going to

---

[2] B.C.E. means "before the Common Era," which is more accurate than B.C. ("before Christ"). C.E. denotes "Common Era," often called A.D., for *anno Domini,* meaning "in the year of our Lord."

say to these ones, "And then will I declare to them, 'I never knew you; depart from me, you workers of lawlessness.'" (Matt. 7:23) What were and are these ones lacking?

Jesus said they were **not doing the will of the Father**, even though they believed they were. The words were important, so again, notice that in 98 C.E., the apostle John, the last surviving apostle, in one of his letters offered that same warning too. He wrote, "The world is passing away, and its lusts; but the one who does the will of God remains forever." (1 John 2:17) Thus, we can see the wisdom of the apostle Paul's counsel to 'Keep testing ourselves to see if you are in the faith. Keep examining ourselves!' Thus, the next question is, what do we need to do to follow this advice? How does one test whether or not they are in the faith? In addition, what does it mean to 'keep examining ourselves after we have tested ourselves?

Keep Testing Yourselves

In a **test**, there is an examination of a person or an object to find something out, e.g., whether it is functioning properly or not. In this **test**, there must be a standard by which the person or object is measured. For example, the "normal" human body temperature is 98.6°F (37°C). Therefore, if we were testing our temperature, it would be measured against the normal body temperature. Anything above or below that would be considered high or low. Another example is the normal resting heart rate for adults, which ranges from 60 to 100 beats a minute. However, our test in this publication is to see if we are truly Christian. However, what we are looking for when we 'test ourselves, to see if we are in the faith,' is **not** the faith, that is the basic Bible doctrines. In our test, we are the subject. What we are testing is, if we are truly walking with God. If we are to test our walk as a Christian, we need to have a perfect standard. Our perfect standard by which to measure ourselves is,

Psalm 19:7-8 Updated American Standard Version (UASV)

7 The law of Jehovah is perfect,
   restoring the soul;
the testimony of Jehovah is sure,
   making wise the simple.
8 The precepts of Jehovah are right,
   rejoicing the heart;

Yes, the Word of God, the Bible is the standard by which we can measure our walk with God. On this, the author of Hebrews wrote, "For the word of God is living and active and sharper than any two-edged sword, and piercing as far as the division of soul and spirit, of both joints and marrow, and able to judge the thoughts and intentions of the heart." (Heb. 4:12) Thus, we must test our walk with God by examining our life course as outlined by Scripture, to find his favor, to be in an approved standing, to be declared righteous before him. Herein, each of the twenty chapters will have a text that they will be built around, a text that defines **what we should be** in the eyes of God. For example, several times Jesus says 'if we are doing _____, we are truly his disciples.' Well, the objective would be to discover what all is involved in doing _____.

Keep Examining Yourselves

The phrase keep *examining yourselves* is self-explanatory, but it involves a self-examination. We may have been a Christian for a number of years, but how many times have we had a spiritual checkup. Every six months we are to go in for a dental cleaning and unless there is a problem, we should get a health screening once a year. The problem with our spirituality is it is far more susceptible to injury than we are physically. The author of Hebrews warns us, "We must **pay much closer attention** to what we have heard, lest we **drift away** from it." (2:1) One chapter later, we are told, "**Take care,** brothers, lest there be in any of you *an evil, unbelieving heart*, leading you to **fall away** from the living God. But exhort one another every day, as long as it is called "today," that none of you may be **hardened by the deceitfulness of sin.**" (3:12-13) This same author warns us about falling away (6:6), becoming sluggish (6:12), and growing weary or fainthearted (12:25).

Why would this be the case? If we are saved, why is it necessary that we keep examining ourselves? Why would we still be susceptible to bad behaviors to the point of drifting away, to the point of having an unbelieving heart, falling away, becoming sluggish, growing weary or fainthearted?

There are four reasons. **(1)** First and foremost, we have inherited sin, which means that we are missing the mark of perfection. **(2)** In addition, our environment can condition us into the bad thinking and behavior. **(3)** We have our human weaknesses, which include inborn tendencies that we naturally lean toward evil, leading us into bad behaviors. **(4)** Moreover, there is the world of Satan and his demons that cater to these human weaknesses, which also leads us down the path of bad thinking and behaviors. After our self-examination, what is needed if we are to overcome any bad thinking or behaviors and how are we to avoid developing them in the future? We will offer more on this in each chapter as well as two appendices at the end, but we offer this for now. It is paramount that we fully understand what all is involved in our human imperfection and never believe that we are so strong spiritually that we would never fall away, slow down, or become sluggish in our walk with God.

Obviously, this should be of the greatest concern to each one of us. We may be a person of good character, and believe that in any situation, we will make the right decisions. However, the moment that **innocent appearing situation** arises, we are plagued with the inner desire toward wrong. We need to address more than what our friends, or our workmates or our spouse may see. We need to look into our inner self, in the hopes of determining, who we really are, and what do we need to do to have a good heart (i.e., inner person).

As we know, we could not function with half a heart. However, we can function, albeit dysfunctional, with a heart that is divided. Yes, we have things outside of us that can contribute to bad thinking, which if left unchecked will lead to bad behavior, but we also have some things within. The apostle Paul bewailed about himself, "For I do not do the good I want, but the evil I do not want is what I keep on doing. Now if I do what I do not want, it is no longer I who do it, but sin that dwells within me." (Romans 7:19-20) This is because all of us are mentally bent toward the doing of wrong, instead of the doing of good. (Gen 6:5; 8:21; Rom 5:12; Eph. 4:20-24; Col 3:5-11) Jeremiah the prophet informs us of the condition of our heart (our inner person), "The heart is deceitful above all things, and desperately sick; who can understand it?" These factors contribute to our being more vulnerable to the worldly desires and the weak human flesh than we may have thought. One needs to understand just how bad human imperfection is before they can fully implement the right **Christian Living Skills**.

Returning to the book of Hebrews, we are told, "solid food belongs to the mature, to those who through practice have their discernment trained to distinguish between good and evil." (5:14) We will have evidence that we are one of the mature ones by training ourselves to distinguish between good and evil. We likely believe that we are already spiritually mature, which may very well be the case. Nevertheless, we are told by Paul to carry out this self-examination and to keep on examining ourselves, to remain that way, and even to improve upon what we currently have by way of maturity. Just as a man or woman in a marathon must continually train their muscles to surpass others in the sport, our discernment (perception) needs to be trained through regularly and rightly applying the Word of God. Throughout this publication, we will apply the inspired words of James, Jesus' half-brother.

James 1:22-25 Updated American Standard Version (UASV)

²² But be doers of the word, and not hearers only, deceiving yourselves. ²³ For if anyone is a hearer of the word and not a doer, he is like a man who looks intently at his natural face³ in a mirror.

²⁴ for he looks at himself and goes away, and immediately forgets what sort of man he was. ²⁵ But he that looks into the perfect law, the law of liberty, and abides by it, being no hearer who forgets but a doer of a work, he will be blessed in his doing.

When we are inundated in the Word of God, it serves as the voice of God, telling us the way in which to walk. Here are some questions to ponder. What are the **SIX factors that have contributed** to a renewed interest in deeper Bible study? Which of these five factors motivates you to do the same? How can we test whether we are truly Christian? What warning did Jesus and the apostle John give to those who believed they were doing the right things? What is involved in examining what we ourselves are? Why must we keep testing ourselves? Why must we keep examining ourselves? Why do we need to understand just how bad human imperfection is before we can fully implement the right Christian Living Skills?

---

³ Lit *the face of his birth*

CHAPTER 1 Motivation for Deeper Bible Study

The Bible is a revelation from our heavenly Father, about our heavenly Father, i.e., his will and purposes. (1 Thess. 2:13) If we take the things we learn and apply them in our lives, we will live a life far more beneficial than those who do not. As we grow in knowledge, we will draw ever closer to God, the Giver of "Every good gift and every perfect gift." (Jam. 1:17) We will discover the beauty of prayer. We will find that God is strengthening us to cope in times of trouble. If we live and walk in harmony with his Word, the opportunity of eternal life awaits us. (Rom. 6:2) However, there is but one problem that lies in our path. We have to know how to study our Bible if we are going to benefit from it. This author in this book will give you the absolute best information in this regard. Moreover, he will make it an interesting read as well as easy to understand. What lies below will serve as motivation as to why Bible study is vital to our spiritual growth, as we learn to walk with God like never before.

The Bible Gives Us Answers to Questions about Life

The Bible gives us answers to questions about this life and the one to come, which can be found nowhere else, and offers illumination to its readers. Those who take in this lifesaving knowledge are freed from the misunderstandings of life that dominate billions of others. For instance, here is one that might come to us as a shock. We are all **Mentally Bent toward Evil.**

Psalm 51:5 Updated American Standard Version (UASV)

⁵ Look, I was brought forth in error,
   and in sin did my mother conceive me.

King David had his adultery with Bathsheba and the subsequent murder of her husband exposed, for which he accepted full responsibility. His words about the human condition give us one reason for the evil of man. He says, "I was brought forth in error." What did King David's inspired words mean? **Error:** (Heb., ʿāwōn; Gr. anomia, paranomia) The Hebrew word *awon* essentially relates to erring, acting illegally or wrongly. This aspect of sin refers to committing a perverseness, wrongness, lawlessness, law breaking, which can also include the rejection of the sovereignty of God. It also focuses on the liability or guilt of one's wicked, wrongful act. This error may be deliberate or accidental; either willful deviation of what is right or unknowingly making a mistake. (Lev. 4:13-35; 5:1-6, 14-19; Num. 15:22-29; Ps 19:12, 13) Of course, if it is intentional; then, the consequence is far more serious. (Num. 15:30-31) Error is in opposition to the truth, and those willfully sinning corrupt the truth, a course that only brings forth flagrant sin. (Isa 5:18-23) We can be hardened by the deceitfulness of sin.–Ex 9:27, 34-35; Heb. 3:13-15.

David stated that his problem was a corrupt heart, saying; **surely, I was sinful at birth.** He entered this world a sinner in nature long before he became a sinner in thinking, words, and actions. In fact, this internal corruption predated his **birth,** actually beginning nine months earlier when he was **conceived** in the womb. It was at conception that the Adamic sin nature was transmitted to him. The problem with what he did, sin, arose from what he was, a sinner.[4]

What is sin? **Sin:** (Heb. *chattath*; Gr. *hamartia*) Any spoken word (Job 2:10; Ps 39:1), wrong action (Lev. 20:20; 2 Cor. 12:21) or failing to act when one should have (Num. 9:13; Jam. 4:17), in mind and heart (Prov. 21:4; Rom. 3:9-18; 2 Pet 2:12-15) that is contrary to God's personality, ways, will and purposes, standards, as set out in the Scriptures. It is also a major sin to lack faith in God, doubting in mind and heart, even subtly in our actions, that he has the ability to carry out his will and purposes. (Heb. 3:12-13, 18-19). It is commonly referred to as missing the mark of perfection.

What is a sinner? **Sinner:** (Gr. *hamartōlos*) In the Scriptures "sinners" is generally used in a more specific way, that is, referring to those willfully living in sin, practicing sin, or have a reputation of sinning.–Matt. 9:10; Mark 2:15; Luke 5:30; 7:37-39; John 9:16; Rom. 3:7; Gal. 2:15; 1 Tim. 1:15; Heb. 7:26; Jam. 4:8; 1 Pet 4:18; Jude 1:15.

David is not here casting the blame onto his mother, as God never intended mothers to conceive and give birth to children who would sin. Nevertheless, when Adam and Eve rebelled, they were expelled from the Garden of Eden, they lost their ability to pass on perfection. Therefore, every child was born missing the mark of perfection. The Hebrew term translated "sin" is *chattath;* in Greek, the word is *hamartia.* Both carry the meaning of missing the mark of perfection, namely, falling short of perfection.

---

[4] Anders, Max; Lawson, Steven (2004-01-01). Holman Old Testament Commentary - Psalms: 11 (p. 266). B&H Publishing. Kindle Edition.

The verbal forms occur in enough secular contexts to provide a basic picture of the word's meaning. In Judges 20:16 the left-handed slingers of Benjamin are said to have the skill to throw stones at targets and "not miss." In a different context, Proverbs 19:2 speaks of a man in a hurry who "misses his way" (RSV, NEB, KJV has "sinneth"). A similar idea of not finding a goal appears in Proverbs 8:36; the concept of failure is implied.[5]

Genesis 6:5 The American Translation (AT)

[5] When the LORD saw that the wickedness of man on the earth was great, and that the **whole bent of his thinking was** never anything but **evil,** the LORD regretted that he had ever made man on the earth.

Genesis 8:21 The American Translation (AT)

[21] I will never again curse the soil, though the **bent of man's mind** may be **evil from his very youth;** nor ever again will I ever again destroy all life creature as I have just done.

All of us have inherited a sinful nature, meaning that we are currently unable to live up to the mark of perfection, in which we were created. In fact, Genesis 6:5 says we all suffer from, 'our whole bent of thinking, which is nothing but evil." Genesis 8:21 says that 'our mind is evil from our very youth.' Jeremiah 17:9 says that our hearts are treacherous and desperately sick." What does all of this mean? It means that prior to the fall, our natural inclination; our natural leaning was toward good. However, after the fall, our natural inclination, our natural leaning was toward bad, wicked, evil.

We should never lose sight of the fact that unrighteous desires of the flesh are not to be taken lightly. (Rom. 7:19, 20) Nevertheless, if it is our desire to have a righteous relationship with God, it will be the stronger desire. Psalm 119:165 says, "Abundant peace belongs to those loving your law, and for them there is no stumbling block." We need to cultivate our love for doing right, which will strengthen our conscience, the sense of what is right and wrong that governs somebody's thoughts and actions, urging us to do right rather than wrong. It is only through studying the Bible that we can train the conscience. Once it is trained, it will prick us like a needle in the heart, when we are thinking of doing something wrong. It will feel like a pain in our heart, sadness, nervousness, which is the voice saying, 'do not do this.' Moreover, if we ignore our voice, it will

---

[5] G. Herbert Livingston, "638 חטא," ed. R. Laird Harris, Gleason L. Archer Jr., and Bruce K. Waltke, *Theological Wordbook of the Old Testament* (Chicago: Moody Press, 1999), 277.

grow silent over time and will stop telling us what is wrong.–Romans 2:14-15.

James 1:14-15 Updated American Standard Version (UASV)

[14] But each one is tempted when he is carried away and enticed by his own desire.[6] [15] Then the desire when it has conceived gives birth to sin, and sin when it is fully grown brings forth death.

We have a natural desire toward wrongdoing, and Satan is the god of this world (2 Cor. 4:3-4), and he caters to the fallen flesh. James also tells us "each one is tempted when he is carried away and enticed by his own desire.[7] Then the desire when it has conceived gives birth to sin, and sin when it is fully grown brings forth death." (James 1:14-15) We resist the devil by immediately dismissing any thought that is contrary to God's values found in his Word. When any wrong thought enters our mind, we do not entertain it for a moment, nor do we cultivate it, causing it to grow. We then offer rational prayers in our head, or better yet, out loud so we can defeat irrational fleshly thinking with rational biblical thinking. The Apostle Peter, referring to the Devil wrote, "Resist him, firm in your faith, knowing that the same kinds of suffering are being experienced by your brotherhood throughout the world." (1 Pet. 5:9) While the Bible helps us better to understand the gravity of our fallen condition, this should not cause us alarm as the Bible also shows us how to control our mental bent toward evil. We can renew our mind (Rom 12:2), acquire the mind of Christ (1 Cor. 2:16)), take off the old person and put on the new person (Eph. 4:20-24; Col 3:9-10), among other things.

The Bible Offers How to Get the Best out of Life Now

Another facet of benefiting from the Bible is that it shows us the way to get the best out of life now, even in imperfection.

1 Timothy 3:2 Updated American Standard Version (UASV)

[2] The overseer must be above reproach, the husband of one wife, **temperate, sober-minded,** respectable, hospitable, able to teach,

All of us can benefit now by being temperate, not just the overseers. What does being temperate mean? Knute Larson wrote, "He must also be **temperate,** or balanced, not given to extremes. *Temperate* comes from a word meaning "sober," or "calm in judgment." It carries the idea of

---

[6] Or "own *lust*"

[7] Or "own *lust*"

objective thinking and clear perspective. A temperate person is free from the influences of passion, lust, emotion, or personal gain.[8]

What did Paul mean by "sober-minded" (rendered self-controlled, LEB, HCSB) and how can we all befit from this as well? **Sober Minded:** (Gr. *nepho*) This denotes being sound in mind, to be in control of one's thought processes and thus not be in danger of irrational thinking, 'to be sober-minded, to be well composed in mind.'[9] Larson wrote, "All Christians are called to be **self-controlled**; this is an evidence of the Spirit's life within. Here Paul required that leaders model this quality. A pastor is to be in control of himself, not given to anger, personal ambition, or passions. He is to be sensible and in charge of his life. Peter told all Christians to be "self-controlled and alert. Your enemy the devil prowls around like a roaring lion looking for someone to devour" (1 Pet. 5:8). Without the power of God's Spirit, the human spirit is left alone to navigate the forces of evil and personal weaknesses. By the Spirit whom God has placed in all believers, we are given the ability to live beyond these evil influences; we are enabled to have a self that is controlled not by fallen nature but by God's kingdom goodness."[10] In just this one verse, simply looking deeper into just two words, we can see what personality changes we need to make that will make us a better Christian, a better person, and help us live a better life even in imperfection.

2 Corinthians 7:1 Updated American Standard Version (UASV)

7 Therefore, having these promises, beloved, let us **cleanse ourselves from all defilement** of flesh and spirit, perfecting holiness in the fear of God.

Richard L. Pratt Jr, wrote, "Paul insisted that the Corinthian believers **purify** themselves **from everything that contaminates.** The tabernacle instructions of Exodus 30:20–21 are evidently in view here. In the Old Testament, ritual washings symbolized the repentance and recommitment of worshipers. Paul applied this principle to the Christian life. Although the ritual washings themselves were not to be observed in the New Testament, the inward reality that they symbolized was to be observed. Note that Paul mentioned **everything.** No defilement is acceptable in the

---

[8] Knute Larson, *I & II Thessalonians, I & II Timothy, Titus, Philemon*, vol. 9, Holman New Testament Commentary (Nashville, TN: Broadman & Holman Publishers, 2000), 183.

[9] '1 Thessalonians 5:6, 8; 2 Timothy 4:5; 1 Peter 1:13; 4:7; 5:8.

[10] Knute Larson, *I & II Thessalonians, I & II Timothy, Titus, Philemon*, vol. 9, Holman New Testament Commentary (Nashville, TN: Broadman & Holman Publishers, 2000), 183.

Christian life, however small it may be. In fact, Paul had in mind both **body and spirit.** Paul probably mentioned the body in light of his discussion of the temptation to religious prostitution. Corinth was full of opportunities for fleshly defilement that led to the defilement of the inner person. Behavior is not just external; it corrupts the spirit of a person as well. Neither the behavior of the body nor the condition of the spirit should be overlooked by believers."[11]

1 Corinthians 6:18 Updated American Standard Version (UASV)

[18] **Flee from sexual immorality.** Every other sin that a man commits is outside the body, but the sexually immoral person sins against his own body.

Sexual Immorality: (Heb. *zanah*; Gr. *porneia*) A general term for immoral sexual acts of any kind: such as adultery, prostitution, sexual relations between people not married to each other, homosexuality, and bestiality.[12] Richard L. Pratt Jr. wrote, **"Flee ... immorality.** It is likely that the apostle had in mind Joseph's example of fleeing Potiphar's wife (Gen. 39:12). Paul instructed the young pastor Timothy in a similar way (2 Tim. 2:22). Rather than moderate resistance to immorality, Paul insisted on radical separation. Paul's radical advice rested on the uniqueness of sexual sin. In contrast with **all other sins,** immorality is **against** one's **own body.** The meaning of these words is difficult to determine. Many sins, such as substance abuse, gluttony, and suicide, have detrimental effects on the body. Paul's words do not refer to disease and/or other damage caused by sin. Instead, his words are linked to the preceding discussion of 6:12–17. There Paul established that Christians' bodies are joined with Christ so that they become "members of Christ" (6:15) himself. Sexual union with a prostitute violates one's body by bringing it into a wrongful "one flesh" union, and by flaunting the mystical union with Christ (6:15). It is in this sense that sexual immorality is a unique sin against the body. It violates the most significant fact about believers' physical existence: their bodies belong to Christ."[13]

In review, what have we discovered in these three texts? Is there any doubt that if we possess the quality of being sober-minded (self-control) that we will not have better health and better relationships. Through

---

[11] Richard L. Pratt Jr, *I & II Corinthians*, vol. 7, Holman New Testament Commentary (Nashville, TN: Broadman & Holman Publishers, 2000), 377.

[12] Numbers 25:1; Deuteronomy 22:21; Matthew 5:32; 1 Corinthians 5:1.

[13] Richard L. Pratt Jr, *I & II Corinthians*, vol. 7, Holman New Testament Commentary (Nashville, TN: Broadman & Holman Publishers, 2000), 101.

'cleansing ourselves from every defilement of body and spirit,' we evade damaging our health. Finally, the marriage is on safe grounds by our 'fleeing from sexual immorality.'

The Bible Offers How to Best Live In an Imperfect World

Another aspect of the Bible is that it will help us to find true happiness in this imperfect world that we live in, with the hope of even greater happiness to come. Bible knowledge helps us to discover the innermost harmony and satisfaction that this imperfect life offers, and gives us faith and hopefulness of an even greater one to come. It assists us to develop such pleasing characteristics as empathy, love, joy, peace, kindness, and faith. (Galatians 5:22, 23; Ephesians 4:24, 32) Such characteristics will help us to be a better spouse, father or mother, son or daughter, friend, coworker, student, and so on.

The Bible helps us to See What the Future Holds

Another facet of the Bible is its prophecies, which will help us to understand where we are in the stream of time, and what is yet to unfold. Notice the conditions that are coming in the text below.

Revelation 21:3-4 Updated American Standard Version (UASV)

³ And I heard a loud voice from the throne, saying, "Behold, the tabernacle of God is among men, and he will dwell[14] among them, and they shall be his people,[15] and God himself will be among them,[16] ⁴ and he will wipe away every tear from their eyes, and death shall be no more, neither shall there be mourning, nor crying, nor pain anymore, for the former things have passed away."

21:3–4. For the third and final time John hears **a loud voice from the throne** (16:17; 19:5). The word for **dwelling** is traditionally translated "tabernacle" or "tent." When the Israelites had lived in the wilderness after the exodus, God's presence was evident through the tent (Exod. 40:34). Part of the reward for Israel's obedience to God was, "I will put my dwelling place [tabernacle] among you, and I will not abhor you. I will walk among you and be your God, and you will be my people" (Lev.

---

[14] Lit *he will tabernacle*

[15] Some mss *peoples*

[16] One early ms and be *their God*

26:11–12). Israel's disobedience, of course, led finally to the destruction of the temple.

The permanent remedy began when God became enfleshed in Jesus: "The Word became flesh and made his dwelling among us" (John 1:14). A form of the same verb translated "made his dwelling" in John 1:14 is now used by the heavenly voice: **he will live with them.** Here, then, is the final eternal fulfillment of Leviticus 26.

They will be his people, and God himself will be with them and be their God is a divine promise often made, particularly in context of the new covenant (Jer. 31:33; 32:38; Ezek. 37:27; 2 Cor. 6:16). In eternity, it will find full completion in its most glorious sense. One striking note here is that the word translated "people," while often singular in Revelation (for example, 18:4), here is plural, literally "peoples." This points to the great ethnic diversity of those in heaven.

The great multitude who came out of the Great Tribulation received the pledge of many blessings including the final removal of any cause for **tears** (7:15–17). Now this promise extends to every citizen-saint of the New Jerusalem. The picture of God himself gently taking a handkerchief and wiping away all tears is overwhelming. It pictures the removal of four more enemies:

- **death**—destroyed and sent to the fiery lake (20:14; 1 Cor. 15:26)

- **mourning**—caused by death and sin, but also ironically the eternal experience of those who loved the prostitute (18:8)

- **crying**—one result of the prostitute's cruelty to the saints (18:24)

- **pain**—the first penalty inflicted on mankind at the Fall is finally lifted at last (Gen. 3:16)

All these belonged to **the old order of things** where sin and death were present. The last thought could also be translated, "The former things are gone." No greater statement of the end of one kind of existence and the beginning of a new one can be found in Scripture.[17]

[17] Kendell H. Easley, *Revelation*, vol. 12, Holman New Testament Commentary (Nashville, TN: Broadman & Holman Publishers, 1998), 394–395.

The Bible helps us Share the Good News

Romans 10:13-17 Updated American Standard Version (UASV)

¹³ For "everyone who calls on the name of the Lord will be saved."""

¹⁴ How then will they call on him in whom they have not believed? And how are they to believe in him of whom they have never heard? And how will they hear without someone to preach? ¹⁵ And how are they to preach unless they are sent? As it is written, "How beautiful are the feet of those who declare good news of good things!"[18]

¹⁶ But they have not all obeyed the gospel. For Isaiah says, "Lord,[19] who has believed what he has heard from us?" ¹⁷ So faith comes from hearing, and hearing through the word of Christ.

¹⁸ But I say, surely they have never heard, have they? Indeed they have;

"Their voice has gone out to all the earth,
   and their words to the ends of the inhabited earth."

10:14a. Calling requires faith. **How ... can they call on the one they have not believed in?** In the Old Testament, calling on the name of the Lord was a metaphor for worship and prayer (Gen. 4:26; 12:8; Ps. 116:4). No one can call out to God who has not believed in him.

10:14b. Faith requires hearing. **And how can they believe in the one of whom they have not heard?** More than anything else, this question is the crux of all missiological activity since the first century. God has ordained that people have to hear (or read, or otherwise understand the content of) the word of God in order to be saved. One who knows the gospel must communicate it to one who does not know it.

10:14c. Hearing requires preaching. **And how can they hear without someone preaching to them?** Since no other media except the human voice was of practical value in spreading the gospel in the first century, **preaching** is Paul's method of choice. And yet, in the media-rich day in which we minister, has anything replaced preaching as the most effective way to communicate the gospel? We thank God for the printed page, and even for cutting-edge presentations of the gospel circling the globe on the internet. But it is still the human voice that cracks with passion, the human

---

¹⁸ Quotation from Isa 52:7; Nah 1:15

¹⁹ Quotation from Isaiah 53:1, which reads, "Who has believed our message? And to whom has the arm of Jehovah been revealed?"

eye that wells with tears of gratitude, and the human frame that shuffles to the podium, bent from a lifetime of Service to the gospel, that reaches the needy human heart most readily. Hearing may not *require* **preaching** in person today, but it always benefits from it.

10:15. Preaching requires sending. **And how can they preach unless they are sent?** Even when his servants were unwilling (e.g., Jonah), God has been sending the message of salvation to the ends of the earth from the beginning. Paul, a "sent one" (apostle, *apostolos*), was sent to the Gentiles, and he needed the church at Rome to help him. But he also wanted them to be available for God to send them. There were many, many Jews in Rome who were still stumbling over the stone in the path of salvation. How would they ever call on the name of the Lord unless someone is sent? Paul wants the church at Rome to get in step with those who have borne good news to Israel before, most specifically those who brought the good news of their deliverance from captivity in Assyria:

Original Context	Isaiah 52:7	Romans 10:15	Paul's Application
"Good news" in its earliest contexts was that of victory in battle. In Isaiah it is deliverance from captivity in Assyria (cf. Isa. 52:4, 11–12), a type of the coming deliverance from sin.	How beautiful on the mountains are the feet of those who bring good news, who proclaim peace, who bring good tidings, who proclaim salvation, who say to Zion, "Your God reigns!"	And how can they preach unless they are sent? As it is written, "How beautiful are the feet of those who bring good news!"	Just as the "good news" was delivered to Israel in the Old Testament, so it still must be delivered in Paul's day. It is a different gospel—a better one—of permanent deliverance from captivity to sin

Six key terms, taken in reverse order, summarize God's plan for taking the good news of the gospel to those in need: send, preach, hear, believe, call, saved.

With a final barrage of scriptures from the Old Testament, Paul proves his point that, in spite of sovereign election from God's side of the equation, Israel is in a state of unbelief by her own choice. Personal responsibility is part of the ministry of the gospel, both in delivering it and in choosing whether or not to receive it. God's responsibility was to get "the gospel" to Israel; it was Israel's responsibility to act on it.

10:16–18. Unfortunately, **not all the Israelites accepted the good news** (the obvious implication being that some did—the remnant; cf. Rom. 9:27; 11:5, 25). Paul uses a situation in Isaiah's day to illustrate:

Original Context	Isaiah 53:1	Romans 10:16	Paul's Application
Isaiah was proclaiming good news of salvation to Israel (Is. 52:7, 10) but at the same time was questioning whether any would believe.	Who has believed our message and to whom has the arm of the Lord been revealed?	For Isaiah says, "Lord, who has believed our message?"	Paul's application of this verse is the same as Isaiah's, just a few centuries later. Israel once again was hearing the good news, but not believing.

The apostle John agreed with Paul's assessment of Israel's condition. Even though the Israelites saw Jesus' miracles with their own eyes, "they still would not believe in him" (John 12:37). John then says this was in fulfillment of Isaiah 53:1, just as Paul did. Paul then reiterates what he said in verses 14–15, that faith can only come through hearing **the message, and the message is heard through the word of Christ.** The word of Christ here is perhaps best taken as "the spoken words about Christ," referring to the preaching of the gospel. **Word** is *rhema*, the uttered or spoken word as opposed to *logos*, the revealed word as expression of thought. A. T. Robertson has *christou* as an objective genitive (Robertson, 4:390), yielding "the spoken message about Christ."

Is it possible that Israel did not hear—either in Isaiah's day, in Jesus' day, or in Paul's day? Paul answers as if the answer would be obvious to anyone who cared to look: **Of course they [heard]**—and he uses another Old Testament quote to prove it, with another fresh application:

Original Context	Psalm 19:4	Romans 10:18	Paul's Application
In its direct application, this psalm supports Paul's contention in Romans 1:20 that creation proves the existence of God.	Their voice goes out into all the earth, their words to the ends of the world. In the heavens he has pitched a tent for the sun,	Their voice has gone out into all the earth, their words to the ends of the world.	Paul uses the "voice" of creation as an analogy for how the gospel has spread to the end of the (Jews') world.

If we parallel Paul's argument in Romans 1:20 with his argument here (Ps. 19:4 being the common element between the two), then just as all people everywhere "are without excuse" (Rom. 1:20) concerning the existence of God, so Jews everywhere are without excuse concerning the existence of their Messiah and his work. Having answered a first objection to Israel's lack of responsibility, Paul answers a second.[20]

The Bible Helps Us Achieve and Maintain Our Spirituality

Matthew 4:4 Updated American Standard Version (UASV)

4 But he answered, "It is written,

"'Man shall not live by bread alone,
but by every word that proceeds out of the mouth of God.'"[21]

John Macarthur wrote, **"4:4 It is written.** All three of Jesus' replies to the devil are taken from Deuteronomy. This one, from Deuteronomy 8:3, states that God allowed Israel to hunger so that He might feed them with manna and teach them to trust Him to provide for them. So the verse is directly applicable to Jesus' circumstances and a fitting reply to Satan's temptation."[22] Indeed, Christians are fed by reading and studying the Word of God. In addition, our faith is strengthened when we experience the benefits of applying God's Word more fully and accurately in our lives as we walk with God, putting him first.

The Bible Helps Us Understand the Will and Purposes of the Creator

When we enter the pathway of walking with our God, we will certainly come across resistance from three different areas. **Our greatest obstacle is ourselves** because we have inherited imperfection from our first parents Adam and Eve. The Scriptures make it quite clear that we are mentally bent toward bad, not good. (Gen 6:5; 8:21, AT) In other words, our natural desire is toward wrong. Prior to sinning, Adam and Eve were perfect, and they had the natural desire of doing good, and to go against

---

[20] Kenneth Boa and William Kruidenier, *Romans*, vol. 6, Holman New Testament Commentary (Nashville, TN: Broadman & Holman Publishers, 2000), 314–316.

[21] Deut. 8:3

[22] MacArthur, John. The MacArthur Bible Commentary (Kindle Locations 38817-38819). Thomas Nelson. Kindle Edition.

that was to go against the grain of their inner person. Scripture also tells us of our inner person, our heart.

Jeremiah 17:9 Updated American Standard Version (UASV)

⁹ The **heart is** more **deceitful** than all else,
   and **desperately sick**;
   who can understand it?

Romans 7:21-24 Updated American Standard Version (UASV)

²¹ I find then the law in me that when I want to do right, that evil is present in me. ²² For I delight in the law of God according to the inner man, ²³ but I see a different law in my members, warring against the law of my mind and taking me captive in **the law of sin** which is in my members. ²⁴ Wretched man that I am! Who will deliver me from this body of death?

1 Corinthians 9:27 Updated American Standard Version (UASV)

²⁷ but **I discipline my body** and make it my slave, so that, after I have preached to others, I myself will not be disqualified.

Ephesians 4:1 Updated American Standard Version (UASV)

4 Therefore I, the prisoner of the Lord, implore you to **walk in a manner worthy** of the calling with which you have been called,

Ephesians 5:15-17 Updated American Standard Version (UASV)

¹⁵ Therefore be careful how you walk, not as unwise men but as wise, ¹⁶ **buying out**²³ **the time,** because the days are evil. ¹⁷ Therefore do not be foolish, but understand what the will of the Lord is.

There are horrific dangers and deceptions that lie within the world that is under the influence of Satan. God recognizes that we are imperfect, knowing that we have human weaknesses that he originally did not intend, meaning that he is aware of how difficult it is to walk in godly wisdom. He is aware that we are all missing the mark of perfection, and that we are all mentally bent toward evil. He knows that our natural desire is to do wrong, and our heart (inner self) is treacherous, and we cannot even know it. It is for this reason that he makes allowances for our imperfection. Jesus Christ offered himself as a ransom, covering our Adamic sin and our human weaknesses when we stumble at times, but only if we demonstrate trust in him.

---

²³ (an idiom, literally 'to redeem the time') to do something with intensity and urgency (used absolutely)–'to work urgently, to redeem the time.'–GELNTBSD

We need to walk not as **unwise** but as **wise**. What does Paul mean by 'wise' and 'unwise' in this text? God has made known to us his plan of salvation, which was a mystery up until the time of Paul's writings. At that time, he had lavished upon them/us, "in all wisdom and insight making known to us the mystery of his will, according to his purpose, which he set forth in Christ." (Eph. 1:8-9) Yes, God has afforded his people wisdom, "that the God of our Lord Jesus Christ, the Father of glory, may give you the Spirit of wisdom and of revelation in the knowledge of him, having the eyes of your hearts enlightened, that you may know what is the hope to which he has called you." (Eph. 1:17-19) It would take a wise person to understand and appreciate the mystery of salvation, and the fact that they are required to bring their life into harmony with God's magnificent plan of saving the world of mankind who are receptive to accepting Christ. To be wise also means that these ones fully grasp the will of the Father (Matt. 7:21), and are carrying out that will to the best of their ability. Therefore, the wise accept, value, and see the significance of wisely walking worthily with God. On the other hand, the unwise are those of the world of humankind who are alienated from God, living their life in the moment, walking in the desires of the flesh, because they see God's Word as foolish.

Turning our attention to verse 16 of Ephesians 5, we see that the wise know how to buy out the opportune time from the world, even though they live in the world, but they do not use it to the fullest extent, unlike the unwise. Why, because they know that the world of wicked mankind is passing away. The wise one buys time back from this wicked world. Some of the areas that can be bought from are watching less television, less time playing on the computer, other forms of entertainment, not always working overtime, or maybe even not taking a promotion that would cause one to miss Christian meetings, so he or she can focus on the better things. Some of these better things are personal family time, family Bible study, personal Bible study, religious services, sharing the Good News with others, congregational responsibilities, and so on. Notice below that we were formerly unwise, but are now the wise.

Ephesians 2:1-3 Updated American Standard Version (UASV)

2 And you being dead in the trespasses and your sins, ² in which you formerly walked according to the age of this world, according to the ruler of the authority of the air, the spirit now working in the sons of disobedience. ³ Among whom also we all formerly lived in the desires of our flesh, doing the desires of the flesh and of the thoughts, and were by nature children of wrath, even as the rest.

Help in Understanding the Bible

The irony is that hundreds of millions of Christians are humble enough to recognize that the Bible is difficult to understand, it is a deep and complex book. There are tens of millions, who believe they understand everything they read, and for them, the Bible is easy to understand. The sad part is that many of the latter do not understand it any better than the former; they are simply putting a modern-day twist on Scripture and having it say what they want it to say. Even Peter in the first century, one of the pillars of the early church, an apostle of Christ, viewed the Apostle Paul's letters as difficult to understand.

2 Peter 3:15-16 Updated American Standard Version (UASV)

[15] and regard the patience of our Lord as salvation; just as also **our beloved brother Paul**, according to the wisdom given him, **wrote to you**, [16] as also **in all his letters**, speaking in them of these things, in which are **some things hard to understand**, which the untaught and unstable distort, as they do also the rest of the Scriptures, to their own destruction.

If we are to appreciate and apply the Bible in our lives, we must first fully understand it. We must know what the author of a Bible book meant by the words that he used, as should have been understood by his original intended audience. Then, we will be able to attach the significance that it has in our lives. If we are unaware of the correct way of interpreting the Scriptures, grammatical-historical interpretation, then we are going to be one of those ones who Peter spoke of as, "the ignorant and unstable twist to their own destruction." Hundreds of millions of Christians unknowingly share an incorrect understanding of Scripture, because they are not aware of the principles of interpretation, and how to apply them correctly. More on Peter's words in a moment.

Our **first step** is *observation*, to get as close to the original text as possible. If we do not read Hebrew or Greek; then, two or three literal translations are preferred (ASV, RSV, NASB, UASV). The **second step** is *interpretation*. What did the author mean by the words that he used, as should have been understood by his original audience. A part of this second step would be what the differences between the biblical audience and us are? The Christian today is separated from the biblical audience by differences in culture, language, situation, time, and often covenant. The **third step** is the *implications* or *principles* in this text? This is perhaps the most challenging step. In it, we are looking for the implications or principles that are reflected in the meaning of the text we identified in the second step. Part of this third step is making sure that we stay within the pattern of the original meaning when we determine any implications for us. The **fourth step** is the *application.* How should individual Christians today live out the implications and principles?

Certainly, no one would suggest that God intended such division and confusion. If each of us can give our own meaning to a text; then, it has no meaning at all, and has lost all authority over our lives. What does the Bible really teach? Look at the different views the Bible scholar have below.

(Inerrancy) *Full inerrancy* in this book means that the original writings are fully without error in all that they state, as are the words. The words were not dictated (automaton), but the intended meaning is inspired, as are the words that convey that meaning. The Author allowed the writer to use his style of writing, yet controlled the meaning to the extent of not allowing the writer to choose a wrong word, which would not convey the intended meaning. Other more liberal-minded persons hold with *partial inerrancy,* which claims that as far as faith is concerned, this portion of God's Word is without error, but that there are historical, geographical, and scientific errors.

There are several different levels of inerrancy. *Absolute Inerrancy* is the belief that the Bible is fully true and exact in every way; including not only relationships and doctrine, but also science and history. In other words, all information is completely exact. *Full Inerrancy* is the belief that the Bible was not written as a science or history textbook, but is phenomenological, in that it is written from the human perspective. In other words, speaking of such things as the sun rising, the four corners of the earth or the rounding off of number approximations are all from a human perspective. *Limited Inerrancy* is the belief that the Bible is meant only as a reflection of God's purposes and will, so the science and history are the understanding of the author's day and is limited. Thus, the Bible is susceptible to errors in these areas. *Inerrancy of Purpose* is the belief that it is only inerrant in the purpose of bringing its readers to a saving faith. The Bible is not about facts, but about persons and relationships, thus, it is subject to error. *Inspired: Not Inerrant* is the belief that its authors are human and thus subject to human error. It should be noted that this author holds the position of **full inerrancy.**

(Creation Account) Were the universe and man created within the past 6,000 to 10,000 years, or are the days creative periods. Or rather, is there a large gap of time between Genesis 1:1 and 1:2, or the literary framework view correctly that asserts that God did not have Moses address how He created the world, nor the length of time in which to do such? This view holds that this account in Genesis 1 is merely a literary outline that summarizes a theology of creation.

(Providence) Is God sovereign over all things, or does God limit his control by granting freedom? (Divine Image) Is the image of God our soul, or is the image of God our God-given authority, or is it our relations? (Human Constitution) Are we made up of a body and soul, or body, soul, and spirit, or are we the person, a soul? (Atonement) Did Christ die in our place, or is it that Christ destroyed Satan and his works, or that Christ displayed God's wrath against sin? (Salvation) Did God from eternity in the past predestine some to salvation, and others to eternal damnation, or is it that God loves everyone, and we can choose to accept or reject that love, with God not coercing them, while they must maintain an approved standing? (Sanctification) Is sanctification a declaration by God, or a holiness in Christ and personal conduct, or resting-faith in the sufficiency of Christ, or is it entire sanctification in perfect love? (Eternal Security) Do we retain our security in the Power of God, or do we need to persist in faith? (Baptism) Are infants to be baptized, or are only believers to be baptized? (Gifts) Is speaking in tongues a true sign of faith, or did speaking in tongues die out after the first century C.E.?[24] (Millennium) Is there to be a rapture before the reign of Christ, or are we working toward and waiting for a coming reign of peace, or is the thousand-year conquest of Satan symbolic? These sorts of questions could go on for hundreds of pages.

Help in Teaching the Bible

If we are to fulfill the great commission, that Jesus gave to every Christian, to proclaim and to teach the Good News, we must accurately understand it ourselves first. It was in the spring of 31 C.E., and Jesus was about to speak to a very large, mixed crowd on a mountainside, who were anxiously awaiting what he would teach them. He did not let them down in the least, as he was nothing short of astounding in what and how he taught them. "And when Jesus finished these sayings, the crowds were astonished at his teaching." Astonished: (Gr. *thambeō;* derivative of *thambos*) This is one who is experiencing astonishment, to be astounded, or amazed as a result of some sudden and unusual event, which can be in a positive or negative sense.[25] What was so special about his way of

---

[24] B.C.E. means "before the Common Era," which is more accurate than B.C. ("before Christ"). C.E. denotes "Common Era," often called A.D., for *anno Domini,* meaning "in the year of our Lord."

[25] Mark 1:27; 10:32; Lu 4:36; 5:9; Acts 3:10.

teaching, in comparison to what they had been hearing from the Jewish religious leaders? He taught with authority from the Scriptures. He quoted or referred to the Old Testament, to support what he was saying. The Jewish religious leaders referred to other Rabbis as their authority.

At the end of his ministry here on earth, Jesus told all of his disciples that they too were to be teachers. He said, "Go therefore and make disciples of all nations ... **teaching them** to observe all that I have commanded you." (Matt. 28:19-20, ESV) The apostle Paul also exhorted Hebrew Christians of their responsibility to teach when they were trying to get away with doing the minimum possible. "For in view of the time **you ought to be teachers,** you have need again for someone to teach you from the beginning the elementary things of the words of God, and you have come to need milk and not solid food." (Hebrews 5:12) Paul also told Timothy, "For a slave of the Lord does not need to fight, but needs to be kind to all, **qualified to teach,** showing restraint when wronged,"– 2 Timothy 2:24.

What about us? Sadly, survey after survey over the last 35 years has shown that 90+ percent of Christians today are in the same position as what Paul had said to the Hebrew Christians. "For in view of the time you ought to be teachers, you have need again for someone to teach you from the beginning the elementary things of the words of God, and you have come to need milk and not solid food." (Heb. 5:12) On this verse, Thomas D. Lea wrote, "First, he said, 'You've been Christians long enough to be teachers, but you still need instruction in the ABCs.' They should have been able to pass on their basic understanding of the Christian message to others. Instead, they needed a good review of the elementary matters themselves. Not only had they failed to move forward in their understanding; they had lost their grasp of the **elementary truths of God's word.** 'If the dark things do not become plain then the plain things will become dark' (Thomas Hewitt). Second, these believers were in need of **milk, not solid food!** The term *milk* represents a beginning level of instruction for Christians. The term solid food describes advanced instruction. Both the milk phase and the solid food phase were important and essential. However, someone who never reached the solid food stage was seriously defective. ... The writer of Hebrews was concerned that his readers should be showing signs of Christian maturity. They were still caught up in issues only 'baby' Christians found to be important."[26] Do not be troubled by these words, as to biblical illiteracy among the

---

[26] Thomas D. Lea, *Hebrews, James,* vol. 10, Holman New Testament Commentary (Nashville, TN: Broadman & Holman Publishers, 1999), 95–96.

Christians today, the church and its leaders bear most of the responsibility by far, with some going to the churchgoer as well.

Joshua 1:8-9 Updated American Standard Version (UASV)

[8] This Book of the Law shall not depart from your mouth, but you shall **meditate** on it **day and night**, so that you may be careful to do according to all that is written in it; for then you will make your way prosperous, and then **you will have good success**. [9] Have I not commanded you? Be strong and courageous! Do not be afraid, and do not be dismayed, for Jehovah your God is with you wherever you go."

We see that we need to **meditate** on God's Word **day and night** (See also Ps. 1:1-3). The day and night are really hyperbole for reading it every day. The Hebrew word behind meditate (*haghah*) can be rendered "mutter." In other words, as we read, we are to read in an undertone, slightly out load, like muttering to oneself. The process of hearing the words increases our retention of the material dramatically. As Bible students we read to understand and remember what we read, and we are obligated to share this good news with others. Gesenius' Hebrew and Chaldee Lexicon (translated by S. Tregelles, 1901, p. 215) say of haghah: "Prop[erly] to speak with oneself, murmuring and in a low voice, as is often done by those who are musing."[27]

The last phrase in verse 8, "you will have good success" can be rendered to "act with insight." How was Joshua to acquire this ability "to act with insight"? He was to meditate on God's Word day and night. What is the equation of Joshua 1:8? If Joshua were to read meditatively (in an undertone) from God's Word daily, applying it in his life, he would be able to act with insight, resulting in his prospering. Of course, the prospering is not financial gain. It is a life of joy and happiness in an age of difficult times. It is avoiding the pitfalls that those in the world around us suffer daily. Moreover, it does not mean that we are to prosper or be successful in an absolute sense because bad things happen to good people. We must add the qualifier, "generally speaking," if we follow God's Word we will have success.

Basics of Biblical Interpretation

Step 1: What is the historical setting and background for the author of the book and his audience? Who wrote the book? When and under what circumstances was the book written? Where was the book written?

---

[27] See also Psalm 35:28; 37:30; 71:24; Isaiah 8:19; 33:18.

Who were the recipients of the book? Was there anything noteworthy about the place of the recipients? What is the theme of the book? What was the purpose for writing the book?

Step 2a: What would this text have meant to the original audience? (The meaning of a text is what the author meant by the words that he used, as should have been understood by his readers.)

Step 2b: If there are any words in our section that we do not understand, or that stand out as interesting words that may shed some insight on the meaning, look them up in a word dictionary.

Step 2c: After reading our section from the three Bible translations, doing a word study, write down what we think the author meant. Then, pick up a trustworthy commentary, like CPH Old or New Testament commentary volume, and see if you have it correct.

Step 3: Explain the original meaning down into one or two sentences, preferably one. Then, take the sentence or two; place it in a short phrase.

Step 4: Now, consider their circumstances, the reason for it being written, what it meant to them, and consider examples from our day that would be similar to theirs, which would fit the pattern of meaning. What **implications** can be drawn from the original meaning?

Step 5: Find the pattern of meaning, i.e., the "thing like these," and consider how it could apply to our modern day life. How should individual Christians today live out the implications and principles?

We know that Scripture makes it clear that there is only one acceptable way of worshiping God, the way outlined in God's Word. Everything that we believe and do needs to be based on that Word, and our understanding of that Word needs to be accurate. There are 41,000 different Christian denominations, and clearly, not all are on the path of doing the will of the Father as outlined in the Bible, for Jesus said, in that day he will say to some, "depart from me, you workers of lawlessness." (Matt 7:23) We can either place our trust in man, who bickers and argues over what the Word of God means, or we can take the Bible's point of view itself. After all, it is the inspired Word of God, which is profitable for teaching, for reproof, for correction, and for training in righteousness, so that the man of God may be complete, equipped for every good work."– 2 Timothy 3:16-17.

Proverbs 3:5-6 Updated American Standard Version (UASV)

5 Trust in Jehovah with all your heart,
   and do not lean on your own understanding.
6 In all your ways acknowledge him,
   and he will make straight your paths.

Milton H. Terry wrote, "It is an old and oft-repeated hermeneutical principle that words should be understood in their literal sense unless such literal interpretation involves a manifest contradiction or absurdity."[28] Robert L. Towns writes, "The Bible is the best interpreter of itself. As we study the Bible, we should learn to compare the Scriptures we are studying with other relevant passages of Scripture to interpret the Bible."[29] This book is the first step, HOW TO STUDY YOUR BIBLE. As to the second step, the reader can take advantage of the *INTERPRETING THE BIBLE: Introduction to Biblical Hermeneutics* by this author (ISBN: 978-1-945757-07-5), so that we are not entirely dependent on the interpretation of others. In other words, we will be able to do as the Bereans did with the Apostle Paul, and for which he commended them,

Acts 17:10-11 Updated American Standard Version (UASV)

Paul and Silas in Berea

10 The brothers immediately sent Paul and Silas away by night to Berea, and when they arrived, they went into the synagogue of the Jews. 11 Now these were more noble-minded than those in Thessalonica, who **received the word with all eagerness,**[30] **examining the Scriptures daily** to see whether these things were so.

Note that they **(1)** "received the word with all eagerness," and then went about **(2)** "examining the Scriptures daily to see if these things were so." If the apostle Paul was to be examined to see if what he said was so, surely uninspired commentators must be examined as well.

---

[28] Robert L. Thomas. *Evangelical Hermeneutics: The New Versus the Old* (p. 280). Kindle Edition.

[29] Towns, *AMG Concise Bible Doctrines* (AMG Concise Series) (Kindle Locations 1011-1012). AMG Publishers. Kindle Edition.

[30] Or with all *readiness of mind*. The Greek word *prothumias* means that one is eager, ready, mentally prepared to engage in some activity.

Are We Willing to Spend Time Each Week to Understand the Bible?

Many want to understand, to be fearless, and capable of sharing Bible truth with others. However, if this is to be the case, we must be willing to buy out a small amount of time from the wicked world under the influence of Satan that surrounds us (2 Cor. 4:3-4; 11:13-15) and invest it into a small study program. Many people want to do many things, but they allow their time to be used on frivolous pursuits. The thought of, 'oh, if only I had started six months ago, I would be so far along now!' Do not let another six months slip by.

Colossians 4:5-6 Updated American Standard Version (UASV)

⁵ Walk in wisdom toward outsiders, buying out for yourselves the time. ⁶ Let your speech always be gracious, seasoned with salt, so that you may know **how you ought to answer each person.**

The recommendation once more is to set aside one hour each day for God. If we are able to spend more time, this is entirely up to us. What must be realized is just how much time we give to the world around us, a world that lies in the hands of Satan. Is it too much to ask that we give one hour a day to the Creator of life? We can simply get up one hour earlier than we normally do, and we will have our study in before the day even gets started. The beautiful thing about that plan is; it will start our day on a spiritual track, meaning a better day from the beginning.

Digging Deeper

Psalm 92:5 Updated American Standard Version (UASV)

⁵ How great are your works, O Jehovah!
Your thoughts are very deep!

1 Corinthians 2:10 Updated American Standard Version (UASV)

¹⁰ For to us God revealed them through the Spirit; for the Spirit searches all things, even **the depths of God.**

There is no doubt that God's thoughts are deep, these deeper things of God are very complex at times, and as Peter tells us in the above, they are *not easy to understand.* Therefore, we must dig deeper by the use of the many wonderful tools on the market, along with prayerful reflection as we carry on in our studies. However, even before we begin that, we need to know (1) HOW TO STUDY YOUR BIBLE, and (2) that our way of INTERPRETING THE BIBLE is correct.

Psalm 139:17-18 Updated American Standard Version (UASV)

[17] How precious to me are **your thoughts**, O God!
How vast is the sum of them!
[18] If I should count them, they would outnumber the sand.
When I awake, I am still with you.

Psalm 119:160 Updated American Standard Version (UASV)

[160] The sum of **your word is truth**,
and every one of your righteous judgments endures forever.

As was true of the Psalmist, we should view God's sharing His thoughts as very precious. We should be very thankful and appreciative that we have access to 'the sum of God's Word' as being truths that He has revealed to us, and therefore, we must dig deeper in the sum of God's Word.

How Does God Communicate With Us Today?

Setting any possible emotionalism[31] aside, we must ask ourselves if God is truly real to us. Can we say that God is our friend? James tells us in his inspired letter, "'Abraham believed God, and it was counted to him as righteousness,'[32] and he was called a friend of God." We all have heard the say, "actions speak louder than words." Abraham's actions evidenced that he had a deep, heartfelt faith, and truly loved God. He showed in his life that he was not just a friend of God in mere words but also in deed. The more we draw closer to God in both word and deed, the more he will draw closer to us.

What are some things that we can do to draw closer to God? The primary ways that we can draw closer to God are through communication with him. In prayer, we communicate with the Father. King David, in prayer, said, "Before him I pour out my complaint;

---

[31] Some have a tendency to be easily swayed by their emotions. They have an exaggerated or undue display of strong feelings, which makes their relationship with the Father and the Son based entirely on emotions. Jesus said, "This is eternal life, that they may know you, the only true God, and the one whom you sent, Jesus Christ." We have to have knowledge of the Father and the Son to know that they are real, which does not negate that we need to have emotions as well. However, a relationship that is based entirely on emotions cannot withstand difficult times.

[32] Quoted from Gen. 15:6

before him I tell about my trouble."[33] (Ps 142:2) How does God communicate with us? The only people in Bible times to receive direct communication from God (namely, spoken audible direction, visions, dreams, and angelic messengers delivered divine messages), were **Patriarchs** like Noah, Abraham, Jacob, Moses, and Joshua. There were also the **Judges** like Gideon, Ehud, and Samson. There were the **Kings** like David, Solomon, Jehu, and Hezekiah. Then there were the **Prophets** like Elijah and Elisha, or Isiah, Jeremiah, and Ezekiel. Then, there were the **Minor Prophets** like Jonah, Micah, and Joel. Then there were **Priests** like Aaron and Ezra. Then, after the Babylonian exile, there were **Governors** like Zerubbabel. After that, we enter the New Testament era with John the Baptist. Then, there were the **Twelve Apostles** like John, Peter, James, and Matthew. Then, there were the **Traveling Apostles** or **Evangelists** like Paul and Philip. There were also more than one hundred **Traveling Companions** of the apostle Paul such as Timothy, Titus, Barnabas, and Tychicus.

Persons such as these might receive a message from God through a dream or night vision, where pictures of God's message or purpose are placed in the mind of the sleeping person. The Bible says, "Then the mystery was revealed to Daniel in a vision of the night." (Dan. 2:19) We are also told, "In the first year of Belshazzar king of Babylon, Daniel saw a dream and visions of his head [that is, in his mind] as he lay in his bed." (Dan 7:1) There were also visions given when a person was awake, which was actually the more common way of communication. We are told, "In the third year of the reign of King Belshazzar a vision appeared to me, Daniel,[34] after the one that appeared to me at the beginning." (Dan. 8:1) Of Ezekiel, it is said, "In the thirtieth year, in the fourth month, on the fifth day of the month, as I was among the exiles by the river Chebar, the heavens were opened, and I saw visions of God." (Eze 1:1) The apostle John tells us, "And this is how I saw the horses in the vision and those seated on them ..." (Rev. 9:17) Then, we have the apostle Peter who fell into a trance, and he saw the heavens open, giving him a pictorial vision of his next assignment. (Ac 10:9-17) There are times when angels served as direct representatives of God and visited persons such as Abraham, Moses, Daniel, the father of John the Baptist, Zechariah, and even Mary. The prophet Zechariah was having a vision of some horsemen and being visited by an angel. Then he said to the angel, 'What are these, my lord?' And the angel who was talking to me said, "I will show you what these

---

[33] THE POWERFUL WEAPON OF PRAYER: A Healthy Prayer Life by Edward D. Andrews (**ISBN**: 978-1-945757-41-9)

[34] Lit *I, Daniel*

36

are." (Gen. 22:11-12, 15-18; Zech. 1:7, 9) The Bible authors "were inspired by God," 'speaking from God as they were moved along by the Holy Spirit.'–2 Timothy 3:16-17; 2 Peter 1:21.

The Bible is a perfect guidebook that was penned to get God's people up unto the time of Armageddon. The only other future books to be written are to come during the millennial reign of Christ. Once the Scriptures were closed in the first century with the death of the last apostle, John, there was no need for any more books to be written or any more prophets. They then and we now have the complete revelation of God to get us to the second coming of Christ. The only person(s) we have needed since the closure of Scriptures in 100 C.E.[35] has been interpreters. There are two **kinds of interpreters**. One is a translator of the Scriptures, like Jerome and his Latin Vulgate, John Wycliffe with the first English Bible (written by hand), William Tyndale with the first English Bible in print, Martin Luther, and the German Bible, to mention just a few. From our modern day era, we have translators on translation committees, who have given us the American Standard Version (ASV), the Revised Standard Version (RSV), the New American Standard Bible (NASB), the English Standard Version (ESV), as well as the forthcoming Updated American Standard Version (UASV).[36] These ones take the written language of our Old Testament Hebrew-Aramaic manuscripts and our Greek New Testament manuscripts and render them into our modern-day languages. We shall call these specialists **Bible Translator Interpreters**. Who are the other interpreters?

All Christians are the other interpreters, ones who convey the meaning of our modern-day translations, namely, what the Bible authors meant by the words that they used. We explain the Bible by giving others the meaning, significance, and understanding of the Word of God. We shall call ourselves, who also are a specialist, **Christian Evangelist Interpreters**. What is an evangelist exactly? Who are all expected to serve in this role? **Evangelism** is the work of a Christian evangelist, of which all true Christians are obligated to partake to some extent, which seeks to persuade other people to become Christian, especially by sharing the basics of the Gospel, but also the deeper message of biblical truths. Why are Christians specialists like the Bible Translator Interpreters? It is because of the groundwork that needs to be laid. **Preevangelism** is laying a foundation for those who have no knowledge of the Gospel, giving them

---

[35] B.C.E. means "before the Common Era," which is more accurate than B.C. ("before Christ"). C.E. denotes "Common Era," often called A.D., for *anno Domini*, meaning "in the year of our Lord."

[36] http://www.uasvbible.org/

background information, so that they are able to grasp what they are hearing. The Christian Evangelist Interpreter is preparing their mind and heart so that they will be receptive to the biblical truths. In many ways, this is known as apologetics.

Again, we quote what the apostle Peter said of the apostle Paul's writings, "some things hard to understand, which the untaught and unstable distort, as they do also the rest of the Scriptures, to their own destruction." (2 Pet. 3:16) The Christian Evangelist Interpreter needs to read, study, and understand the verses of scripture, in order to obey the command by Jesus to teach and make disciples. (Matt. 24:14; 28:19-20; Ac 1:8) In order to teach another, we must clearly understand the Word of God ourselves first. Otherwise, how do we, 2,000-years removed from Peter, who felt the Scriptures were hard to understand, make it understandable to others? When we fully, completely, and accurately understand the Word of God; then, we can give reasons as to why it says what it say, and what the author meant by what he wrote. Moreover, we are also able to express it in our own words. There are two reasons why need to be absolutely certain that what we are conveying is accurate. **First**, it reflects poorly on us, our church and our denomination, and more importantly on God. **Second**, Peter said it himself, "the untaught and unstable distort, as they do also the rest of the Scriptures, **to their own destruction**." Whether we distort the Word of God intentionally (false teachers), or unintentionally because we were too busy in Satan's world to buy out the time to understand better, it all ends the same way, our destruction.

We need to understand the cultural differences in the Scriptures, the Bible backgrounds, as we are 2,000-years removed from the New Testament era and 2,500-3,500-years removed from the Old Testament era. We need to appreciate original language words that are in Hebrew, Aramaic, and Greek. **This does not mean** that we need necessarily to learn Biblical Hebrew and Greek. Some tools can aid us in this. We need to take what the author meant out of the text, not read our twenty-first-century mindset into the text. We need to understand the context. Context is the words, phrases, or passages that come before and after a particular word or passage in a speech or piece of writing and help to explain its full meaning. Context is also the circumstances or events that form the environment within which something exists or takes place. We need to be observant as we study, taking not of persons, place, things, and circumstances. Discover who wrote it, what the purpose was, what is being conveyed when it was written, and why it was written. Are we reading historical texts like Kings and Chronicles, or poetical like the

Psalms, apocalyptic such as Daniel or Revelations, prophetic like Isaiah or Jeremiah, the laws like Leviticus, Numbers, and Deuteronomy, or letters like Ephesians, Galatians, Hebrews, or the Gospels? What do we know about the people involved? Can we say that we know anything about Alexander, Demas, Hermogenes, Asyncritus, Hermas, Julia, Philologus, and Phygelus? What are some of the keywords that we can investigate further? What is the main theme of the Bible book we are studying? Interpret literally, unless the author did not mean for it to be taken literally. We need to understand how to apply what the author meant to our lives.

What if we have not been properly trained in how to study God's Word properly? You are now holding the best book on that subject. It can be very disheartening to struggle through Bible reading and study when we do not know how to study properly, to interpret the Scriptures correctly. In addition, it is difficult to form a long for personal Bible study if we have had no training. We have taken a long way around to answer, how does God talk to us today? Should we expect dreams, visions, a voice from heaven, or a visit from an angel? What about a prophet, should we expect that God would raise up another prophet? No, those days ended over 2,000-years ago. God speaks to us when we regularly read his word, the Bible, and meditate on it.

Roadblocks to Regular and Consistent Bible Reading and Study

Psalm 119:97 Updated American Standard Version (UASV)

[97] Oh how I love your law!
  It is my meditation all the day.

Literally billions of men and women have a Bible. However, while they may own a Bible and even carry the Bible to their church meetings, can they honestly say that they love God's Word? Is a person's claim that they love the Word of God true if they are irregular and inconsistent in reading and studying it? Certainly not, the claim would be false based on their actions. On the other hand, there are **former** atheists, who had absolutely no respect for the Bible, who now read and study it daily now that they have converted to Christianity. They have grown to love God's Word, and now are very much like the Psalmist, meditating on the Word of God "all the day." Let us now look at some roadblocks that has gotten in the way for some, so that they had not read and studied their Bible consistently.

A. IT REQUIRES DISCIPLINE

Today, many associate discipline with *punishment* that is designed to teach somebody obedience. For Christians they see discipline as *church rules*: the system of rules used in a Christian denomination in order to keep the church organized, clean, and pure. This is not how the word is being used here. The primary meaning of discipline is **training to ensure proper behavior:** the practice or methods of teaching and enforcing acceptable patterns of behavior. Someone, who regularly and consistently cleans their house, mows their lawn, makes their doctor's visits, cooks family meals, holds down a job, is a disciplined person. The same holds true of reading and studying the Bible, as well as preparing for and attending church meetings. If they are failing to do so; then, the Word of God is not their priority. Moreover, by extension, growing close to God is not their priority either because only by growing in the knowledge of God can one draw closer to him.

Without seeming too insulting, it really comes down to being lazy. If we fail to carry out regular Bible study, prepare for Sunday's Christian meeting, and even fail to attend that Sunday, yet we go out shopping later that day, or turn on the football games, where are our priorities? Thus, a lack of discipline has become a problem that we must overcome. If we have the time to do things that we desire to do; then, these things are close to our heart. What do we do during our seven-day week? Do we read newspapers and magazines? Do we surf the internet and regularly post on social media? Do we go shopping? Do we watch sports? Do we have a garden that we care for, a pet that we are taking care of, go out to eat, take in a movie, and so on. Then, we need to 'buy out'[37] the time from other activities in order to read and study the Bible regularly. (Eph. 5:16) If we fail to buy out this time; then, our claim that we love God and his Word is simply untrue. We may try to rationalize why we are too busy, but that will be irrational thinking. We need to have a genuine love for God and for people that need saving, being willing to make personal sacrifices, if we are going to grow in knowledge, so are to share biblical truths with others, to make disciples. (Matt. 22:37-39; 28:19-20; Phil. 4:13) We must cultivate qualities that make us a better Christian, a better disciple, to draw closer to God, namely discipline.

B. INEXPERIENCED AND UNSKILLED BIBLE STUDENT

Experience is knowledge or skill gained through being involved in or exposed to something over a period. I am not mechanically inclined. My

---

[37] (an idiom, literally 'to redeem the time') to do something with intensity and urgency (used absolutely)—'to work urgently, to redeem the time.'–GELNTBSD

father died when I was four, I had no older brother to train me, no uncles, and so I grew up without learning how to repair go-carts, mini bikes, cars, or motorcycles. I also never learned how to fix things around the house. All of my friends through life had these skills, which was a blessing and a curse. It was a blessing because I had a friend that would repair things for me. I was always clumsy around tools and had no real self-confidence in this area.

The same is true with Bible study. If we have always been told that the Bible is easy to understand, just interpret it as you read it because it is straightforward, we were extremely misinformed. Here again, is what the apostle Peter said about the apostle Paul's writings, "also in all his letters, speaking in them of these things, in which are some things **hard to understand**, which **the untaught** and **unstable distort**, as they do also the rest of the Scriptures, **to their own destruction**." (2 Pet. 3:16) This is not the apostle Peter that Jesus found on a fishing boat, whom Jesus said 'be my disciple,' or the apostle Peter that denied Jesus three times. Rather this is the apostle Peter 35-years later, who was one of the main leaders of the entire church, who had decades of study and teaching under his belt, not to mention being an inspired author himself. This experienced and highly knowledgeable, wise apostle Peter, felt that some things in Paul's letters were "**hard to understand**." We are 2,000 years removed, of a different language, culture, and historical setting, and we are going to be so bold as to say, the Bible is easy to understand. Peter also said the '**untaught were distorting the Scriptures**.' There is the important correlation if you are untaught; you have no choice but to distort the Scriptures. Sadly, Peters last words should be a wake-up call of all of us, 'distorting the Scriptures, **to our own destruction**.' One thing that this book will bring its readers is this; we will acquire the skills on *HOW TO STUDY YOUR BIBLE*. We will also learn how to use the Bible study tools as well.

C. LACKING REASONS, ENTHUSIASM & MOTIVATION

If we were never disciplined to regularly and consistently take care of the important things in life and we lack the experience and skills to do so, how are we going to have enthusiasm and the motivation? **Reasons** are defined as a motive or cause for acting or thinking in a particular way. **Enthusiasm** is defined as a passionate interest in or eagerness to do something. **Motivation** is defined as the act of giving somebody a reason or incentive to do something. It is the intention of this author to give the reader many motives, to help form a passionate interest and eagerness, as well as incentives to regularly and consistently read and study their Bible.

D. A COMPLETE HEART

We cannot be **halfhearted** or in want of heart, or even **double hearted.** (Ps 12:2; Pro. 10:13) As a reader of hearts, God can see any insincere or feigned behavior on our part. He is well aware of our actions and thinking, even when we are alone. He knows our heart condition, what we are trying to do with our lives. If our heart is good, and we love God's Word, he will know. (Josh. 1:8-9; Ps. 1:1-3; 119:97, 101, 105, and 165) A person who is **halfhearted** is lukewarmly worshiping God. (Ps 119:113; Re. 3:16) a person who is **double hearted** (literally, with a heart and a heart), is trying to serve two masters, or deceivingly saying one thing while thinking something else completely. (1 Ch. 12:33; Ps 12:2) Jesus clearly condemned such double hearted hypocrisy (Matt 15:7-8) A person being in **want of heart** is one who lacks good sense.

If we are not buying out the appropriate amount of time for reading and Studying God's word, this is because we lack a complete heart. It is because we are not aware of our spiritual needs. Worse still, we might be aware of our spiritual needs but have chosen to ignore them, which will result in a calloused, unfeeling heart. Jesus pointed out that humans have an inborn, essential spiritual need. We long to be fed by God's Word, which gives meaning to our life. In dealing with the heart, let us look at one of Jesus illustrations. The parable of the sower talks about three different types of soil, which can be viewed as three different types of heart conditions.

Matthew 13:3-9, 18-23 Updated American Standard Version (UASV)

The Parable of the Sower

³ Then he told them many things by parables, saying: "Behold, a sower went out to sow; ⁴ and as he was sowing, some seeds fell alongside the road, and the birds came and ate them up. ⁵ Others fell on the rocky places, where they did not have much soil; and immediately they sprang up, because they had no depth of soil. ⁶ But when the sun had risen, they were scorched; and because they had no root, they withered away. ⁷ Others fell among the thorns, and the thorns came up and choked them. ⁸ Still others fell upon the good soil and they began to yield fruit, this one a hundredfold, that one sixty, the other thirty. ⁹ The one who has ears, let him hear."

The Parable of the Sower Explained

¹⁸ "Hear then the parable of the sower: ¹⁹ When anyone hears the word of the kingdom and does not understand it, the evil one comes and snatches away what has been sown in his heart. This is what was sown

along the path. ²⁰ As for what was sown on rocky ground, this is the one who hears the word and immediately receives it with joy, ²¹ yet he has no root in himself, but endures for a while, and when tribulation or persecution arises on account of the word, immediately he falls away. ²² As for what was sown among thorns, this is the one who hears the word, but the cares of the world and the deceitfulness of riches choke the word, and it proves unfruitful. ²³ As for what was sown on good soil, this is the one who hears the word and understands it. He indeed bears fruit and yields, in one case a hundredfold, in another sixty, and in another thirty."

13:3–8. The **many things** Jesus spoke in parables certainly included what was written in 13:3–52. It is possible that there were other parables that Matthew did not record.

The parable of the sower requires little comment, because Jesus himself explained the parable in 13:18–23. Note that the farmer sowed seed or several different kinds of soil. The soil **along the path** (13:4) would likely have been hard-packed from much traffic. There would be little or no vegetation or loose soil to hide or bury the seeds, so the birds could easily find them. **The birds** represent the devil, "the evil one" (13:19). Note also the variable quality of even the good soil (13:8); even among that which is conducive to fruit bearing, some soils do better than others.

As is common in storytelling today, Jesus used patterns of threes—three bad soils and three variations on the good soil. Usually the first two examples set a pattern, and the third example departs from that pattern, revealing the central message of the story. In this parable, the first three soils set the pattern of poor response to the seeds, and the fourth soil was the contrasting positive example.

13:9. Jesus repeated the challenge that Matthew first recorded in 11:15, after identifying John the Baptizer with "Elijah, who was to come." He will repeat the same wording in 13:43, and the challenge is explained thoroughly in the following context (13:10–17).

In fact, the distinction between those who have **ears** to hear and those who do not is central to understanding all of Matthew 11–13. In chapters 11–12, the conflicts revealed the contrast between those who willfully chose to disbelieve in the face of overwhelming evidence, and those who humbly accepted the evidence and responded in faith and obedience to the Messiah. Those who had **ears** to hear would not only find understanding about the parable, but would realize that the parable was talking about their willingness to hear. Those who did not have "ears to hear" would go on in denial about the parable's implications about their own unwillingness to hear.

13:18–19. These verses connect Jesus' explanation of the parable of the sower and the soils (13:18–23) with the disciples' privilege as hearers of the truth. Jesus was saying to them. "Because you have responded to what you have already seen with eyes, ears, and hearts of faith and humble obedience, I will show you even more. You have proven faithful with little, so I will trust you with much."

Jesus identified the **seed** as **the message about the kingdom**—its arrival in Jesus and the way to participate in this kingdom. The "message about the kingdom" is probably identical to the "good news of the kingdom" in 4:23; 9:35. 24:14.

The soils were the issue. Throughout the parable's explanation, Jesus compared the four kinds of soil with various kinds of people who had been exposed to his teaching. The first soil, that "along the path" (13:4), was packed and hardened by traffic. It represented the person who **does not understand** the word he had heard. The person represented by the hardened soil is one who chooses not to understand rather than a person who wants to understand but cannot. Such a person may actually understand Jesus' teaching in a literal sense but refuse to accept its truth. The biblical concept of "understanding" goes beyond the idea of mental comprehension. It sometimes includes volitional acceptance. In 21:45, the chief priests and Pharisees knew the meaning of Jesus' parable concerning them, but they refused to accept its truth.

The person who refuses to accept the word of God will fall victim to the **evil one** (Satan, represented by the birds in 13:4), who **comes and snatches away what was sown in his heart.** If given even the slightest opportunity, Satan and his evil forces—archenemies of the kingdom of God—are able to remove or distort the truth, thus making that person even less likely to accept the truth in the future. This is one manifestation of the principle Jesus taught in 12:30: "He who is not with me is against me." To refuse to accept his word is to move away from him. There can be no objective neutrality.

Many people who were exposed to the words and works of the Messiah (especially the religious leaders) fell into this category. They rejected him without any second thoughts.

13:20–21. The rocky soil (13:5–6) receives extra attention in both the parable and its explanation because this person's response to the truth follows a two-stage pattern. His initial response is unreserved and emotional—joyful acceptance—but only because the circumstances are favorable. The cost of commitment is not yet obvious. This person's commitment is not deeply rooted. We might say that the truly committed "pay their dues up front," but the marginally committed cancel their membership when payment comes due. The cost of commitment to the Messiah comes in the form of **trouble** (*thlipsis*, "tribulation") or persecution (*diogmos*) that come **because of the word**. As quickly as this individual had committed, just as quickly he defected, distancing himself from the **word** or message.

There is debate as to whether such a person is truly saved. This question cannot be answered from Jesus' words, because it is not related to his purpose in the parable, and he does not make the answer clear. It is doubtful than the person was expressing true faith from the start.

13:22. The soil with **thorns** (13:7) is also assumed to produce some initial growth, as did the **rocky places** (13:20). But the influence which draws this person away from a sustained interest is not persecution but competing "gods"—**the worries of this life and the deceitfulness of wealth**. Rather than being driven from the truth by hardship, this person is lured away from the truth by promises of something better. Of course, these promises will never be fulfilled, because these competing gods or masters are deceitful.

Is this kind of person saved? The language may lean somewhat toward believing that this person had responded initially with sincere faith, for the seedling is not said to die (as we can presume with the rocky soil, 13:21), but rather to become choked and **unfruitful**. Still, without perseverance, there is no final evidence of salvation.

We have already seen in Matthew an example of a person who started following Jesus, but then began giving excuses for why he needed to postpone his commitment (8:21–22). But even more prominent in this category would be Judas Iscariot, who sold out Jesus for thirty coins (26:14–16, 20–25, 48–50; 27:1–10).

13:23. All three of the preceding "soils" had heard the word. So also the fourth **good soil** hears the word, but this one also **understands**. This person *chooses* to understand and accept the truth, also accepting the One who is truth (John 14:6). None of the other soils bore any fruit, but this soil yielded much fruit. Jesus did not clarify what caused the variability between the fruitfulness of various faithful followers. One factor may be the degrees of faith. Perhaps another factor has to do with the variety of tasks given to different believers by God. Some may have greater potential for bearing fruit than others (cf. the different number of talents and different levels of return in 25:14–30). **Crop** represents the tangible results of a life of faith, including godly character (Gal. 5:22–23) and other souls brought into the kingdom (Matt. 9:37–38; cf. John 15:1–17).

In Matthew, where the focus is primarily on Jesus, we are given little opportunity to see examples of the disciples' responses of faith. The rest of the New Testament, however, is filled with stories about the fruit of faithful hearts. Prominent examples include Peter, John, Philip, Stephen, Paul, and Timothy.[38]

Reasons for Consistent and Regular Reading and Bible Study

A. CULTIVATE OBEDIENCE AS IT PROTECTS YOU

Many times this author has heard that God loves us unconditionally. This is not true. There are many conditions in the Bible that his servants are expected to believe, accept as absolute truth, and apply in their lives. Yes, obedience is a condition. If we lived a life of constant disobedience, would we expect that God would just overlook that because God is love? We must be mindful that God's great love does not negate his other qualities, such as justice. R. C. Sproul says, "There are many facets to the question and countless reasons why we ought to study the Bible. I could plead with you to study the Bible for personal edification; I could try the art of persuasion to stimulate your quest for happiness. I could say that the study of the Bible would probably be the most fulfilling and rewarding educational experience of your life. I could cite numerous reasons why you would benefit from a serious study of Scripture. But ultimately the main reason why we should study the Bible is that it is our duty. If the Bible were the most boring book in the world, dull, uninteresting and seemingly irrelevant, it would still be our duty to study it. If it's literary style were awkward and confusing, the duty would remain. We live as human beings under an obligation by divine mandate to study God's Word diligently. He is our Sovereign, it is his Word, and he commands that we study it. A duty is not an option. If you have not yet begun to respond to that duty, then you need to ask God to forgive you and to resolve to do your duty from this day forth." (Sproul 2016, 21)

---

[38] Stuart K. Weber, *Matthew*, vol. 1, Holman New Testament Commentary (Nashville, TN: Broadman & Holman Publishers, 2000), 192–197.

Is it not sad that knowing the Bible's direction can bring us great happiness is not enough of a reason to have a consistent and regular reading and Bible study? Knowing that a sound foundational knowledge of the Word of God will bring us the most fulfilling and rewarding educational experience of our life is not enough. We, as imperfect humans need to be forced to do what is good for us. How many have suffered a heart attack before they started exercising and eating correctly? Sadly, we must be commanded, forced, demanded to do the right and most beneficial things in life. Deuteronomy 5:33 tells us, "You shall walk in all the way that the Lord your God has commanded you, that you may live, and that it may go well with you, and that you may live long in the land that you shall possess." Joshua 1:8 tells us, "This Book of the Law shall not depart from your mouth, but you shall meditate on it day and night, so that you may be careful to do according to all that is written in it. For then you will make your way prosperous, and then you will have good success." Jeremiah 7:23 tells us " But this command I gave them: 'Obey my voice, and I will be your God, and you shall be my people. And walk in all the way that I command you, that it may be well with you.'"

If the command to embed ourselves in the Word of God is not enough, here is one that we can deduct from the Scriptures, which does not end well if we do not have a deep and correct understanding of God's Word. At Matthew 7:21, Jesus tells us, "Not everyone who says to me, 'Lord, Lord,' will enter the kingdom of heaven, but the one who does the will of my Father who is in heaven." What is the first and foremost question we should ask? What is the will of the Father? Jesus brings up those who wrongly believed that they were doing the will of the Father in verse 22. "On that day many will say to me, 'Lord, Lord, did we not prophesy in your name, and cast out demons in your name, and do many mighty works in your name?'" However, Jesus has some very bad news for these ones in verse 23. "And then I will declare to them, 'I never knew you; depart from me, you who practice lawlessness.'" The apostle John tells us at 1 John 2:17, "The world is passing away, and its lusts; but the one who does the will of God remains forever." Who will live forever? Oh, yeah, "whoever does the will of God." There it is again, the will of the Father. We already noted that the will of the Father is the key. Thus, the second most important question is, what is the only way of knowing the will of the Father? Yes, the only way to know is by deep study of God's Word.

The laws and commands within God's Word are not an option. The path to eternal life is not clear unless we have the mind of Christ, a biblical worldview, which comes from study, so as to see more clearly.

The Psalmist wrote, "Your word is a lamp to my feet and a light to my path." (Ps. 119:105) Right before telling us that it is only by the will of the Father, Jesus said, "Enter through the narrow gate; for the gate is wide and the way is broad that leads to destruction, and there are many who enter through it. For the gate is small and the way is narrow that leads to life, and there are few who find it." This is the path to eternal life, and few are finding it, although many are on what they believe to be the right path.–Matthew 7:13-14.

B. BEING GUIDED THROUGH LIFE AS YOU STUDY THROUGH GOD'S WORD

The cynic would view God's commandments to us are weighing us down and stripping us of our freedoms. The Bible student with his heart and mind being receptive to the Word of God will realize that these commandments are actually a blessing, which gives us access to a better life now and the eternal one to come.

The term *commandment(s)* translates the Hebrew word (*miṣ·wā(h)*), which means "command, order, commandment, i.e., an authoritative directive, either written or verbal, given as instruction or prescription to a subordinate (1Sa 13:13; 1Ki 2:43)."[39] All Christians are sons and daughters of the commandment. Psalm 119:76 says, "May your loyal love please comfort me according to your promise to your servant." An outstanding way in which God comforts his people is by giving them exhortation and guidance. (Ps. 119:105) God's commandments will guide us in the short term (daily) and the long-term (throughout our lives).

The term *law* translates the Hebrew word (*tô·rā(h)*), which means "law, regulation, i.e., a legal prescription of something that should or must be done (Ex 12:49; Lev 6:2); 2. LN 33.224–33.250 teaching, instruction, i.e., information that is imparted to a student (Ps 78:1; Pr 1:8); 3. LN 33.35–33.68 Torah, the Law, i.e., a written code (Ne 8:2)."[40] The author of Psalm 119 faced trials more extreme than most of us will ever know. Enemies of God ridiculed him and smeared him with falsehood. The princes were seeking his demise and persecuted him. At every turn, he life was in danger, and he was surrounded by wickedness. Even still, the Psalmist sang, "Oh how I love your law! It is my meditation all the day." Ps 119:97) The Psalmist found great joy in life regardless of his hardships

---

[39] James Swanson, *Dictionary of Biblical Languages with Semantic Domains : Hebrew (Old Testament)* (Oak Harbor: Logos Research Systems, Inc., 1997).

[40] James Swanson, *Dictionary of Biblical Languages with Semantic Domains : Hebrew (Old Testament)* (Oak Harbor: Logos Research Systems, Inc., 1997).

from those in opposition to him because he knew the law guided his every move. Apply God's law in his life, he became wiser than his enemies, keeping him safe in the darkest of times. Being obedient to the law also gave him a clean conscience, which brought him peace.—Psalm 119:1, 9, 65, 93, 98, 165.

The term *orders* ("precepts" in the ASV, ESV, LEB, CSB, NASB et al) translates the Hebrew word (*piq·qû·dîm*, which means instructions procedures, rule of personal conduct. "precepts, directions, regulation, i.e., a principle instructing to do a certain action, which is to be obeyed by all in same society of the covenant (Ps 19:9[EB 8]; 103:18; 111:7; 119:4, 15, 27, 40, 45, 56, 63, 69, 78, 87, 93, 64. 100, 104, 110, 128, 134, 141, 159, 168, 173+)."[41] With heartfelt gratefulness, the psalmist speaks of these "orders" or "precepts." He writes, "Consider how I love your orders! O Jehovah, according to your loyal love preserve my life." "From your orders I get understanding; therefore I hate every false way." "I understand more than the aged, for I keep your orders."–Psalm 119:159, 104, 100.

The term *regulation* ("statutes" in the ASV, ESV, LEB, CSB, NASB et al) translates the Hebrew word (*ḥōq*), which means "**regulation**, decree, statute, ordinance, i.e., a clear communicated prescription of what one should do (Ge 47:26; Ex 15:25)."[42] Over and over again the Psalmist asks God, "Teach me your regulations" (vss. 12, 26, 64, 68, 124, 135), and he also praises God for doing so. "Let my lips utter praise, for you teach me your regulations." (Ps 119:171) The Psalmist not only wanted to learn the regulations set out by God but also desired to observe them. "I will keep your regulations; do not utterly forsake me!"–Ps. 119:8.

The term *testimonies* translates the Hebrew word (*'ē·dūt*), which means "**statute**, stipulation, regulation, i.e., a principle or contingent-particular point of law, having authority to give consequences for not keeping, with a possible focus that these commands serve as a warning, urging, or witness to the covenant agreement (1Ki 2:3; Ps 19:8[EB 7])."[43] The focus is on the fact that these commands are serving as a warning that is gone over again and again, repeatedly, i.e., a reminder. The Psalmist greatly appreciated these reminders and frequently tells of having kept them. (Ps. 119:22, 88, 129, 167, 168) The Psalmist sang, "Incline my heart to your testimonies [reminders], and not to dishonest gain." (Ps. 119:36)

---

[41] IBID

[42] IBID

[43] IBID

The Psalmist had no shame when it came to talking about God's testimonies. "I will also speak of your testimonies [reminders] before kings and shall not be put to shame."–Ps. 119:46.

The above five terms "commandment(s)," "law," "orders," "regulations," and "testimonies," is used by the Psalmist as he refers to matters that has much in common with the Word of God. Another term that is a bit different is the Hebrew (*miš·pāṭ*) "judgment." As God's people, we are to have a reverential (wholesome) fear of his judgments. The Psalmist writes, "My flesh trembles[44] for fear[45] of you, and I am afraid of your judgments." (Ps. 119:120) This **is not** dreading the Father; it is dreading displeasing the Father. The Psalmist tells us I will praise you with an upright heart when I <u>learn</u> your righteous <u>judgments</u>." (Ps. 119:7) He goes on to say, "With my lips I <u>declare</u> all the <u>judgments</u> of your mouth." (Ps. 119:13) He then says, "My soul is crushed with <u>longing</u> for your <u>judgments</u> at all times." (Ps. 119:20) He also says, "I have sworn an oath and confirmed it, to <u>keep</u> your righteous <u>judgments</u>." (Ps. 119:106) The Psalmist follows with, "Hear my voice according to your loyal love; O Jehovah, according to **your justice give me life**. Great is your mercy, O Jehovah; **give me life** according to your <u>judgments</u>.–Ps. 119:149, 156.

Another word that the author of Psalm 119 seems to be fond of is (Heb. *'im·rā(h)*) "promise." It is rendered "word," "saying" (Gen 4:23), "instruction," "teach" (Deut. 32:2), a "prayer" (Ps. 17:6), a "promise" (Ps. 119:41), and "a word" (or promise). (Ps. 119:133). The Psalmist uses it most often in references to God's "promises" throughout Psalm 119. He writes, "Let your **loyal love come to me**, O Jehovah, your salvation **according to your** <u>promise</u>." (Ps. 119:41) He then says, "I entreat your face[46] with all my heart; **be gracious** to me **according to your** <u>promise</u>." (Ps. 119:58) He goes on, "**Sustain me according to your** <u>promise</u>, that I may live, and let me not be put to shame in my hope." (Ps. 119:116) The Psalmist then says, "<u>Make my steps steady</u> according to your <u>promise</u>, and do not let any error have dominion over me." (Ps. 119:133) In his last use, he writes, "Let my plea come before you; **deliver me according to your** <u>promise</u>." The Psalmist uses the same word in reference to God's "word," i.e., a promise, assurance, or guarantee, namely, God gives us his "word." The Word of God, i.e., the Scriptures are God's "word" to us. The Psalmist says, "In my heart I treasure up your **word**, so that I may not

---

[44] This (Heb. *sā·mǎr*) is literally to "bristle up" from some fearful expectation.

[45] This (Heb. *pā·ḥǎd*) is literally "to shake" because of fear, terror or dread over an expectation or anticipation of an impending judgment.

[46] I.E. *your favor*

sin against you." Many verses later he says, "I rejoice at your **word** like one who finds great spoil." Yes, having God's word and promises is like finding a great treasure.

C. GOD'S WORD IN YOUR LIFE

How Will You Know Unless You Study

- The Bible Gives Us Answers to Questions about Life
- The Bible Offers How to Get the Best out of Life Now
- The Bible Offers How to Best Live In an Imperfect World
- The Bible helps us to See What the Future Holds
- The Bible helps us Share the Good News
- The Bible Helps Us Achieve and Maintain Our Spirituality
- The Bible Helps Us Understand the Will and Purposes of the Creator
- Knowing and Applying God's Word Can Protect Us from False Teachers
- Knowing and Applying God's Word Can Help Us Deal with Our Human Imperfection

"Deep study is no guarantee that mature faith will result, but shallow study guarantees that immaturity continues." Dr. Lee M. Fields

Merely reading the Bible is no use at all without we study it thoroughly, and hunt it through, as it were, for some great truth. Dwight L. Moody

Remember, Christ's scholars must study upon their knees. Charles Spurgeon

Beginning with the Right Mindset

Ezra 7:10 Updated American Standard Version (UASV)

[10] For Ezra had **prepared his heart** to study the Law of Jehovah, and to do it and to teach its regulations and judgments in Israel.

Psalm 119:15-16 Updated American Standard Version (UASV)

[15] I will **meditate on** your precepts
  and **keep my eyes on** your ways.
[16] I will **delight in** your statutes;
  I will **not forget** your word.

How Powerful Are the Scriptures?

Hebrews 4:12 Updated American Standard Version (UASV)

[12] For the word of God is **living and active** and sharper than any two-edged sword, and piercing as far as the division of soul and spirit, of both joints and marrow, and able to judge the thoughts and intentions of the heart.

Joshua 1:8 Updated American Standard Version (UASV)

[8] This Book of the Law shall **not depart from your mouth**, but you shall **meditate on it day and night**, so that you may be careful to do according to all that is written in it; for then you will make your way prosperous, and then you will have good success.

Ephesians 6:17 Updated American Standard Version (UASV)

[17] And take the helmet of salvation, and the sword of the Spirit, which is **the word of God**.

Studying the Bible Helps with Life and Temptation

Proverbs 4:10-13 Updated American Standard Version (UASV)

[10] Hear, my son, and **accept my words**,
  that the years of your life may be many.
[11] In the way of **wisdom** I have taught you;
  I have led you in the paths of uprightness.
[12] When you walk, your step will not be hampered,
  and if you run, you will not stumble.
[13] Keep hold of **instruction**; do not let go;
  guard her, for she is your life.

Bible Study Can Protect Us from False Teachers

Matthew 24:4-5 Updated American Standard Version (UASV)

⁴ And Jesus answered them, "See that no one leads you astray. ⁵ For many will come in my name, saying, 'I am the Christ,' and they will lead many astray.

Matthew 24:9-11 Updated American Standard Version (UASV)

⁹ "Then they will deliver you up to tribulation, and will kill you, and you will be hated by all nations because of my name. ¹⁰ And then many will fall away,⁴⁷ will betray⁴⁸ one another, and will hate one another. ¹¹ And many **false prophets** will arise and will lead many astray.

2 Corinthians 4:3-4 Updated American Standard Version (UASV)

³ And even if our gospel is veiled, it is veiled to those who are perishing. ⁴ In their case **the god of this world** has **blinded** the minds of the unbelievers, to keep them from seeing the light of the gospel of the glory of Christ, who is the image of God.

2 Corinthians 11:13-15 Updated American Standard Version (UASV)

¹³ For such men are **false apostles**, deceitful workers, **disguising themselves** as apostles of Christ. ¹⁴ And no wonder, for even Satan disguises himself as an angel of light. ¹⁵ Therefore it is not a great thing if his servants also disguise themselves as servants of righteousness, whose end will be according to their deeds.

1 Thessalonians 3:5 Updated American Standard Version (UASV)

⁵ For this reason, when I could endure it no longer, I sent to learn about your faith, for fear that **the tempter** might have tempted you, and our labor would be in vain.

1 Timothy 4:1-3 Updated American Standard Version (UASV)

4 But the Spirit explicitly says that in later times some will fall away from the faith, paying attention to **deceitful spirits and doctrines of demons,** 2 by means of the hypocrisy of men who **speak lies,** whose conscience is seared as with a branding iron, ³ men who forbid marriage and command to abstain from foods that God created to be partaken of with thanksgiving by those who have faith and accurately know the truth.

---

⁴⁷ Lit *be caused to stumble*

⁴⁸ Or *hand over*

1 Timothy 6:3-5 Updated American Standard Version (UASV)

³ If anyone **teaches a different doctrine** and does not agree with the sound words, those of our Lord Jesus Christ, and with the teaching according to godliness, ⁴ he is conceited and understands nothing; but has a sick interest in controversial questions and disputes about words, out of which arise envy, strife, abusive language, evil suspicions, ⁵ and constant friction between men of depraved mind and deprived of the truth, who consider godliness to be a means of gain.

2 Timothy 2:15-17 Updated American Standard Version (UASV)

¹⁵ Do your best to present yourself to God as one approved, a workman who does not need to be ashamed, **rightly handling**[49] **the word of truth.** ¹⁶ But avoid empty speeches that violate what is holy, for they will lead to more and more ungodliness, ¹⁷ and their word will spread like gangrene; Hymenaeus and Philetus are among them.

2 Timothy 4:3-4 Updated American Standard Version (UASV)

³ For there will be a time when they **will not put up with sound teaching,** but in accordance with their own desires, they will accumulate teachers for themselves to have their ears tickled,[50] ⁴ and will turn away their ears from the truth and will turn aside to myths.

1 Peter 5:8-9 Updated American Standard Version (UASV)

⁸ Be sober-minded;[51] be watchful. Your adversary the devil prowls around like a roaring lion, **seeking someone to devour.** ⁹ Resist him and be firm in the faith, knowing that the same sufferings are being experienced by your brothers in the world.

2 Peter 2:1-3 Updated American Standard Version (UASV)

2 But **false prophets** also arose among the people, just as there will also be false teachers among you, who will secretly introduce destructive heresies, even denying the Master who bought them, bringing swift destruction upon themselves. ² Many will follow their acts of shameless conduct,[52] and because of them the way of the truth will be spoken of

---

[49] Or *accurately handling* the word of truth; *correctly teaching* the word of truth

[50] Or *to tell them what they want to hear*

[51] **Sober Minded:** (Gr. *nepho*) This denotes being sound in mind, to be in control of one's thought processes and thus not be in danger of irrational thinking, 'to be sober-minded, to be well composed in mind.'–1 Thessalonians 5:6, 8; 2 Timothy 4:5; 1 Peter 1:13; 4:7; 5:8

[52] Or *their sensuality; their licentious ways; their brazen conduct*

abusively; ³ and in their greed they will exploit you with false words; their judgment from long ago is not idle, and their destruction is not asleep.

Jude 1:4 Updated American Standard Version (UASV)

⁴ Certain men have **crept in among you** who were long ago appointed for this judgment, ungodly men⁵³ who turn the grace of our God into an excuse for licentiousness⁵⁴ and who prove false to our only Master and Lord, Jesus Christ.

Acts 17:11 Updated American Standard Version (UASV)

¹¹ Now these were more noble-minded than those in Thessalonica, who received the word with all eagerness,⁵⁵ **examining the Scriptures daily** to see whether these things were so.

1 John 4:1 Updated American Standard Version (UASV)

4 Beloved ones, do not believe every spirit, but **test the spirits** to see whether they are from God, for many false prophets have gone out into the world.

Studying the Bible Helps Us Serve God Better

2 Timothy 3:16-17 Updated American Standard Version (UASV)

Every scripture is inspired by God and useful for teaching, for reproof, for correction, and for training in righteousness, that the person dedicated to God may be capable and equipped for every good work.

2 Timothy 2:15 Updated American Standard Version (UASV)

Be diligent to present yourself approved to God as a workman who does not need to be ashamed, accurately handling the word of truth.

---

⁵³ Lit *irreverential (ones)*

⁵⁴ Or loose conduct; shameless conduct (Gr *aselgeia*) behavior completely lacking in moral restraint, usually with the implication of sexual licentiousness—'licentious behavior, extreme immorality.'

⁵⁵ Or with all *readiness of mind.* The Greek word *prothumias* means that one is eager, ready, mentally prepared to engage in some activity.

Studying the Bible Makes Us Better Disciple Makers

Matthew 24:14 Updated American Standard Version (UASV)

¹⁴ And this gospel of the kingdom will be **proclaimed** in all the inhabited earth⁵⁶ as a testimony to all the nations, and then the end will come.

Matthew 28:19-20 Updated American Standard Version (UASV)

¹⁹ Go therefore and **make disciples** of all the nations, baptizing them in the name of the Father and the Son and the Holy Spirit, ²⁰ **teaching** them to observe all that I commanded you; and look, I am with you always, even to the end of the age."

Acts 1:8 Updated American Standard Version (UASV)

⁸ But you will receive power when the Holy Spirit has come upon you; and you will be my **witnesses** in both Jerusalem and in all Judea and Samaria, and **to the extremity of the earth**."

Hebrews 5:11-6:1 Updated American Standard Version (UASV)

¹¹ Concerning whom we have much to say, and it is hard to explain, since you have become dull of hearing.⁵⁷ ¹² For in view of the time **you ought to be teachers**, you have need again for someone to teach you from the beginning the elementary things of the sayings⁵⁸ of God, and you have come to need milk and not solid food. ¹³ For everyone who partakes of milk is unacquainted with the word of righteousness, for he is an infant. ¹⁴ But solid food belongs to the mature, to those who through practice have their discernment trained to distinguish between good and evil.

6 Therefore, leaving behind the elementary doctrine about the Christ, let us press on to maturity, not laying again a foundation of repentance from dead works and faith in God,

---

⁵⁶ Or *in the whole world*

⁵⁷ **Hearing, Dull of:** (Gr. *Nōthros tais akoais*) This is an idiom, which literally means that one has 'lazy ears.' In other words, they are slow to learn, to understand, to react, lacking intellectual perception, with the implication that this is so because they are lazy. Have we become lethargic in the truth, to the point of having lazy ears? Are we slow to learn, to understand, to react, lacking intellectual perception?–Heb. 5:11.

⁵⁸ **Sayings:** (Gr. *logia, on* [only in the plural]) A saying or message, usually short, especially divine, gathered into a collection.–Acts 7:38; Romans 3:2; Hebrews 5:12; 1 Peter 4:11.

Studying the Bible Helps Us In Our Defending God's Word

2 Timothy 2:2 Updated American Standard Version (UASV)

² and the things which you have heard from me in the presence of many witnesses, entrust these to faithful men who will be able to **teach** others also.

1 Peter 3:15 Updated American Standard Version (UASV)

¹⁵ but sanctify Christ as Lord in your hearts, always being prepared to make a defense[59] to anyone who asks you for a reason for the hope that is in you; yet do it with gentleness and respect;

We Cannot Live On Food Alone

Matthew 4:4 Updated American Standard Version (UASV)

⁴ But he answered, "It is written,

"'Man shall not live by bread alone,
but by every word that proceeds out of the mouth of God.'"[60]

God's Word Does Not Fail

Isaiah 55:11 Updated American Standard Version (UASV)

¹¹ so shall my word be that goes out from my mouth;
  it shall not return to me empty,
but it shall **accomplish** that which I purpose,
  and shall succeed in the thing for which I sent it.

Luke 1:37 Updated American Standard Version (UASV)

³⁷ For **nothing** will be impossible with God."

God Guides and Directs Us Through His Word

Isaiah 30:20-21 Updated American Standard Version (UASV)

²⁰ And though Jehovah[61] give you the bread of distress and the water of oppression, yet **your Teacher**[62] will no longer hide himself, but your

---

[59] Or *argument*; or *explanation*

[60] A quotation from Deut. 8:3

[61] One of 134 scribal changes from *YHWH* to *Adhonai.*

eyes shall behold your Teacher. [21] And your ears shall hear a word behind you, saying, "**This is the way,** walk in it," when you turn to the right or when you turn to the left.

Isaiah 48:17-18 Updated American Standard Version (UASV)

[17] Thus says Jehovah,
  your Redeemer, the Holy One of Israel:
"I am Jehovah your God,
  who teaches you to profit,
  who **leads you** in the way you should go.
[18] Oh that you had paid attention to my commandments!
  Then your peace would have been like a river,
  and your righteousness like the waves of the sea;

Isaiah 54:13 Updated American Standard Version (UASV)

[13] All your sons shall be **taught** by Jehovah,
  and great shall be the peace of your sons.

Studying the Bible Is an Evident Demonstration that We Love, Respect and Honor God and His Word

Colossians 3:17 Updated American Standard Version (UASV)

[17] And whatever you do, **in word or deed,** do all in the name of the Lord Jesus, **giving thanks to God** the Father through him.

Psalm 119:96-98 Updated American Standard Version (UASV)

[96] I have seen a limit to all perfection,
  but your **commandment** is exceedingly broad.

[97] Oh how **I love your law!**
  It is my **meditation** all the day.
[98] Your commandment makes me wiser than my enemies,
  for it is ever with me.

Psalm 119:47-48 Updated American Standard Version (UASV)

[47] for I find my **delight in your commandments,**
  which I **love.**
[48] And I will lift up my hands toward your commandments, which I love,
  and I will meditate on your statutes.

---

[62] Lit *your teachers.* The Hebrew verb is plural to denote grandeur or excellence.

Studying the Bible Is a Path to What Leads to Salvation

John 5:39-40 Updated American Standard Version (UASV)

39 You **search the Scriptures**[63] because you think that in them you have eternal life; and it is these that bear witness about me. 40And yet you do not want to come to me that you may have life.

Store God's Word in Your Heart

Psalm 119:11-12 Updated American Standard Version (UASV)

11 In my heart I **treasure** up your word,
    so that I may not sin against you.
12 Blessed are you, O Jehovah;
    teach me your regulations!

Psalm 37:31 Updated American Standard Version (UASV)

31 The law of his God is in his heart;
    his steps do not slip.

Scripture is God-Breathed and Fully Inerrant

2 Peter 1:20-21 Updated American Standard Version (UASV)

20 But know this first, that no prophecy of Scripture comes from one's own interpretation, 21 for no prophecy was ever produced by the will of man, but men carried along by the Holy Spirit spoke from God.

Proverbs 30:5-6 Updated American Standard Version (UASV)

5 Every word of God proves true;
    he is a shield to those who take refuge in him.
6 Do not add to his words,
    lest he reprove you and you be found a liar.

Studying the Bible Transforms Your Life

Romans 12:1-2 Updated American Standard Version (UASV)

12 Therefore I urge you, brothers, by the mercies of God, to present your bodies a living and holy sacrifice, acceptable to God, which is your rational service.[64] 2 And do not be conformed to this world, but be

---

[63] The Scriptures do give us the path, the direction, the guidance to what leads to eternal life. Jesus was not condemning the study of Scripture for that purpose. He was condemning their motive, studying the Scripture, not out of love for God's Word, but for dishonest gain. The Jewish religious leaders also misinterpreted the Scriptures.

[64] Lit *the reasonable (or rational, logical) service of you*

transformed by the renewing of your mind, so that you may prove what the will of God is, that which is good and acceptable[65] and perfect.

Ephesians 4:23-24 Updated American Standard Version (UASV)

[23] and to be renewed in the spirit of your minds, [24] and put on the new man,[66] the one created according to the likeness of God in righteousness and loyalty of the truth.

Colossians 3:8-10 Updated American Standard Version (UASV)

[8] But now you must put them all away: anger, wrath, malice, slander, and obscene talk from your mouth. [9] Do not lie to one another, seeing that you have put off the old man[67] with its practices [10] and have put on the new man[68] who is being renewed through accurate knowledge[69] according to the image of the one who created him,

Keep This In Mind

Matthew 5:6 Updated American Standard Version (UASV)

[6] "Blessed are those who hunger and thirst for righteousness, for they shall be satisfied.

Romans 15:4 Updated American Standard Version (UASV)

[4] For whatever was written in former days was written for our instruction, that through endurance and through the encouragement of the Scriptures we might have hope.

---

4. Paul explains why he can appeal to Scripture in this way. *Everything that was written in the past* means "all that was written in Scripture"; it is not an endorsement of every piece of literature that comes down from earlier ages. But we should bear in mind that *everything* is comprehensive:[70] Paul is not saying that there are some good things in the

---

[65] Or *well-pleasing*

[66] An interpretive translation would have, "put on the new person," because it does mean male or female.

[67] Or *old person*

[68] Or *new person*

[69] *Epignosis* is a strengthened or intensified form of *gnosis* (*epi*, meaning "additional"), meaning, "true," "real," "full," "complete" or "accurate," depending upon the context. Paul and Peter alone use *epignosis.*

[70] ὅσα, "whatever things"; NIV is not an exact translation but gives the sense of it. Notice that προεγράφη is followed up by ἐγράφη, "a classical idiom by which the

Bible, but that all of it was written for[71] our[72] instruction (cf. 4:23–24). "Our" evidently has some emphasis: although it was written in earlier ages it was intended for *our* instruction (cf. 1 Cor. 9:9–10).[73] The reason[23] for their being written was that *we might have hope*. The present tense of the verb points to continuous possession, and the article before *hope* seems to show that it is not the general hope of mankind of which Paul is writing, but the specifically Christian hope, the hope that is given by what Christ has done in winning our salvation, the hope that leaves no doubts and sustains Christ's people in the darkest days (see the note on 4:18).[74]

Paul speaks of two things important in bringing this about: *endurance* and *the encouragement of the Scriptures*. It is not clear whether we should take both *endurance* and *encouragement* as deriving from the Scriptures (as GNB, "through the patience and encouragement which the Scriptures give us") or whether we should see Paul as specifically linking only *encouragement* with the Scriptures (as Moffatt, "by remaining stedfast and drawing encouragement from the scriptures").[75] Of course the Christian's *endurance* and *encouragement* both come from God, and it may well be said that Scripture has a part in producing both. The question here is whether Paul is linking them both with the Bible or only one; his construction seems to show that only

---

preposition in a compound is omitted, without weakening the sense, when the verb is repeated" (M, I, p. 115). προεγράφω is used in a different sense in Gal. 3:1.

[71] εἰς conveys the thought of purpose, "with a view to".

[72] This is Paul's one use of ἡμέτερος in Romans (it is found once each in 2 Timothy and Titus, and eight times in all in the New Testament). His "our" refers to the Christians, which leads to the conclusion, "This statement is a bold generalization expropriating all Scriptures for the infant church" (Denis Farkasfalvy in William R. Farmer and Denis M. Farkasfalvy, *The Formation of the New Testament Canon* [New York, 1983], p. 105).

[73] διδασκαλία may be used in the active sense, "instruction", or in the passive, "that which is taught"; here it is the active (BAGD). The word occurs 15 times in the Pastorals, and 19 times in the Pauline corpus out of 21 times in the New Testament.

[74] Cf. William Watty, "May I therefore suggest that this is our unique contribution to the world of to-day? It is to offer the Biblical message of hope from the God of hope to a world of shattered hopes" (ET, LXXXVII [1975–76], p. 50).

[75] Paul has διά before τῆς ὑπομονῆς and another διά before τῆς παρακλήσεως. It is this repetition of the preposition that seems to show that the two are separated. If he were saying that both qualities are derived from Scripture we would expect only one διά. Käsemann says that the first διά "denotes an accompanying circumstance, the second is causal.... Scripture gives comfort and leads to patience" (p. 383). NEB has "that through the encouragement they give us we may maintain our hope with fortitude", but there seems no reason for linking "hope" with "fortitude".

encouragement is here said to derive from the Bible. The apostle often speaks of *endurance*[76] and of *encouragement*.[77] Both are important. We need steadfastness in our Christian life and we need the encouragement the Bible can give; our life is a very poor thing without either.[78]

---

[76] ὑπομονή is found in Paul in exactly half its New Testament occurrences (16 out of 32; six in Romans); see the note on 2:7. It is often taken to mean "patience", but this is too negative a virtue for this word. It is rather "fortitude" or *endurance*. Griffith Thomas quotes A. Beet on the importance of this word in the present context: "Our Christian character is seldom so severely tried as when we are put to inconvenience by the spiritual childishness of members of the Church."

[77] παράκλησις is found in Paul 20 times out of 29 in the New Testament, three being in Romans. See the note on the corresponding verb in 12:1. It is often understood of comfort (as KJV), and it can refer to exhortation, but *encouragement* seems right in this place.

[78] Leon Morris, *The Epistle to the Romans*, The Pillar New Testament Commentary (Grand Rapids, MI; Leicester, England: W.B. Eerdmans; Inter-Varsity Press, 1988), 499–500.

CHAPTER 2 How the Bible Came Down to Us

We have a young man, who is a has been on the run from the Catholic church for many years, all the while working as a printer and a translator of the English Bible. Many times, there was a pounding at the door, only to find that this translator and his apprentice has left moments earlier. The Catholic Church viewed the Bible in the language of the common people as illegal literature, because the people were too illiterate to understand the Word of God.[79] The Bible had been locked up in the dead language of Latin for almost a thousand years. Who was the translator? He was William Tyndale, i.e., "God's Outlaw," who had been pursued by the false friend of the Catholic Church, as though he were the worst criminal on the planet in the early 16th-century. While King James is credited with the most popular Bible that has ever been published, it was actually William Tyndale who should be credited, because the 1611 King James Version was 97 percent Tyndale's English translation. The Word of God has had many enemies since the first book, Genesis, was published, some 3,500 years ago.

HOW WE GOT THE OLD TESTAMENT

The Old Testament, the inspired Word of God, how was it copied, maintained as to the textual reliability, and handed down throughout the past three thousand five hundred years?

It should be appreciated that what we possess today is nothing short of Word of God that the Old Testament writers penned throughout a 1,600-year period, from the time of Moses to Malachi. While it certainly is not probable that God personally preserved these documents by the same way that he miraculously inspired the Scriptures to be error free; there is little doubt that he blessed the work of those who worked on the copies, and has blessed our attempts at restoring the text. Skeptics would consider it as mere coincidence that, we have a storehouse of manuscript treasure for both the Old Testament and New Testament documents while secular writings are nowhere near so fortunate. The secular writings of antiquity are reflected in but a handful of manuscripts for any given author. Moreover, they are hundreds of years removed from the date of

---

[79] We will see that another group assigned with the task of dispensing the Word of God has similar feeling about its readers.

the original copy, making them less trustworthy; while the Old Testament and New Testament are preserved in tens of thousands of manuscripts, with a number being within a century or two from the original copy[80] (especially the NT).

Isaiah 40:8 Updated American Standard Version (UASV)

[8] The grass withers, the flower fades,
　　but the word of our God will stand forever.

The Bible reader has every right to ask if the book that he carries has been tainted throughout the centuries of copying and recopying. What we possess today, is it a complete reflection of what was penned so many centuries ago? Does the evidence suggest that the manuscripts have been transmitted faithfully from the original-language texts so that the reader of God's Word can feel safe that the Bible is trustworthy? We know that scribal errors have crept into the text, after centuries of copying by hand, but have the textual scholars been able to ascertain what the original text was? There are many excellent books that cover the trustworthiness of the text of the Old and New Testaments; we will not be able to go into in great detail herein, because of limited space, but we can lay an excellent foundation, and suggest further reading. However, what is covered will be very informative and beneficial to examine.[81]

Men that were chosen by God penned the original manuscripts in Hebrew and a very small portion in Aramaic languages. Moses was the first in the late 16th-century B.C.E.,[82] who wrote the first five books of the Bible, down to about 443 B.C.E., with Malachi penning the book that bears his name, and Nehemiah writing the book that bears his name, totaling 39 canonical books for the Hebrew Old Testament. There are no original manuscripts in existence today. Around 642 B.C.E., in the time of King Josiah, Hilkiah, the high priest "found the Book of the Law" of Moses, very likely the original copy, which had been stored away in the house of God. At this point, it had survived for some 871 years. Jeremiah

---

[80] When we use the term "original" reading or "original" text in this publication, it is a reference to the exemplar manuscript by the New Testament author (e.g., Paul) and his secretary (e.g., Tertius) from which other copies was made for publication and distribution into the Christian communities. It should be noted that the author likely penned some books without the use of a secretary, such as the apostle John in First and Second John.

[81] THE TEXT OF THE NEW TESTAMENT: The Science and Art of Textual Criticism by Don Wilkins and Edward D. Andrews, ISBN-13: 978-1-945757-44-0

[82] B.C.E. means "before the Common Era," which is more accurate than B.C. ("before Christ"). C.E. denotes "Common Era," often called A.D., for *anno Domini*, meaning "in the year of our Lord."

was so moved by the particular discovery that he wrote about the occasion at 2 Kings 22:8-10. About 180 years later, in 460 B.C.E., Ezra wrote about the same incident as well. (2 Chron. 34:14-18) Ezra was very interested in this, not only because of the importance of the event itself but he "was a skilled scribe in the Law of Moses, which Jehovah, the God of Israel, had given." (Ezra 7:6, UASV) Considering Ezra's position, the fact he was a historian, a scribe, he would have had access to all of the scrolls of the Old Testament that had been copied and handed down up to his time. In some cases, some were likely the inspired originals from the authors themselves. It would seem that Ezra was well qualified to be the custodian of the manuscripts in his day.–Nehemiah 8:1-2

Period of Manuscript Copying

In the days of Ezra and beyond, there would have been an increasing need of copying the Old Testament manuscripts. As you may recall from your personal Bible study, the Babylonians took the Jews into captivity for seventy years. Most of the Jews did not return upon their release in 537 B.C.E., and after that. Tens of thousands stayed in Babylon while others migrated throughout the ancient world, settling in the commercial centers. However, the Jews would pilgrimage back to Jerusalem several times each year, for religious festivals. Once there, they would be reading from the Hebrew Old Testament and sharing in the worship of God. Over a century later in Ezra's day, the need to travel back to Jerusalem was no longer a concern, as they carried on their studies in places of worship known as synagogues, where they read aloud from the Hebrew Scriptures and discussed their meaning. As one might imagine, the scattered Jewish populations throughout the ancient world would have been in need of their own personal copies of the Hebrew Scriptures.

Within the synagogues, there was a storage room, known as the Genizah.[83] Over time, manuscripts would wear out to the point of tearing. Thus, it would have been placed in the Genizah and replaced with new copies. Before long, after the old manuscripts were built up in the Genizah, they would eventually need to be buried in the earth. They performed this duty, as opposed to just burning them, so the holy name of God, Jehovah (or Yahweh), would not be desecrated. Throughout many centuries, many thousands of Hebrew manuscripts were disposed of in this way. Gratefully, the well-stocked Genizah of the synagogue in Old

---

[83] The Genizah was storehouse for Hebrew books: a repository for Hebrew documents and sacred books that were no longer in use, e.g. because they are old and worn, but must not be destroyed.

Cairo was saved from this handling of their manuscripts, perhaps because it was enclosed and overlooked until the middle of the 19th century. In 1890, as soon as the synagogue was being restored, the contents of the Genizah were checked, and its materials were gradually either sold or donated. From this source, manuscripts that were almost complete and thousands of fragments have found their way to Cambridge University Library and other libraries in Europe and America.

Throughout the world, scholars have counted and cataloged about 6,300 manuscripts of all or portions of the Hebrew Old Testament. Textual scholars of the Hebrew Scriptures, for the longest time, had to be content with Hebrew manuscripts that only went back to the tenth century C.E. This, of course, meant that the Hebrew Old Testament was about 1,400 hundred years removed from the last book that had been penned. This, then, always left the question of the trustworthiness of those copies. However, all of that changed in 1947, in the area of the Dead Sea, there was discovered a scroll of the book of Isaiah. In following years more of these precious scrolls of the Hebrew Scriptures were found as caves in the Dead Sea area yielded an enormous amount of manuscripts that had been concealed for almost 1,900 years. Specialists in the area of paleography[84] have now dated some of these as far back as the third and second century B.C.E. The Dead Sea Scrolls as they have become known, vindicated the trust that had been placed in the Masoretic texts[85] that we have possessed all along. A comparative study of the approximately 6,000 manuscripts of the Hebrew Scriptures gives a sound basis for establishing the Hebrew text and reveals faithfulness in the transmission of the text.

The Hebrew Language

Hebrew is the language in which the thirty-nine inspired books of the Old Testament were penned, apart from the Aramaic sections in Ezra 4:8–6:18; 7:12–26; Dan. 2:4b–7:28; Jer. 10:11, as well as a few other words and phrases from Aramaic and other languages. The language is not called "Hebrew" in the Old Testament. At Isaiah 19:18 it is spoken of as "the language [Literally "lip"] of Canaan." The language that became known as "Hebrew" is first shown in the introduction to Ecclesiasticus, an

---

[84] Paleography is the study of ancient writings: the study of ancient handwriting and manuscripts

[85] Hebrew Bible: the traditional text of the Hebrew Bible revised and annotated by Jewish scholars between the 6th and 10th centuries C.E.

Apocrypha[86] book. Moses, being raised in the household of Pharaoh, would have been given the wisdom of Egypt, as well as the Hebrew language of his ancestors. This would have made him the perfect person to look through any ancient Hebrew documents that may have been handed down to him, giving him the foundation for the book of Genesis.

Later, in the days of the Jewish kings, Hebrew came to be known as "Judean" (UASV) that is to say, the language of Judah (Neh. 13:24; Isa. 36:11; 2 Ki. 18:26, 28). As we enter the period of Jesus, the Jewish people spoke an expanded form of Hebrew, which would become Rabbinic Hebrew. Nevertheless, in the Greek New Testament, the language is referred to as the "Hebrew" language, not the Aramaic. (John 5:2; 19:13, 17; Acts 22:2; Rev. 9:11) Therefore, for more than 2,000 years, Biblical Hebrew served God's chosen people, as a means of communication.

However, once God chose to use a new spiritual Israel, made up of Jew and Gentile, there would be a difficulty within the line of communication as not all would be able to understand the Hebrew language. It became evident, 300 years before the rise of Christianity; there was a need for the Hebrew Scriptures to be a translation into the Greek language of the day, because of the Jewish diaspora who lived in Egypt. Down to our day, all or portions of the Bible have been translated into about 2,287 languages.

Even the Bible itself expresses the need of translating it into all languages. Paul, quoting Deuteronomy 32:43, says, "Rejoice, O Gentiles ["people of the nations"], with his people." And again, 'Praise the Lord, all you Gentiles, and let all the peoples extol him.'" (Rom 15:10) Moreover, all Christians are given what is known as the Great Commission, to "go therefore and make disciples of all nations." (Matt 28:19-20) In addition, Jesus stated, "this gospel of the kingdom will be proclaimed throughout the whole world as a testimony to all nations." (Matt 24:14) All of the above could never take place without translating the original language into the languages of the nations. What is more, ancient translations of the Bible that are extant (still in existence) in manuscript form have likewise aided in confirming the high degree of textual faithfulness of the Hebrew manuscripts.

Earliest Translated Versions

Versions are translations of the Bible from Hebrew, Aramaic, and Greek into other languages (or Hebrew into Greek). Translation work has

---

[86] The Old Testament Apocrypha are unauthentic writings: writings or reports that are not regarded as authentic.

made the Word of God accessible to billions of persons, who are incapable of understanding the original Biblical languages. The early versions of the Scriptures were handwritten and were, therefore, in the form of manuscripts. However, since the beginning of the printing press in 1455 C.E., many additional versions, or translations, have appeared, and these have been published in great quantities. Some versions have been prepared directly from Hebrew and Greek Bible texts, whereas others are based on earlier translations.

The Septuagint

The Septuagint is the common term for the Old Greek translation of the Hebrew Scriptures. The word means "seventy" and is frequently shortened by using the Roman numeral LXX, which is a reference to the tradition 72 Jewish translators (rounded off), who are alleged to have produced a version in the time of Ptolemy II Philadelphus (285-246 B.C.E.). The first five books of Moses being done around 280 B.C.E., with the rest being completed by 150 B.C.E. As a result, the name Septuagint came to denote the complete Hebrew Scriptures translated into Greek.

Acts 8:26-38 Updated American Standard Version (UASV)

Philip and the Ethiopian Eunuch

[26] But an angel of the Lord spoke to Philip saying, "Get up and go south to the road that descends from Jerusalem to Gaza." (This is a desert road.) [27] And he rose and went. And there was an Ethiopian, a eunuch, a court official of Candace, queen of the Ethiopians, who was in charge of all her treasure; who had come to worship in Jerusalem, [28] and he was returning and sitting in his chariot, and was reading the prophet Isaiah. [29] And the Spirit said to Philip, "Go over and join this chariot." [30] So Philip ran to him and heard him reading Isaiah the prophet and asked, "Do you understand what you are reading?" [31] And he said, "How can I, unless someone guides me?" And he invited Philip to come up and sit with him. [32] Now the passage of the Scripture that he was reading was this:

"He was led as a sheep to slaughter
 and like a lamb before its shearer is silent,
 so he opens not his mouth.
[33] In his humiliation was taken away.
 Who can describe his generation?
For his life is taken away from the earth."[87]

---

[87] A quotation from Isaiah 53:7–8

[34] And the eunuch answered Philip and said, "I beg you, of whom does the prophet say this? Of himself or of someone else?" [35] Then Philip opened his mouth, and beginning from this Scripture he declared to him the good news about Jesus. [36] And as they went along the road they came to some water; and the eunuch said, "Look! Water! **What prevents me from being baptized?"**[88] [38] And he commanded the chariot to stop, and they both went down into the water, Philip and the eunuch, **and he baptized him.**

The Eunuch court official was an influential man, who was in charge of the treasury of the queen of Ethiopia and to whom Philip preached. He was a proselyte [convert] to the Jewish religion who had come to Jerusalem to worship God. He had been reading aloud from the scroll of Isaiah (53:7-8 as our English Bible has it sectioned), and was puzzled as to whom it was referring to; however, Philip explained the text, and the Eunuch was moved to the point of being baptized. The Eunuch was not reading from the Hebrew Old Testament; rather he was reading from the Greek translation, known as the Greek Septuagint. This work was very instrumental to both Jews and Christians in the Greek-speaking world in which they lived.

What contributed to the Hebrew Old Testament being translated into Greek and when and how did it occur? What was the need that brought the Septuagint about? How has it affected the Bible throughout these last 2,200 years? What impact does the Septuagint still have for the translator today?

The Greek-Speaking Jews and the Septuagint

In 332 B.C.E., Alexander the Great had just finished destroying the Phoenician city of Tyre, and was now entering Egypt, but was received as a great deliverer, not as a conqueror. It was here that he would found the city of Alexandria, bringing mankind one of the great learning centers of all time in the ancient world. The result of Alexander's conquering much of the then known world was the spread of Greek culture and the Greek language. Alexander himself spoke Attic Greek, which was the dialect that spread throughout the territories that he conquered. As the Attic dialect spread, it interacted with other Greek dialects, as well as the local languages, resulting in what we call Koine Greek or common Greek spreading throughout this vast realm.

---

[88] p45, 74 ℵ AB C 33 81 614 vg syrp, h copsa, bo eth omit vs 37; E, many minuscules, itgig, h vgmss syrh with * copG67 arm, And Philip said, "If you believe with all your heart, you may." And he replied, "I believe that Jesus Christ is the Son of God."

By the time of the third century B.C.E., Alexandria had a large population of Jews. King Nebuchadnezzar of Babylon destroyed Jerusalem and exiled its people to Babylon centuries before. Many Jews had fled to Egypt at the time of the destruction. The returning Jews in 537, were scattered throughout southern Palestine, migrating to Alexandria after it was founded. The need of a Greek translation of the Hebrew Scriptures arose out of the necessity for the Jews in their worship services and education within the Jewish community of Alexandria.

Many of the Jews in Alexandria could no longer understand the Hebrew language, with others simply letting it grow out of practice. Most could only speak the common Greek of the Mediterranean world. However, they remained Jews in custom and culture and wanted to be able to understand the Scriptures that affected their everyday lives and worship. Therefore, the time was right for the production of the first translation of the Hebrew Scriptures.

Aristobulus of Paneas (c. 160 B.C.E.) wrote that the Hebrew law was translated into Greek, being completed during the reign of Ptolemy Philadelphus (285-246 B.C.E.). We cannot be certain as to what Aristobulus meant by the term "Hebrew law." Some have suggested that it encompassed only the Mosaic Law, the first five books of the Bible while others suggested that it was the entire Hebrew Scriptures.

Useful in the First Century

The Septuagint was put to use at great length by Greek-speaking Jews both prior to and throughout first-century Christianity. Just after Jesus ascension, at Pentecost 33 C.E., almost a million Jews customarily gathered in Jerusalem for the Passover and Festival of Weeks, coming from such places as the districts of Asia, Egypt, Libya, Rome, and Crete, places that spoke Greek. There is little doubt that these were using the Septuagint in their services. (Acts 2:9-11) As a result, the Septuagint played a major role in spreading the Gospel message in the Jewish and proselyte communities. For example, we can look to Stephen.[89]

Acts 6:8-10 Updated American Standard Version (UASV)

---

[89] "The first Christian martyr; foremost of those chosen to bring peace to the quarreling church (Acts 6:1–7) and so mighty in the Scriptures that his Jewish opponents in debate could not refute him (Acts 6:10) as he argued that Jesus was the Messiah. Saul of Tarsus heard Stephen's speech to the Jewish Sanhedrin accusing the Jewish leaders of rejecting God's way as their forefathers had (Acts 6:12–7:53). Saul held the clothes of those who stoned Stephen to death; he saw him die a victorious death." (Brand, Draper and Archie 2003, p. 1534)

⁸ And Stephen, full of grace and power, was performing great wonders and signs among the people. ⁹ But some men from what was called the Synagogue of the Freedmen, both <u>Cyrenians</u> and <u>Alexandrians</u> and some from <u>Cilicia</u> and <u>Asia</u>, rose up and disputed with Stephen. ¹⁰ But they were not able to withstand the wisdom and the Spirit with which he was speaking.

In his defense, Stephen gave a long history of the Israelite people, and at one point he said,

Acts 7:12-14 Updated American Standard Version (UASV)

¹² But when Jacob heard that there was grain in Egypt, he sent our fathers the first time. ¹³ On the second visit Joseph made himself known to his brothers, and the family of Joseph became known to Pharaoh. ¹⁴ And Joseph sent and summoned Jacob his father and all his kindred, <u>seventy-five persons in all</u>.

This account comes from Genesis chapter 46, verse 27, which reads, "All the persons of the house of Jacob who came into Egypt <u>were seventy</u>." The Hebrew Old Testament reads seventy, but it is the Septuagint that reads seventy-five. Therefore, Stephen was referencing the Septuagint in his defense before the synagogue of the Freedmen.

The Apostle Paul traveled about 10,282 miles on his missionary tours,[90] which brought him into contact with Gentiles, who feared the God of the Bible and the devout Greeks who worshiped God. (Acts 13:16, 26; 17:4) These became worshipers or fearers of God because they had access to the Septuagint. The Apostle Paul used the Septuagint quite often in his ministry, and his letters.–Genesis 22:18; Galatians 3:8

The Greek New Testament contains about 320 direct quotations, as well as a combined 890 quotations and paraphrases from the Hebrew Old Testament. Most of these are from the Septuagint. Therefore, those Septuagint quotes and paraphrases became a part of the inspired Greek New Testament. Jesus had said, "you will be my witnesses in Jerusalem and in all Judea and Samaria, and to the end of the earth." (Acts 1:8) He had also foretold, "this gospel of the kingdom will be proclaimed throughout the whole world." (Matt 24:14) For this to take place, it had to be translated into other languages, to reach the people earth wide.

---

[90] Stanford University recently unveiled ORBIS, a site that lets you calculate the time and cost required to travel by road or ship around the Roman world in A.D. 200. (University 2012)

Still Beneficial Today

The Septuagint's great purpose today is the light that it sheds on textual variants that crept into the Hebrew Old Testament text, as it was being copied throughout the centuries. An example of this can be found at Genesis 4:8, which reads,

Genesis 4:8 Updated American Standard Version (UASV)

[8] Cain said to Abel his brother. "Let us go out into the field."[91] And it came about when they were in the field, that Cain rose up against Abel his brother and killed him.

The portion "let us go out to the field" is not in the tenth century C.E. Hebrew manuscripts. However, it is found in the earlier Septuagint manuscripts, as well as the Samaritan Pentateuch,[92] the Peshitta,[93] and the Vulgate.[94] **First**, the Hebrew that is used to introduce speech [*yomer*, "to say something"] is in the Hebrew text, "Cain Spoke." However, no speech follows in the Hebrew text. Many scholars argue that these words were in the original Hebrew text, but were omitted accidentally very early. **Second**, a few others, on the other hand, claim that the Hebrew that is used to introduce speech [*yomer*, "to say something"] is used in three other passages, with nothing being said. Therefore, they maintain that the more difficult and shorter reading is original, which would mean that the Greek translators added the words to complete the meaning. This book supports the first textual argument, along with the majority of scholars. Herein, we see how the Septuagint can help in identifying textual errors that may have crept into the Hebrew text over centuries of copying.

The text of the LXX is largely close to that of the Masoretes and Vulgate. For instance, Genesis 4:1-6 is identical in both the LXX, Vulgate and the Masoretic Text. Similarly, Genesis 4:8 to the end of the chapter is the same. There is only one visible difference in that chapter, at 4:7

---

[91] **Genesis 4:8**: SP LXX It Syr inserts these bracketed words; Vg, "Let us go outdoors"; MT omits; some MSS and editions have an interval here.

[92] This version only encompasses the first five books, and is really a transliteration of the Hebrew text into Samaritan script, developed from the ancient Hebrew script.

[93] The Syriac version of the Bible, written around the 4th century.

[94] A Latin version of the Bible, produced by Saint Jerome in the 4th century.

Genesis 4:7, LXX and English Translation (NETS)	Genesis 4:7, Masoretic and English Translation from MT (Judaica Press)	Genesis 4:7, Latin Vulgate and English Translation (Douay-Rheims)
οὐκ ἐὰν ὀρθῶς προσενέγκῃς, ὀρθῶς δὲ μὴ διέλῃς, ἥμαρτες; ἡσύχασον· πρὸς σὲ ἡ ἀποστροφὴ αὐτοῦ, καὶ σὺ ἄρξεις αὐτοῦ.	הֲלֹא אִם תֵּיטִיב שְׂאֵת וְאִם לֹא תֵיטִיב לַפֶּתַח חַטָּאת רֹבֵץ וְאֵלֶיךָ תְּשׁוּקָתוֹ וְאַתָּה תִּמְשָׁל בּוֹ:	nonne si bene egeris recipes sin autem male statim in foribus peccatum aderit sed sub te erit appetitus eius et tu dominaberis illius
If you offer correctly but do not divide correctly, have you not sinned? Be still; his recourse is to you, and you will rule over him.	Is it not so that if you improve, it will be forgiven you? If you do not improve, however, at the entrance, sin is lying, and to you is its longing, but you can rule over it.	If thou do well, shalt thou not receive? but if ill, shall not sin forthwith be present at the door? but the lust thereof shall be under thee, and thou shalt have dominion over it.

However, the Hebrew text is the foundation and most trustworthy text. Thus, it is used to correct the Septuagint text as well. It is by the comparison of the Hebrew manuscripts, and the many early versions that we discover any textual errors, and establish the original reading. This can give us confidence that we are reading the Word of God. Old Testament textual scholar, Paul D. Wegner writes,

> The job of the textual critic is very similar to that of a detective searching for clues as to the original reading of the text. It is reminiscent of the master detective Sherlock Holmes who could determine a number of characteristics of the suspect from the slightest of clues left at the crime scene. In our case the "crime scene" is the biblical text, and often we have far fewer clues to work from than we would like. Yet the job of the textual critic is extremely important, for we are trying to determine the exact reading of a text in order to know what God has said and expects from us.[95]

---

[95] Paul D. Wegner, A Student's Guide to Textual Criticism of the Bible: Its History, Methods & Results (Downers Grove, Ill.: InterVarsity Press, 2006), 22-23.

We have complete copies of the Septuagint that go back to the fourth century C.E., and many other fragments that date much earlier.

The Aramaic Targums

The Aramaic word for "interpretation" or "paraphrase" is *targum*. (Brand, Draper and Archie 2003, p. 1558) After the exile from Babylon in 539 B.C.E., the Jews living in the territory of the Persian Empire came to use the common language of Aramaic. Therefore, it became necessary to have a translation of the Hebrew Old Testament in the Aramaic language. They probably assumed their current form by about the fifth century C.E. Although they are simply free paraphrases of the Hebrew text and not an accurate translation, they are a source of rich background to the text and give assistance in determining some problematic passages. In addition, "the material is of interest to NT scholars who attempt to understand the Judaism of which Jesus was a part." (IBID,. 1558)

The Latin Versions

Romans 15:24-25 Updated American Standard Version (UASV)

[24] whenever **I journey to Spain,** I hope that I will see you in passing and to be helped on my way there by you after I have first enjoyed your company for a time. [25] But now I am about to travel to Jerusalem to minister to the holy ones. (Bold mine)

The apostle Paul penned those words on his third missionary journey in Rome about 56 C.E. We cannot be certain if Paul ever made his journey to Spain. However, Clement of Rome describes Paul (c. 95 C.E.) as "having taught righteousness to the whole world and having reached the farthest limits of the West."[96] This very well could have included Spain. Regardless, through the efforts of Paul and his more than one hundred traveling companions, as well as other Christian missionaries after him, the Word of God did reach Spain by the second century C.E. As a result, the conditions were right for the Christians in Spain to have the Bible translated into Latin. Latin was the official language of Imperial Rome. However, it was not the common language of the people throughout the Roman Empire the first century C.E. By the last half of the second century C.E., Spain had long been under Roman rule, and Latin had become the common language.

The Latin translations of the Bible were used in the Western part of the Roman Empire to the Reformation. In fact, they are still in use today

---

[96] Michael William Holmes, *The Apostolic Fathers: Greek Texts and English Translations*, Third ed. (Grand Rapids, MI: Baker Books, 2007), 53.

in conjunction with translations from Latin into the common language, in the Roman Catholic Church.

Old Latin Versions (180 C.E.) came into existence prior to the end of the second century C.E. in Carthage, North Africa. Today we have thirty-two Old Latin manuscripts, Codex Vercellenis (it^a) being the oldest, dating to the fourth century. None of the Old Latin manuscripts is a complete New Testament, but most of the New Testament is preserved when we consider them all. Scholars typically speak of two basic types of Old Latin text: the African and the European. The sigla that represent the manuscripts of the Itala are italic lower-case letters, such as it^a (Vercellenis) Gospels; 4th c., it^{aur} (Aureus) Gospels; 7th c., it^b (Veronensis) Gospels; 5th c., it^d (Cantabrigiensis—the Latin text of Bezae) Gospels, Acts, 3 John; 5th c., it^e (Palatinus) Gospels; 5th c., it^f (Brixianus) Gospels; 6th c., it^{ff2} (Corbeiensis II) Gospels; 5th c., it^{g1} (Sangermanensis) Matthew; 8th–9th c., and it^{gig} (Gigas) Gospels; Acts; 13th c.

This version has been the primary text used by many of the Catholic translators in turning out other versions in the many languages of Western Christianity. How did the Vulgate come about? The Latin word *vulgatus* means "common, that which is popular." Latin was once the official language of the Roman Empire. Even though Greek was the common language that most people spoke up until the fourth century C.E., there was still a need for Latin translations of the New Testament, which were produced in the second century, and are known as the Old Latin texts. However, as times passed, especially after Constantine the Great legalized Christianity in 313 C.E., the differences in the Old Latin texts eventually became unbearable.

When the Latin Vulgate was first produced, it was in common, or popular, Latin of the day, which would have been understood without difficulty by the average people of the Western Roman Empire. In 382 C.E., Pope Damasus commissioned the leading Bible scholar of the time, Jerome, his advisor, to revise the Old Latin text. Jerome made two revisions of the Old Latin Psalms, in comparison with the Greek Septuagint. His translation of the Vulgate Bible was made directly from the original Hebrew language of the Old Testament and Greek language of the New Testament and was, therefore, not a version of a version. This approach created considerable controversy at the time. Jerome worked on his Latin translation from the Hebrew from about 390 to 405 C.E. The completed work included apocryphal books, which were also in copies of the Septuagint by this time. However, Jerome plainly distinguished between the books that were canonical and those that were not. There are no less than 10,000 Latin manuscripts today, as well as 9,300 other early versions.

The Hebrew Texts

The Sopherim

The Sopherim (scribes) were copyist from the days of Ezra down to the time of Jesus. While they were very serious about their task as a copyist, they did take liberties in making textual changes at times. Whether this was what Jesus had in mind cannot be know for certain, but Jesus condemned these scribes, for assuming powers that did not belong to them.–Matthew 23:2, 13.

The Consonantal Text

The Hebrew alphabet consists of 23 consonants, with no vowels. Unlike English though, Hebrew was not written from left to right but right to left. In the beginning, the reader had to supply the vowel sounds from his knowledge of the language. This would be like our abbreviations within the English language, such as "ltd" for limited. The Hebrew originally consisted of words made up only of consonants. Hence, "consonantal text" means the Hebrew text without any vowel markings. The consonantal text of the Hebrew manuscripts come to be fixed in form between the first and second centuries C.E., even though manuscripts with variants within the text continued to be produced for some time. Changes were no longer made, unlike the previous period of the Sopherim.

The Masoretic Text

Between the 6th and 10th centuries C.E., the Masoretes setup vowel point, and accent mark system. This would help the reader to pronounce the vowel sounds properly, meaning that there would be a standard, and no need to have the pronunciation handed down by oral tradition. Because the Masoretes saw the text as sacred, they made no changes to the text itself but chose to record notes within the margins of the text. Unlike the Sopherim before them, they did not take any textual liberties. Moreover, they drew attention to any textual issues, correcting them within the margins.

The devotement of the vocalizing and accent marking of the Masoretic text throughout this period was done by three different schools, that is, the Babylonian, Palestinian, and Tiberian. The Hebrew text that we now possess in the printed Hebrew Bibles is known as the

Masoretic Text, which came from the Tiberian school. The Masoretes of Tiberias, a city on the western shore of the Sea of Galilee, established this method.

Unlike the Tiberian school, which placed their vowel signs below the consonants, the Palestinian school positioned the vowel signs above the consonants. Only an insignificant number of such manuscripts came down to us from the Palestinian school, showing that this system of vocalization was flawed. The Babylonian method of vowel pointing was likewise placed above the consonants. A manuscript possessing the Babylonian pointing is the Petersburg Codex of the Prophets, of 916 C.E., preserved in the Leningrad Public Library, U.S.S.R. This codex contains the books of Isaiah, Jeremiah, Ezekiel, as well as the "minor" prophets, with marginal notes. Textual scholars have readily studied this manuscript and compared it with the Tiberian text. While it uses the system of vocalization that places the vowels above the text, it follows the Tiberian text as regards the consonantal text and its vowels and Masora. The British Museum has a copy of the Babylonian text of the Pentateuch, which is substantially in agreement with the Tiberian text.

The Dead Sea Scrolls

In the spring of 1947, a Bedouin shepherd threw a stone into a cave, marking an event that would be heard around the world, making the name "Dead Sea Scrolls" more known than any other associated with archaeology. As he released one of his rocks into the cave, the sound of a breaking earthenware jar came back at him. Upon further examination, he discovered the first of the Dead Sea Scrolls.

The discovery of the scrolls rise to fame has been partly fueled by the controversy among scholars and the media. Sadly, this has left a public scandal, where those, not in the know, are thrown back and forth by confusion and misinformation. Stories have spread about an enormous conspiracy, driven by anxiety that the scrolls disclose details that would damage the faith of Christians and Jews as well. Nevertheless, what is the real importance of these scrolls? More than 63 years have now gone by; is it possible that the facts can be known?

The Dead Sea Scrolls: What are They?

The Dead Sea Scrolls are manuscripts of the Old Testament. Many of them are in Hebrew, with some being in Aramaic and a small number in Greek. Many of these scrolls and fragments date to the third and second

Century B.C.E., almost 300 years before the birth of Jesus Christ. There were seven lengthy manuscripts in various stages of deterioration that had been acquired from the Bedouin. Soon other caves were being searched, with new discoveries of scrolls and fragments in the thousands. A total of eleven caves near Qumran, by the Dead Sea, were discovered between 1947 and 1956.

Since, it has been determined that there are 800 manuscripts, once all the scrolls and fragment are considered. About 200 manuscripts, or about twenty-five percent, are copies of portions of the Old Testament. The other seventy-five percent, or 600 manuscripts, belong to ancient non-Biblical Jewish writings, divided between Apocrypha[97] and Pseudepigrapha.[98]

Various scrolls that produced the greatest interest for the scholars were formerly unknown texts. Among these were the interpretations on matters of the Jewish law, detailed instructions for the community of the Qumran sect, eschatological works that disclose interpretations about the outcome of Bible prophecy and the end times, as well as liturgical poems and prayers. Among them too were unique Bible commentaries, the oldest examples of verse-by-verse[99] commentary on Biblical passages.

The Dead Sea Scrolls: Who Wrote Them?

After carefully dating these fragile documents, it has been determined that they were copied or composed sometime between the third century B.C.E and the first century C.E. A handful of scholars have suggested that these scrolls were hidden in the caves by Jews that fled just before the destruction of Jerusalem in 70 C.E. However, the vast majority of scholars find this to be mere speculation, because the content of the scrolls tells something quite different. For example, many scrolls reveal an outlook

---

[97] "The Protestant designation for the fourteen or fifteen books of doubtful authenticity and authority that are not found in the Hebrew Old Testament but are in manuscripts of the LXX; most of these books were declared canonical by the Roman Catholic church at the Council of Trent in 1546, and they call these books deuterocanonical (second canon)."—Geisler 1986, 637.

[98] "A word meaning "false writings" and used to designate those spurious and unauthentic books of the late centuries B.C. and early centuries A.D. These books contain religious folklore and have never been considered canonical by the Christian church."—Geisler 1986, 642.

[99] Of course, there were no verses in the ancient texts, as they were simply running text. It was Rabbi Isaac Nathan, while working on a concordance, numbered the Bible into verses in 1440 C.E. Robert Estienne (Stephanus) introduced his system for dividing the Bible's text into numbered verses in 1550 C.E., which we still use today.

and customs that were in conflict with the religious leaders in Jerusalem. The Dead Sea Scrolls disclose a community that held the belief that God did not approve of the priests and temple service in Jerusalem. On the other hand, they believed that God saw their form of worship in the desert as a substitute temple service until the return of the Messiah. Therefore, it is highly unlikely that the authorities at Jerusalem's temple would be in possession of such scrolls.

The Qumran community likely had a scriptorium (a room in a monastery for storing, copying, illustrating, or reading manuscripts); it is probable that people who became a part of the community brought scrolls in with them when they joined. Therefore, the Dead Sea Scrolls are a broad library collection. As applies to any extensive collection of books, the subject matter will be a wide range of thought, which will not reflect the thinking or religious worldview of any given reader within the community. Nevertheless, those texts, which encompass numerous copies, are more likely to take into account the general beliefs of the Qumran community as a whole.

The Hebrew Text Behind Today's Translations

We go clear back to the Second Rabbinic Bible of Jacob ben Chayyim (c. 1470 – before 1538), which was published in 1524-25. The second edition became the prototype of future Hebrew Bibles down to the twentieth century. It contained an enormous text-critical apparatus of Masoretic notes, which has never since been equaled in any edition.

"In London, Christian David Ginsburg, an emigrant Polish Jew, and Christian convert, produced a critical edition of the complete Hebrew Bible (1894, 1908, 1926) revised according to the Masora and early prints with variant readings from manuscripts and ancient versions. It was soon displaced by the Biblica Hebraica (1906, 1912) by Rudolf Kittel and Paul Kahle, two German biblical scholars. The third edition of this work, completed by Albrecht Alt and Otto Eissfeldt (Stuttgart, 1937), finally abandoned Ben Hayyim's text, substituting that of the Leningrad Codex (B 19a). It has a dual critical apparatus with textual emendations separated from the manuscript and versional variants. Since 1957 variants from the so-called Judaean Desert scrolls have been included. In progress at the Hebrew University of Jerusalem in the early 1970s was the preparation of a new text of the entire Hebrew Bible based on the Aleppo Codex to include all its own Masoretic notes together with textual differences found in all pertinent sources. A sample edition of the Book of Isaiah appeared in 1965."[100] The 1906 Hebrew scholar Rudolf Kittel released his first edition of the Hebrew text entitled Biblia Hebraica, or "The Hebrew Bible." We have every edition, such as the 7th, 8th, and 9th editions (1951-55). These are titled as Biblia Hebraica (BHK) and Biblia Hebraica Stuttgartensia (BHS).

HOW WE GOT THE NEW TESTAMENT

Below is a short overview of the copying process of the Greek text of the New Testament. We will cover its transmission in the Greek of the time, as well as other languages that it has been translated into; not to mention the trustworthiness of the critical text that we have today.

The first-century Christians, at Pentecost 33 C.E., had Holy Spirit come upon about 120 disciples waiting in Jerusalem, resulting in their speaking in many languages about "the mighty works of God." (Ac 2:1-4, 11) On that same day, about 3,000 were baptized. (Ac 2:37-41) Within a short time, the Jewish religious leaders were complaining of these disciples, "You have filled Jerusalem with your teaching." (Ac 5:27-28, 40-42) With what result? "The number of the disciples multiplied greatly in Jerusalem." (Ac 6:7) The early Christians spread throughout the then known world.

Areas of Intense Activity	Areas Touched by Activity
Rome	Spain
Macedonia	Italy
Greece	Malta
Black Sea	Mediterranean Sea
Asia	Illyricum
Bithynia	Mesopotamia
Pontus	Media
Galatia	Parthia
Cappadocia	Caspian Sea
Pamphylia	Elam
Syria	Arabia
Jerusalem	Cyrene
Cyprus	Libya
Crete	Egypt
Babylon	Ethiopia
Persian Gulf	Red Sea

[100] biblical literature - The Christian canon | Britannica.com.   May 22, 2017 https://www.britannica.com/topic/biblical-literature/The-Christian-canon

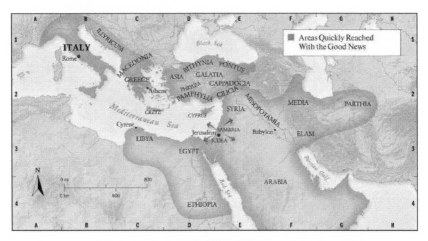

it-2 p. 744

The early Christian congregations were not isolated from one another. The Roman roads and maritime travel connected all the regions from Rome to Greece, to Asia, to Syria and Palestine and Egypt.[101] From the days of Pentecost 33 C.E. onward, Jewish or Jewish proselyte Christians returned to Egypt with the good news of Christ. (Acts 2:10) Three years after that, the Ethiopian eunuch traveled home with the good news as well. (Acts 8:26–39). Apollos of Alexandria, Egypt, a renowned speaker, came out of Egypt with the knowledge of John the Baptizer and arrived in Ephesus in about 52 C. E. (Acts 18:24-25) The apostle Paul traveled approximately 10,282 miles throughout the Roman Empire establishing congregations.[102] The apostles were a restraint to the apostasy and division within the whole of the first-century Christian congregation. (2 Thess. 2:6-7; 1 John 2:18) It was not until the second century that the next generation of Christian leaders gradually caused divisions.[103] However, the one true Christianity that Jesus started and the apostles established was strong, active, and able to defend against Gnosticism, Roman persecution, and Jewish hatred.

---

[101] People of the first three centuries sent and received letters and books from all over the Roman Empire. Hurtado has given us two examples: the Shepherd of Hermas was written in Rome and found its way to Egypt within a few decades; Irenaeus' Against Heresies was written in Gaul and made it to Egypt (Oxyrhynchus) within short order.

[102] http://orbis.stanford.edu/

[103] This apostasy and divisiveness did not just come into the Christian congregation out of nowhere. It started developing in the first-century, but was restrained by apostolic authority.

It is conceivable that by 55 C.E., there would have been a thriving congregation in Alexandrian Egypt, with its huge Jewish population.[104] "Now those who had been scattered because of the persecution that arose over Stephen went through as far as Phoenicia and Cyprus and Antioch, speaking the word to no one except Jews." (Acts 11:19) While this indicates a traveling north to Antioch, it does not negate a traveling south to Egypt. Antioch is obviously mentioned because it played a significant role as a commencement for first century Christianity, in particular for the apostle Paul.

The Coptic Church claims the Gospel writer Mark as its founder and first patriarch. Tradition has it that he preached in Egypt just before the middle of the first-century. At any rate, Christianity spread to Egypt and North Africa at an early date. In fact, it became a prominent religious center, with a noted scholar named Pantaenus, who founded a catechetical school in Alexandria, Egypt, about 160 C.E. In about 180 C.E. another prominent scholar, Clement of Alexandria, took over his position. Clement put this religious, educational institution on the map as a possible center for the whole of the Christian church throughout the Roman Empire. The persecution that came about the year 202 C.E. forced Clement to flee Alexandria, but one of the most noted scholars of early Christian history, Origen, replaced him. In addition, Origen took this scholarly environment to Caesarea in 231 C.E. and started yet another prominent school and scriptorium (i.e., room for copying manuscripts).

What does all of this mean? Of course, we cannot know absolutely, but textual scholar Philip W. Comfort[105] and others believe that the very early Alexandrian manuscripts that we now possess are a reflection of what would have been found throughout the whole of the Greco-Roman Empire from about 125–300 C.E. If we were to discover other early manuscripts from Antioch, Constantinople, Carthage, or Rome, they would be very similar to the early Alexandrian manuscripts. This means that these early papyri are a primary means of establishing the original text, and we are in a far better position today than were Westcott and Hort in 1881.

First-Century Manuscripts. All of the twenty-seven books of the New Testament were penned between 45 C.E. and 98 C.E. Yes, it has been

---

[104] Macquarie University, *Ancient History Documentary Research Center* (AHDRC), Papyri from the Rise of Christianity in Egypt (PCE),

http://www.anchist.mq.edu.au/doccentre/PCEhomepage.html.

[105] Philip W. Comfort, *The Quest for the Original Text of the New Testament* (Eugene, Oregon: Wipf and Stock Publishers, 1992).

discussed that there were likely changes made to some of the authors' books before it was released for publication. After looking at the rough draft of the book of Romans for example, likely both Paul and Tertius made some corrections, with Tertius producing the master copy after that to be the authorized publication, which would have been used to make other copies. Another example would be the Gospel of John. The last verse of chapter 20 seems to close the Gospel of John, which reads, "but these are written so that you may believe that Jesus is the Christ, the Son of God and that by believing you may have life in his name." The style of chapter 21 is that of the apostle John, and he clearly added it before publishing the authoritative copy to be used to make copies. This is not suggesting that there are two editions of John. It is suggesting that before John published the authoritative edition, he decided himself to add chapter 21. On this Andreas J. Köstenberger writes,

> Throughout the Johannine narrative, Jesus is repeatedly identified as Christ and Son of God. If the Gospel were to conclude with 20:30–31, this purpose statement would, at least on those grounds, provide sufficient closure. In fact, it has been conjectured that John originally planned to finish his Gospel at this point and only later appended an additional chapter. Alternatively, it has been suggested that someone other than John, perhaps some of his disciples, added chapter 21 after the apostle's death (e.g., Roberts 1987). This is possible. However, the presence of an epilogue seems required by the opening prologue in order to preserve balance and symmetry of structure. The prologue, in turn, is tied in so closely with the remainder of the Gospel that its composition cannot be easily relegated to a later follower of John. Hence, both prologue and epilogue frame the Gospel in such a way that they form an integral part of the theological and literary fabric of the entire narrative. Particularly notable is the way in which the relationship between Peter and the beloved disciple is resolved in terms of noncompetition. Another crucial element of resolution is the identification of the beloved disciple as the Fourth Evangelist. What is more, not only do language and style in chapter 21 not differ significantly from chapters 1–20, but also there are actually positive terminological links between this final chapter and the rest of the Gospel. Also, there is no textual evidence that the Gospel ever circulated in any form other than the present, canonical one (Ellis 1992: 18; Mahoney 1974: 12 [cited in Minear 1983: 86]). Finally, ending the Gospel immediately after Jesus' encounter with Thomas would have

seemed rather abrupt. For these reasons it must be maintained that the epilogue constitutes an integral part of John's Gospel. It is part of John's overall literary plan and provides the culmination of various strands carefully woven earlier in the Gospel. In fact, both the prologue and the epilogue can be shown to be integrally connected to the body of the Gospel by way of anticipation and resolution.[106]

Again, while there may have been some corrections and even some additions, it was done under the authority of the author himself before the authorized publication of the book. Once the official publication was released, there were no more changes by the author. Moreover, it is highly unlikely that anyone would have made any substantial changes to these documents while the authors were alive, or even during the lives of their coworkers and traveling companions. This is not to say that absolutely no copyist errors would have crept in during this period. However, it is highly unlikely that anyone would have been so bold as to alter the text of the author while he or his coworkers were around and could have challenged any such alterations. The New Testament authors had coworkers, such as Apollos, Barnabas, Silas, Timothy, Titus, Sopater, Secundus, Gaius, and Trophimus, to mention just a few. They also had secretaries, such as Tertius and Silvanus (or Silas), as well as Timothy possibly serving as Paul's secretary, as Timothy appears in the six letters that also bear his name in the greeting.[107] Then, there were also the 70 intimate disciples of Jesus Christ, who was with him throughout his ministry, as well as the 500 that saw the resurrected Jesus. The apostle John himself did not die until about 100 C.E.

---

[106] Andreas J. Köstenberger, *John*, Baker Exegetical Commentary on the New Testament (Grand Rapids, MI: Baker Academic, 2004), 583–586.

[107] **1 & 2 Thessalonians 1:1** (NASB) 1 Paul and Silvanus and Timothy, To the church of the Thessalonians ...

2 Corinthians 1:1 (NASB) 1 Paul, an apostle of Christ Jesus by the will of God, and Timothy *our* brother, To the church of God which is at Corinth ...

Philippians 1:1 (NASB) 1 Paul and Timothy, bond-servants of Christ Jesus, To all the saints in Christ Jesus who are in Philippi ...

Colossians 1:1 (NASB) 1 Paul, an apostle of Jesus Christ by the will of God, and Timothy our brother, ...

Philemon 1 (NASB) [1]Paul, a prisoner of Christ Jesus, and Timothy our brother, To Philemon ...

In addition, the authors themselves spoke of their writings as being authoritative and that no one should alter the copy that they had published. The apostle Paul wrote to the Galatians that they should consider as "accursed" anyone (even angels) who proclaimed a gospel contrary to the one they had preached. (Gal. 1:6-9) Paul went on to write, "the gospel that was preached by me is not according to man [i.e., human origin]. For I neither received it from man, nor was, I taught it, but I received it through a revelation [Lit., uncovering; disclosure] of Jesus Christ." (Gal. 1:11-12) The apostle Paul charged that 'the Corinthian Christians had put up with false teachers, readily enough, who proclaim another Jesus and another gospel.' (2 Cor. 11:3-4) Paul and Silas wrote to the Thessalonians that they continually thanked God that when the Thessalonians received the Word of God, which they had heard from them, they accepted it not as the word of men, but for what it really is, the **Word of God.** (1Thess. 2:3) Paul then closed that letter by commanding them "by the Lord, have this letter read aloud to all the brothers." (1 Thess. 5:27) In 2 Thessalonians Paul 'requested that they not be quickly shaken from their composure or be disturbed either by a spirit or a word or a letter as if from us.' (2:2) Paul closed the letter with a greeting in his own hand, to authenticate it. (3:17) Lastly, John closed the book of Revelation with a warning to everyone about adding to or taking away from what he had written therein. (Rev. 22:18-19) The New Testament authors were well aware that future scribes could intentionally alter the Word of God, so they warned them of the consequences.

We pause a moment to look at yet another author of the New Testament. The apostle Peter wrote about 64 C.E.,

2 Peter 1:12-18 New American Standard Bible (NASB)

[12] Therefore, I will always be ready to remind you of these things, even though you already know them, and have been established in the truth which is present with you. [13] I consider it right, as long as I am in this earthly dwelling, to stir you up by way of reminder, [14] knowing that the laying aside of my earthly dwelling is imminent, as also our Lord Jesus Christ has made clear to me. [15] And I will also be diligent that at any time after my departure you will be able to call these things to mind.

[16] For we did not follow cleverly devised tales when we made known to you the power and coming of our Lord Jesus Christ, but we were eyewitnesses of His majesty. [17] For when He received honor and glory from God the Father, such an utterance as this was made to Him by the Majestic Glory, "This is My beloved Son with whom I am well-

pleased"—[18] and we ourselves heard this utterance made from heaven when we were with Him on the holy mountain.

Peter was making it clear that he was sharing firsthand accounts and not devised tales. Here again, like the other New Testament authors, Peter warns his readers of false teachers, who corrupt the truth and distort the Scriptures, such as Paul's letters. Again, like Paul and John, warning that this would be to their own destruction.

2 Peter 3:15-16 New American Standard Bible (NASB)

[15] and regard the patience of our Lord *as* salvation; just as also our beloved brother Paul, according to the wisdom given him, wrote to you, [16] as also in all *his* letters, speaking in them of these things, in which are some things hard to understand, which the untaught and unstable distort, as *they do* also the rest of the Scriptures, to their own destruction.

Yes, "It is especially interesting that Peter writes of the distortion of Paul's letters along with 'the other Scriptures.' The implication is that the letters of Paul were already regarded as Scripture at the time Peter wrote."[108] Verse 16 shows that Peter "is aware of several Pauline letters. This knowledge again raises the dating issue. We know that Paul himself on one occasion had requested that churches share his letters: 'After this letter has been read to you, see that it is also read in the church of the Laodiceans and that you, in turn, read the letter from Laodicea' (Col 4:16). However, it is a big jump in time from Colossians to the first concrete evidence we have of people who know more than one letter. This evidence shows up in *1 Clement*, who not only knows Romans but can also write to the Corinthians, 'Take up the epistle of the blessed Apostle Paul' (*1 Clem.*[109] 47:1). It appears later in *2 Clement* and in Ignatius's *Ephesians*.[110] Thus, we are on solid ground when we accept that a collection of the Pauline letters existed by the end of the first century.[111] It is also likely that some Pauline letters circulated independently of a

---

[108] Allen Black and Mark C. Black, *1 & 2 Peter*, The College Press NIV Commentary (Joplin, MO: College Press Pub., 1998), 2 Pe 3:16.

[109] *1 Clem.* First Epistle of Clement to the Corinthians

[110] Ignatius, *Eph.* 12:2, refers to Paul, "who in all his Epistles makes mention of you in Christ Jesus." (Although one wonders how Ignatius thought the Ephesians were mentioned in every Pauline letter he knew.) On the evidence for 2 Clement's knowledge of a collection, see Karl P. Donfried, *The Setting of Second Clement in Early Christianity* (NovTSup 38; Leiden: E. J. Brill, 1974), 93–95.

[111] Jack Finegan, "The Original Form of the Pauline Collection," *HTR* 49 (1956) 85–104. See also Walter Schmithals, "Zur Abfassung und ältesten Sammlung der pauli nischen Hauptbriefe" ["On the Composition and Earliest Collection of the Major Epistles of Paul"], *ZNW* 51 (1960) 225–45.

collection (which is what one would expect as one church hears that another has a letter that might prove helpful in their situation),[112] and that there were collections of a few Pauline letters before there was a collection of all of his letters.[113] All of this is quite logical since Paul was a valued teacher in his circle of communities and, as he left an area and especially as he died, his letters were his continuing voice. Thus, churches would share letters and, as they obtained funds (a few hundred dollars to a couple of thousand dollars in today's money), they would make copies. Copies would turn into collections, particularly as it was possible to use one scroll for several of the shorter letters. Probably by the end of the first century, the complete collection (i.e., all extant letters) was circulating to at least a limited degree (remember, these copies did not come cheap). The issue is which stage in this process 2 Peter is indicating."[114]

This author would argue that the stage Peter was referring to was when "there were collections of a few Pauline letters before there was a collection of all of his letters." It is most likely that Peter's first letter was written about 62-64 C.E., while **Peter's second letter was written about 64 C.E.**[115] At the time Peter penned his second letter, several of Paul's letters from the 50s were available to Peter. (Romans [56], 1 & 2 Corinthians [55], Galatians [50-52], and 1 & 2 Thessalonians [50, 51]) He could have had access to those from the early 60s as well. (Ephesians [60-61], Philippians [60-61], Colossians [60-61], Titus [61-64], Philemon [60-61], and Hebrews [61]) The only ones that were clearly unavailable would have been 1 & 2 Timothy [61, 64] and possibly Titus [61-64]. Thus, Peter's reference to "in all his [Paul's] letters, speaking in them of these things," we garner several insight. It highly suggests (1) there were collections of Paul's letters, (2) Peter and the early church viewed them as "Scripture" in the same sense as the Old Testament Scriptures, (3) which were not to be changed, and that (4) apostolic author's written works were being collected and preserved for posterity.

Second-Century Manuscripts: Once we enter the second-century almost all firsthand witnesses of Jesus Christ would have died, and most of the younger traveling companions, fellow workers and students of the

---

[112] Harry Gamble, "The Redaction of the Pauline Letters and the Formation of the Pauline Corpus," *JBL* 94 (1971) 403–18.

[113] Mary Lucetta Mowry, "The Early Circulation of Paul's Letters," *JBL* 63 (1944) 73–86.

[114] Peter H. Davids, *The Letters of 2 Peter and Jude,* The Pillar New Testament Commentary (Grand Rapids, MI: William B. Eerdmans Pub. Co., 2006), 302–303.

[115] Clinton E. Arnold, *Zondervan Illustrated Bible Backgrounds Commentary: Hebrews to Revelation.,* vol. 4 (Grand Rapids, MI: Zondervan, 2002), 153.

apostles would be getting up there in age. However, there were some, like Polycarp, who was born to Christian parents about 69 C.E. in Asia Minor, in Smyrna. As he grew into a man, he was known for his kindness, self-discipline, compassionate treatment of others, and thorough study of God's Word. Soon enough he became an elder in the Christian congregation at Smyrna. Polycarp was very fortunate to live in a time, where he was able to learn from the apostles themselves. In fact, the apostle John was one of his teachers. "By any standard, Polycarp must be reckoned as one of the more notable figures in the early postapostolic church. Already bishop of Smyrna in Asia Minor when his friend and mentor, Ignatius of Antioch [c. 35 C.E. – c. 108 C.E.], addressed one of his letters to him (ca. A.D. 110; cf. above, p. 131), he died a martyr's death (see the *Martyrdom of Polycarp*) several decades later at age eighty-six (ca. 155–160), having served as bishop for at least forty and possibly sixty or more years. Irenaeus (who met Polycarp as a child) and Eusebius both considered him a significant link in the chain of orthodox apostolic tradition. His life and ministry spanned the time between the end of the apostolic era and the emergence of catholic [i.e., universal] Christianity, and he was deeply involved in the central issues and challenges of this critical era: the growing threat of persecution by the state, the emerging Gnostic movement (he is particularly known for his opposition to one of the movement's most charismatic and theologically innovative teachers, Marcion), the development of the monepiscopal form of ecclesiastical organization, and the formation of the canon of the New Testament. Polycarp's only surviving document[116] is a letter to the Philippians, written in response to a letter from them (cf. 3.1; 13.1). It reveals, in addition to a direct and unpretentious style and a sensitive pastoral manner, a deep indebtedness to the Scriptures (in the form of the Septuagint) and early Christian writings, including *1 Clement* (with which Polycarp seems to be particularly familiar).[117] While apparently no New Testament books are cited as "Scripture" (the reference to Ephesians in 12.1 is a possible

---

[116] The attempt by H. von Campenhausen ("Polykarp und die Pastoralen," repr. *Aus der Frühzeit des Christentums* [Tübingen: Mohr/Siebeck, 1963], 197–252) to show that Polycarp also authored the pastoral Epistles has met with little acceptance.

[117] Schoedel (*Polycarp*, 4–5) suggests that it is "fairly certain" that the letter "reflects more or less direct contact" with the following writings: Psalms, Proverbs, Isaiah, Jeremiah, Ezekiel, Tobit, Matthew, Luke, Acts, Romans, 1–2 Corinthians, Galatians, Ephesians, Philippians, 1–2 Timothy, 1 John, 1 Peter, and *1 Clement*. Metzger (*Canon*, 61–62) adds to the New Testament list 2 Thessalonians and Hebrews while deleting Acts and 2 Corinthians.

exception), the manner in which Polycarp refers to them indicates that he viewed them as authoritative documents.[118]

Christ "gave gifts to men." "He gave some as apostles, and some as prophets, and some as evangelists, and some as pastors and teachers." (Eph. 4:8, 11-13, NASB) The Father moved these inspired ones along by Holy Spirit, as they set forth God's Word for the Christian congregation, "to stir [them] up by way of reminder," repeating many things already written in the Scriptures. (2 Pet. 1:12-13; 3:1; Rom 15:15) Thus, then, we have internal New Testament evidence from Second Peter of about 64 C.E. that "there were collections of a few Pauline letters before there was a collection of all of his letters." Outside of Scripture, we find evidence of a collection of at least ten of Pauline letters that were collected together by 90-100 C.E.[119] We can be certain that the early Christians were collecting the inspired Christian Scriptures as early as the middle of the first century C.E. to the early second century C.E.

Clement of Rome (c. 96 C.E.) was acquainted with Paul's letter to the church at Corinth, saying Paul wrote under the inspiration of the Spirit. We have Clement of Rome (c. 30-100 C.E.), Polycarp of Smyrna (69-155 C.E.), Ignatius of Antioch (c. 35 C.E. – c. 108 C.E.), who wove Scripture of the Greek New Testament in with their writings, showing their view of them as inspired Scripture. Justin Martyr, who died about 165 C.E., used the expression "it is written" when quoting from Matthew. Theophilus of Antioch who died about 181 C.E., declared "concerning the righteousness which the law enjoined, confirmatory utterances are found both with the prophets and in the Gospels because they all spoke inspired by one Spirit of God."[120] Theophilus then uses such expressions as "**says the Gospel**" (quoting Matt, 5:28, 32, 44, 46; 6:3) and "**the divine word** gives us instructions, in order that "we may lead a quiet and peaceable life."[121] And it teaches us to render all things to all,[122] "honour to whom

---

[118] Michael William Holmes, *The Apostolic Fathers: Greek Texts and English Translations*, Third ed. (Grand Rapids, MI: Baker Books, 2007), 272–273.

[119] Jack Finegan, "The Original Form of the Pauline Collection," *HTR* 49 (1956) 85–104. See also Walter Schmithals, "Zur Abfassung und ältesten Sammlung der pauli nischen Hauptbriefe" ["On the Composition and Earliest Collection of the Major Epistles of Paul"], *ZNW* 51 (1960) 225–45.

[120] Theophilus of Antioch, "Theophilus to Autolycus," in *Fathers of the Second Century: Hermas, Tatian, Athenagoras, Theophilus, and Clement of Alexandria (Entire)*, ed. Alexander Roberts, James Donaldson, and A. Cleveland Coxe, trans. Marcus Dods, vol. 2, The Ante-Nicene Fathers (Buffalo, NY: Christian Literature Company, 1885), 114.

[121] 1 Tim. 2:2

[122] Rom. 13:7, 8

honour, fear to whom fear, tribute to whom tribute; to owe no man anything, but to love all."[123]

Inspiration and Inerrancy in the Writing Process

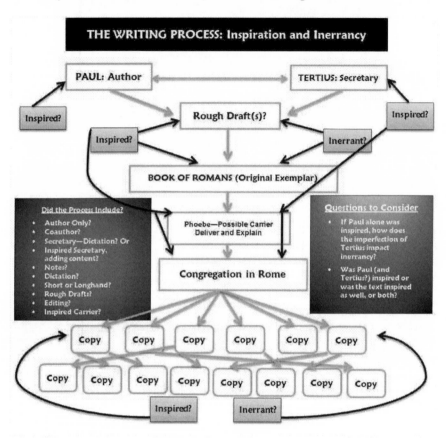

All Scripture is Inspired by God

In this context, inspiration is **the state** of a human being moved by the Holy Spirit, which results in an inspired, fully inerrant written Word of God.

---

[123] Theophilus of Antioch, "Theophilus to Autolycus," in *Fathers of the Second Century: Hermas, Tatian, Athenagoras, Theophilus, and Clement of Alexandria (Entire)*, ed. Alexander Roberts, James Donaldson, and A. Cleveland Coxe, trans. Marcus Dods, vol. 2, The Ante-Nicene Fathers (Buffalo, NY: Christian Literature Company, 1885), 115.

Chicago Statement on Biblical Inerrancy ICBI (Bold mine)

Article VII

We affirm that **inspiration** was the work in which God by His Spirit, through human writers, gave us His Word. The origin of Scripture is divine. The mode of divine **inspiration** remains largely a mystery to us. We deny that **inspiration** can be reduced to human insight, or to heightened states of consciousness of any kind.

Article VIII

We affirm that God in His Work of **inspiration** utilized the distinctive personalities and literary styles of the writers whom He had chosen and prepared. We deny that God, in causing these writers to use the very words that He chose, overrode their personalities.

Article IX

We affirm that **inspiration**, though not conferring omniscience, guaranteed true and trustworthy utterance on all matters of which the Biblical authors were moved to speak and write. We deny that the finitude or fallenness of these writers, by necessity or otherwise, introduced distortion or falsehood into God's Word.

Article X

We affirm that **inspiration**, strictly speaking, applies only to the autographic text of Scripture, which in the providence of God can be ascertained from available manuscripts with great accuracy. We further affirm that copies and translations of Scripture are the Word of God to the extent that they faithfully represent the original. We deny that any essential element of the Christian faith is affected by the absence of the autographs. We further deny that this absence renders the assertion of Biblical **inerrancy** invalid or irrelevant.

Article XI

We affirm that Scripture, having been given by divine inspiration, is infallible, so that, far from misleading us, it is true and reliable in all the matters it addresses. We deny that it is possible for the Bible to be at the same time infallible and errant in its assertions. Infallibility and inerrancy may be distinguished, but not separated.

Inerrancy of Scripture

Inerrancy of Scripture is the result of the state of a human being moved by Holy Spirit from God, which results in an inspired, fully inerrant written Word of God.

Article XII

We affirm that Scripture in its entirety is inerrant, being free from all falsehood, fraud, or deceit. We deny that Biblical infallibility and inerrancy are limited to spiritual, religious, or redemptive themes, exclusive of assertions in the fields of history and science. We further deny that scientific hypotheses about earth history may properly be used to overturn the teaching of Scripture on creation and the flood.

Article XIII

We affirm the propriety of using inerrancy as a theological term with reference to the complete truthfulness of Scripture. We deny that it is proper to evaluate Scripture according to standards of truth and error that are alien to its usage or purpose. We further deny that inerrancy is negated by Biblical phenomena such as a lack of modern technical precision, irregularities of grammar or spelling, observational descriptions of nature, the reporting of falsehoods, the use of hyperbole and round numbers, the topical arrangement of material, variant selections of material in parallel accounts, or the use of free citations.

Article XV

We affirm that the doctrine of inerrancy is grounded in the teaching of the Bible about inspiration. We deny that Jesus' teaching about Scripture may be dismissed by appeals to accommodation or to any natural limitation of His humanity.

Article XVI

We affirm that the doctrine of inerrancy has been integral to the Church's faith throughout its history. We deny that inerrancy is a doctrine invented by Scholastic Protestantism, or is a reactionary position postulated in response to negative higher criticism.

Authoritative Word of God

The authoritative aspect of Scripture is that God by way of inspiration gives the words the authors chose to use power and authority,

92

so that the outcome (i.e., originals) is the very Word of God, as though God were speaking to us himself.

Article I

We affirm that the Holy Scriptures are to be received as the **authoritative** Word of God. We deny that the Scriptures receive their authority from the Church, tradition, or any other human source.

2 Timothy 3:16-17 New American Standard Bible (NASB)

[16] All Scripture is inspired by God and profitable for teaching, for reproof, for correction, for training in righteousness; [17] so that the man of God may be adequate, equipped for every good work.

What does this mean? The phrase "inspired by God" (Gr., *theopneustos*) literally means, "Breathed out by God." A related Greek word, *pneuma,* means "wind," "breath," life, "Spirit." Since *pneuma* can also mean "breath," the process of "breathing out" can rightly be said to be the work of the Holy Spirit inspiring the Scriptures. The result is that the originals were accurate, fully inerrant and authoritative. Thus the Holy Spirit moved human writers so that the result can truthfully be called the Word of *God,* not the word of man.

2 Peter 1:21 New American Standard Bible (NASB)

[21] for no prophecy was ever made by an act of human will, but men moved by the Holy Spirit spoke from God.

The Greek word here translated "men moved by (NASB)," *phero,* is used in another form in Acts 27:15, 17, which describes a ship that was driven along by the wind. So the Holy Spirit, by analogy, 'navigated the course' of the Bible writers. While the Spirit did not give them each word by dictation,[124] it certainly kept the writers from inserting any information that did not convey the will and purpose of God.

The heart of what the International Council on Biblical Inerrancy (ICBI) stood for is apparent in "A Short Statement," produced at the Chicago conference in 1978:

---

[124] (Wilkins) Exactly how the Spirit guided the writers is a mystery, and the words "thus says the Lord" in prophecy most likely do introduce a dictated message. However, those familiar with Greek can easily see stylistic differences between the NT writers which seem to reflect different personalities, and rule out verbatim dictation from a single source.

1. God, who is Himself Truth and speaks truth only, has inspired Holy Scripture in order thereby to reveal Himself to lost mankind through Jesus Christ as Creator and Lord, Redeemer and Judge. Holy Scripture is God's witness to Himself.

2. Holy Scripture, being God's own Word, written by men prepared and superintended by His Spirit, is of infallible divine authority in all matters upon which it touches: it is to be believed, as God's instruction, in all that it affirms, obeyed, as God's command, in all that it requires; embraced, as God's pledge, in all that it promises.

3. The Holy Spirit, Scripture's divine Author, both authenticates it to us by His inward witness and opens our minds to understand its meaning.

4. Being wholly and verbally God-given, Scripture is without error or fault in all its teaching, no less in what it states about God's acts in creation, about the events of world history, and about its own literary origins under God, than in its witness to God's saving grace in individual lives.

5. The **authority of Scripture** is inescapably impaired if this total divine **inerrancy** is in any way limited or disregarded, or made relative to a view of truth contrary to the Bible's own; and such lapses bring serious loss to both the individual and the Church.

Publishing Industry of the Ancient World

Most people today would not imagine the ancient world's having a large publishing industry, yet this was the case. The ancient writings of famous authors were great pieces of literature that were highly sought after from the moment they were penned, much as today. Thus, there was a need for the scriptorium[125] to fill orders for both pagan and civil literature, as well as the Bible books. There was a need for hundreds of copies, and as Christianity displaced paganism, the need would grow exponentially.

The **Autograph** ("self-written") was the text actually written by a New Testament author, or the author and scribe as the author dictated to him. If the scribe was taking down dictation (Rom. 16:22; 1 Pet. 5:12), he

---

[125] A scriptorium was a room for storing, copying, illustrating, or reading manuscripts.

may have done so in shorthand.[126] Whether by shorthand or longhand, we can assume that both the scribe and the author would check the scribe's work. The author would have authority over all corrections since the Holy Spirit did not inspire the scribe. If the inspired author wrote everything down himself as the Spirit moved him, the finished product would be the autograph. This text is also often referred to as the **Original**. Hence, the terms *autograph* and *original* are often used interchangeably. Sometimes textual critics prefer to make a distinction, using "original" as a general reference to the text that is correctly attributed to a biblical author. This designation does not focus on the process of how a book or letter was written.

The *original* can also be referred to as the first **Authorized Text (Archetypal Manuscript)**, i.e., the text first used to make other copies. We should also point out that some textual critics debate whether the original or autograph of any given book was actually the first text used to make copies, and they prefer to call the latter the **Initial Text** instead, not requiring that it actually be the autograph. Conservative critics would maintain that they are the same. Neither term should be confused with what is known as an ordinary **Exemplar**, any authorized text of the book from which other copies were made. The original text necessarily was the very first exemplar used to make copies, but after that other copies of high quality were used as exemplars. We will frequently use this term to refer to any copy that a scribe employed as his text for making another copy. Usually, a scribe would have a main or primary exemplar from which he makes most of his copy and one or more secondary exemplars with which to compare what he found in his main exemplar. As we will see, scribes sometimes substituted text from other exemplars for what they found in their main exemplars.

We have mentioned the **Scriptorium**, a room where multiple scribes or even one scribe worked to produce the manuscript(s). A lector would read aloud from the exemplar, and the scribe(s) would write down his words. The **Corrector** was one who checked the manuscripts for needed corrections. Corrections could be by three primary persons: **(1)** the copyist himself, **(2)** the official corrector of the scriptorium, or **(3)** a person who had purchased the copy. When textual scholars speak of the **Hand**, this

---

[126] "The usual procedure for a dictated epistle was for the amanuensis (secretary) to take down the speaker's words (often in shorthand) and then produce a transcript, which the author could then review, edit, and sign in his own handwriting. Two New Testament epistles provide the name of the amanuensis: Tertius for (Romans 16:22) and Silvanus (another name for Silas) for 1 Peter 5:12." Philip Comfort, *Encountering the Manuscripts: An Introduction to New Testament Paleography & Textual Criticism* (Nashville, TN: Broadman & Holman, 2005), 06.

primarily refers to a person who is making the copy, distinguishing his level of training. Paleographers have set out four basic levels of handwriting. First, there was the *common hand* of a person who was untrained in making copies. Second, there was the documentary hand of an individual who was trained in preparing documents. The third level was the *reformed documentary* hand of a copyist who was experienced in the preparation of documents and copying literature; and fourth was the *professional hand*, the scribe experienced in producing literature.[127]

We must keep in mind that we are dealing with an oral society. Therefore, the apostles, who had spent three and a half years with Jesus, first published the Good News orally. The teachers within the newly founded Christian congregations would repeat this information until it was memorized. Thereafter, those who had heard this gospel would, in turn, share it with others (Acts 2:42, Gal 6:6). In time, they would see the need for a written record so Matthew, Luke, Mark, and John would pen the Gospels, and other types of New Testament books would be written by Paul, James, Peter, and Jude. We can see from the first four verses of Luke that Theophilus[128] was being given a written record of what he had already been taught orally. In verse 4, Luke says to Theophilus, "[My purpose is] that you may know the exact truth about the things you have been taught."

The appearance of the written record did not mean the end of oral publication. Both oral and written would be used together. Most did not read the written records themselves, as they would hear them read in the congregational meetings by the lector. Paul and his letters came to be used in the same way as he traveled extensively, but was just one man and could only be in one place at a time. It was not long before he took advantage of the fact that he could be in one place and dispatch letters to other locations through his traveling companions. These traveling companions would not only deliver the letters but would know the issues well enough to address questions that might be asked by the leaders of the congregation to which they had been dispatched. In summary, the

---

[127] Philip Comfort, *Encountering the Manuscripts: An Introduction to New Testament Paleography & Textual Criticism* (Nashville, TN: Broadman & Holman, 2005), 17-20.

[128] Theophilus means "friend of God," was the person to whom the books of Luke and Acts were written (Lu 1:3; Ac 1:1). Theophilus was called "most excellent," which may suggest some position of high rank. On the other hand, it simply may be Luke offering an expression of respect. Theophilus had initially been orally taught about Jesus Christ and his ministry. Thereafter, it seems that the book of Acts, also by Luke, confirms that he did become a Christian. The Gospel of Luke was partially written to offer Theophilus assurances of the certainty of what he had already learned by word of mouth.

first century saw the life and ministry of Jesus Christ, the Son of God, as well as his death, resurrection, and ascension. After that, his disciples spread this gospel orally for at least 15 years before Matthew penned his gospel. The written was used in conjunction with the oral message.

In the first-century C.E., the Bible books were being copied individually. In the late first century or the beginning of the second century, they began to be copied in groups. At first, it was the four gospels and then the book of Acts with the four gospels, as well as a collection of the Apostle Paul's writings. Each of the individual books of the New Testament were penned, edited, and published between 44 and 98 C.E. A group of the apostle Paul's letters and the gospels were copied and published between 90 to 125 C.E. The entire 27 books of the New Testament were not published as a whole until about 290 to 340 C.E.

Thus we have the 27 books of the New Testament that were penned individually in the second half of the first century. Each of these would have been copied and recopied throughout the first century. Copies of these copies would, of course, be made as well. Some of the earliest manuscripts that we now have indicated that a professional scribe copied them. Many of the other papyri provide evidence that a semi-professional hand copied them, while most of these early papyri give evidence of being made by a copyist who was literate and experienced at making documents. Therefore, either literate or semi-professional copyist produced the vast majority of our early papyri, with some being made by professionals.

Sadly, we do not have the autographs. Even if we did, we would have no way to authenticate them. We do however have copies of New Testament manuscripts that go back to the second and third centuries C.E. Over the centuries this copying of copies continued. The authors were inspired so that the originals were error-free. However, this is not the case with those who made copies; they were not under the influence of the Holy Spirit while making their copies. Therefore these copies must have contained unintentional mistakes, as well as intentional changes, differing from the originals and from each other. However, this is not as disconcerting as it may first appear. By far, most of the copyist errors are trivial, such as differences in spelling, word order and such. Moreover, they are easily analyzed and corrected, so that we know what the original did state. It is true that other copyist errors, a very small portion, are noteworthy, arising from the copyist's desire to correct something in the text that he perceived as erroneous or problematic. However, these changes have little to no effect on doctrines because other passages addressing the same doctrines provide the means to analyze and correct the copyist's "corrections."

In the language of textual criticism, changes to the original text introduced by copyists are called "variant readings." A variant reading is a different reading in the extant [existing] manuscripts for any given portion of the text. The process of textual criticism basically is an examination of variant readings in various ancient manuscripts in an effort to reconstruct the original wording of a written text. These variants in our copies of the New Testament manuscripts are largely the reason for the rise of the science of textual criticism in the 16th century. Thereafter, we have had hundreds of scholars working very hard over the following five centuries to restore the New Testament text to its original state. Keep in mind that textual criticism is not just performed on the Old and New Testament texts, but in all other ancient literature as well: Plato (428/427–348/347 B.C.E.), Herodotus (c. 484–c. 425 B.C.E.), Homer (Ninth or Eighth Century B.C.E.), Livy (64or 59 B.C.E.–17 C.E.), Cicero (106–43 B.C.E.), and Virgil (70–19 B.C.E.). However, as the Bible is the greatest work of all time, which has directly influenced the lives of countless Christians, it is the most important field.

It is here that we should also expound a little more on the "criticism" portion of the term textual criticism. It may be helpful if for a moment we address biblical criticism in general, which is divided into two branches: lower criticism and higher criticism. Lower criticism, also known as textual criticism, is an investigation of manuscripts by those who are known as textual scholars, seeking to establish the original reading, which is only available in the thousands of extant copies. Higher criticism, also known as literary criticism, is the investigation of the restored text with the goal of identifying any sources that may lie behind it. Therefore we can say the following:

Lower criticism (i.e., textual criticism), has been the bedrock of scholarship over the last 500 years. It has given us a master text, i.e., a critical text, which is a reflection of the original published Greek New Testament. It has done nothing but contributes to the furtherance of Bible scholarship, removing interpolations, correcting scribal errors, and giving us a restored text, allowing us to produce better translations of the New Testament.

In contrast, **higher criticism** (i.e., literary criticism) has attempted to provide rationalized explanations for the composition of Bible books, ignoring the supernatural element and very often eliminating the traditional authorship of the books. Late dating of the composition of Bible books is very common, and the historicity of biblical accounts is called into question. It would not be an overstatement to say that the effect has often been to challenge and undermine the Christian's confidence in the New Testament. Fortunately, some conservative scholars[129] have rightly criticized higher critics for their illogical or unreasonable approaches in dissecting God's Word.

Importance of Textual Criticism

Christian Bible students need to be familiar with Old and New Testament textual criticism as two of the most important foundational studies. Why? If we fail to establish what was originally penned with reasonable certainty, how are we to do a translation, or even to interpret what we think is the actual Word of God? We are fortunate in that there are far more existing New Testament manuscripts today than any other book from ancient history. This gives New Testament textual scholars vastly more to work with in establishing the original words of the text. Some ancient Greek and Latin classics are based on one existing manuscript, while with others there are just a handful and a few exceptions that have a few hundred available. However, for the New Testament over 5,838 Greek manuscripts have been cataloged,[130] 10,000 Latin manuscripts, and an additional 9,300 other manuscripts in such languages as Syriac, Slavic, Gothic, Ethiopic, Coptic, and Armenian.

The other difference between the New Testament manuscripts and those of the classics is that the existing copies of the New Testament date much closer to the originals. In the case of the Greek classics, some of the manuscripts are dated about a thousand years after the author had penned the book. Some of the Latin classics are dated from three to seven hundred years after the time the author wrote the book. When we look at the Greek copies of the New Testament books, some portions are within decades of the original author's book. Sixty-two Greek papyri, along with five majuscules[131] date from 110 C.E. to 300 C.E.

---

[129] Such Bible scholars as Robert L. Thomas, Norman L. Geisler, Gleason L. Archer, F. David Farnell, and Joseph M. Holden among many others have fought for decades to educate readers about the dangers of higher criticism.

[130] As of January 2016

[131] Large lettering, often called "capital" or uncial, in which all the letters are usually the same height.

Distribution of Greek New Testament Manuscripts

- The **Papyrus** is a copy of a portion of the New Testament made on papyrus. At present, we have 127-catalogued New Testament papyri, many dating between 110-350 C.E., but some as late as the 6th century C.E.

- The **Majuscule** or **Uncial** is a script of large letters commonly used in Greek and Latin manuscripts written between the 3rd and 9th centuries C.E. that resembles a modern capital letter but is more rounded.

- The **Minuscule** is a small cursive style of writing used in manuscripts from the 9th to the 16th centuries.

- The **Lectionary** is a schedule of readings from the Bible for Christian church services during the year, in both majuscules and minuscules, dating from the 4th to the 16th centuries C.E.

We should clarify that of the approximate 24,000 total manuscripts of the New Testament, not all are complete books. There are fragmented manuscripts which have just a few verses; but there are manuscripts that contain an entire book, others that contain numerous books, and some that have the entire New Testament, or nearly so. This is to be expected since the oldest manuscripts we have were copied in an era when copying the whole New Testament was not the norm, but rather a single book or a group of books (i.e., Paul's letters). This still does not negate the vast riches of manuscripts that we possess.

What can we conclude from this short introduction to textual criticism? There is some irony here, in that secular scholars have no problem accepting the wording of classic authors, with their minuscule amount of evidence. However, they discount the treasure trove of evidence that is available to the New Testament textual scholar. Still, this should not surprise us as the New Testament has always been under-appreciated and attacked in some way, shape, or form over the past 2,000 years.

On the contrary, in comparison to classical works, we are overwhelmed by the quantity and quality of existing New Testament manuscripts. We should also keep in mind that seventy-five percent[132] of the New Testament does not even require the help of textual criticism because that much of the text is unanimous and thus we know what it says. Of the other twenty-five percent, about twenty percent make up trivial scribal mistakes that are easily corrected. Therefore, textual criticism

---

[132] The numbers in this paragraph are rounded for simplicity purposes.

focuses mainly on a small portion of the New Testament text. The facts are clear: the Christian, who reads the New Testament, is fortunate to have so many manuscripts, with so many dating so close to the originals, with 500 hundred years of hundreds of textual scholars who have established the text with a level of certainty unimaginable for ancient secular works.

The Iliad is dated to about 1260–1180 B.C.E. The most notable Iliad manuscripts are from the 9th, 10th, and 11th centuries C.E. That would make these manuscripts over 2,000 years removed from their original.

Once we get to into the middle to the end of the second century C.E., it now comes down to whether those who came before **would stress the written documents as Scripture by**

- the apostles, who had been personally selected by Jesus (Matthew, John, and Peter),

- Paul, who was later selected as an apostle by the risen Jesus himself,

- the half-brothers of Jesus Christ (James and Jude),

- as well as Mark and Luke, who were close associates and traveling companions of Paul and Peter.

We can see from the above that this largely was the case. We know that major church leaders across the Roman Empire had done just that. We know that Irenaeus of Asia Minor (180 C.E.) fully accepted 25 of 27 books of the New Testament but had some doubt about Hebrews and uncertain about James. We know that Clement of Alexandria (190 C.E.) fully accepted 26 of 27 books of the New Testament but may not have been aware of 3 John. We know that Tertullian of North Africa (207 C.E.) fully accepted 24 of 27 books but may not have been aware of 2, 3 John, or Jude. We know that Origen of Alexandria (230 C.E.) and Eusebius of Palestine (320 C.E.) fully accepted 27 of 27 books of the New Testament books. It has been estimated that by the close of the second century C.E., there were over 60,000 copies of major parts of the Greek New Testament in existence. This is an enormous number, even if it was only one in every fifty professing Christians, who possessed a copy.

However, would there be evidence that these church leaders running back to the days of the apostles would influence the copyists? In addition, were the copyists professionals? In other words, even if some of the copyists did not see the documents as Scripture, would the church leaders and long-standing traditions motivate them to copy them with accuracy? In addition, would the professional scribe copy accurately even if he did not view them as Scripture? Additionally, if the scribe did view the texts as Scripture, the inspired Word of God, was it plenary inspiration (every word), or that the meaning was inspired? Generally, speak, from what we know about the Alexandrian scribes, they would have sought to reproduce an accurate copy regardless of their views. We can say that there were other scribes, who saw the message as inspired; thus, their focus was not on retaining every single word, or word order. It seems that they felt they could alter the words without damaging the intended meaning of the author. These copyists added and removed words here and there, rearranged words, and substituted words, all in the name of improving the text but not intending to alter the meaning. It has to be mentioned that there were some untrained copyists, who simply produced inaccurate copies, regardless of how they viewed the text.

Then, there are those scribes who willfully altered the text, with the intention of improving the text. Some were seeking to harmonize the gospel accounts. An extreme example would be Tatian, a noteworthy, apologetic writer of the second century C.E. In an account of his conversion to nominal Christianity, Tatian claims, "I sought how I might be able to discover the truth," which gives us his intent. About 170 C.E., Tatian compiled a harmonized account of the life and ministry of Jesus Christ, combining the four Gospels into a single narrative (Diatessaron means "of the four"). Another one who willfully revised the New Testament was Lucian of Antioch (c. 240-312 C.E.). Lucian produced the Syrian text, renamed Byzantine text. About 290 C.E., some of his associates, made various subsequent alterations, which deliberately combined elements from earlier types of text, and this text was adopted about 380 C.E. At Constantinople, it became the predominant form of the New Testament throughout the Greek-speaking world. The text was also edited, harmonizing parallel accounts, grammar corrections, modifying abrupt transitions, to produce a smooth text. Nevertheless, this was not a faithfully accurate copy. Still, others willfully altered the text to have it support their doctrinal position. Marcion (c. 85-c. 160 C.E.), a semi-Gnostic of the second century C.E. is a leading example. In fact, the idea of forming a catalog of authoritative Christian writings did not come to mind until Marcion. One such catalog was the Muratorian Fragment, Italy (170 C.E.) The list shows 24 books of the New Testament as being accepted without question as Scriptural and canonical, some uncertainty of 2 Peter, and Hebrews and James was not listed, possibly unaware. In the end, we must admit that there were heretics that altered the text to get it to align with their doctrinal positions, but also Orthodox Christians who also altered the text to strengthen their doctrinal positions.

Encouraged to action, these disciples of Jesus Christ sprang into a teaching (Gk *katecheo*), i.e., an instruction that ultimately spread out into every corner of the then known world. (Col. 1:23) You would have had a teacher practicing and preparing Jesus' life and teachings, with his congregation orally, repeating, memorizing what had been taught by Jesus himself. The congregation would have then taken that from house to house while others like Paul and his other 100+ traveling companions, took the same message from city to city, and from country to country, preaching "the good news!" (Rom. 10:15) The good news was three-fold: (1) Christ's ransom sacrifice, (2) his resurrection and hope for others, and (3) the Kingdom of God. – 1 Corinthians 15:1-3, 20-22, 50; James 2:5

Scripture under Attack

Jesus had told his followers, "'a slave is not greater than his master.' If they persecuted me, they will also persecute you. If they kept my word, they will keep yours also.'" (John 15:20) Certainly, the growth of Christianity from 120 disciples on Pentecost 33 C.E. to over one million by the middle of the second century was a frightening thought to the pagan mind as well as Judaism. Thus, shortly after the death and resurrection of Jesus Christ, the pagan population, Judaism and the Roman government began the very persecution of which Jesus had warned. However, it was in the fourth century, under the Roman Emperor Diocletian, a program of persecution began with the intent of wiping out Christianity. In 303 C.E., Diocletian spread a series of progressively harsh edicts against Christians. This brought about what some historians have called "The Great Persecution."

Diocletian's first edict ordered the burning of copies of the Scriptures and the destruction of Christian houses of worship. Harry Y. Gamble wrote, "Diocletian's edict of 303 ordering the confiscation and burning of Christian books is itself important evidence, in both its assumptions and results. At the start of the fourth century, Diocletian took it for granted that every Christian community, wherever it might be, had a collection of books and knew that those books were essential to its viability." (Gamble 1995, 150) Church historian Eusebius of Caesarea, Palestine, in his *Ecclesiastical History*, reported, "all things in truth were fulfilled in our day, when we saw with our very eyes the houses of prayer cast down to their foundations from top to bottom, and the inspired and sacred Scriptures committed to the flames in the midst of the market-places." (Cruse 1998, VIII, 1. 9-11.1) The Christians who were most affected by the persecution lived in Palestine, Egypt, and North Africa. In fact, just three months after Diocletian's edict, the mayor of the North African city of

Cirta, which was destroyed in the beginning of the 4th century and was rebuilt by the Roman Emperor Constantine the Great, is said to have ordered the Christians to give up all of their "writings of the law" and "copies of scripture." It is quite clear that the intent of Diocletian and local leaders was to wipe out the Word of God.

The authorities had many Christians who obey the decrees by handing over their copies of the Scriptures. Nevertheless, some refused to give up their copies of God's Word. Bishop Felix of Thibiuca (d. 303 C.E.) in Africa was martyred during the Great Persecution alongside Audactus, Fortunatus, Januarius, and Septimus.[133] Felix resisted the command of the local magistrate Magnillian (Lat. *Magnillianus*) to surrender his congregation's copies of the Christian Scriptures. One account has Felix and the others being taken to Carthage and decapitated on July 15, 303 C.E. Other Christian leaders deceived the leaders by handing in their pagan writings, safeguarding their Scriptures.

The Diocletian persecution was, in the end, unsuccessful. Many Christian libraries escaped the persecution of Diocletian. Two of our best collections today, the Beatty and Bodmer papyri survived the fires. Alfred Chester Beatty (1875-1968), at the age of 32 had amassed a fortune. As a collector of books, he had Over 50 papyrus codices, both religious and secular, which are dated earlier than the fourth century C.E. There are seven consisting of portions of Old Testament books, three consisting of portions of the New Testament (P45 c. 250, P46 c. 175–225, and P47 c. 250-300). Martin Bodmer (1899-1971) was also a wealthy collector, who discovered twenty-two papyri in Egypt in 1952, which contained parts from the Old and New Testaments, as well as other early Christian literature. Particularly noteworthy are the New Testament Bodmer papyri, which consists of P66 dating to c. 200 C.E. and P75 dating to c. 175 C.E. Many in rural Egypt would have heard of the persecution in Alexandria, likely making great efforts to remove their manuscripts from their congregations, hiding them until the persecution lifted.

The men known as the *readers* in the early Christian congregations, who read from the Scriptures during the meeting, carried the burden of preserving the Word of God beyond preserving accurate copies.[134] They also would have guarded them during times of persecution. Because of

---

[133] These men may have been deacons but, apart from their joint martyrdom with Felix, their identities are unknown at the time of this writing.

[134] Some may have been scribes as well but not all. Retaining accurate, fresh copies for the congregation entailed reaching out to scribes or scriptoriums, to acquire copies for their congregation.

the mass persecution against Alexandria, Egypt,[135] we owe the primary preservation of our New Testament manuscripts to those congregations within rural Egypt. During times of persecution, manuscripts would not have been housed in the congregation but rather would have been hidden in homes. Because of the dry sands of Egypt, the professional scribal practices, the courage of the Christians, we not only owe the Egyptian Christians for the preservation of the New Testament but also for the original *words* that made up the New Testament. If we look at the manuscripts copied right after the Diocletian persecution (Codex Vaticanus and Sinaitic c. 350 C.E.), they are reflective of the manuscripts from rural Egypt that survived, such as P[4, 64, 67] from Coptos, P[13] from Oxyrhynchus, and P[46] from Fayum and P[75] from Abu Mana. (P. W. Comfort 1992, 16-17)

The Range of Textual Criticism

The Importance and scope of New Testament textual criticism could be summed up in the few words used by J. Harold Greenlee; it is "the basic biblical study, a prerequisite to all other biblical and theological work. Interpretation, systemization, and application of the teachings of the NT cannot be done until textual criticism has done at least some of its work. It is, therefore, deserving of the acquaintance and attention of every serious student of the Bible." (Greenlee, *Introduction to New Testament Textual Criticism* 1995, 7)

It is only reasonable to assume that the original 27 books written first-hand by the New Testament authors have not survived. Instead, we only have what we must consider to be imperfect copies. Why the Holy Spirit would miraculously inspire 27 fully inerrant texts, and then allow human imperfection into the copies, is not explained for us in Scripture. We do know that imperfect humans have had the tendency to worship relics that traditions hold to have been touched by the miraculous powers of God or to have been in direct contact with one of his special servants of old. Ultimately, though, all we know is that God had his reasons for allowing the New Testament autographs to be worn out by repeated use. From time to time we hear of the discovery of a fragment possibly dated to the first century, but even if such a fragment is eventually verified, the dating alone can never serve as proof of an autograph; it will still be a copy in all likelihood.

---

[135] This is not to say that no manuscripts survived the persecution in Alexandria, it is possible that some got through the flames.

As for errors in all the copies, we have, however, we can say is that the vast majority of the Greek text is not affected by errors at all. The errors occur in the form of variant readings, i.e., portions of the text where different manuscripts disagree. Of the **small amount** of the text that is affected by variant readings, the vast majority of these are minor slips of the pen, misspelled words, etc., or intentional but easily analyzed changes, and we are certain what the original reading is in these places. A **far smaller number** of changes present challenges to establishing the original reading. It has always been said and remains true that no major doctrine is affected by a textual problem. In fact, only rarely does a textual issue change the meaning of a verse.[136] Still, establishing the original text wherever there are variant readings is vitally important. Every word matters!

The Printed Text of the Greek New Testament

Separated Into Families

We have textual traditions or families of texts, which grew up in a certain region. For example, we have the **Alexandrian text-type**, which Westcott and Hort called the Neutral text that came from Egypt. Then, there is the **Western text-type**, which came from Italy and Gaul as well as North Africa and elsewhere. There was also the **Caesarean text-type**, which came from Caesarea and is characterized by a mixture of Western and Alexandrian readings (B. M. Metzger, A Textual Commentary on the Greek New Testament 1994, Page xxi). The **Byzantine text-type**, also called **Majority Text**, came from Constantinople (i.e., Byzantium).

In short, early Christianity gave rise to what is known as "local texts." Christian congregations in and near cities, such as Alexandria, Antioch, Constantinople, Carthage, or Rome, were making copies of the Scriptures in a form that would become known as their text-type. In other words, manuscripts grew up in certain areas, just like a human family, becoming known as that text-type, having their own characteristics. In reality, it is not as simple as this because there are mixtures of text-types within each text-type. However, generally, each text-type resembles itself more than it does the others. It should also be remembered that most of our extant manuscripts are identical in more than seventy-five percent of

---

[136] Leading textual scholar Daniel Wallace tells us, after looking at all of the evidence, that the percentage of instances where the reading is uncertain and a well-attested alternative reading could change the meaning of the verse is a quarter of one percent, i.e., 0.0025%

their texts. Thus, it is the twenty-five percent of variation that identifies a manuscript as a certain text-type, i.e., what one could call "agreement in error."

Therefore, the process of classifying manuscripts for centuries was to label them a certain text-type, such as Alexandrian, Western, Caesarean, or Byzantine. However, this practice is fading because technology has allowed the textual scholar to carry out a more comprehensive comparison of all readings in all manuscripts, supposedly blurring the traditional classifications. The new method primarily responsible is the Coherence-Based Genealogical Method (CBGM). In this method, an "initial text" is reconstructed that is considered "relatively close to the form of the text from which the textual tradition of a New Testament book has originated." (Stephen C. Carlson)

The original New Testament authors were inspired of God, and error-free. The copyists were not inspired, and errors did show up in the texts as a result. These errors help us to place these texts into certain families. Very early in the transmission process copies of the originals worked their way to these four major religious centers and the copying traditions that distinguish these text-types began to take place. The Alexandrian text-type is the earliest and reflects the work of professional and semi-professional scribes who treated the copying process with respect. The text is simple, without added material, and lacking the grammatical, stylistic polish sometimes imposed by Byzantine scribes. The Western text-type is an early second century. These manuscripts reflect the work of scribes that were given to paraphrasing. Scribes freely changed words, phrases, clauses, and whole sentences as they felt it necessary. At times, they were simply trying to harmonize the text, or even add apocryphal material to spice it up. The Caesarean text-type is a mixture of Western and Alexandrian readings. The Byzantine text-type shows the hand of scribes who, as noted, attempted to smooth out both grammar and style, often with a view to making the text easier to understand. These scribes also combined differing readings from other manuscripts that contained variants. The period of 50 to 350 C.E. certainly saw its share of errors (variants) entering into the text, but the era of corruption is the period when the Byzantine text would become the standard text.

The Corruption Period

To round out our understanding of this early history, we need at least a short overview of what happened after 350 C.E. After Constantine legalized Christianity, giving it equal status with the pagan religions, it was much easier to have biblical manuscripts copied. In fact, Constantine ordered 50 copies of the whole of the Bible for the church in Constantinople. Over the next four centuries or so, the Byzantine Empire and the Greek-speaking church were the dominant factors in making the Byzantine text the standard. It was not a matter of its being the better, i.e., more accurate text. From the eighth century forward, the Byzantine text had displaced all others.

After the invention of the Guttenberg printing press in 1455, it would be this Byzantine text which would become the first printed edition by way of Desiderius Erasmus in 1516. Thanks to an advertisement by the publishers it was referred to as the Textus Receptus, or the "Received Text."[137] Over the next four centuries, many textual scholars attempted to make minor changes to this text based on the development of the science of textual criticism, but to no real effect on its status as the Greek text of the church. Worse still, it would be this inferior text what would lay the foundation of all English translations until the *Revised English Version* of 1881 and the *American Standard Version* of 1901. It was not until 1881 that two Cambridge scholars, B. F. Westcott and F. J. A. Hort, replaced the Textus Receptus with their critical text. It is this critical edition of the Westcott and Hort text that is the foundation for most modern translations and all critical editions of the Greek New Testament, UBS[5], and the NA[28].

Desiderius Erasmus and the Greek Text

> I WOULD have these words translated into all languages, so that not only Scots and Irish, but Turks and Saracens too might read them . . . I long for the ploughboy to sing them to himself as he follows his plough, the weaver to hum them to the tune of his shuttle, the traveler to beguile with them the dullness of his journey. (Clayton 2006, 230)

Dutch scholar Desiderius Erasmus penned those words in the early part of the 16th century. Like his English counterpart, William Tyndale, it was his greatest desire that God's Word be widely translated and that even the plowboy would have access to it.

Much time has passed since the Reformation, and 98 percent of the world we live in today has access to the Bible. There is little wonder that

---

[137] (Wilkins) The nuance between "receive" and "accept" is often overlooked in discussing the TR, and the Latin "receptus" could just as well mean "accepted" (i.e. "the text accepted by all"), which I suspect was the intent of the advertisement.

the Bible has become the best seller of all time. It has influenced people from all walks of life to fight for freedom and truth. This was especially true during the Reformation of Europe throughout the 16th century. These leaders were of great faith, courage, and strength, such as Martin Luther, William Tyndale, while others, like Erasmus, were more subtle in the changes that they brought. Thus it has been said of the Reformation that Martin Luther only opened the door to it after Erasmus picked the lock.

There is not a single historian of the period who would deny that Erasmus was a great scholar. Remarking on his character, the *Catholic Encyclopedia* says: "He had an unequalled talent for form, great journalistic gifts, a surpassing power of expression; for strong and moving discourse, keen irony, and covert sarcasm, he was unsurpassed." (Vol. 5, p. 514) Consequently, when Erasmus went to see Sir Thomas More, the Lord Chancellor of England, just before Erasmus revealed himself, More was so impressed with his exchange that he shortly said: "You are either Erasmus or the Devil."

The wit of Erasmus was evidenced in a response that he gave to Frederick, elector of Saxony, who asked him what he thought about Martin Luther. Erasmus retorted, "Luther has committed two blunders; he has ventured to touch the crown of the pope and the bellies of the monks." (*Cyclopedia of Biblical, Theological, and Ecclesiastical Literature*: Vol. 3 – p, 279) However, we must ask what type of influence did the Bible have on Erasmus and, in turn, what did he do to affect its future? First, we will look at the early years of Erasmus' life.

Erasmus' Early Life

He was born in Rotterdam, the Netherlands, in 1466. He was not a happy boy, living in a home as the illegitimate son of a Dutch priest. He was faced with the double tragedy of his mother's death at seventeen, and his father shortly thereafter. His guardians ignored his desire to enter the university; instead, they sent him to the Augustinian monastery of Steyn. Erasmus gained a vast knowledge of the Latin language, the classics as well as the Church Fathers. In time, this life was so detestable to him that he jumped at the opportunity, at the age of twenty-six, to become secretary to the bishop of Cambrai, Henry of Bergen, in France. This afforded him his chance to enter university studies in Paris. However, he was a sickly man, suffering from poor health throughout his entire life.

It was in 1499 that Erasmus was invited to visit England. It was there that he met Thomas More, John Colet, and other theologians in London, which fortified his resolution to apply himself to Biblical studies. In order to understand the Bible's message better, he applied himself more fully in his study of Greek, soon being able to teach it to others. It was around this time that Erasmus penned a treatise entitled *Handbook of the Christian Soldier*, in which he advised the young Christian to study the Bible, saying: "There is nothing that you can believe with greater certitude than what you read in these writings." (Erasmus and Dolan 1983, 37)

While trying to escape the plague and make a living in an economy that had bottomed worse than our 20th-century Great Depression, Erasmus found himself at Louvain, Belgium, in 1504. It was there that he fell in love with the study of textual criticism while visiting the Praemonstratensian Abbey of Parc near Louvain. Within the library, Erasmus discovered a manuscript of Italian scholar Lorenzo Valla: *Annotations on the New Testament*. Thereupon Erasmus commissioned to himself the task of restoring the original text of the Greek New Testament.

Erasmus moved on to Italy and subsequently pushed on to England once again. It is this trip that brought to mind his original meeting with Thomas More, meditating on the origin of More's name (moros, Greek for "a fool"); he penned a satire which he called "Praise of Folly." In this work, Erasmus treats the abstract quality "folly" as a person, and pictures it as encroaching in all aspects of life, but nowhere is folly more obvious than amid the theologians and clergy. This is his subtle way of exposing the abuses of the clergy. It is these abuses that had brought on the Reformation, which was now festering. "As to the popes," he wrote, "if they claim to be the successors of the Apostles, they should consider that the same things are required of them as were practiced by their predecessors." Instead of doing this, he perceived, they believe that "to teach the people is too laborious; to interpret the scripture is to invade the prerogative of the schoolmen; to pray is too idle." There is little wonder that it was said of Erasmus that he had "a surpassing power of expression"! (Nichols 2006, Vol. 2, 6)

The First Greek Text

While teaching Greek at Cambridge University in England, Erasmus continued with his work of revising the text of the Greek New Testament. One of his friends, Martin Dorpius, attempted to persuade him that the Latin did not need to be corrected from the Greek. Dorpius made the same error in reasoning that the "King James Only" people make, arguing: "For is it likely that the whole Catholic Church would have erred for so many centuries, seeing that she has always used and sanctioned this translation? Is it probable that so many holy fathers, so many consummate scholars would have longed to convey a warning to a friend?" (Campbell 1949, 71) Thomas More joined Erasmus in replying to these arguments, making the point that what matters is having an accurate text in the original languages.

In Basel, Switzerland, Erasmus was about to be harassed by the printer Johannes Froben. Froben was alerted that Cardinal Ximenes of Toledo, Spain, had been putting together a Greek and Latin Testament in 1514. However, he was delaying publication until he had the whole Bible completed. The first printed Greek critical text would have set the standard, with any other being all but ignored. Erasmus published his first edition in 1516, while the Complutensian Polyglot (Greek for "many languages") was not issued until 1522.

The fact that Erasmus was terribly rushed resulted in a Greek text that contained hundreds of typographical errors alone.[138] Textual scholar Scrivener once stated: '[It] is in that respect the most faulty book I know' (Scrivener 1894, 185). This comment did not even take into consideration the blatant interpolations into the text that were not part of the original. Erasmus was not oblivious to the typographical errors, which were corrected in a good many later editions. This did not include the textual errors. It was his second edition of 1519 that was used by Martin Luther in his German translation and William Tyndale's English translation. This is exactly what Erasmus wanted, writing the following in that edition's preface: "I would have these words translated into all languages. . . . I long for the ploughboy to sing them to himself as he follows his plough."

Unfortunately, the continuous reproduction of this debased Greek New Testament gave rise to its becoming the standard, called the Textus Receptus ("Received Text"), reigning 400 years before it was dethroned by the critical text of B. F. Westcott and F. J. A. Hort in 1881. Regardless of its imperfections, the Erasmus critical edition began the all-important work of textual criticism, which has only brought about a better critical text, as well as more accurate Bible translations.

Erasmus was not only concerned with ascertaining the original words; he was just as concerned with achieving an accurate understanding of those words. In 1519, he penned *Principles of True Theology* (shortened to *The Ratio*). Herein he introduces his principles for Bible study, his interpretation rules. Among them is the thought of never taking a quotation out of its context nor out of the line of thought of its author.

---

[138] In fact, his copy of Revelation being incomplete, Erasmus simply retranslated the missing verses from the Latin Vulgate back into Greek.

Erasmus saw the Bible as a whole work by one ultimate author, and as such it should interpret itself.

Erasmus Contrasted With Luther

Erasmus penned a treatise called *Familiar Colloquies* in 1518, in which again he was exposing corruption in the Church and the monasteries. Just one year earlier, in 1517, Martin Luther had nailed his 95 theses on the church door at Wittenberg, denouncing the indulgences, the scandal that had rocked numerous countries. Many people likely thought that these two could bring about change and reform. This was not going to be a team effort, though, as the two were at opposite ends of the spectrum on how to bring reform about. Luther would come to condemn Erasmus because he was viewed as being too moderate, seeking to make change peacefully within the Church.

The seemingly small bond they may have shared (by way of their writings against the Church establishment) was torn apart in 1524 when Erasmus wrote his essay *On the Freedom of the Will*. Luther believed that salvation results from "justification by faith alone" (Latin, *sola fide*) and not from priestly absolution or works of penance. In fact, Luther was so adamant in his belief of "justification by faith alone" that in his Bible translation, he added the word "alone" to Romans 3:28. What Luther failed to understand was that Paul was writing about the works of the Mosaic Law. (Romans 3:19, 20, 28) Thus, Luther denied the principle that man possesses a free will. However, Erasmus would not accept such faulty reasoning, in that it would make God unjust because this would suggest that man would be unable to act in such a way as to affect his salvation.

As the Reformation was spreading throughout Europe, Erasmus saw complaints from both sides. Many of the religious leaders who supported the reform movement chose to leave the Catholic Church. While they could not predict the result of their decision, they moved forward, many meeting their deaths. This would not be true of Erasmus, though, for he withdrew from the debate, yet he did refuse to be made cardinal. His approach was to try to appease both sides. Thus, Rome saw his writings as being that of a heretic, prohibiting them, while the reformers denounced him as refusing to risk his life for the cause. Here was a man emotionally broken over criticism, but in fear of burning bridges with Rome, so he cautiously sat on the sideline.

The affairs of Erasmus in relation to the Reformation can be summarized as follows: "He was a reformer until the Reformation became a fearful reality; a jester at the bulwarks of the papacy until they began to give way; a propagator of the Scriptures until men betook themselves to the study and the application of them; depreciating the mere outward forms of religion until they had come to be estimated at their real value; in short, a learned, ingenious, benevolent, amiable, timid, irresolute man, who, bearing the responsibility, resigned to others the glory of rescuing the human mind from the bondage of a thousand years. The distance between his career and that of Luther was therefore continually enlarging, until they at length moved in opposite directions, and met each other with mutual animosity."— (McClintock and Strong 1894, 278).

The greatest gain from the Reformation is that the common person can now hold God's Word in his hand. In fact, the English-language person has over 100 different translations from which to choose. From these 16th-century life and death struggles, in which Erasmus shared, there has materialized dependable and accurate Bible translations. Consequently, the "plowboy" of 98 percent of the world can pick up his Bible, or at least part of it.

The Textus Receptus

The Dark Ages (5th to 15th centuries C.E.), was a time when the Church had the Bible locked up in the Latin language, and scholarship and learning were nearly nonexistent. However, with the birth of the Morning Star of the Reformation, John Wycliffe (1328-1384), and the invention of the printing press in 1455, the restraints were loosened, and there was a rebirth of interest in the Greek language. Moreover, with the fall of Constantinople to the Turks in 1453 C. E., many Greek scholars and their manuscripts were scattered abroad, resulting in a revival of Greek in the Western citadels of learning.

About fifty years later, or at the beginning of the sixteenth century, Ximenes, archbishop of Toledo, Spain, a man of rare capability and honor, invited foremost scholars of his land to his university at Alcala to produce a multiple-language Bible—not for the common people, but for the educated. The outcome would be the Polyglot, named Complutensian, corresponding to the Latin of Alcala. This would be a Bible of six large volumes, beautifully bound, containing the Old Testament in four languages (Hebrew, Aramaic, Greek, and Latin) and the New Testament in two (Greek and Latin). For the Greek New Testament, these scholars had only a few manuscripts available to them, and those of late origin. One may wonder why this was the case when they were supposed to have access to the Vatican library. This Bible was completed in 1514, providing the first printed Greek New Testament, but it did not receive approval by the pope to be published until 1520 and was not released to the public until 1522.

Froben, a printer in Basel, Switzerland became aware of the completion of the Complutensian Polyglot Bible and of its pending consent by the pope to be published. Immediately, he saw a prospect of making profits. He at once sent word to Erasmus, who was the foremost European scholar of the day and whose works he had published in Latin, pleading with him to hurry through a Greek New Testament text. In an attempt to bring the first published Greek text to completion, Erasmus was only able to locate, in July of 1515, a few late cursive manuscripts for collating and preparing his text. It would go to press in October of 1515 and would be completed by March of 1516. In fact, Erasmus was in such a hurried mode that he rushed the manuscript containing the Gospels to the printer without first editing it, making such changes as he felt were necessary on the proof sheets. Because of this terrible rush job, the work contained hundreds of typographical errors, as we noted earlier. Erasmus himself admitted this in his preface, remarking that it was "rushed through rather than edited." Bruce Metzger referred to the Erasmian text as a "debased form of the Greek testament." (B. M. Metzger 1964, 1968, 1992, 103)

As one would expect, Erasmus was moved to produce an improved text in four succeeding editions of 1519, 1522, 1527, and 1535. Erasmus' editions of the Greek text, we are informed, ultimately proved an excellent achievement, even a literary sensation. They were inexpensive, and the first two editions totaled 3,300 copies, in comparison to the 600 copies of the large and expensive six-volume Polyglot Bible. In the preface to his first edition, Erasmus stated, "I vehemently dissent from those who would not have private persons read the Holy Scriptures, nor have them translated into the vulgar tongues." (Baer 2007, 268)

Except for everyday practical consideration, the editions of Erasmus had little to vouch for them, for he had access only to five (some say eight) Greek manuscripts of relatively late origin, and none of these contained the entire Greek New Testament. Rather, these comprised one or more sections into which the Greek texts were normally divided: (1) the Gospels; (2) Acts and the general epistles (James through Jude); (3) the letters of Paul; and (4) Revelation. In fact, of some 5,750 Greek New Testament manuscripts that we now have, only about fifty are complete.

Consequently, Erasmus had but one copy of Revelation (twelfth-century). Since it was incomplete, he merely retranslated the missing last six verses of the book from the Latin Vulgate back into Greek. He even frequently brought his Greek text in line with the Latin Vulgate; this is why there are some twenty readings in his Greek text not found in any other Greek manuscript.

Martin Luther would use Erasmus' 1519 edition for his German translation, and William Tyndale would use the 1522 edition for his English translation. Erasmus' editions were also the foundation for later Greek editions of the New Testament by others. Among them were the four published by Robert Estienne (Stephanus, 1503-59). The third of these, published by Stephanus in 1550, became the Textus Receptus or Received Text of Britain and the basis for the King James Version. This took place through Theodore de Beza (1519-1605), whose work was based on the corrupted third and fourth editions of the Erasmian text. Beza would produce nine editions of the Greek text, four being independent (1565, 1589, 1588-9, 1598), and the other five smaller reprints. It would be two of Beza's editions, that of 1589 and 1598, which would become the English Received Text.

Beza's Greek edition of the New Testament did not even differ as much as might be expected from those of Erasmus. Why do I say, as might be expected? Beza was a friend of the Protestant reformer, John Calvin, succeeding him at Geneva, and was also a well-known classical and biblical scholar. In addition, Beza possessed two important Greek manuscripts of the fourth and fifth century, the D and D^p (also known as D^2), the former of which contains most of the Gospels and Acts as well as a fragment of 3 John, and the latter containing the Pauline epistles. The Dutch Elzevir editions followed next, which were virtually identical to those of the Erasmian-influenced Beza text. It was in the second of seven of these, published in 1633 that there appeared the statement in the preface (in Latin): "You therefore now have the text accepted by everybody, in which we give nothing changed or corrupted." On the continent, this edition became the Textus Receptus or the Received Text. It seems that this success was in no small way due to the beauty and useful size of the Elzevir editions.

The Restoration Period

For the next 250 years, until 1881, textual scholarship was enslaved to the Erasmian-oriented Received Text. As these textual scholars[139] became familiar with older and more accurate manuscripts and observed the flaws in the Received Text, instead of changing the text, they would publish their findings in introductions, margins, and footnotes of their editions. In 1734, J. A. Bengel of Tübingen, Germany, made an apology for again printing the Received Text, doing so only "because he could not publish a text of his own. Neither the publisher nor the public would have stood for it," he complained. (Robertson 1925, 25)

The first one to break free from this enslavement to the Textus Receptus, in the text itself, was Bible scholar J. J. Griesbach (1745-1812). His principal edition comes to us in three volumes, the first in Halle in 1775-7, the second in Halle and London in 1796-1806, and the third at Leipzig in 1803-7. However, Griesbach did not fully break from the Textus Receptus. Nevertheless, Griesbach is the real starting point in the development of classifying the manuscripts into families, setting down principles and rules for establishing the original reading, and using symbols to indicate the degree of certainty as to its being the original reading. We will examine his contributions in more detail below.

Karl Lachmann (1793-1851) was the first scholar fully to get out from under the influence of the Textus Receptus. He was a professor of ancient classical languages at Berlin University. In 1831, he published his edition of the Greek New Testament without any regard to the Textus Receptus. As Samuel MacAuley Jackson expressed it: Lachmann "was the first to found a text wholly on ancient evidence; and his editions, to which his eminent reputation as a critic gave wide currency, especially in Germany, did much toward breaking down the superstitious reverence for the textus receptus." Bruce Metzger had harsh words for the era of the Textus Receptus as well:

> So superstitious has been the reverence accorded the Textus Receptus that in some cases attempts to criticize it or emend it have been regarded as akin to sacrilege. Yet its textual basis is essentially a handful of late and haphazardly collected minuscule manuscripts, and in a dozen passages its reading is

---

[139] Brian Walton (1600-61), Dr. John Fell (1625-86), John Mill 1645-1707), Dr. Edward Wells (1667-1727, Richard Bentley (1662-1742), John Albert Bengel (1687-1752), Johann Jacob Wettstein (1693-1754), Johann Salomo Semler (1725-91), William Bowyer Jr. (1699-1777), Edward Harwood (1729-94), and Isaiah Thomas Jr. (1749-1831)

supported by no known Greek witnesses. (B. M. Metzger 1964, 1968, 1992, 106)

Subsequent to Lachmann came Friedrich Constantine von Tischendorf (1815-74), best known for his discovery of the famed fourth-century Codex Sinaiticus manuscript, the only Greek uncial manuscript containing the complete Greek New Testament. Tischendorf went further than any other textual scholar to edit and made accessible the evidence contained in leading as well as less important uncial manuscripts. Throughout the time that Tischendorf was making his valuable contributions to the field of textual criticism in Germany, another great scholar, Samuel Prideaux Tregelles (1813-75) in England made other valued contributions. Among them, he was able to establish his concept of "Comparative Criticism." That is, the age of a text, such as Vaticanus 1209, may not necessarily be that of its manuscript (i.e., the material upon which the text was written), which was copied in 350 C.E., since the text may be a faithful copy of an earlier text, like the second-century P[75]. Both Tischendorf and Tregelles were determined defenders of divine inspiration of the Scriptures, which likely had much to do with the productivity of their labors. If you take an opportunity to read about the lengths to which Tischendorf went in his discovery of Codex Sinaiticus, you will be moved by his steadfastness and love for God's Word.

The Climax of the Restored Text

The critical text of Westcott and Hort of 1881 has been commended by leading textual scholars over the last one hundred and forty years, and still stands as the standard. Numerous additional critical editions of the Greek text came after Westcott and Hort: Richard F. Weymouth (1886), Bernhard Weiss (1894–1900); the British and Foreign Bible Society (1904, 1958), Alexander Souter (1910), Hermann von Soden (1911–1913); and Eberhard Nestle's Greek text, *Novum Testamentum Graece*, published in 1898 by the Württemberg Bible Society, Stuttgart, Germany. The Nestle in twelve editions (1898–1923) to subsequently be taken over by his son, Erwin Nestle (13th–20th editions, 1927–1950), followed by Kurt Aland (21st–25th editions, 1952–1963), and lastly, it was co-edited by Kurt Aland and Barbara Aland (26th–27th editions, 1979–1993).

Many of the above scholars gave their entire lives to God and the Greek text. Each of these could have an entire book devoted to them and their work alone. The amount of work they accomplished before the era of computers is nothing short of astonishing. Rightly, the preceding history should serve to strengthen our faith in the authenticity and general integrity of the Greek New Testament. Unlike Bart D. Ehrman, men like Sir Frederic Kenyon have been moved to say that the books of the Greek New Testament have "come down to us substantially as they were written." And all this is especially true of the critical scholarship of the almost two hundred years since the days of Karl Lachmann, due to which all today can feel certain that what they hold in their hands is a mirror reflection of the Word of God that was penned in twenty-seven books, some two thousand years ago.

The Arrival of the Critical Text

New Testament textual criticism goes back to Origen (185-254), in the third century of our common era. The historical roots of textual scholarship actually reach back to the 3rd-century B.C.E. in the Library of Alexandria. We are going to the 18th-19th centuries for the purposes of this chapter.

From 1550, the New Testament Greek text was in bondage to the popularity of the Textus Receptus as though the latter were inspired itself, and no textual scholar would dare make changes regardless of the evidence found in older, more accurate manuscripts that later became known. The best textual scholars would offer was to publish these new findings in the introductions, margins, and footnotes of their editions. Bengel, as we noted above, apologized for repeating the printing of the Textus Receptus "because he could not publish a text of his own. Neither the publisher nor the public would have stood for it." (Robertson 1925, 25)

Karl Lachmann (1793-1851), Professor of Classical and German Philology at Berlin, was the first to make a clean break with the influential Textus Receptus. In 1831, he published at Berlin his edition of the Greek text overthrowing the Textus Receptus. Ezra Abbot says of Lachmann, "He was the first to found a text wholly on ancient evidence; and his editions, to which his eminent reputation as a critic gave wide currency, especially in Germany, did much toward breaking down the superstitious reverence for the textus receptus." (Schaff, Companion to the Greek Testament, 1883, 256-7)

Johann Jakob Griesbach [1745-1812]

Griesbach obtained his master's degree at the age of 23. He was educated at Frankfurt, and at the universities of Tubingen, Leipzig, and Halle. Griesbach became one of Johann Salomo Semler's most dedicated and passionate students. It was Semler (1725 – 1791) who persuaded him to focus his attention on New Testament textual criticism. Even though it was Semler who introduced Griesbach to the theory of text-types, Griesbach is principally responsible for the text-types that we have today. Griesbach made the Alexandrian, Byzantine, and Western text-types appreciated by a wide range of textual scholars over two centuries.

After his master's degree, Griesbach traveled throughout Europe examining Greek manuscripts: Germany, the Netherlands, France, and England. Griesbach would excel far beyond any textual scholar who had preceded him, publishing his Greek text first at Halle in 1775-77, followed by London in 1795-1806, and finally in Leipzig in 1803-07. It would be his latter editions that would be used by a number of Bible translators, such as Archbishop Newcome, Abner Kneeland, Samuel Sharpe, Edgar Taylor, and Benjamin Wilson.

Griesbach was the first to include manuscript readings that were earlier than what Erasmus had used in his Greek text of 1516 C.E. The Society for New Testament Studies comments on the importance of his research: "Griesbach spent long hours in the attempt to find the best readings among the many variants in the New Testament. His work laid the foundations of modern textual criticism, and he is, in no small measure, responsible for the secure New Testament text which we enjoy today. Many of his methodological principles continue to be useful in the process of determining the best readings from among the many variants which remain." (B. Orchard 1776-1976, 2005, xi)

Of Griesbach, Paul D. Wegner writes, "While Griesbach sometimes would rely too heavily on a mechanical adherence to his system of recensions, by and large, he was a careful and cautious scholar. He was also the first German scholar to abandon the Textus Receptus in favor of what he believed to be, by means of his principles, superior readings."

(Wegner, A Student's Guide to Textual Criticism of the Bible: Its History Methods & Results 2006, 214)

His choosing the shorter reading of the Lord's Prayer at Luke 11:3-4 evidences Griesbach's ability as a textual scholar. He made this decision based on only a handful of minuscule and uncials, patristic, and versional evidence. A few short years later, the Vaticanus manuscript would confirm that Griesbach's choice was correct. Today we have one of the oldest and most valued manuscripts, P[75], and it has the shorter reading as well. Many scribes from the fourth century onward harmonized Luke's form of the prayer with Matthew's Gospel.

Luke 11:3-4 New American Standard Bible (NASB / NU)	Luke 11:3-4 New King James Version (NKJV / TR)
[3] 'Give us each day our daily bread. [4] 'And forgive us our sins, For we ourselves also forgive everyone who is indebted to us. And lead us not into temptation.'"	[3] Give us day by day our daily bread. [4] And forgive us our sins, For we also forgive everyone who is indebted to us. And do not lead us into temptation, **But deliver us from the evil one.**"

Karl Lachmann [1793-1851]

After two and a half centuries, in 1831 a German classical philologist and critic, Karl Lachmann, had the courage to publish an edition of the New Testament text he prepared from his examination of the manuscripts and variants, determining on a case-by-case basis what he believed the original reading was, never beholding to the Textus Receptus. However, he did not include his textual rules and principles in his critical text. He simply stated that these principles could be found in a theological journal. "Karl Lachmann, a classical philologist, produced a fresh text (in 1831) that presented the Greek New Testament of the fourth century."[140]

---

[140] (P. Comfort, Encountering the Manuscripts: An Introduction to New Testament Paleography and Textual Criticism 2005, 294)

The *Interpreter's Dictionary of the Bible* sums up Lachmann's six textual criteria as follows:

- Nothing is better attested than that in which all authorities agree.

- The agreement has less weight if part of the authorities are silent or in any way defective.

- The evidence for a reading, when it is that of witnesses of different regions, is greater than that of witnesses of some particular place, differing either from negligence or from set purpose.

- The testimonies are to be regarded as doubtfully balanced when witnesses from widely separated regions stand opposed to others equally wide apart.

- Readings are uncertain which occur habitually in different forms in different regions.

- Readings are of weak authority which are not universally attested in the same region.[141]

It was not Lachmann's intention to restore the text of the New Testament back to the original, as he believed this to be impossible. Rather, his intention was to offer a text based solely on documentary evidence, setting aside any text that had been published prior to his, producing a text from the fourth century. Lachmann used no minuscule manuscripts, but instead, he based his text on the Alexandrian text-type, as well as the agreement of the Western authorities, namely, the Old Latin and Greek Western Uncials if the oldest Alexandrian authorities differed. He also used the testimonies of Irenaeus, Origen, Cyprian, Hilary, and Lucifer. As A. T. Robertson put it, Lachman wanted "to get away from the tyranny of the Textus Receptus." Lachmann was correct in that he could not get back to the original, at least for the whole of the NT text, as he simply did not have the textual evidence that we have today, or even what Westcott and Hort had in 1881. Codex Sinaiticus had yet to be discovered, and Codex Vaticanus had yet to be photographed and edited. Moreover, he did not have the papyri that we have today.

---

[141] Biographies of Textual Critics - SkyPoint,
http://www.skypoint.com/members/waltzmn/Bios.html (accessed June 10, 2016).

Samuel Prideaux Tregelles [1813-1875]

Tregelles was an English Bible scholar, textual critic, and theologian. He was born to Quaker parents at Wodehouse Place, Falmouth on January 30, 1813. He was the son of Samuel Tregelles (1789–1828) and his wife Dorothy (1790–1873). His education began at Falmouth Grammar School. He lost his father at the young age of fifteen, compelling him to take a job at the Neath Abbey iron works. However, he had a gift and a love of language, which led him in his free time to the study of Hebrew, Greek, Aramaic, Latin, and Welsh. He began the study of the New Testament at the age of twenty-five, which would become his life's work.

Tregelles discovered that the Textus Receptus was not based on any ancient witnesses, and he determined that he would publish the Greek text of the New Testament grounded in ancient manuscripts, as well as the citations of the early church fathers, exactly as Karl Lachmann was doing in Germany. In 1845, he spent five months in Rome, hoping to collate Codex Vaticanus in the Vatican Library. Philip W. Comfort writes, "Samuel Tregelles (self-taught in Latin, Hebrew, and Greek) devoted his entire life's work to publishing one Greek text (which came out in six parts, from 1857 to 1872).[142] As is stated in the introduction to this work, Tregelles's goal was 'to exhibit the text of the New Testament in the very words in which it has been transmitted on the evidence of ancient authority.'[143] During this same era, Tischendorf was devoting a lifetime of labor to discovering manuscripts and producing accurate editions of the Greek New Testament."[144]

---

[142] Because he was very poor, Tregelles had to ask sponsors to help him with the cost of publishing. The text came out in six volumes over a fifteen-year period—the last being completed just prior to his death. I consider myself fortunate to own a copy of Tregelles's *Greek New Testament* with his signature.

[143] See Prolegomena to Tregelles's *Greek New Testament*.

[144] (P. Comfort, Encountering the Manuscripts: An Introduction to New Testament Paleography and Textual Criticism 2005, 100)

Friedrich Constantin von Tischendorf [1815-1874]

Tischendorf was a world leading biblical scholar who rejected higher criticism, which led to his noteworthy success in defending the authenticity of the Bible text. He was born in Lengenfeld, Saxony, in northern Europe, the son of a physician, in the year 1815. Tischendorf was educated in Greek at the University of Leipzig. During his university studies, he was troubled by higher criticism of the Bible, as taught by famous German theologians, who sought to prove that the Greek New Testament was not authentic. Tischendorf became convinced, however, that thorough research of the early manuscripts would prove the trustworthiness of the Bible text.

We are indebted to Tischendorf for dedicating his life and abilities to searching through Europe's finest libraries and the monasteries of the Middle East for ancient Bible manuscripts, and especially for rescuing the great Codex Sinaiticus from destruction. However, our highest thanks go to our heavenly Father, who has used hundreds of men since the days of Desiderius Erasmus, who published the first printed Greek New Testament in 1516, so that the Word of God has been accurately preserved for us today. We can be grateful for the women of the twentieth and now the twenty-first century who have given their lives to this great work as well, such as Barbara Aland.

Westcott's and Hort's 1881 Master Text

The climax of this restoration era goes to the immediate successors of these men, the two English Bible scholars B. F. Westcott and F. J. A. Hort, upon whose text the United Bible Society is based, which is the foundation for all modern-day translations of the Bible. Westcott and Hort began their work in 1853 and finished it in 1881, working for twenty-eight years independently of each other, yet frequently comparing notes. As the Scottish biblical scholar Alexander Souter expressed it, they "gathered up in themselves all that was most valuable in the work of their predecessors. The maxims which they enunciated on questions of the text are of such importance." (Souter 1913, 118) They took all imaginable factors into consideration in laboring to resolve the difficulties that conflicting texts presented, and when two readings had equal weight, they indicated that in their text. They emphasized, "Knowledge of documents should precede final judgment upon readings" and "all trustworthy restoration of corrupted texts is founded on the study of their history." They followed Griesbach in dividing manuscripts into families, stressing the significance of manuscript genealogy. In addition, they gave due weight to internal evidence, "intrinsic probability" and "transcriptional probability," that is, what the original author most likely wrote and wherein a copyist may most likely have made a mistake.

Westcott and Hort relied heavily on what they called the "neutral" family of texts, which involved the renowned fourth-century vellum Vaticanus and Sinaiticus manuscripts. They considered it quite decisive whenever these two manuscripts agreed, particularly when reinforced by other ancient uncial manuscripts. However, they were not thoughtlessly bound to the Vaticanus manuscript as some scholars have claimed, for by assessing all the elements they frequently concluded that certain minor interpolations had crept into the neutral text that was not found in the group more given to interpolations and paraphrasing, i.e., the Western manuscript family. E. J. Goodspeed has shown that Westcott and Hort departed from Vaticanus seven hundred times in the Gospels alone.

According to Bruce M. Metzger, "the general validity of their critical principles and procedures is widely acknowledged by scholars today." In 1981 Metzger said,

> The international committee that produced the United Bible Societies Greek New Testament, not only adopted the Westcott and Hort edition as its basic text, but followed their methodology in giving attention to both external and internal consideration.

Philip Comfort offered this opinion:

> The text produced by Westcott and Hort is still to this day, even with so many more manuscript discoveries, a very close reproduction of the primitive text of the New Testament. Of course, I think they gave too much weight to Codex Vaticanus alone, and this needs to be tempered. This criticism aside, the Westcott and Hort text is extremely reliable. (...) In many instances where I would disagree with the wording in the Nestle

/ UBS text in favor of a particular variant reading, I would later check with the Westcott and Hort text and realize that they had often come to the same decision. (...) Of course, the manuscript discoveries of the past one hundred years have changed things, but it is remarkable how often they have affirmed the decisions of Westcott and Hort.[145]

Setting Straight the Indefensible Defenders of the Textus Receptus

While Karl Lachmann was the one to overthrow the Textus Receptus, it would be B. F. Westcott and F. J. A. Hort in 1881 who would put the nails in the coffin of the Textus Receptus. The 1881 British Revised Version (RV), also known as the English Revised Version (ERV) of the King James Version, and the 1881 New Testament Greek text of Westcott and Hort did not sit well with the King-James-Version-Only[146] advocate John William Burgon (1813–1888), E. H. A. Scrivener (1813–1891), and Edward Miller (1825–1901), the latter authoring *A Guide to the Textual Criticism of the New Testament* (1886). We do not have the space nor the time to offer a full-scale argument against the King James Version Only and the Textus Receptus Only groups. However, we will address what amounts to their main arguments. This should help the reader to see how desperate and weak their arguments are.

Bible scholar David Fuller brings us the first argument in his book, *Which Bible*, where he writes, "Burgon regarded the good state of preservation of B (Codex Vaticanus) and ALEPH (Codex Sinaiticus) in spite of their exceptional age as proof not of their goodness but of their badness. If they had been good manuscripts, they would have been read to pieces long ago. We suspect that these two manuscripts are indebted for their preservation, solely to their ascertained evil character .... Had B (Vaticanus) and ALEPH (Sinaiticus) been copies of average purity, they must long since have shared the inevitable fate of books which are freely used and highly prized; namely, they would have fallen into decadence and disappeared from sight. Thus, the fact that B and ALEPH are so old is

---

[145] Philip Comfort, *Encountering the Manuscripts: An Introduction to New Testament Paleography & Textual Criticism*, (Nashville, 2005), p. 100.

[146] A connected group of Christians promotes the King James Only movement. It is their position that the King James Version of the Bible is superior to all other English translations, and that all English translations based on the Westcott and Hort text of 1881 (foundation text of UBS5 and NA28) are corrupt due to the influence of the Alexandrian Greek manuscripts.

a point against them, not something in their favour. It shows that the Church rejected them and did not read them. Otherwise, they would have worn out and disappeared through much reading."

Thus, Vaticanus and Sinaiticus, leading representatives of the Alexandrian family of manuscripts, are in such great condition because they are full of errors, alterations, additions, and deletions, so they would have had little chance of wear and tear, never having been used by true believers. This argument is simply the weakest and most desperate that this author has ever heard. **First,** many of the papyrus Alexandrian manuscripts are in terrible shape, some being 200 years older than codices Vaticanus and Sinaiticus, which would mean that they must have been read very often by true believers. **Second,** a number of old Byzantine and Western manuscripts are in good condition as well, which by this argument would indicate that they are also guilty of never having been read because they were full of errors, alterations, additions, and deletions, so they would have had little chance of wear and tear. **Third,** the size of Sinaiticus with the Old Testament, the New Testament, and apocryphal books, among other books would have weighed about 50+ lbs. This book was not read in the same manner that Christians would read their Bibles today. The same would be true of Codex Vaticanus as well. **Fourth,** both were written on extremely expensive and durable calfskin. **Fifth,** the period of copying the Byzantine text type was c. 330 – 1453 C.E. and it progressed into the most corrupt period for the Church (priests to the popes: stealing, sexual sins, torture, and murder); so much so, it ends with the Reformation. Thus, the idea of **true believers** wearing out manuscripts is ludicrous. **Sixth,** the Bible was locked up in Latin. Jerome's Latin Vulgate, produced in the 5th century to make the Bible accessible to all, became a means of keeping God's Word hidden. Almost all Catholic priests were biblically illiterate, so one wonders who were these so-called true believers and how were they reading God's Word to the point of wearing it out. For centuries, manuscripts were preserved, even when the Catholic priests could no longer understand them.

Burgon, Miller, and Scrivener in their **second argument** maintained that the Byzantine text was used by the church for far more centuries, which proved its integrity, as God would never allow the church to use a corrupt text. B. F. Westcott wrote, "A corrupted Bible is a sign of a corrupt church, a Bible mutilated or imperfect, a sign of a church not yet raised to complete perfection of the truth." (*The Bible in the Church,* 1864, 1875) The reader can determine for himself or herself if it is mere coincidence that as the church grew corrupt, the most corrupt manuscript of all grew right along with it for a thousand years.

As was stated earlier, Lucian produced the Syrian text, renamed the Byzantine text. About 290 C.E., some of his associates made various subsequent alterations, which deliberately combined elements from earlier types of text, and this text was adopted about 380 C.E. At Constantinople, it became the predominant form of the New Testament throughout the Greek-speaking world. The text was also edited, with harmonized parallel accounts, grammar corrections, and abrupt transitions modified to produce a smooth text. This was not a faithfully accurate copy. As we had just learned earlier under the corruption period, after Constantine legalized Christianity, giving it equal status with the pagan religions, it was much easier for those possessing manuscripts to have them copied. In fact, Constantine had ordered 50 copies of the whole of the Bible for the church in Constantinople. Over the next four centuries or so, the Byzantine Empire and the Greek-speaking church **were the dominant factors** as to why this area saw their text becoming the standard. It had nothing to do with it being the better text, i.e., the text that more accurately reflected the original. From the eighth century forward, the corrupt Byzantine text was the standard text and had displaced all others; it makes up about 95 percent of all manuscripts that we have of the Christian Greek Scriptures.

Burgon, Miller, and Scrivener in their **third argument** continued with the belief that it would be foolish to set aside thousands of manuscript witnesses (the Byzantine text-type) for a few *supposedly* early manuscript witnesses (the Alexandrian text-type). But in truth, the majority of anything does not automatically mean that it is the best or even correct. Today we can easily produce thousands of copies of a faulty manuscript with a machine, and every copy displays the same errors. If we were to hand-copy the same manuscript a thousand times, obvious errors probably would be corrected in many copies, but new errors would be introduced, many of them probably the result of a well-intended "correction." A textual criticism principle that has been derived from this observation is that manuscripts should be weighed (i.e. for value), not counted.

In their **fourth argument,** Burgon, Miller, and Scrivener maintained that the Byzantine text-type was actually older and superior to the Alexandrian text-type. To refute this, we can go back to our patristic quotations, which reveal the Alexandrian text-type as earlier than the Byzantine text-type. Greenlee writes, "The fallacy in this argument was that the antiquity of a 'Syrian' (i.e., Byzantine) reading could be shown only when the Byzantine text was supported by one of the pre-Byzantine texts, which proved nothing in favor of the Byzantine, since WH maintained that Syrian readings were largely derived from the pre-Syrian texts. That the traditional text was intrinsically superior was more nearly a matter of subjective opinion; but extensive comparison of text-types has left most scholars convinced that the late text [Byzantine] is in general inferior, not superior."[147]

Metzger (whom I cite at length) writes,

The Alexandrian text, which Westcott and Hort called the Neutral text (a question-begging title), is usually considered to be the best text and the most faithful in preserving the original. Characteristics of the Alexandrian text are brevity and austerity. That is, it is generally shorter than the text of other forms, and it does not exhibit the degree of grammatical and stylistic polishing that is characteristic of the Byzantine type of text. Until recently the two chief witnesses to the Alexandrian text were codex Vaticanus (B) and codex Sinaiticus (ℵ), parchment manuscripts dating from about the middle of the fourth century. With the acquisition, however, of the Bodmer Papyri, particularly P^{66} and P^{75}, both copied about the end of the second or the beginning of the third century, evidence is now available that the Alexandrian type of text goes back to an archetype that must be dated early in the second century. The Sahidic and Bohairic versions frequently contain typically Alexandrian readings .... It was the corrupt Byzantine form of text that provided the basis for almost all translations of the New Testament into modern languages down to the nineteenth century. During the eighteenth century scholars assembled a great amount of information from many Greek manuscripts, as well as from versional and patristic witnesses. But, except for three or four editors who timidly corrected some of the more blatant errors of the Textus Receptus, this debased form of the New Testament text was reprinted in edition after edition. It was only in the first part of the nineteenth century (1831) that a German classical scholar, Karl Lachmann, ventured to apply to the New Testament the criteria that he had used in editing texts of the classics. Subsequently other critical editions appeared, including those prepared by Constantin von Tischendorf, whose eighth edition (1869–72) remains a monumental thesaurus of variant readings, and the influential edition prepared by two Cambridge scholars, B. F. Westcott and F. J. A. Hort (1881). It is the latter edition that was taken as the basis for the present United Bible Societies' edition. During the twentieth century, with the discovery of several New Testament manuscripts much older than any that had hitherto been available, it has become possible to produce editions of the New Testament that

---

[147] (Greenlee, Introduction to New Testament Textual Criticism 1995, 76-7)

approximate ever more closely to what is regarded as the wording of the original documents.[148]

History of the Nestle-Aland Edition

It seems best to allow the German Bible Society and the Institute for New Testament Textual Research to tell their own history:

In 1898, Eberhard Nestle published the first edition of his Novum Testamentum Graece. Based on a simple yet ingenious idea it disseminated the insights of the textual criticism of that time through a hand edition designed for university and school studies and for church purposes. Nestle took the three leading scholarly editions of the Greek New Testament at that time by Tischendorf, Westcott/Hort and Weymouth as a basis. (After 1901 he replaced the latter with Bernhard Weiß's 1894/1900 edition.) Where their textual decisions differed from each other Nestle chose for his own text the variant which was preferred by two of the editions included, while the variant of the third was put into the apparatus.

The text-critical apparatus remained rudimentary in all the editions published by Eberhard Nestle. It was Eberhard Nestle's son Erwin who provided the 13th edition of 1927 with a consistent critical apparatus showing evidence from manuscripts, early translations and patristic citations. However, these notes did not derive from the primary sources, but only from editions.

This changed in the nineteen-fifties, when Kurt Aland started working for the edition by checking the apparatus entries against Greek manuscripts and editions of the Church Fathers. This phase came to a close in 1963 when the 25th edition of the Novum Testamentum Graece appeared; later printings of this edition already carried the brand name "Nestle-Aland" on their covers.

---

[148] Bruce Manning Metzger, United Bible Societies, *A Textual Commentary on the Greek New Testament, Second Edition a Companion Volume to the United Bible Societies' Greek New Testament (4th Rev. Ed.)* (London; New York: United Bible Societies, 1994), xx, xxv.

The 26th edition, which appeared in 1979, featured a fundamentally new approach. Until then the guiding principle had been to adopt the text supported by a majority of the critical editions referred to. Now the text was established on the basis of source material that had been assembled and evaluated in the intervening period. It included early papyri and other manuscript discoveries, so that the 26th edition represented the situation of textual criticism in the 20th century. Its text was identical with that of the 3rd edition of the UBS Greek New Testament (GNT) published in 1975, as a consequence of the parallel work done on both editions. Already in 1955 Kurt Aland was invited to participate in an editorial committee with Matthew Black, Bruce M. Metzger, Alan Wikgren, and at first Arthur Vööbus, later Carlo Martini (and, from 1982, Barbara Aland and Johannes Karavidopoulos) to produce a reliable hand edition of the Greek New Testament.

The first edition of the GNT appeared in 1966. Its text was established along the lines of Westcott and Hort and differed considerably from Nestle's 25th edition. This holds true for the second edition of the GNT as well. When the third edition was prepared Kurt Aland was able to contribute the textual proposals coming from his preliminary work on the 26th edition of the Nestle-Aland. Hence the process of establishing the text for both editions continued to converge, so that eventually they could share an identical text. However, their external appearance and the design of their apparatus remains different, because they serve different purposes. The GNT is primarily intended for translators, providing a reliable Greek initial text and a text-critical apparatus showing variants that are relevant for translation. In the case of the passages selected for this purpose the evidence is displayed as completely as possible. The Novum Testamentum Graece is produced primarily for research, academic education and pastoral practice. It seeks to provide an apparatus that enables the reader to make a critical assessment of the reconstruction of the Greek initial text.

The text of the 26th edition of the Nestle-Aland was adopted for the 27th edition also, while the apparatus underwent an extensive revision. The text remained the same, because the 27th edition was not "deemed an appropriate occasion for introducing textual changes". Since then the situation has changed, because the Editio Critica Maior (ECM) of the Catholic Letters is now available. Its text was established on the basis of all the relevant material from manuscripts and other sources. The ECM text

> was adopted for the present edition following approval by the editorial committee of the Nestle-Aland and the GNT.[149]

This makes more certain for us the Apostle Peter's words: "But the word of the Lord endures forever." (1 Peter 1:25, NASB) We can have the same confidence that the One who inspired the Holy Scriptures, giving us His inerrant Word, has also used his servants to preserve them throughout the last two thousand years, "who desires all men to be saved and to come to the knowledge of the truth." (1 Tim. 2:4, NASB) The beloved Bruce Manning Metzger was right; the text of the New Testament was transmitted; then, it entered a 1,400-year period of corruption, and has been enjoying a 500-year period of restoration.

---

[149] Nestle Aland Novum Testamentum Graece: History, http://www.nestle-aland.com/en/history/ (accessed June 12, 2016).

CHAPTER 3 Understanding Bible Translation Differences

This is a short introduction to the basics of Bible translation, with later chapters readdressing some areas herein, in greater detail.

John Wycliffe (1330?-84), was a Catholic priest and renowned Oxford theologian. He is credited with producing the first complete English Bible. Of course, this was a handwritten edition and produced from the Latin Vulgate and not the original language of Hebrew and Greek. It is William Tyndale (1494–1536), who produced the first printed edition of the New Testament from the original languages of Hebrew and Greek. Our modern English translations begin with the 1901 American Standard Version.

Those who wish to read the Bible, likely only have access to translations, as it was originally written in ancient Hebrew, some Aramaic, and Greek. As of 2010, there are 6,900 languages spoken in the world today, with 2,100 still needing the Bible translated into their language. (Wycliffe Translators)[150] The English-speaking world has over 100 different translations while others have just one. In fact, the Bible has even been translated into Klingon, the made-up language of the television show *Star Trek*. If we are one of the fortunate ones who have a choice, we certainly want to choose the Bible that is literal, accurate, clear, natural, and easy-to-understand.

The question that begs to be asked is, 'why the need for so many English translations?' There are several reasons, but as is true with many things in life, it can be taken to the extreme. The primary reason is that the English language changes over time. We no longer speak the way of the King James Version or the American Standard Version. Another reason is that other methods of translating have come on the scene in the 1950s, which has caused a plethora of new translations: the easy-to-read dynamic equivalents and the paraphrases. Another basic reason is that even literal translation will differ in minute ways is because of textual, literary and grammatical problems that translators must make choices over.

---

[150] http://www.wycliffe.org/About/Statistics.aspx

The Words and Their Meaning

After the translation committee has established, which critical [master] text they are going to work from, they must still work the evidence of each word that has significant variants. Once it has been determined what the original language word is, its meaning must be established. The Hebrew Old Testament has hundreds of words that have not been found outside of the Old Testament itself. Let us look at an example.

1 Samuel 13:21 King James Version (KJV)

[21]Yet they had a file [Heb., *pim*] for the mattocks, and for the coulters, and for the forks, and for the axes, and to sharpen the goads.

What was a pim? It would not be uncovered until 1907 when archaeology discovered the first pim weight stone at the ancient city of Gezer. The translation, like the above King James Version, struggled in their translation of the word "pim." Today, translators know that the pim was a weight measure of about 7.82 grams, or as the English Standard Version has it, "two-thirds of a shekel," a common Hebrew unit of weight that the Philistines charged for sharpening the Israelites plowshares and mattocks.

Weight inscribed with the word pym Z. Radovan/www.BibleLandPictures.com[151]

---

[151] http://biblia.com/books/zibbcot02/1Sa14.1-14

1 Samuel 13:21 Updated American Standard Version (UASV)

²¹ The charge was a pim [Heb. *pim*] for the plowshares and for the mattocks, for the three-pronged fork, for the axes, and for fixing the oxgoad.

The Greek New Testament does not face the same challenges, as there are a mere handful of words that does not appear outside of the New Testament literature. We can look at one example though from Jesus' model prayer.

Matthew 6:11 Updated American Standard Version (UASV)

¹¹ Give us this day our daily [Gr., *epiousion*] bread,

Here, "*epiousion*" is defined in the lexicon as either "daily" bread or "bread for tomorrow."[152] The policy of almost all modern translations is to use both words if a given Hebrew or Greek word can be taken in two different ways. Generally, they select one for the translation, the other will be placed in a footnote as "or."

The Punctuation in Translation

For centuries, there was no punctuation in the earliest Greek manuscripts of the Bible. Punctuation marks started to be introduced by copyist and translators, in accordance with their interpretation of context, as well as their understanding of Bible doctrine. There is one verse, which captures the seriousness of the modern translator, making the choice of punctuation, i.e., Luke 23:43. Depending on where the translation places the comma, you have a completely different outcome.

(1) Jesus answered him, "Truly I tell you, today you will be with me in paradise." Alternatively,

(2) Jesus answered him, "Truly I tell you today, you will be with me in paradise."

With number **(1)**, you have Jesus telling the criminal that sided with him eventually, "today you will be with me in paradise." With number **(2)**, you have Jesus telling the criminal today, "you will be with me in paradise." In other words, number **(2)** tells us that the criminal was being told this day, the day he and Jesus were speaking, that he would be with Jesus in paradise. This would mean that the criminal would die with the

---

[152] William Arndt, Frederick W. Danker and Walter Bauer, *A Greek-English Lexicon of the New Testament and Other Early Christian Literature*, 3rd ed. (Chicago: University of Chicago Press, 2000), 376.

guarantee of an immediate future resurrection. Moreover, if the criminal were resurrected that day, it would conflict with the fact Jesus was not resurrected that day. Jesus remained in the tomb for parts of three days.

The Grammar in Translation

The grammar of Hebrew and Greek can present multiple problems. The initial problem is which words should be transliterated. The Hebrew word 'adam' means "Adam" or "man." When should it be translated "Adam," and when should it be translated "man."

Genesis 1:26 Updated American Standard Version (UASV)

26 And God went on to say, "Let us make man ['*adam*] in our image, after our likeness.

Genesis 3:17 Updated American Standard Version (UASV)

17 And to Adam ['*adam*] he said,

By looking at both the ancient translations, as well as the modern ones, we see a major disagreement. At Genesis 2:7 the Targum Pseudo-Jonathan uses "Adam." The Greek Septuagint does not use Adam until 2:16; and the Latin Vulgate, at 2:19. Moving to modern translations, we find the New American Standard Bible at 2:20, the New International Version at 2:21; the New English Bible at 3:21; and the New Revised Standard Version at 5:1. Other difficult choices are with the Greek word Christos, which means "Christ," or "anointed one." Additionally, Should the Greek verb *baptizo*, be transliterated as "baptize," or translated as "immerse?" Moreover, should the Hebrew word *sheol* and the Greek word *hades* be transliterated, as it is confusing when it is translated as "hell," as "death," "grave," as well as other renderings? Should Gehenna, Tartarus, and others be transliterated as opposed to translating them?

Another translation issue of late is the gender-inclusive issue. The question before a translation committee is whether the masculine-oriented Bible should stay that way. What these gender-inclusive translators fail to understand is this: to deviate, in any way, from the pattern, or likeness of how God brought his Word into existence, merely opens the Bible up to a book that reflects the age and time of its readers. If we allow the Bible to be altered because the progressive women's movement feels offended by masculine language, it will not be long before the Bible gives way to the homosexual communities being offended by God's Words in the book of Romans; so modern translations will then tame that language, so as to not cause offense. I am certain that we thought that we would never see the day of two men, or two women being married by priests, but that day has been upon us for some time now. In fact, the American government is debating whether to change the definition of marriage. Therefore, it is suggested that the liberal readers not take the warning here as radicalism, but more like reality.

The Most Important Choice

The most important decision a Christian can make is, 'which translation should be my study Bible?' If we are to make an informed choice on which translation, is best, we need to consider the following questions: What are the different types of translations available to us, and how is each to be best used? Of the different types, what are the strong points and weaknesses? Thus, if there are weaknesses, why should you be cautious? For the purpose of this chapter, we are only considering the English language translation. In addition, while we could demonstrate with both Hebrew and Greek, to keep it simple we will only use Greek in the examples. In addition, we will use the actual Greek font, but this will not affect those who do not know Greek. The different types of translations cover a wide-range of styles, but there are three basic categories.

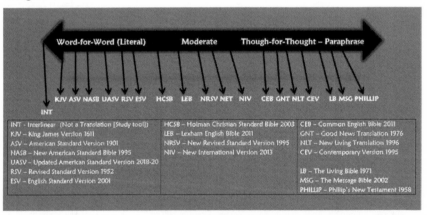

One can look at these three different styles of translations as different stages in the Bible translation process. The interlinear stage is not a Bible translation. The interlinear stage is a very rough stage of sorts, in that it does not have a smooth, clear, natural, flow, nor is it in an easy-to-understand format. However, the interlinear is a tool, and not meant to be smooth as you will see below. The literal translation is a much smoother and clearer translation when compared with an interlinear, and should be our choice of a study Bible. The dynamic equivalent is much smoother and easy-to-read, with the paraphrase being very conversational-informal (every day). However, one has to ask, at what point are we moving beyond the **Word** of God, and into a smooth, clear, easy-to-understand translation, that has hidden or obscured the original language text.

The interlinear Study Tool: This study tool could be known as a hyper-literal translation. The interlinear follows the original language **without** any concern for English grammar and syntax. Beneath the Hebrew or Greek words of the original language text, depending upon which testament you are working with, the lexical English equivalent is placed. The Greek New Testament, 2004 (UBS[4]); The Nestle-Aland Greek New Testament, 2004 (NA[27]); The Lexham Greek-English Interlinear New Testament, 2008-2010 (LGNTI); The Lexham Hebrew-English Interlinear Old Testament, 2004 (LHB).

The Literal Translation: The literal translation is commonly called the word-for-word translation. Unlike the interlinear, the literal translation follows the original language **with** concern for English grammar and syntax. The literal translation seeks to render the original language words and style into a corresponding English word and style. Again, they seek to retain the original syntax and sentence structure, and the style of each Bible writer **as far as possible**. For example, we have the King James Version, 1611 (KJV); American Standard Version, 1901 (ASV); Revised Standard Version, 1952 (RSV); New American Standard Bible, 1995 (NASB); English Standard Version, 2001 (ESV); and the Updated American Standard Version, 2018 (UASV).

Dynamic Equivalent Dishonesty

There has become a pattern for those who favor a dynamic equivalent translation, to use an interlinear Bible, which is not a translation, and refers to it as a word for word translation, because they know that this phrase is tied to translations like the KJV, ASV, RSV, ESV, and NASB. Below is an example from Duvall and Hays in the third edition of Grasping God's Word (GGW).

Grasping God's Word by J. Scott Duvall and Daniel J. Hays is a great book, so please take what is said with a grain of salt. However, what is quoted below is very dishonest, wrong, misleading, and shows the length one will go to, to biasedly express their preference in translation philosophy. Within the table below are the egregious words from GGW.

Approaches to Translating God's Word

The process of translating is more complicated than it appears. Some people think that all you have to do when making a translation is to define each word and string together all the individual word meanings. This assumes that the source language (in this case, Greek or Hebrew) and the receptor language (such as English) are exactly alike. If life could only be so easy! In fact, no two languages are exactly alike. For example, look at a verse chosen at random–from the story of Jesus healing a demon-possessed boy (Matt. 17:18). The word-for-word English rendition is written below a transliteration of the Greek:

Kai epetimēsen autō ho Iēsous kai exēlthen ap' autou to daimonion

And rebuked it the Jesus and came out from him the demon

kai etherapeuthē ho pais apo tēs hōras ekeinēs

and was healed the boy from the hour that

Should we conclude that the English line is the most accurate translation of Matthew 17:18 because it attempts a literal rendering of the verse, keeping also the word order? Is a translation better if it tries to match each word in the source language with a corresponding word in a receptor language? Could you even read an entire Bible "translated" in this way?[153]

Because these authors favor the dynamic equivalent translation philosophy, they misrepresent the literal translation philosophy here, to the extent of dishonesty. They give you, the reader, an interlinear rendering of Matthew 17:18, and then refer or infer that it is a literal translation, which by association would include the ASV, RSV, NASB, ESV, and the UASV. Again, an interlinear is not a Bible translation; it is a Bible study tool for persons who do not read Hebrew or Greek. What is placed under the Greek is the lexical rendering, while not considering grammar and syntax, i.e., they are the words in isolation. Now, to demonstrate that J. Scott Duvall and Daniel J. Hays are being disingenuous at best, let us look at the literal translations, to see if they read anything like the interlinear that Duvall and Hays used; or rather, do the literal translations

---

[153] Duvall, J. Scott; Hays, J. Daniel (2012-05-01). *Grasping God's Word: A Hands-On Approach to Reading, Interpreting, and Applying the Bible* (Kindle Locations 494-507). Zondervan. Kindle Edition.

consider grammar and syntax when they bring the Greek over into their English translation.

ASV	NASB	UASV
[18] And Jesus rebuked him; and the demon went out of him: and the boy was cured from that hour.	[18] And Jesus rebuked him, and the demon came out of him, and the boy was cured at once.	[18] And Jesus rebuked him, and the demon came out of him and the boy was healed from that hour.
RSV	ESV	CSB
[18] And Jesus rebuked him, and the demon came out of him, and the boy was cured instantly.	[18] And Jesus rebuked the demon, and it came out of him, and the boy was healed instantly.	[18] Then Jesus rebuked the demon, and it came out of him, and from that moment the boy was healed.

As can be clearly seen from the above four literal translations (ASV, NASB, UASV, and the RSV) and the essentially literal ESV and the optimally literal CSB, they are nothing like the interlinear that Duvall and Hays tried to pawn off on us as a word-for-word translation, i.e., a literal translation. The reader can decide for himself if this is misleading or dishonest.

The Dynamic or Functional Equivalent: This is actually going beyond the Word of God. This method of translation is fine for those few verses that would be misunderstood or even meaningless if it were left literal. For example, 1 Peter 3:3 reads, "Do not let your adorning [*kosmos*, literally "world"] be external, the braiding of hair and the putting on of gold jewelry, or the clothing you wear." It would be nonsensical if it were left literally to read, "Do not let your **world** be external, the braiding of hair and the putting on of gold jewelry, or the clothing you wear."

The DE or thought-for-thought translation philosophy (dynamic equivalent) seeks to render the biblical meaning of the original language text as accurately as possible into an English informal (conversational) equivalent. For example, to mention just a few, we have Today's English Version, 1976 (TEV, GNB); Contemporary English Version, 1995 (CEV); New Living Translation (second edition), 2004 (NLT).

Paraphrase translations are the furthest removed from the interlinear stage. The translators of these Bibles, if we dare to call them such, render the original language into the target language as freely as they feel it needs to be, with the target audience being their most important concern. For example, we have The Living Bible, 1971 (TLB) and The Message Bible, 2002 (MSG).

The Moderate Translation: Like anything in life, there is a tendency to strike a balance between two polarizing worlds, such as the literal translation and the dynamic equivalent. These versions of the Bible endeavor to express the words as well as the meaning and essence of the original-language expressions while also making the text easier to read. For example, we have the New English Translation, 1996 (NET); Holman Christian Standard Bible, 2003 (HCSB); and the New International Version, 2011 (NIV). However, this gesture is a slippery slope for two reasons (1) there is no need to drop below a literal translation level, to do so is to dilute the Word of God. (2) In addition, a step toward the dynamic equivalent is usually followed by another step before long. For example, the 1984 New International Version was an attempt at the middle ground, but the 2011 edition of the NIV went another step toward the dynamic equivalent camp.

Translation Philosophy

The debate as to where one should be in the spectrum of literal versus dynamic equivalent, i.e., their translation philosophy has been going on since the first translation of the Hebrew (Aramaic) into Greek, i.e., the Septuagint (280-150 B.C.E.). However, if we were to look to the first printed English translation of 1526 by William Tyndale, we would find a literal translation philosophy that ran for almost four-hundred-years. It was not until the 20th century that we find the wholesale overthrow of the literal translation philosophy. For every literal English translation that we have today, there are dozens of dynamic equivalent translations. Just to name a few, we have the Contemporary Version, the Good News Translation, the Easy to Read Version, the New Life Version, the New Living Translation, God's Word, the New Century Version, the New International Reader's Version, and the like. Below, we will offer a deeper discussion of these translation philosophies than we had in the previous chapter, which had simply served as an introduction to the subject.

Interlinear Study Tool

The interlinear Bible page is set up with the left column where you will find the original language text, with the English word-for-word lexical gloss beneath each original language word; generally, the right column contains an English translation like the ESV, NASB, or the NIV. The interlinear translation in the left column and the modern-day English translation in the right column are parallel to each other. This allows the student to make immediate comparisons between the translation and the interlinear, helping one to determine the accuracy of the translation.

THE GOSPEL ACCORDING TO
MATTHEW

CHAPTER 1

KATA   ΜΑΘΘΑΙΟΝ
ACCORDING TO MATTHEW

1.1 Βίβλος γενέσεως   Ἰησοῦ Χριστοῦ υἱοῦ Δαυὶδ
A RECORD   OF [THE] GENEALOGY OF JESUS CHRIST   SON   OF DAVID

υἱοῦ Ἀβραάμ.
SON   OF ABRAHAM.

1.2 Ἀβραὰμ ἐγέννησεν τὸν Ἰσαάκ, Ἰσαὰκ δὲ
ABRAHAM   FATHERED   -   ISAAC,   AND~ISAAC

ἐγέννησεν τὸν Ἰακώβ, Ἰακὼβ δὲ ἐγέννησεν τὸν Ἰούδαν
FATHERED   -   JACOB,   AND~JACOB   FATHERED   -   JUDAH

καὶ τοὺς ἀδελφοὺς αὐτοῦ, **1.3** Ἰούδας δὲ ἐγέννησεν τὸν
AND THE BROTHERS   OF HIM,   AND~JUDAH   FATHERED   -

Φάρες καὶ τὸν Ζάρα ἐκ τῆς Θαμάρ, Φάρες δὲ
PEREZ   AND   -   ZERAH   BY   -   TAMAR,   AND~PEREZ

ἐγέννησεν τὸν Ἐσρώμ, Ἐσρὼμ δὲ ἐγέννησεν τὸν
FATHERED   -   HEZRON,   AND~HEZRON   FATHERED   -

Ἀράμ, **1.4** Ἀρὰμ δὲ ἐγέννησεν τὸν Ἀμιναδάβ,
ARAM,   AND~ARAM   FATHERED   -   AMMINADAB,

Ἀμιναδὰβ δὲ ἐγέννησεν τὸν Ναασσών, Ναασσὼν δὲ
AND~AMMINADAB   FATHERED   -   NASHON,   AND~NASHON

ἐγέννησεν τὸν Σαλμών, **1.5** Σαλμὼν δὲ ἐγέννησεν τὸν
FATHERED   -   SALMON,   AND~SALMON   FATHERED   -

Βόες ἐκ τῆς Ῥαχάβ, Βόες δὲ ἐγέννησεν τὸν Ἰωβὴδ ἐκ
BOAZ   BY   -   RAHAB,   AND~BOAZ   FATHERED   -   OBED   BY

τῆς Ῥούθ, Ἰωβὴδ δὲ ἐγέννησεν τὸν Ἰεσσαί,
-   RUTH,   AND~OBED   FATHERED   -   JESSE,

1.6 Ἰεσσαὶ δὲ ἐγέννησεν τὸν Δαυὶδ τὸν βασιλέα.
AND~JESSE   FATHERED   -   DAVID   THE   KING.

Δαυὶδ δὲ ἐγέννησεν τὸν Σολομῶνα ἐκ τῆς   τοῦ
AND~DAVID   FATHERED   -   SOLOMON   BY   THE [WIFE]   -

An account of the genealogy[a] of Jesus the Messiah,[b] the son of David, the son of Abraham.

2 Abraham was the father of Isaac, and Isaac the father of Jacob, and Jacob the father of Judah and his brothers, [c]and Judah the father of Perez and Zerah by Tamar, and Perez the father of Hezron, and Hezron the father of Aram, [4]and Aram the father of Aminadab, and Aminadab the father of Nahshon, and Nahshon the father of Salmon, [5]and Salmon the father of Boaz by Rahab, and Boaz the father of Obed by Ruth, and Obed the father of Jesse, [6]and Jesse the father of King David.

And David was the father of Solomon by the wife of Uriah, [7]and Solomon the father of Rehoboam, and Rehoboam the father of Abijah, and Abijah the father of Asaph, [c]and Asaph the father of Jehoshaphat, and Jehoshaphat the father of Joram, and Joram the father of Uzziah, [8]and Uzziah the father of

[a] Or birth
[b] Or Jesus Christ
[c] Other ancient authorities read Asa

The New Greek-English Interlinear NT by Tyndale Publishing

The interlinear and the English equivalent in the left column are not generated by taking the English word(s) from the translation on the right and then placing them under the original language text. Whether we are dealing with Hebrew or Greek as our original language text, each word will have two or more English equivalents. What factors go into the choice of which word will go under the original language word? One factor is the period in which the book was written. As the New Testament was penned in the first century, during the era of Koine Greek, as

141

opposed to classical Greek of centuries past, and then there is the context of what comes before and after the word under consideration.

Therefore, the translator will use his training in the original language, or a lexicon to determine if he is working with a noun, verb, the definite article, adjective, adverb, preposition, conjunction, participle, and the like. Further, say he is looking at the verb, it must be determined what mood it is in (indicative, subjunctive, imperative, etc.), what tense (present, future, aorist, etc.), what voice (active, middle, passive, etc.), and so forth. In addition, the English words under the original language text are generated from grammatical form, the alterations to the root, which affect its role within the sentence, for which he will look to the Hebrew or Greek grammar reference.

The best lexicon is the 3rd edition Greek-English Lexicon of the New Testament and other Early Christian Literature, (BDAG) ten years in the making, this extensive revision of Bauer, the standard authority worldwide, features new entries, 15,000 additional references from ancient literature, clearer type, and extended definitions rather than one-word synonyms. Providing a more panoramic view of the world and language of the New Testament, it becomes the new indispensable guide for translators. The second best lexicon is the Greek-English Lexicon: With a Revised Supplement, 1996: Ninth Revised Edition - Edited By H.G. Liddell, R. Scott by H.G. Liddell & R. Scott. Each word is given in root form along with important variations, and an excellent representation of examples from classical, Koine and Attic Greek sources follows. This lexicon is appropriate for all classical Greek and general biblical studies. By far the best traditional Hebrew lexicon currently available is The Hebrew and Aramaic Lexicon of the Old Testament (HALOT) (vols. 1-5; trans. M. E. J. Richardson; Brill, 1994-2000). However, the price is beyond most students and scholars. A more affordable edition, which I highly recommend, is available, Hebrew and Aramaic Lexicon of the Old Testament (Unabridged 2-Volume Study Edition) (2 vols. trans. M. E. J. Richardson; Brill, 2002).

There are numerous lexicons on the market, which would be fine tools for the Bible student. Many scholars would concur that Biblical lexicons have four main weaknesses:

(1) They are geared toward the translations of the 20th century, as opposed to new translations.

(2) They primarily contain only information from the Bible itself, as opposed to possessing information from Greek literature overall.

(3) They are too narrow as to the words of say the New Testament, attempting to harmonize a word and its meaning. The problem with this agenda is that a word can have numerous meanings, some being quite different, depending on its context, even by the same author.

(4) Most Biblical lexicons have not escaped the etymological fallacy, determining the meaning of a word based on its origin and past meaning(s). Another aspect being that the meaning of a word is based on the internal structure of the word. A common English example of the latter is "butterfly." The separate part of "butter" and "fly" do not define "butterfly." Another example is "ladybird."

> 7 μὴ θαυμάσῃς ὅτι εἶπόν σοι,   Δεῖ
> Not marvel   that I said to you it is necessary
>
> ὑμᾶς γεννηθῆναι ἄνωθεν
> you to be born from above
>
> 154

⁷ Do not marvel that I said to you, 'It is necessary for you to be born again.'[155]

As you can see the interlinear translation reads very rough, as it is following the Greek sentence structure. The Updated American Standard Version rearranges the words according to English grammar and syntax. Do not be surprised that at times words may need to be left out of the English translation, as they are unnecessary. For example, The Greek language sometimes likes to put the definite article "the" before personal name, so in the Greek, you may have "the Jesus said." In the English, it would be appropriate to drop the definite article. At other times, it may be appropriate to add words to complete the sense in the English translation. For example, at John 4:26, Jesus said to the Samaritan woman, "I, the one speaking to you, am he." *The word "he" is not in the Greek text but is implied, so it is added to complete the sense. Please see the image on the next page.

---

[154] Kurt Aland et al., *The Greek New Testament, Fourth Revised Edition (Interlinear with Morphology)* (Deutsche Bibelgesellschaft, 1993; 2006), Jn 3:7.

[155] Edward Andrews et al., *The Updated American Standard Version* (Christian Publishing House, 2014; 2018), Jn 3:7.

26λέγει αὐτῇ ὁ Ἰησοῦς, Ἐγώ εἰμι, ὁ λαλῶν σοι
Says to her the Jesus I am the one speaking to you

Literal: I am the one speaking to you
ESV: "I who speak to you <u>am he.</u>"

The Greek New Testament, (Interlinear)

Here in John chapter 4, you have Jesus being spoken to by a Samaritan woman. She is inquiring about the coming Messiah, and Jesus does something with the Samaritan woman that he has not done even with his disciples, He discloses who he really is, "I am the one [i.e., the Messiah]. The ESV, like the other translations that we have considered, is aware that there is an implied predicate pronoun in the sentence "I am [he] the one speaking to you."

Literal Translation

Once the interlinear level has taken place, it is now time to adjust our English lexical glosses into sentences. Each word will possess its own grammatical indicator. As the translator begins to construct his English sentence, he will adjust according to the context of the words surrounding his focus. As you will see shortly, in the examples below, the translator must transition the words from the Greek order, to correct English grammar and syntax. This is a delicate balance faced by the literal translation team. As they must determine how close they will cling to the Hebrew or Greek word order in their English translation. The reader will find that the KJV, ASV, NASB, ESV and the UASV will allow a little roughness for the reader, for them an acceptable sacrifice as they believe that meaning is conveyed by the word order at times. An overly simplified example might be Christ Jesus as opposed to Jesus Christ, with the former focusing on the office ("Christ" anointed one), while the latter focuses on the person.

Even though it is impossible to follow the word order of the original in an English translation, the translator will attempt to stay as close as possible to the effective and persuasive use that the style of the original language permits. In other words, what is stated in the original language is rendered into the English, as well as the way that it is said, as far as possible? This is why the literal translation is known as a "formal equivalence." As a literal translation, it "is designed so as to reveal as much of the original form as possible. (Ray 1982, p. 47)

It should be noted that this writer favors the literal translation over the dynamic equivalent, and especially the paraphrase. The literal translation gives us what God said; there is no concealing this by going beyond into the realms of what a translator interprets these words as saying. It should be understood that God's Word to man is not meant to be read like a John Grisham novel. It is meant to be meditated on, pondered over, and absorbed quite slowly; using many tools and helps along the way. There is a reason for this; it being that the Bible is a sifter of hearts. It separates out those who really want to know and understand God's Word (based on their evident demonstration of buying out the opportune time for study and research), from those who have no real motivation, no interest, just going through life. Even though, literal translation method needs to be done in a balanced manner, and should not be taken too far.

There are times when a literal word-for-word translation is **not** in the best interest of the reader and could convey a meaning contrary to the original.

(1) As we have established throughout this book, but have not stated directly, no two languages are exactly equivalent in grammar, vocabulary, and sentence structure.

Ephesians 4:14 Updated American Standard Version (UASV

14 So that we may no longer be children, tossed to and fro by the waves and carried about by every wind of teaching, by the trickery [lit., dice playing] of men, by craftiness with regard to the scheming of deceit;

The Greek word *kybeia* that is usually rendered "craftiness" or "trickery," is literally "dice-playing," which refers to the practice of cheating others when playing dice. If it was rendered literally, "carried about by every wind of doctrine, by the trickery dice-playing of men," the meaning would be lost. Therefore, the meaning of what the original author meant by his use of the Greek word *kybeia*, must be the translator's choice.

Romans 12:11 Updated American Standard Version (UASV)

11 Do not be slothful in zeal,[156] be fervent in spirit, serving the Lord;

When Paul wrote the Romans, he used the Greek word *zeontes*, which literally means, "boil," "seethe," or "fiery hot." Some serious Bible students may notice the thought of "boiling in spirit," as being "fervent in

---

[156] Or *diligent*

spirit or better "aglow with the spirit," or "keep your spiritual fervor." Therefore, for the sake of making sense, it is best to take the literal "boiling in spirit," determine what is meant by the author's use of the Greek word *zeontes*, "keep your spiritual fervor", and render it thus.

Matthew 5:3 New International Version, ©2011 (NIV)

³ "Blessed are the poor in spirit, for theirs is the kingdom of heaven.

Matthew 5:3 GOD'S WORD Translation (GW)

³"Blessed are those who [are poor in spirit] recognize they are spiritually helpless. The kingdom of heaven belongs to them.

This one is a tough call. The phrase "poor in spirit" carries so much history, and has been written as to what it means, for almost 2,000 years that, even the dynamic equivalent translations are unwilling to translate its meaning, not its words. Personally, this writer is in favor of the literal translation of "poor in spirit." Those who claim to be literal translators should not back away because "poor in spirit" is ambiguous, and there is a variety of interpretations. The above dynamic equivalent translation, God's Word, has come closest to what was meant. Actually, "poor" is even somewhat of an interpretation, because the Greek word *ptochos* means "beggar." Therefore, "poor in spirit" is an interpretation of "beggar in spirit." The extended interpretation is that the "beggar/poor in spirit" is aware of his or her spiritual needs as if a beggar or the poor would be aware of their physical needs.

(2) As we have also established in this chapter a word's meaning can be different, depending on the context that it was used.

2 Samuel 8:3 Updated American Standard Version (UASV)

³ Then David struck down Hadadezer, the son of Rehob king of Zobah, as he went to restore his authority [lit. hand] at the River.

1 Kings 10:13 Updated American Standard Version (UASV)

¹³ King Solomon gave to the queen of Sheba all her desire which she requested, besides what he gave her according to his royal bounty [li. hand]. Then she turned and went to her own land, she together with her servants.

Proverbs 18:21 Updated American Standard Version (UASV)

²¹ Death and life are in the power [lit. hand] of the tongue, and those who love it will eat its fruits.

The English word "hand" has no meaning outside of its context. It could mean, "end of the arm," "pointer on a clock," "card players," "round in a card game," "part in doing something," "round of applause," "member of a ship's crew," or "worker." The Hebrew word "*yad*," which means "hand," has many meanings as well, depending on the context, as it can mean "control," "bounty," or "power." This one word is translated in more than forty different ways in some translations. Let us look at some English sentences, to see the literal way of using "hand," and then add what it means, as a new sentence.

- Please give a big *hand* to our next contestant. Please give a big *applause* for our next contestant.
- Your future is in your own *hands*. Your future is in your own *power*. Your future is in your own *possession*.
- Attention, all *hands*! Attention, all *ship's crew*!
- She has a good *hand* for gardening. She has a good *ability* or *skill* for gardening.
- Please give me a hand; I need some help.
- The copperplate writing was beautifully written; she has a nice hand.

At times, even a literal translation committee will not render a word the same every time it occurs, because the sense is not the same every time. The only problem we have is that the reader must now be dependent on the judgment of the translator to select the right word(s) that reflect the meaning of the original language word accurately and understandably. Let us look at the above texts from the Hebrew Old Testament again, this time doing what we did with the English word "hand" in the above. It is debatable if any of these verses really needed to be more explicit, by giving the meaning in the translation, as opposed to the word itself.

2 Samuel 8:3: who went to restore his *hand* at the Euphrates River – who went to restore his control at the Euphrates River

1 Kings 10:13: she asked besides what was given her by the *hand* of King Solomon - she asked besides what was given her by the *bounty* of King Solomon

Proverbs 18:21: Death and life are in the *hand* of the tongue - Death and life are in the power of the tongue

We can look to one example translation, who touts the fact that it is a literal translation, i.e., the English Standard Version (ESV). In fact, it waters that concept down by qualifying its literalness, saying that it is an essentially literal translation. Essentially means being the most basic element or feature of something. In this case, the ESV is the most basic element or feature of a literal translation. In the course of 13 years of using the ESV, this author has discovered that it unnecessarily abandons its literal translation philosophy quite regularly. Dr. William Mounce was the head of the translation committee that produced the ESV, and he leans toward or favors the dynamic equivalent translation philosophy. He has since left the ESV committee and has become the head of the New International Version committee, which is being more and more of a dynamic equivalent, with each new edition. This is not to say that the ESV is not a splendid translation because it is.

Dynamic Equivalent Translation

Translators who produce what are frequently referred to as free translations, take liberties with the text as presented in the original languages. How so? They either insert their opinion of what the original text could mean or omit some of the information contained in the original text. Dynamic equivalent translations may be appealing because they are easy to read. However, their very freeness at times obscures or changes the meaning of the original text.

Ecclesiastes 9:8 (NLT)	Ecclesiastes 9:8 (CEV)	Ecclesiastes 9:8 (GNT)	Ecclesiastes 9:8 (NCV)
[8] Wear fine clothes, with a splash of cologne!	[8] Dress up, comb your hair, and look your best.	[8] Always look happy and cheerful.	[8] Put on nice clothes and make yourself look good.

First, the above dynamic equivalents do not even agree with each other. What does **Ecclesiastes 9:8** really say.

Ecclesiastes 9:8 (NASB)	Ecclesiastes 9:8 (ESV)	Ecclesiastes 9:8 (UASV)	Ecclesiastes 9:8 (HCSB)
[8] Let your clothes be white all the time, and let not oil be lacking on your head.	[8] Let your garments be always white. Let not oil be lacking on your head.	[8] Let your garments be always white, and let not your head lack oil.	[8] Let your clothes be white all the time, and never let oil be lacking on your head.

What does the metaphorical language of "white garments" and "oil on your head" symbolize? Does **"white garments"** mean to "wear fine clothes," "dress up," "look happy," or "put on nice clothes"? In addition, does "oil on your head" means "a splash of cologne," "comb your hair" or "make yourself look good"? Duane Garrett says, "Wearing white clothes and anointing the hair (v. 8) symbolize joy and contrast with the familiar use of sackcloth and ashes as a sign of mourning or repentance."[157] Let us also look at an exegetical commentary as well as a book on Bible backgrounds.

John Peter Lange et al., A Commentary on the Holy Scriptures: Ecclesiastes	James M. Freeman and Harold J. Chadwick, Manners & Customs of the Bible
White garments are the expression of festive joy and pure, calm feelings in the soul, comp. Rev. 3:4 f.; 7:9 ff. Koheleth could hardly have meant a literal observance of this precept, so that the conduct of Sisinnius, Novatian bishop of Constantinople, who, with reference to this passage, always went in white garments, was very properly censured by Chrysostom as Pharisaical and proud. Hengstenberg's view is arbitrary, and in other respects scarcely corresponds to the sense of the author: "White garments are here to be put on as an expression of the confident hope of the future glory of the people of God, as Spener had himself buried in a white coffin as a sign of his hope in a better future of the Church." **And let thy head lack no ointment.** As in 2 Sam. 12:20; 14:2; Isa. 61:3; Amos 6:6; Prov. 27:9; Ps. 45:8, so here appears the anointing oil, which keeps the hair smooth and makes the face to shine, as a	In any area with strong sunlight, white clothing is preferred because white reflects the sunlight and so decreases the heating effect of it. In addition, white garments in the East were symbols of purity, and so were worn on certain special occasions. The symbols and custom were adopted by the West and is reflected especially in the wedding ceremony. The oil was symbolic of joy. Together they signified purity and the joy of festive occasions. In the Bible there are several references to white garments symbolizing purity, righteousness, or holiness. In Daniel 7:9, the clothing worn by the "Ancient of Days ... was as white as snow." When Jesus was transfigured, "his clothes became as white as the light" (Matthew 17:2). The angels appeared in white robes when they appeared to the soldiers guarding Jesus' tomb and when the women went to the tomb after He had risen (Matthew 28:3, Mark 16:5,

---

[157] Duane A. Garrett, *Proverbs, Ecclesiastes, Song of Songs*, vol. 14, The New American Commentary (Nashville: Broadman & Holman Publishers, 1993), 331.

symbol of festive joy, and a contrast to a sorrowing disposition. There is no reason here for supposing fragrant spikenard (Mark 14:2), because the question is mainly about producing a good appearance by means of the ointment, comp. Ps. 133:2. Ver. 9.[158]	Luke 24:4, and John 20:12), and also when Christ ascended into heaven (Acts 1:10). In the ages to come, the redeemed will be clothed in white (Revelation 7:13 and 19:14).[159]

We can see that the three sources interpret the metaphorical language of "white garments" and "oil on your head" as purity and joy. Would we get this by way of the four dynamic equivalents in the above? Would "Wear fine clothes, with a splash of cologne" (NLT) get us to the correct meaning? We should not replace metaphorical language because we feel it is too difficult for the reader to understand. They should buy out the time, just as this writer has done, by going to commentaries, word study books, and Bible background books. Let us look at one more informative Bible background book,

9:8. clothed in white. Scholars have understood the color white to symbolize purity, festivity or elevated social status. In both Egypt Story of Sinuhe) and Mesopotamia (Epic of Gilgamesh) clean or bright garments conveyed a sense of well-being. Moreover, the hot Middle-Eastern climate favors the wearing of white clothes to reflect the heat.

9:8. anointed head. Oil preserved the complexion in the hot Middle Eastern climate. Both the Egyptian *Song of the Harper* and the Mesopotamian Epic of Gilgamesh described individuals clothed in fine linen and with myrrh on their head. (Walton, Matthews and Chavalas 2000, p. 574)

As we are about to take up the subject of the paraphrase, let us consider the above Ecclesiastes 9:8 and the surrounding verses in a paraphrase.

---

[158] John Peter Lange et al., *A Commentary on the Holy Scriptures: Ecclesiastes* (Bellingham, WA: Logos Bible Software, 2008), 126.

[159] James M. Freeman and Harold J. Chadwick, *Manners & Customs of the Bible* (North Brunswick, NJ: Bridge-Logos Publishers, 1998), 338.

Ecclesiastes 9:8 (The Message)

[7-10] Seize life! Eat bread with gusto,
Drink wine with a robust heart.
Oh yes, God takes pleasure in your pleasure!
Dress festively every morning.
Don't skimp on colors and scarves.
Relish life with the spouse you love
Each and every day of your precarious life.
Each day is God's gift. It's all you get in exchange
For the hard work of staying alive.
Make the most of each one!
Whatever turns up, grab it and do it. And heartily!
This is your last and only chance at it,
For there's neither work to do nor thoughts to think
In the company of the dead, where you're most certainly headed.

Paraphrase Translation

A paraphrase is "a restatement of a text, passage, or work giving the meaning in another form."[160] The highest priority and characteristic is the rephrasing and simplification. Whatever has been said in the above about the dynamic equivalent can be magnified a thousand fold herein. The best way to express the level this translation will be to go to a paraphrase and set it side-by-side with the dynamic equivalent and literal translations. Below we have done that, i.e., **Isaiah 1:1-17**. It is recommended that we read verses 1-4 in the Message Bible, then in the New Living Translation, and then in the English Standard Version. Thereafter, read verses 5-9 in the same manner, followed by verses 10-12, and 13-17. This way we will taste the flavor of each with just a small bit at a time, so you do not lose the sense of the previous one by too much reading.

Isaiah 1:1-9 The Message (MSG)	Isaiah 1:1-9 New Living Translation (NLT)	Isaiah 1:1-9 Updated American Standard Version (UASV)
[1]The vision that Isaiah son of Amoz saw regarding Judah and Jerusalem during the times of the kings of	[1] These are the visions that Isaiah son of Amoz saw concerning Judah and Jerusalem.	1 The vision of Isaiah the son of Amoz, which he saw concerning Judah and Jerusalem in the

---

160 Inc Merriam-Webster, *Merriam-Webster's Collegiate Dictionary.*, Eleventh ed. (Springfield, Mass.: Merriam-Webster, Inc., 2003).

Judah: Uzziah, Jotham, Ahaz, and Hezekiah. 2-4Heaven and earth, you're the jury.

Listen to God's case:
"I had children and raised them well,
and they turned on me.
The ox knows who's boss,
the mule knows the hand that feeds him,
But not Israel.
My people don't know up from down.
Shame! Misguided God-dropouts,
staggering under their guilt-baggage,
Gang of miscreants,
band of vandals—
My people have walked out on me, their God,
turned their backs on The Holy of Israel,
walked off and never looked back.

5-9"Why bother even trying to do anything with you
when you just keep to your bullheaded ways?
You keep beating your heads against brick walls.
Everything within you protests against

He saw these visions during the years when Uzziah, Jotham, Ahaz, and Hezekiah were kings of Judah.

2 Listen, O heavens! Pay attention, earth!
This is what the LORD says:
"The children I raised and cared for
have rebelled against me.
3 Even an ox knows its owner,
and a donkey recognizes its master's care—
but Israel doesn't know its master.
My people don't recognize my care for them."
4 Oh, what a sinful nation they are—
loaded down with a burden of guilt.
They are evil people,
corrupt children who have rejected the LORD.
They have despised the Holy One of Israel
and turned their backs on him.

5 Why do you continue to invite punishment?
Must you rebel forever?

---

days of Uzziah, Jotham, Ahaz, and Hezekiah, kings of Judah.

The Wickedness of Judah

2 Hear, O heavens, and give ear, O earth;
for Jehovah has spoken:
"Sons I have brought up and raised,
but they have revolted against me.
3 An ox knows its owner,
and the donkey its master's manger,
but Israel does not know,
my people do not understand."

4 Woe to the sinful nation,
a people weighed down with error,
brood of wicked men,
sons who act corruptly!
They have abandoned Jehovah,
they
have despised the Holy One of Israel,
they have turned their backs on him.

5 Where will you be stricken again,
as you continue in your rebellion??
The whole head is sick,

you.
From the bottom of your feet to the top of your head,
nothing's working right.
Wounds and bruises and running sores—
untended, unwashed, unbandaged.
Your country is laid waste,
your cities burned down.
Your land is destroyed by outsiders while you watch,
reduced to rubble by barbarians.
Daughter Zion is deserted—
like a tumbledown shack on a dead-end street,
Like a tarpaper shanty on the wrong side of the tracks,
like a sinking ship abandoned by the rats.
If God-of-the-Angel-Armies hadn't left us a few survivors,
we'd be as desolate as Sodom, doomed just like Gomorrah.

Your head is injured,
and your heart is sick.
⁶ You are battered from head to foot—
covered with bruises, welts, and infected wounds—
without any soothing ointments or bandages.
⁷ Your country lies in ruins,
and your towns are burned.
Foreigners plunder your fields before your eyes
and destroy everything they see.
⁸ Beautiful Jerusalem stands abandoned
like a watchman's shelter in a vineyard,
like a lean-to in a cucumber field after the harvest,
like a helpless city under siege.
⁹ If the LORD of Heaven's Armies
had not spared a few of us,
we would have been wiped out like Sodom,
destroyed like Gomorrah.

and the whole heart faint.
⁶ From the sole of the foot even to the head,
there is no soundness in it,
but bruises and sores
and raw wounds;
they are not pressed out or bound up
or softened with oil.

⁷ Your land is desolate;
your cities are burned with fire;
in your very presence
foreigners devour your land;
it is desolate, as overthrown by foreigners.
⁸ And the daughter of Zion is left
like a shelter in a vineyard,
like a hut in a cucumber field,
like a city besieged.

⁹ Unless Jehovah of armies
had left us a few survivors,
we would be like Sodom,
we would have become like Gomorrah.

Literal Contrasted With Dynamic Equivalent

In short, the dynamic equivalent translator seeks to render the biblical meaning of the original language text as accurately as possible into an English informal (conversational) equivalent. Alternatively, the literal translation seeks to render the original language words and style into a corresponding English word and style.

Again, there are two major divisions in translation philosophy. We have the word-for-word and the thought-for-thought. A literal translation is one-step removed from the original, and something is always lost or gained, because there will never be 100 percent equivalent transference from one language to the next. A thought-for-thought translation is one more step removed than the literal translation in many cases and can block the sense of the original entirely. A thought-for-thought translation slants the text in a particular direction, cutting off other options and nuances.

A literal word-for-word translation makes every effort to represent accurately the authority, power, vitality, and directness of the original Hebrew and Greek Scriptures and to transfer these characteristics in modern English. The literal translations have the goal of producing as literal a translation as possible where the modern-English idiom permits and where a literal rendering does not conceal the thought. Again, there are times when the literal rendering would be unintelligible, and so one must interpret what the author meant by the words that he used.

Literal Translation	Dynamic Equivalent
Focuses on form	Focuses on meaning
Emphasizes source language	Emphasizes receptor language
Translates what was said	Translates what was meant
Presumes original context	Presumes contemporary context
Retains ambiguities	Removes ambiguities
Minimizes interpretative bias	Enhances interpretative bias
Valuable for serious Bible study	Valuable for commentary use
Awkward receptor language style	Natural receptor language style

The alteration of one word can remove an enormous amount of meaning from the Word of God. Let us consider 1 Kings 2:10 as an example.

Literal Translation	Dynamic Equivalent
1 Kings 2:10 (ESV) ¹⁰ Then David **slept** with his fathers and was buried in the city of David.	1 Kings 2:10 (GNT) ¹⁰ David **died** and was buried in David's City.
1 Kings 2:10 (ASV) ¹⁰ And David **slept** with his fathers, and was buried in the city of David.	1 Kings 2:10 (NLT) ¹⁰ Then David **died** and was buried with his ancestors in the City of David.
1 Kings 2:10 (NASB) ¹⁰ Then David slept with his fathers and was buried in the city of David.	1 Kings 2:10 (GW) ¹⁰ David **lay down in death** with his ancestors and was buried in the City of David.
1 Kings 2:10 (UASV) ¹⁰ Then David **slept** with his fathers and was buried in the city of David.	1 Kings 2:10 (NIRV) ¹⁰ David joined the members of his family who had already **died**. His body was buried in the City of David.
1 Kings 2:10 (RSV) ¹⁰ Then David **slept** with his fathers, and was buried in the city of David.	1 Kings 2:10 (NCV) ¹⁰ Then David **died** and was buried with his ancestors in Jerusalem.

One could conclude that the (dynamic equivalent) thought-for-thought translations are conveying the idea in a more clear and immediate way, but is this really the case? There are three points that are missing from the thought-for-thought translation:

In the scriptures, "sleep" is used metaphorically as death, also inferring a temporary state where one will wake again, or be resurrected. That idea is lost in the thought-for-thought translation. (Ps 13:3; John 11:11-14; Ac 7:60; 1Co 7:39; 15:51; 1Th 4:13)

Sleeping with or lying down with his father also conveys the idea of having closed his life and having found favor in God's eyes as did his forefathers.

When we leave out some of the words from the original, we also leave out the possibility of more meaning being drawn from the text. Missing is the word *shakab* ("to lie down" or "to sleep"), *'im* ("with") and 'ab in the plural ("forefathers"). Below are verses that enhance our understanding of death, by way of sleep, as being temporary for those who will be awakened by a resurrection.

Psalm 13:3 Updated American Standard Version (UASV)

³ Consider and answer me, Jehovah my God;
   give light to my eyes
lest I sleep *the sleep of* death,

John 11:11-14 Updated American Standard Version (UASV)

¹¹ After saying these things, he said to them, "Our friend Lazarus has fallen asleep, but I go to awaken him." ¹² The disciples said to him, "Lord, if he has fallen asleep, he will get well." ¹³ Now Jesus had spoken of his death, but they thought that he meant taking rest in sleep. ¹⁴ Then Jesus told them plainly, "Lazarus has died,

Acts 7:60 Updated American Standard Version (UASV)

⁶⁰ Then falling on his knees, he cried out with a loud voice, "Lord, do not hold this sin against them!" Having said this, he fell asleep.[161]

1 Corinthians 7:39 Updated American Standard Version (UASV)

³⁹ A wife is bound for so long time as her husband is alive. But if her husband should fall asleep (*koimethe*) [in death], she is free to be married to whom she wishes, only in the Lord.[162]

1 Corinthians 15:51 Updated American Standard Version (UASV)

⁵¹ Behold, I tell you a mystery; we will not all sleep, but we will all be changed,

1 Thessalonians 4:13 Updated American Standard Version (UASV)

¹³ But we do not want you to be ignorant,[163] brothers, about those who are asleep, so that you will not grieve as do the rest who have no hope.

Those who argue for a though-for-thought translation will say the literal translation "slept" or "lay down" is no longer a way of expressing death in the modern English-speaking world. While this may be true to some extent, the context of chapter two, verse 1: "when David was about to die" and the latter half of 2:10: "was buried in the city of David" resolves that issue. Moreover, while the reader may have to meditate a

---

[161] I.e. died

[162] The ASV, ESV, NASB, and other literal translation do not hold true to their literal translation philosophy here. This does not bode well in their claim that literal is the best policy. We are speaking primarily to the ESV translators, who make this claim in numerous books.

[163] Or *uninformed*

little longer, or indulge him/herself in the culture of different Biblical times, they will not be deprived of the full potential that a verse has to convey. (Grudem, et al. 2005, pp. 20-21)

A Word of Caution

The dynamic equivalent and paraphrase can and does obscure things from the reader by overreaching in their translations. This can be demonstrated on the moral standards found in 1 Corinthians 6:9-10.

1 Corinthians 6:9-10 The Message

9-10 Don't you realize that this is not the way to live? Unjust people who don't care about God will not be joining in his kingdom. Those who use and abuse each other, use and abuse sex, use and abuse the earth and everything in it, don't qualify as citizens in God's kingdom.

1 Corinthians 6:9-10 Updated American Standard Version (UASV)

9 Or do you not know that the unrighteous will not inherit the kingdom of God? Do not be deceived; neither fornicators, nor idolaters, nor adulterers, nor men of passive homosexual acts, nor men of active homosexual acts,[164] 10 nor thieves, nor the covetous, nor drunkards, nor revilers, nor swindlers, will inherit the kingdom of God.

If you compare the MSG with the UASV, you will notice that the MSG does not even list the specifics defined by the apostle Paul on precisely what kind of conduct we should shun.

Matthew 7:13 Today's English Version (TEV)

13"Go in through the narrow gate, because the gate to **hell** is wide and the road that leads to it is easy, and there are many who travel it.

Matthew 7:13 Updated American Standard Version (UASV)

13 "Enter through the narrow gate; for the gate is wide and the way is broad that leads to **destruction**, and there are many who enter through it.

The Greek word *apōleian* means "destruction," "waste," "annihilation," "ruin." Therefore, one has to ask, 'why did the TEV translation committee render it "hell"? It has all the earmarks of theological bias. The translation committee is looking to promote the

---

[164] The two Greek terms refer to passive men partners and active men partners in consensual homosexual acts

doctrine of eternal torment, not destruction. The objective of the translator is to render it the way that it should be rendered. If it supports a certain doctrine, this should be accepted, if not, then this should be accepted as well. The policy is that God does not need an overzealous translator to convey his doctrinal message.

1 Corinthians 11:10

10 διὰ   τοῦτο ὀφείλει ἡ   γυνὴ ἐξουσίαν ἔχειν ἐπὶ τῆς
Through this   owes the woman authority to have on the

κεφαλῆς   διὰ   τοὺς ἀγγέλους
head   because of the messengers

Literal	Dynamic Equivalent	Dynamic Equivalent
1 Corinthians 11:10 (UASV) ¹⁰ This is why the woman ought to have a symbol of authority on her head, because of the angels.	1 Corinthians 11:10 (GNT) ¹⁰ On account of the angels, then, a woman should have a covering over her head to show that she is under her husband's authority.	1 Corinthians 11:10 (CEV) ¹⁰ And so, because of this, and also because of the angels, a woman ought to wear something on her head, as a sign of her authority.

As we can see, the English lexical glosses of the interlinear are literally carried over into the Source Language word for word, keeping the exact form. This is called a **gloss** in the world of the Bible translator. While this does not convey much meaning to the average English reader, it does to one who has studied Biblical Greek. However, the Bible student would have a literal translation as a study Bible. The literal translation, as you can see, will keep the form as far as is possible, as well as the wording. The Dynamic Equivalent advocates will argue that this does not sound natural. Well, for those that want the Word of God in its undiluted form, as accurately as possible, we will accept a little unnatural sounding at times. Soon, we will see the danger of going beyond translation into interpretation.

Our literal translation contains ambiguity. Is the writer talking about *women* or *wives*? Is the woman to have her own authority, or is something or someone else to have authority over her? This is just fine, because it ambiguity has many benefits, as you will see. First, as a quick aside, the work of interpretation will weed out those pseudo-Christians,

158

who do not want to put any effort into their relationship with God, who do not want to buy out the time to understand. Now, the reader has the right to determine for himself or herself which is the correct interpretation. The translator should not steal this right from them, for the translator or the translation committee, could be wrong, and life or death may be uncertain.

Seeing two dynamic equivalents side-by-side helps you to see that they have arrived at two different conclusions and both cannot be right. The *Today's English Version* believes that the "woman" here is really the "wife," as it refers to the "husband." It also believes that the wife is to be under the husband's authority. On the other hand, the *Contemporary English Version* does not commit to the argument of "woman" versus "wife," but does understand the verse to mean the woman has her *own* authority. She has the authority to act as she feels she should, as long as she wears something as a sign of this.

A good translation will do the following:

(1) Accurately render the original language words and style into the corresponding English word and style that were inspired by God.

(2) Translate the meaning of words literally, when the wording and construction of the original text allow for such a rendering in the target language.

(3) Transfer the correct meaning (sense) of a word or a phrase when a literal rendering of the original-language word or a phrase would garble or obscure the meaning.

(4) After considering, the objectives of the first three points, as far as possible, use natural, easy-to-understand language that inspires reading.

Are there such translations available on the market? Yes, the author recommends that you use the NASB Zondervan Study Bible by Kenneth L. Barker, Donald W. Burdick, John H. Stek and Walter W. Wessel (Jan 6, 2000), as your primary study Bible. Of course, you should consider other literal translations as time permits. In addition, use the dynamic equivalents as mini-commentaries, as that is what they are.

CHAPTER 4 The Process of Doing Bible Research

Wise King Solomon, also known as the Teacher or Preacher, "taught the people knowledge, and he **pondered and made a thorough search** in order to arrange many proverbs. The Teacher **sought to find delightful words** and to record **accurate words of truth**." (Eccl. 12:9-10) Luke, the author of our third Gospel, "followed all things accurately from the beginning" (Luke 1:3), as he compiled the life and times of Jesus Christ. Both of these men of God were doing research.

Research is the systematic investigation into and study of materials and sources in order to establish facts and reach conclusions. So, Bible research would be the systematic investigation into and Word of God and Bible study materials (word dictionaries, commentaries, historical setting, Bible backgrounds, Bible encyclopedias), in order to establish facts and reach conclusions.

Research should be a part of every Christin's life and personal study. There is a difference between **Bible study** and **Bible research**. Bible study is the devotion of time and attention to acquiring knowledge of God's Word, especially by means of Bible study tools like a commentary, among others. Bible research is a systematic investigation in order to establish facts, so as to reach a conclusion. What might move a Christian from Bible study into the Bible research mode? During your Bible study, you come across some biblical terms that you do not fully understand. During your personal study, you come across a Christian quality that you need to strengthen, like patience. Someone raises a Bible question to you and you want to discover the answer, so as to make a reply. A Bible critic might have challenged you online, ask a difficult Bible question. While you are not trying to necessarily win over the Bible critics that likely has a closed mind, you are trying to provide a response to those that see the critics question, so that they know there is an answer.

Who our audience is a very important factor in the type of Bible study tools that we might look at. Do they have a basic understanding of God's Word? What do they need to know? You then need to identify the objective. Are you trying to *explain*? Are you trying to *convince*? Are you trying to *refute* something? Are you trying to *reason*? Are you trying to *overturn false reasoning*? Are you trying to *motivate*? Are you seeking to *convert* this one to the faith? Are you trying to leave a biblical thought as a planted seed?

Explaining involves giving your listener more information so as to make it clear. It may be that they understand the basic facts, so you may need to expound more on the *when* or *how* of what was stated. In order to convince, you must give them reasonable and rational reasons, outlining *why* something is so and *why* what you are saying is true. Thus, this is a presentation of evidence. If you are refuting something, this will mean that you must have a thorough knowledge of what you know to be true as well as the other sides opposing arguments, having previously made a careful analysis of the evidence. You are not just looking for strong arguments but how you can present them respectfully, so as to not cause offense, but rather to *motivate*. It means you are reaching the heart of your listener, *reasoning* with them, maybe even *overturning* false beliefs, so as to move them to research the subject objectively (**not** influenced by personal feelings or opinions in considering and representing facts) as opposed to subjectively (based on or influenced by personal feelings, tastes, or opinions).

Now that we have who our audience is, what is next? Who we are talking to will determine just how much information will be needed to convince. Then, we have to consider how much time we have in order to research thoroughly. Are you on the internet where you have but minutes as discussions pass quickly? Or is this a person you will see again and you have plenty of time to pull your research together. A word of caution and the right perspective on presenting evidence. You are researching for more than your listener. You are also researching for your benefit, as it strengthens your faith as well, and this information will be needed again and again because some Bible questions are often asked. The word of caution is this, many time you put hours into researching something; then, you present it well, and the listener just blows it off without even really listening or reading what you prepared. This may make you feel like, 'Why do I even try?' Nevertheless, remember, the information benefit you too.

What Bible study tools will we need in our lifetime of research? If our budget is low, we can get things as we can. Be very cautious of the outdated tools from the 1800s that are free on the internet. Something like R. A. Torrey's books on Bible difficulties might be very good but a dictionary or an encyclopedia might have inaccurate information because our understanding of the original language words has advanced over the last 150 years. Software is a way to grow your library without having to have all of those physical books. Basically, you need Bible dictionaries, Bible word study books, Bible encyclopedias, Bible background books, Bible commentaries, Bible atlas, and so on.

However, you need to read and study other kinds of books as well. You will need to read books on Christian apologetics, which help you to understand how to reason from the Scriptures. You need to read an apologetic book on things like inerrancy of Scripture, Bible difficulties, reasoning from the Scriptures and so on. You will need to read books on how to interpret the Bible. A word of caution here too. Not all Christian authors are equal. The vast majority of Bible scholars today are liberal to moderate, meaning they doubt parts of the Bible, they have liberal social positions, and they are using higher criticism in their interpretive process, which tears the Bible apart, giving you the author's views, not what the original authors, inerrant, authoritative Bible author said or meant.

So, as you build your library, you need to be very cautious as you compile it. Always, remember that a literal translation of God's Word is truth. (John 17:17) Jesus is the central person in the fulfillment of the Father's will and purposes. Therefore, Colossians 2:3 says of Jesus: "in whom are hidden all the treasures of wisdom and knowledge." You need to stay with truly conservative resources and conservative authors. How can you know who is conservative and who is not? One way is to ask your pastor. Another is to become friends on social media with Bible scholars that are conservative. Therein, you can ask, "what book would you recommend for biblical interpretation, textual criticism, the history of the church, and so on. Aside from basic Bible study tools, you need to have a foundational understanding of some important subject areas. Apologetics, biblical archaeology, biblical interpretation, how to study, Christian living, Christian evangelism, textual criticism, translation process, and philosophy, among others.

Proverbs 2:1-5 Updated American Standard Version (UASV)

2 My son, if you receive my words
   and **treasure** up my commandments with you,
² making your ear **attentive** to wisdom
   and **inclining your heart** to discernment;¹⁶⁵
³ For if you **cry for** discernment¹⁶⁶
   and **raise your voice** for understanding,
⁴ if you **seek it** like silver
   and **search for it** as for hidden treasures,
⁵ then you will understand the fear of Jehovah
   and find the knowledge of God.

---

¹⁶⁵ The Hebrew word rendered here as "discernment" (*tevunah*) is related to the word *binah*, translated "understanding." Both appear at Proverbs 2:3.

¹⁶⁶ See 2.2 ftn.

⁶ For Jehovah gives wisdom;
  from his mouth come knowledge and understanding;

Basic Bible Study Tools

We have only mentioned some of the basic tools; now we need to spend a brief moment talking about them. Again, many of the Christian publishing houses today offer books by conservative, moderate and liberal authors. Therefore, as Forest Gump might say, "it is like a box of Chocolate, you never know what you are going to get."[167]

Study Bible

The most important tool in your study chest is the study Bible. The goal and purpose of the upcoming Updated American Standard Version (UASV) are as follows. "Our primary purpose is to give the Bible readers what God said by way of his human authors, not what a translator thinks God meant in its place, Truth Matters! Our primary goal is to be accurate and faithful to the original text. The meaning of a word is the responsibility of the interpreter (i.e., reader), not the translator.], Translating Truth! The Updated American Standard Version will be one of the most faithful and accurate translations to date."[168] There is no other translation to date that stays faithful to these translation principles. Yes, a few have these principles, but they also abandon them quite often during their translation process. Thus, follow the link below to the UASV website. Know when it is coming available. In the meantime, these other translation are still worthy of your attention. It is recommended that you use The Holy Bible, English Standard Version. ESV® Permanent Text Edition® (2016). Copyright © 2001 by Crossway Bibles, a publishing ministry of Good News Publishers. We also recommend The Christian Standard Bible. Copyright © 2017 by Holman Bible Publishers.

Cross References: In the translation, you will find a column of cross references. The verses that they take you to might be based on the verse as a whole, a section of the verse, even a particular word within the verse. This gives you other verses in the Bible that use the same term. Keep in mind; the translator may not have chosen the cross reference verse with the same intention of why you are looking at it.

---

[167] life is like a box of chocolates – Wiktionary (Saturday, September 02, 2017) https://en.wiktionary.org/wiki/life_is_like_a_box_of_chocolates

[168] http://www.uasvbible.org/

Study Notes: The study note are normally at the bottom of the page. The study notes may be brief, say a sentence or two, as well extensive, a paragraph or two. The study notes will cover such things as the Bible background, historical setting, original language word meaning, textual, as well doctrinal. A word of caution here as well. The translator is offering his doctrinal position when it comes to the doctrinal footnotes. Never assume he is correct.

Subject or Topical Index: Some study Bible have a subject or topical index at the back of the Bible, some in the front of the Bible. This will offer you brief information on persons, places, and things within God's Word.

Glossary of Bible Terms: Some study Bibles have a glossary of Bible terms that will give you brief definitions of such terms as confession, sin, righteousness, adultery, antichrist, and son. These definitions may be a simple sentence or even two paragraphs or more. The glossary helps the reader understand selected words according to their Bible-specific usage.

Maps and Archaeology: Almost all Bible have maps at the end of the Bible. Some study Bibles have archaeological sections near the maps, which will introduce the readers to significant archaeological finds over the last two-hundred years.

Choosing a Bible: You must have a very good literal translation that is the Word of God in English. The upcoming Updated American Standard Version (UASV) will be your best choice in the near future. Until then, the English Standard Version (ESV) of 2001 or the Christian Standard Bible of 2017 is your best choices for a study Bible. The New American Standard Bible (NASB) of 1995 is your best choice for a literal translation for now. If you use an interpretive translation as an aid to your literal translation, such as the (CEB, NIV, CEV, ERV, GNT, NLT), just know that they are mini commentaries, and are not to serve as a translation.

Bible Dictionary

We also need a very good Bible dictionary. A trusted Bible dictionary is found in Chad Brand et al., eds., *Holman Illustrated Bible Dictionary* (Nashville, TN: Holman Bible Publishers, 2003). Another is by Walter A. Elwell and Philip Wesley Comfort, *Tyndale Bible Dictionary*, Tyndale Reference Library (Wheaton, IL: Tyndale House Publishers, 2001).

Bible Encyclopedia

Christians who want to dig a little deeper, you may want to invest in a Bible encyclopedia. If you are looking for something a little more extensive yet still very easy for the non-academics to understand, it will be by Hobert K. Farrell, *Baker Encyclopedia of the Bible* (Grand Rapids, MI: Baker Book House, 1988), 270. Another long trusted source would be by D. H. Engelhard, Geoffrey W. Bromiley, *The International Standard Bible Encyclopedia*, Revised (Wm. B. Eerdmans, 1979–1988).

Bible Concordance

Robert L. Thomas, The Lockman Foundation, New American Standard Exhaustive Concordance of the Bible: Updated Edition (Anaheim: Foundation Publications, Inc., 1998).

Bible Study Software

This is a lifetime investment. It is a digital library that offers you deeper research, faster, and easier than you have ever imagined.

Logos Bible Software (https://www.logos.com/): is a digital library application designed for electronic Bible study. In addition to basic eBook functionality, it includes extensive resource linking, note-taking functionality, and linguistic analysis for study of the Bible both in translation and in its original languages. It is developed by Faithlife Corporation. As of February 2017, Logos Bible Software is in its seventh version. Logos Bible Software is compatible with more than 43,000 titles related to the Bible from 200 publishers, including Baker, Bantam, Catholic University of America Press, Eerdmans, Harvest House, Merriam Webster, Moody Press, Oxford University Press, Thomas Nelson, Tyndale House, and Zondervan. Logos also recently published its own Lexham Bible Reference series, featuring new scholarship on the original Biblical languages.

Accordance Bible Software (http://www.accordancebible.com/): it is a Bible study program for Apple Macintosh and iPhone, and now Windows developed by OakTree Software, Inc. The program is used for both private and academic study.

BibleWorks (http://bibleworks.com/): Whether you're preparing a sermon, doing complex morphological analysis, or writing a seminary paper, scholars agree that BibleWorks is indispensable. You'll find everything you need for close exegesis of the original text in its 200+ Bible translations in 40 languages, 50+ original language texts and morphology databases, dozens of lexical-grammatical references, plus a wealth of practical reference works! Instead of providing a loose collection of books, BibleWorks tightly integrates its databases with the most powerful morphology and analysis tools.

Handle God's Word Aright

2 Timothy 2:15 Updated American Standard Version (UASV)

[15] Do your best to present yourself to God as one approved, a workman who does not need to be ashamed, rightly handling[169] the word of truth.

If we are teaching ourselves, regular and diligent personal study of the Bible is vital, no matter how long we have been serving God.

On **2 Timothy 2:15**, New Testament Bible scholar Knute Larson writes,

> Timothy, by contrast, must do his best to **present [himself] to God as one approved, a workman who does not need to be ashamed.** Timothy, and all who follow Christ, are to consecrate themselves to God, working diligently for his approval. The teacher whom God approves has no need of shame in his presence.
>
> God bestows his approval on the one who exhibits truth, love, and godliness in daily living, and who **correctly handles the word of truth.** The false teachers were mishandling God's words, using them for their own benefit. Timothy was commissioned to handle the words of God correctly. All preaching should present the truth clearly, cutting through erroneous ideas or inaccurate opinions. (Larson 2000, p. 286)

The English Standard Version renders the participial clause of 2:15 "rightly handling the word of truth," while the Holman Christian Standard Bible renders it "correctly teaching the word of truth," and the New American Standard Bible, "accurately handling the word of truth." The Greek word, *orthotomeo*, means "to give accurate instruction—'to teach correctly, to expound rightly.' ... 'do your best ... to teach the

---

[169] Or *accurately handling* the word of truth; *correctly teaching* the word of truth

word of truth correctly' 2 Tm 2:15."[170] This is all that can be asked of any Christian, that 'we do our best to teach the word of truth correctly.'

What can help us to teach the word of truth correctly? If we are to teach another, we must correctly and clearly understand the Word ourselves. When we clearly understand something, we are able to give reasons as to why it is so. Moreover, we are able to express it in our own words. If we are to understand the Bible correctly, we must read it within the context of the verses that surround it, the chapter it is within, the Bible book it is within, the Testament that it is in, and the Bible as a whole. According to the Merriam-Webster Dictionary, immediate context (i.e., of a word, phrase, clause or sentence) is "the words that are used with a certain word or phrase and that help to explain its meaning."[171] The meaning of a text is what the author meant by the words that he used. On this Robert H. Stein writes,

> Great confusion can result if we do not pay careful attention to context. For instance, both Paul (Rom. 4:1–25) and James (2:14–26) use the term "faith" (pistis). Yet we will misunderstand both if we assume that by faith they mean "a body of beliefs." We will misunderstand Paul if we assume that he means "a mere mental assent to a fact," and we will misunderstand James if we assume that he means "a wholehearted trust." It is evident from the context that Paul means the latter (cf. Rom. 4:3, 5) and that James means the former (cf. 2:14, 19). (Stein 1994, p. 59)

Stein also wrote, "A context is valuable because it assists the reader in understanding the meaning the author has given the text." Another example would be Paul's statement at Galatians 5:13 (ESV), "For you were called to freedom, brothers. Only do not use your freedom as an opportunity for the flesh, but through love serve one another." If we were looking at this verse alone, not considering what is before and after, we would be asking, what does Paul mean by "freedom"? Was he speaking of freedom from sin and death, freedom from being enslaved to false beliefs, freedom from corruption, or was it something entirely different? If we consider the context, we get our answer. The context tells us the "freedom" that Paul spoke of was our being freed from "the curse of the law," as Christ became the curse for us. (Gal. 3:13, 19-24; 4:1-5) If

---

[170] Louw, Johannes P.; Nida, Eugene A. (**Greek-English Lexicon of the New Testament based on Semantic Domains**)

[171] http://www.merriam-webster.com/dictionary/context (Sunday, September 03, 2017)

we look at Galatians 3:10, "Paul quotes Deuteronomy 27:26 to prove that, contrary to what the Judaizers claimed, the law cannot justify and save. It can only condemn. The breaking of any aspect of the law brought a curse on the person who broke the law. Since no one can keep the law perfectly, we are all cursed. Paul, with this argument, destroys the Judaizers' belief that a person is saved through the law."[172] Thus, Paul was referring to the freedom that Christians possess. Just because we are not under the Mosaic Law, a law that imperfect man cannot keep perfectly, this is no excuse to use our "freedom as an opportunity for the flesh." Rather, if we truly understand and value our freedom, we will slave for one another because of our love for one another. However, those in the Galatian congregation who lacked that love were engaged in vicious infighting and quarreling.–Galatians 5:15.

There is another meaning of the word "context," i.e., background, conditions, historical setting, and situation. Some call the surrounding text context and the historical setting context. Either way, the second meaning here is just as important. The background information that must be considered is, who penned the book, when and where was it written and under what historical setting. Why was the author moved to pen the book, or more realistically, why did God move him to write the book? Within any book on Bible backgrounds, the author will discuss the social, moral, and religious practices of the time Bible book was written.

Correctly handling the word of truth goes deeper than simply explaining a biblical truth accurately. We do not want to use our knowledge of God's Word in an intimidating way. Of course, we want to defend the truth offensively and defensively, following the example of Jesus, who used Scripture to defeat Satan the Devil when under temptation. Nevertheless, figuratively speaking, we do not use the Bible to club others over the head. (Deut. 6:16; 8:3; 10:20; Matt. 4:4, 7, 10) Rather, we want to follow counsel that Peter gave, "in your hearts honor Christ the Lord as holy, **always being prepared to make a defense** to anyone who asks you for a reason for the hope that is in you; **yet do it with gentleness and respect.**"–1 Peter 3:15.

New Testament Bible scholar Richard L. Pratt Jr. offered the following on 2 Corinthians 10:3-5,

> Paul responded by reminding the Corinthians that his ministry was successful warfare. He had previously described his gospel ministry as a parade of victory in war, and he used

---

[172] (Anders, *Holman New Testament Commentary:* vol. 8, Galatians, Ephesians, Philippians, Colossians 1999, p. 37)

similar military analogies elsewhere as well. His apostolic effort was a war he was sure to win.

Paul admitted that he and his company live[d] in the world, but insisted that they did not wage war as the world does. They did not employ the intimidation, coercion, and violence normally associated with worldly authorities. Instead of employing the weapons of the world, Paul relied on divine power. These weapons appeared weak by worldly standards, but they were actually very powerful. The preaching of the cross brought great displays of God's power in the lives of believers everywhere, including Corinth.

Consequently, Paul was certain that he was on a course to demolish the strongholds or fortifications of arguments and every pretension that anyone set up against the knowledge of God. As Paul traveled the world proclaiming the gospel of Christ, he encountered pretentious disbelief supported by clever arguments and powerful personalities. But through the "weakness" of preaching Christ, Paul went about taking captive every thought to make it obedient to Christ. (Pratt Jr 2000, p. 417)

2 Corinthians 10:3-5 Updated American Standard Version (UASV)

[3] For though we walk in the flesh, we do not war according to the flesh, [4] for the weapons of our warfare are not of the flesh[173] but powerful to God for destroying strongholds.[174] [5] We are destroying speculations and every lofty thing raised up against the knowledge of God, and we are taking every thought captive to the obedience of Christ,

---

[173] That is *merely human*

[174] That is *tearing down false arguments*

CHAPTER 5 The Correct Method of Bible Study

Introduction to the Correct Method

It is highly important that we get at what the author meant by his words that he used. It is highly important that **we do not** impose our 21ˢᵗ mindset **into** the text (**eisegesis**, taking out of the text). What we want to do is take the meaning **out of** the text, which is known as **exegesis**. We are going to take a look at a passage of Scripture, 1 Corinthians 8:1-3. Then, we will answer the challenges of interpreting such a passage.

1 Corinthians 8:1-13 Updated American Standard Version (UASV)

8 Now concerning food offered to idols: we know that "all of us possess knowledge." This "knowledge" puffs up, but love builds up. ² If anyone thinks he knows anything, he does not yet know it as he ought to know it. ³ But if anyone loves God, he is known by him.

⁴ Therefore, concerning the eating of food sacrificed to idols, we know that "an idol is nothing in the world" and that "there is no God but one." ⁵ For even if there are so-called gods whether in heaven or on earth, as indeed there are many gods and many lords, ⁶ yet for us there is one God, the Father, from whom are all things and for whom we exist, and one Lord, Jesus Christ, through whom are all things and through whom we exist.

⁷ However not all men have this knowledge; but some, being accustomed to the idol until now, eat food as if it were sacrificed to an idol; and their conscience being weak is defiled. ⁸ But food does not bring us close to God. Neither if we do not eat do we lack, nor if we do eat do we have more."[175] ⁹ But take care that this right of yours does not somehow become a stumbling block to the weak. ¹⁰ For if someone should see you who has knowledge reclining for a meal in an idol's temple, will not his conscience, if he is weak, be strengthened to eat things sacrificed to idols? ¹¹ For through your knowledge he who is weak is ruined, the brother for whose sake Christ died. ¹² Thus, sinning against your brothers and wounding their conscience when it is weak, you sin

---

[175] Meaning "we are neither the worse if we do not eat, nor the better if we do eat."—NASB.

170

against Christ. [13] Therefore, if food causes my brother to stumble, I will never eat meat again, so that I will not cause my brother to stumble.

Cultural Differences

For the Western world of Christians, the cultural differences are very foreign to us. Culture relates to the ideas, customs, and social behavior of society. This would involve religious practices, language, dress, ideas about relationships, and about gender. What is Paul talking about here? Is he talking about physical food, or is he painting some kind of word picture? It can seem as though Paul is getting extremely complex on us and is difficult to follow. The context of this passage will help us appreciate who is being addressed and what is being said.

We have a rare opportunity to look inside the first-century Corinthian Christian congregation. These Christian had problems that they were struggling with, meaning that they had many questions that needed to be answered. The congregation was divided into different factions, some following different men instead of Christ. There was a shocking case of sexual immorality that was being permitted. Some were dealing with a religiously divided household. The question of whether they had to remain with their unbelieving mated needed to be answered. Were they permitted to eat meat from the market that had been used in a sacrifice to idols? The Corinthians needed direction on how they were to conduct their Christian meetings. What position were women to have within the congregation? Some within the congregation rejected the resurrection. Yes, there were many problems. The apostle mission within this first letter was to address these problems and to restore them spiritually.

The question is how do we apply God's Word in our lives today? As was said earlier, we do not read our meaning into the text. We are seeking what Paul meant by the words that he used as would have been understood by his readers. Then, we need to see if this information was simply historical content that was to help one's understanding of the situation. Or, was it principles that are eternal and thus apply to us. Was it cultural specific to their time, or does it carry over to our time? What of idioms, symbolic and figurative language, hyperbole? The technical term for this is prescriptive or descriptive. Was a verse prescribed for all time or was it prescribed for that moment? Was a verse simply describing the historical setting to give readers a better understanding?

Thus, some will take the Bible more serious if they see reasons for doing so. Show them God's initial purpose for life in the Garden of Eden, why God has permitted wickedness since the rebellion in Eden,[176] where he places us in the stream of Bible history and the hope of an unending life in the Kingdom of God. Some people have practical reasons for their skepticism about the Bible. However, these may not have an impact on the atheist, since an atheist does not believe in God. Therefore, you would have to establish this truth of God's existence with him first.

1 Timothy 2:3-4 Updated American Standard Version (UASV)

[3] This is good, and it is acceptable in the sight of God our Savior, [4] who desires all men to be saved and to come to **an accurate knowledge**[177] **of truth.**

Do not just open the Bible and read Scriptures, but rather help people come to an accurate knowledge of truth. An evangelist wants a listener to feel confident that the believer can do that. In other words, we must speak with authority. If one seems timid, stumbling over words, or unsure of one's self, the listener will conclude we do not have authority on God's Word. Would anyone get heart surgery from a heart surgeon who could not explain the procedure or seemed unsure of himself? Hardly! Why then, would an evangelist expect someone to invest in the idea of a God, life eternal, and other doctrines like the resurrection hope, from someone that comes off as unsure?

Bible Reading and Study Program

There has long been a trend for pastors and religious leaders to recommend a one-year Bible reading program, which we would not recommend for the serious student of God's Word. At best, a one-year reading program will help its reader to know a few Bible stories, and introduce them to a several Bible characters, as well as coming away with many principles to help in their walk with God. Instead, we recommend a **five-year Bible Reading / Study Program.** With this Bible reading / study program, the reader will know far more of the Bible stories, the

---

[176] Why has God Permitted Wickedness and Suffering?

http://bit.ly/2qHkwYR

Why is Life So Unfair?

http://bit.ly/2p43Ai9

Does God Step in and Solve Our Every Problem Because We are Faithful?

http://bit.ly/2qLdxgN

[177] *Epignosis* is a strengthened or intensified form of *gnosis* (*epi,* meaning "additional"), meaning, "true," "real," "full," "complete" or "accurate," depending upon the context. Paul and Peter alone use *epignosis.*

background behind those stories, what the author actually meant by what he wrote, and be able to explain hundreds of Bible difficulties[178] that exist from Genesis to Revelation, and far more.

Psalm 1:2 Updated American Standard Version (UASV)

[2] but his delight is in the law of Jehovah,
and on his law he meditates day and night.

We should begin every study by thanking God for his Word, i.e., the Bible, and his helping us to understand it. We may **read** the Bible from cover to cover fifty times in our life, each time taking one year, which will give us a very basic understanding of the Bible stories and accounts within it. However, we not only want to know what is in it, but we also want to be able to (1) understand it, (2) to share it and (3) to defend it. For this, we need to **study** it from cover to cover three to five times in our life, each time taking about three to five years, depending on the business of our family life.

Imagine that our spouse has spent several hours making us dinner. The sweat and toil of overseeing so many things going on at one time: several on the stovetop, in the oven, and in the microwave, and having it all are done at the same time. Now, imagine the pain of heart, if we sat down, and rushed through the meal, to get away to something that interests us more. God spent 1,600 years, with forty plus authors, throughout atrocious times of six world powers that persecuted his people, to bring us sixty-six books that came together to make but one book. He does not want his servants rushing through that well-prepared spiritual meal. One of God's authors makes just that point,

Joshua 1:8 Updated American Standard Version (UASV)

[8] This Book of the Law shall not depart from your mouth, but you shall meditate on it day and night, so that you may be careful to do according to all that is written in it; for then you will make your way prosperous, and then you will have good success.

Does Joshua expect us literally to meditate in a study of God's Word day and night from Genesis to Revelation? No, but **it does mean** that we should give our time to God so that we are studying at a pace that will allow for some serious meditation. When we study the Bible in a

---

[178] These so-called Bible difficulties are what Bible critics call errors and contradictions. However, they are not errors and contradictions, but rather difficulties because we are far removed from their time and culture, as well as their languages, which was Hebrew, Aramaic, and Greek.

meditative way, it will allow us to take notice of what the author truly meant, and how that meaning can influence our lives today. A good commentary, like the Holman Old and New Testament commentary volumes, will enable us to investigate the Bible verse-by-verse, even investigating many important words, the historical setting, hard to understand passages, all for the purpose of applying it in our lives, striking us in a deeply personal way. Getting the sense of God's guidance gives us resilient incentive to put it into practice.

Bible Hebrew Language Bible scholar, Lee M. Fields writes, "'Deep' Bible study is no guarantee that mature faith will result, but shallow study guarantees that immaturity continues." – *Hebrew for the Rest of Us*, (p. xiii)

Before We Begin Our Study Program

We need to study a book on Biblical interpretation. Therefore, the Bible student should **study the following books during the program.** However, Roy B. Zuck's Basic Bible Interpretation and Andrews' INTERPRETING THE BIBLE should be studied first.

- BASIC BIBLE INTERPRETATION by Roy B. Zuck

- INTERPRETING THE BIBLE: Introduction to Biblical Hermeneutics by Edward D. Andrews

- HOW TO INTERPRET THE BIBLE: An Introduction to Hermeneutics by Kieran Beville

- THE EVANGELISM HANDBOOK: How All Christians Can Effectively Share God's Word in Their Community by Edward D. Andrews

- CONVERSATIONAL EVANGELISM [Second Edition] by Edward D. Andrews

- THE CHRISTIAN APOLOGIST: Always Being Prepared to Make a Defense [Second Edition] By Edward D. Andrews

- BASICS OF BIBLICAL CRITICISM: Helpful or Harmful? [Second Edition]

Books that one needs in this five-year Bible reading program are New American Standard Bible (NASB) 1995 by The Lockman

Foundation.[179] A translation that supersedes even the English Standard Version (ESV) and the New American Standard Bible (NASB) as to literalness and trustworthiness is the upcoming Updated American Standard Version (UASV)[180] One will also need the *Holman Old and New Testament Commentary Volumes*.[181] If one's finances are limited, buy these *Holman Commentary* volumes one at a time. Doing it that way means that we would only have to buy one volume every two to four months. One will also need to buy the *Holman Illustrated Bible Dictionary*. In addition, we will need The Big Book of Bible Difficulties: Clear and Concise Answers from Genesis to Revelation (2008) by Norman L. Geisler and Thomas Howe. One will also need *The IVP Bible Background Commentary* (*Old and New Testament Volumes*), which may be expensive. Therefore, if you can buy them one at a time, or get them used on Amazon.com, this would be best for those on a limited income. Lastly, every Christian needs to know how to interpret the Bible correctly. For this Bible study program, the first book should be *Basic Bible Interpretation* by Roy B. Zuck.

The first Bible reading would be Genesis 4:1-26. The student would begin by praying that God would provide understanding, and help apply his Word and grow in knowledge. The student then meditatively reads those verses. After that, use the *Holman Old Testament Commentary* on Genesis by Stephen J. Bramer. The student would read the corresponding chapter to the Bible verses. Then, examine the section in the volume Deeper Discoveries. The Deeper Discoveries section helps the reader to understand the most important words, phrases, backgrounds, and teaching of each chapter. After completing this portion of the study, pick up The Big Book of Bible Difficulties: Clear and Concise Answers from Genesis to Revelation. We want to see if there are any Bible difficulties, which fall within this section of Bible reading, Genesis 4:1-26. The students will have seven Bible difficulties to read the concluding portion of the study. I have added one of the difficulties identified by Andrews so that students can see they are written to be easily understood.

---

[179] We want to use a good literal translation (UASV, ESV, NASB, CSB, or LEB) because literal translations bring you closer to the original, while the interpretive translations (NIV somewhat, NLT, TEV, CEV), distance you from the originals.

[180] http://uasvbible.org/

[181] If you feel that you are a more advanced student of the Bible, you can replace Holman Commentary volumes with the Old and New Testament volumes of The New American Commentary.

Genesis 4:3 Why was Cain's offering unacceptable to God?

There are two aspects of Cain's offering, which found him unapproved before God: **(1)** his attitude and **(2)** the type of offering.

Eventually, Cain and Abel came before God with their offerings. "Cain brought of the fruit of the ground an offering to Jehovah." (Gen 4:3, ASV) "Abel also brought of the firstborn of his flock and of their fat portions." (Gen 4:4, ESV) It is likely that both Cain and Abel were close to 100 years old at the time, as Adam was 130 years old when he fathered his third son, Seth. (Gen 4:25; 5:3)

We can establish that the two sons became aware of their sinful state and sought our God's favor. How they garnered this knowledge is guesswork, but it is likely by way of the father, Adam. Adam likely informed them about the coming seed and the hope that lie before humankind.[182] Therefore, it seems that they had given some thought to their condition and stand before God, and realized that they needed to try to atone for their sinful condition. The Bible does not inform us just how much time they had given to this need before they started to offer a sacrifice. Rather, God chose to convey the more important aspect, each one's heart attitude, which gives us an inside look at their thinking.

Some scholars have suggested that Eve felt that Cain was the "seed" of the Genesis 3:15 prophecy that would destroy the serpent, "she conceived and bore Cain, saying, 'I have gotten a man with the help of the LORD.'" (Gen 4:1) It might be that Cain shared in this belief and had begun to think too much of himself, and thus the haughty spirit. If this is the case, he was very mistaken. His brother Abel had a whole other spirit, as he offered his sacrifice in faith, "By faith Abel offered to God a more acceptable sacrifice than Cain, through which he was commended as righteous, God commending him by accepting his gifts." (Heb. 11:4)

It seems that Abel was capable of discerning the need for blood to be involved in the atoning sacrifice while Cain was not, or simply did not care. Therefore, it was the heart attitude of Cain as well. Consequently, "but on Cain and his offering he did not look with favor. So Cain was very angry, and his face was downcast." (Gen 4:5, NIV) It may well be

---

[182] Adam's family must have received God's revelation about the necessity of sacrifice to create and maintain fellowship with God. The background to this was probably the sacrifice that God performed to provide the clothing to cover Adam and Eve's shame (see Gen. 3:21). Anders, Max; Gangel, Kenneth; Bramer, Stephen J. (2003-04-01). Holman Old Testament Commentary – Genesis: 1 (p. 56). Holman Reference. Kindle Edition.

that Cain had little regard for the atoning sacrifice, giving it little thought, going through the motions of the act only. However, as later biblical history would show, Jehovah God is not one to be satisfied with formal worship. Cain had developed a bad heart attitude, and Jehovah well knew that his motives were not sincere. The way Cain reacted to the evaluation of his sacrifice only evidenced what Jehovah already knew. Instead of seeking to improve the situation, "Cain was very angry, and his face was downcast." (Gen 4:5) As you read the rest of the account, it will become clearer as to the type of temperament Cain had before God.

Genesis 4:6-16 Updated American Standard Version (UASV)

⁶ Then Jehovah said to Cain, "Why are you angry, and why has your face fallen? ⁷ If you do well, will there not be a lifting up?[183] And if you do not do well, sin is crouching at the door. Its desire is for you, but you must rule over it."

⁸ Cain said to Abel his brother. "Let us go out into the field."[184] And it came about when they were in the field, that Cain rose up against Abel his brother and killed him.

⁹ Then Jehovah[185] said to Cain, "Where is Abel your brother?" And he said, "I do not know. Am I my brother's keeper?" ¹⁰ He said, "What have you done? The voice of your brother's blood is crying to me from the ground. ¹¹ Now you are cursed from the ground, which has opened its mouth to receive your brother's blood from your hand. ¹² When you cultivate the ground, it will no longer yield its strength to you; you will be a fugitive and a wanderer on the earth." ¹³ Cain said to Jehovah, "My punishment is greater than I can bear! ¹⁴ Behold, you have driven me today away from the ground, and from your face I shall be hidden. I shall be a fugitive and a wanderer on the earth, and whoever finds me will kill me." ¹⁵ So Jehovah said to him, "Therefore whoever kills Cain, vengeance will be taken on him sevenfold." And Jehovah put a mark on Cain, so that no one finding him would slay him.

¹⁶ Then Cain went out from the presence of Jehovah, and dwelt in the land of Nod,[186] east of Eden.

---

[183] This is a shortening of the Hebrew idiom "to lift up the face," which means "to accept" favorably

[184] **Genesis 4:8**: SP LXX It Syr inserts these bracketed words; Vg, "Let us go outdoors"; MT omits; some MSS and editions have an interval here.

[185] The Tetragrammaton, God's personal name, יהוה (*JHVH/ YHWH*), which is found in the Hebrew Old Testament 6,828 times.

[186] I.e. wandering

The last section of the study opens the *Zondervan Illustrated Bible Background Commentary* to read the chapter from this, as well. This may seem overwhelming for one study period. When we first sit, and see how many verses are in the chapter that will be studied that day, open the books and see how long they are as well. If the material seems too long, break it into two or even three study sessions. In **study session one**, do the Bible reading and the corresponding Holman Commentary Chapter and Deeper Discoveries. In **study session two**, do the Bible difficulties from the *Big Book of Bible Difficulties* and the chapter *Zondervan Illustrated Bible Background Commentary*.

Basics in Biblical Interpretation

Step 1: What is the historical setting and background for the author of the book and his audience? Who wrote the book? When and under what circumstances was the book written? Where was the book written? Who were the recipients of the book? Did you find anything noteworthy about the place of the recipients? What is the theme of the book? What was the purpose for writing the book?

Step 2a: What would this text mean to the original audience? (The meaning of a text is what the author meant by the words that he used, as should have been understood by his readers.)

Step 2b: If there are any words in this section that one does not understand, or that stand out as interesting words that may shed some insight on the meaning, look them up in a word dictionary, such as *Mounce's Complete Expository Dictionary of Old and New Testament Words*.

Step 2c: After reading this section from the three Bible translations, do a word study and write down what you think the author meant. Then, pick up a trustworthy commentary, like Holman Old or New Testament commentary volume, and see if you have it correct.

Step 3: Explain the original meaning in one or two sentences, preferably one. Then, take the sentence or two and place it in a short phrase.

Step 4: Now, consider their circumstances, the reason for it being written, what it meant to them, and consider examples from today that would be similar to that time, which would fit the pattern of meaning. What **implications** can be drawn from the original meaning?

Step 5: Find the pattern of meaning, the "thing like these," and consider how it could apply in modern life. How should individual Christians today live out the implications and principles?

Biblical Interpretation Explained In Greater Detail

Step 1: What is the historical setting and background for the author of the book and his audience? Who wrote the book? When and under what circumstances was the book written? Where was the book written? Who were the recipients of the book? Did you find anything noteworthy about the place of the recipients? What is the theme of the book? What was the purpose for writing the book? The first step is observation, to get as close to the original text as possible. If you do not read Hebrew or Greek; then, two or three literal translations are preferred (ESV, NASB, and HCSB). The above Bible background information may seem daunting, but it can all be found in the Holman Bible Handbook or the Holman Illustrated Bible Dictionary.

Step 2a: What would this text have meant to the original audience? (The meaning of a text is what the author meant by the words that he used, as should have been understood by his readers.) Once someone has an understanding of step 1, read and reread the text in its context. In most Bibles, there are indentations or breaks where the subject matter changes. Look for the indentations that are before and after the text, and read and read that whole section from three literal translations. If there are no indentations, read the whole chapter and identify where the subject matter changes.

Step 2b: If there are any words in the section that one does not understand, or that stands out as interesting words that may shed some insight on the meaning, look them up in a word dictionary, such as *Mounce's Complete Expository Dictionary of Old and New Testament Words*. For example, if the text was Ephesians 5:14, ask what Paul meant by "sleeper" in verse 14. If it was Ephesians 5:18, what did Paul mean by using the word "debauchery" in relation to "getting drunk with wine." I would recommend *Mounce's Complete Expository Dictionary of Old and New Testament Words* by William D. Mounce (Sep 19, 2006) Do not buy the Amazon Kindle edition until they work out a difficulty. If you have Logos Bible Software, it would be good to add this book if it did not come with the package.

Step 2c: After reading the section from the three Bible translations, do a word study and write down what you think the author meant. Then, pick up a trustworthy commentary, like Holman Old or New

Testament commentary volume, checking to see if you have it correct. It can be more affordable to buy one volume each time a project is assigned so that it is spread out over time. If one cannot afford each volume of these commentary sets, Holman has a one-volume commentary on the entire Bible. Also, check with the pastor of your church because he may allow you to take a volume home for the assignment.

Step 3: Explain the original meaning in one or two sentences, preferably one. Then, take the sentence or two and place it in a short phrase. If you look in the Bible for Ephesians chapter five, you will find verses 1-5 or 6 are marked off as a section, and the phrase that captures the sense of the meaning, is "imitators of God." Then, verses 6-16 of that same chapter can be broken down to "light versus darkness" or "walk like children of light."

Step 4: Consider their circumstances, the reason for it being written, what it meant to them, and consider examples from our day that would be similar to the time they lived, which would fit the pattern of meaning. What **implications** can be drawn from the original meaning? Part of this fourth step ensures the Bible student stays within the pattern of the original meaning to determine any implications for the reader.

An example would be the admonition that Paul gave the Ephesian congregation at 5:18, "do not get drunk with wine." Was Paul talking about beer that existed then, too? Surely, he was not explicitly referring to whiskey, which would be centuries before it was invented. Yes, Paul refers to the others because they provide implications that can be derived from the original meaning.

Step 5: Find the pattern of meaning, the "thing like these," and consider how it could apply in modern life. How should individual Christians today live out the implications and principles?

Preparing for Christian Meetings

Almost every church hands out a weekly flyer of some sort to its flock, which outlines the upcoming week's meetings, as well as what is to be studied or heard in those meetings. Almost every church has a Bible study or book study meeting once a week, where the groups work their way through a publication. Usually, the publication is a study publication, meaning that it has review questions throughout the chapters or at the end of each chapter.

These books are designed as a Bible study course. How is it to be used? We suggest the following program: The review questions go with specific paragraphs. Read all of the chapter questions first, ponder over them. Then, read however many paragraphs go with the first question. After that, look up any Scriptures cited in the paragraph. Now, read the first question and highlight the answer in the paragraph(s). Also, write any additional thoughts in the margin of the study book. Then, if any of the verses are standouts, look them up in a commentary, digging a little deeper. If there are any highly important words in that verse, look them up in a word study dictionary. Now, write down any other important points that you learned. You are now done with the first question and its corresponding paragraphs. When you have finished all the chapter questions, in the same manner, go back and review all the questions.

Phrase-By-Phrase Research of a Verse.

It is best to study a Bible verse phrase-by-phrase. Let us use Matthew 24:14 as our example. It reads, "And this gospel of the kingdom will be proclaimed in all the inhabited earth[187] as a testimony to all the nations, and then the end will come." What did Jesus mean by **the gospel of the kingdom**? What is the **kingdom**? What did Jesus mean by **it will be proclaimed**? What was meant by **in all the inhabited earth**? What is meant by **in all the inhabited earth**? What did Jesus mean by **a testimony to all the nations**? Finally, what was meant by **then the end will come**? Well, let's investigate these phrases.

Matthew 24:14

this gospel or good news: The Greek word *euangelion* is made up from the words *eu*, meaning "good; well" and *aggellos*, "one who brings news; one who proclaims or announces good news." It is rendered "gospel" in some English Bibles. The related term rendered "evangelizer" (Greek, *euaggelistes*) means "a proclaimer of good news."—Ac 21:8; Eph. 4:11; 2 Tim. 4:5.

the Kingdom: Namely, God's Kingdom. Throughout the Greek New Testament the "good news" or "gospel" is closely tied into the kingdom of God. This was the theme of Jesus Christ's ministry.

The Greek word basileia is a reference to a royal government, as well as to the region and the peoples under the rule of a king. Of the 162

---

187 Or *in the whole world*

occurrences of this Greek word in the Greek New Testament, 55 of them can be found in the Gospel of Matthew, with most of them referring to God's heavenly rule. In fact, Matthew uses the term to frequently, his gospel could be called the Kingdom Gospel.

proclaimed: The Greek word (*kēryssō*) basically means to **announce**, in an official capacity (Rev 5:2); **2.** LN 33.207 **tell**, announce publicly (Mk 5:20); **3.** LN 33.256 **preach**, proclaim with the goal to persuade, urge, warn to comply (Ro 10:14; 1Pe 3:19; Mk 16:15, 20)."[188] The promise is that the gospel will be proclaimed in all of the inhabited earth, not that every person ever living would hear the gospel. What will happen to the unevangelized. See the CPH Blog article: THE UNEVANGELIZED: What Happens to People Who Have Never Heard the Gospel?[189]

all the inhabited earth . . . all the nations: Both expressions highlight the scope of the evangelism work. In a broad sense, the Greek word for "inhabited earth" (*oikoumenē*) refers to the **earth** as the dwelling place of humankind. (Lu 4:5; Ac 17:31; Ro 10:18; Re 12:9; 16:14) In the first century, this term would have referred to the **immense Roman Empire** where the Jews had been dispersed. (Lu 2:1; Ac 24:5)[190] In its general sense, the Greek word for "nation" (*ethnos*) refers to "a people, a large group based on various cultural, physical or geographic ties,"[191] who are basically related to one another by blood, who share a common language.

end: The Greek here (*telos*) is referring to as a point in time, where combination of events take place, and Satan's rule over the earth comes to an end and he is abyssed.

---

[188] James Swanson, *Dictionary of Biblical Languages with Semantic Domains: Greek (New Testament)* (Oak Harbor: Logos Research Systems, Inc., 1997).

[189] http://tiny.cc/nfyiny

[190] **earth**, the world (Lk 4:5; Ro 10:18); 2. LN 1.83 **empire**, the entire Roman world (Ac 11:28; 17:6; 24:5; Lk 2:1); 3. LN 9.22 **people**, humankind (Lk 21:26; Ac 17:31; Rev 3:10; 12:9) - James Swanson, Dictionary of Biblical Languages with Semantic Domains: Greek (New Testament) (Oak Harbor: Logos Research Systems, Inc., 1997).

[191] James Swanson, *Dictionary of Biblical Languages with Semantic Domains: Greek (New Testament)* (Oak Harbor: Logos Research Systems, Inc., 1997).

CHAPTER 6 Bible Background

Biblical archaeology is the scientific study of ancient cultures through the examination of their material remains such as buildings, graves, tools, and other artifacts usually dug up from the ground. The biblical archaeologist in Bible lands remove the soil of the earth in a very careful and methodical manner, so as to examine rocks, ruined walls, buildings, city remains as well as pottery, clay tablets, written inscriptions, coins, and other ancient remains, or artifacts, with the purpose of recording information that can aid in the discovery of what happened. This painstaking work has improved our understanding of 2,500 years of Bible times, from the days of Noah stepping off the ark in about 2369 B.C.E. to the death of the Apostle John in 100 C.E. We have gained immense knowledge of their languages, places of residence, food and meals, clothing, home life, marriage, health, education, the peoples around them, economy, cities and towns, recreation and sports. Our knowledge of all the regions of Bible history has grown immeasurably: Palestine, Egypt, Persia, Assyria, Babylonia, Asia Minor, Greece, and Rome. Archaeology is a relatively new science, as it has only been around for about 200-years.

Historical-Cultural Elements

The Bible is filled with a rich history of people, places, and events, and God's interactions with them, personally at times, through materialized angels at other times, but by far, through human representatives.

All Christians desire a full or accurate understanding of the meaning of the Bible. However, most are not aware that they must have knowledge of the historical-cultural and geographical background of the Bible. Without such, much of the Bibles, true message will be lost, because the reader would be attempting to impose their modern day mindset on an ancient society, as opposed to bridging that gap, getting back to the Bible times setting.

Judges 16:2-3

2 The **Gazites** were told, "Samson has come here." And they surrounded the place and set an ambush for him all night at **the gate of the city**. They kept quiet all night, saying, "Let us wait till the light of the morning; then we will kill him." 3 But Samson lay till midnight, and at

midnight he arose and **took hold of the doors of the gate of the city and the two posts, and pulled them up,** bar and all, and **put them on his shoulders** and **carried them to the top of the hill that is in front of Hebron.**

City gate from Balawat—Zondervan Illustrated Bible Backgrounds

Every Christian is aware of Samson's superhuman strength that he received through God. However, some biblical accounts come to life when the reader is aware of the background information. What Samson pulled out of the ground and threw on his shoulders at Judges 16:2-3, weighed a minimum of 400-500 pounds, with some suggesting closer to 2,000 pounds. If this feat of strength is not enough to grow our appreciation of Samson' great power, the simple statement that he "carried them to the top of the hill that is in front of Hebron," will do just that. Gaza, the city, mentioned here is at sea level, while Hebron is about 3,000 feet above sea level, a serious climb indeed! However, there is more. Hebron is 37 miles from Gaza, uphill all the way! Knowing the weight of the gate and posts, the distance traveled, and that it was uphill, makes Samson's colossal feat take on a completely new magnitude, does it not?

If most Christians were aware of the need for having some understanding of Bible backgrounds, they would eagerly find the appropriate books that would aid them in this area. It seems that when a pastor adds some Bible background into his sermon, it really enhances what is being said, and is a part of the conversation after the meeting is over by most of the congregants. Learning of the historical setting is paramount in much of the Bible if the reader is going to have an accurate understanding of the text. Many Christians are hungering for this sort of information, which will make their studies come to life. Please see the footnote below, for a section of our Amazon bookstore that will recommend some books that cover this area.[192]

Places of Residence

Amos 5:19

19   as if a man fled from a lion,
     and a bear met him,
or went into the house and leaned his hand against the wall,
     and a serpent bit him.

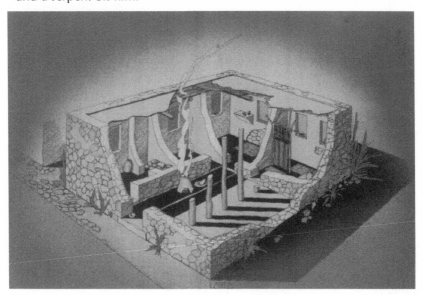

Home in First-Century Palestine

Homes in Bible times were not viewed the same as those of our modern day Western world. They spent most of the day outside, using the home for protection from the weather, and a place to sleep. In the plains, where one could find little good-quality limestone and sandstone,

---

[192] http://astore.amazon.com/bibletranslat-20?_encoding=UTF8&node=9

sunbaked or, sometimes, kiln-baked mud bricks were used for the walls of homes. Snakes could be found in the crevices of the walls because they too enjoyed the warmth of sun-baked bricks.—Amos 5:19.

Joshua 2:15

[15] Then she let them down by a rope through the window, for her house was built into the city wall so that she lived in the wall.

Some houses were built on the top of wide city walls. (Jos 2:15) Some cities had double walls surrounding it. The space between the two walls was filled with dirt.

The mound, or "tell," of Jericho was surrounded by a great earthen rampart, or embankment, with a stone retaining wall at its base. The retaining wall was some 12–15 ft high. On top of that was a mudbrick wall 6 ft thick and about 20–26 ft high (Sellin and Watzinger 1973: 58). At the crest of the embankment was a similar mudbrick wall whose base was roughly 46 ft above the ground level outside the retaining wall. This is what loomed high above the Israelites as they marched around the city each day for seven days. Humanly speaking, it was impossible for the Israelites to penetrate the impregnable bastion of Jericho.

Within the upper wall was an area of approximately 6 acres, while the total area of the upper city and fortification system together was half again as large, or about 9 acres. Based on the archaeologist's rule of thumb of 100 persons per acre, the population of the upper city would have been about 600. From excavations carried out by a German team in the first decade of this century, we know that people were also living on the embankment between the upper and lower city walls. In addition, those Canaanites living in surrounding villages would have fled to Jericho for safety. Thus, we can assume that there were several thousand people inside the walls when the Israelites came against the city.[193]

---

[193] http://www.biblearchaeology.org/

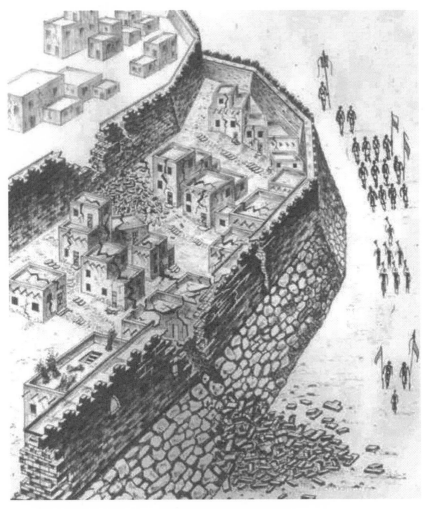

www.bible-architecture.info

Mark 2:1-4

[1] And when he returned to Capernaum after some days, it was reported that he was at home. [2] And many were gathered together, so that there was no more room, not even at the door. And he was preaching the word to them. [3] And they came, bringing to him a paralytic carried by four men. [4] And when they could not get near him because of the crowd, they removed the roof above him, and when they had made an opening, they let down the bed on which the paralytic lay.

WATTLE AND MUD ROOF Reconstruction of the roof of a typical rural home.
Zondervan Illustrated Bible Backgrounds

While the homes of our Western world have roofs that were built on a slant, the ones of Bible times were often flat. In the image above, we can see the roof larger wooden beams running from wall to wall, with smaller beams wooden rafters running across the beams. These wooden rafters, in turn, were covered with branches, reeds. Then, a layer of earth several inches thick was added, followed by a thick coating of plaster of clay or clay and lime. It would have been quite easy for the four men to climb up on the flat roof, pull up the paralyzed man, and dig through such a roof and lower in him in on the cot, so that Jesus might heal him. Rather than be angry at such an intrusion, Jesus was moved by such great faith.

Acts 1:13

[13] And when they had entered, they went up to the upper room, where they were staying, Peter and John and James and Andrew, Philip and Thomas, Bartholomew and Matthew, James the son of Alphaeus and Simon the Zealot and Judas, the son of James.

While most have likely not given any serious consideration, as to why the disciples met in an upper room, aside from the fact it was likely the home of someone that was sympathetic to their needs; it also accommodated their needs in size as well.

188

A historical tradition locates the "upper room" in the Cenacle on Mount Zion. Zondervan Illustrated Bible Backgrounds.

To accommodate a crowd of this size (later 120 people meet in the room), the home was probably owned by a fairly wealthy person. Archaeologists have recovered the remains of a few homes in the Herodian quarter from this period owned by wealthy citizens. One of these homes, the so-called "Palatial Mansion," had a room that measured thirty-six by twenty-one feet (nearly seven hundred square feet). Early Christian tradition, however, identifies this home with the "Cenacle".[194]

Food and Meals

Bread

Matthew 16:6, 11-12

[6] Jesus said to them, "Watch and beware of the leaven of the Pharisees and Sadducees." [11] How is it that you fail to understand that I did not speak about bread? Beware of the leaven of the Pharisees and Sadducees." [12] Then they understood that he did not tell them to beware of the leaven of bread, but of the teaching of the Pharisees and Sadducees.

---

[194] Clinton E. Arnold, Zondervan Illustrated Bible Backgrounds Commentary Volume 2: John, Acts., 227 (Grand Rapids, MI: Zondervan, 2002).

Leaven in Scripture often denotes sin or corruption. Initially, the disciples did not understand that Jesus was speaking symbolically to them. He was warning them about the hypocrisy of the Pharisees and false teachings of the Sadducees. Jesus would also mention Herod and his followers, saying, "Watch out; beware of the leaven of the Pharisees and the leaven of Herod." (Mark 8:15) He was exposing the hypocrisy and political deceitfulness of Herod and his followers. He also bravely condemned the Pharisees as hypocrites concerned only with superficial displays of devotion.—Matthew 23:25-28.

Milk

Exodus 23:19

19 "The best of the firstfruits of your ground you shall bring into the house of the Lord your God. "You shall not boil a young goat in its mother's milk.

What would be the reason for God prohibiting the Israelites from boiling a kid (young goat) in its mother's milk? This prohibition appears three times in the Mosaic Law. (Ex 23:19; 34:26; Deut. 14:21) This prohibition helps the reader to appreciate Jehovah God's decency, his concern for his created beings, and his sensitivity.

If we pause for a moment and consider what God created the milk for; to nourish the young goat and help it grow. Therefore, to boil a young goat in its mother's milk would be contrary to the arrangement that God had set in place.

There are other suggestions as to why God established this prohibition: (1) it was an idolatrous practice, (2) it was an occult practice to improve the productivity of the land, (3) the belief that milk and meat were difficult to digest, (4) it would be disrespectful to the feast of ingathering, (5) and so on.

In reality, the Law had a number of comparable restrictions against brutality toward animals and protections against working in opposition to the natural order of things. For example, the Law encompassed instructions that prohibited sacrificing an animal except when it had been with its mother for at least seven days, sacrificing both an animal and its young on the same day, and taking from a nest both a mother and her eggs or young.—Leviticus 22:27, 28; Deuteronomy 22:6, 7.

Honey

Proverbs 16:24 (ESV)

24 Gracious words are like a honeycomb,
   sweetness to the soul and health to the body.

Proverbs 24:13-14 (ESV)

13 My son, eat honey, for it is good,
   and the drippings of the honeycomb are sweet to your taste.
14 Know that wisdom is such to your soul;
   if you find it, there will be a future,
   and your hope will not be cut off.

Ezekiel 3:2-3 (ESV)

2 So I opened my mouth, and he gave me this scroll to eat. 3 And he said to me, "Son of man, feed your belly with this scroll that I give you and fill your stomach with it." Then I ate it, and it was in my mouth as sweet as honey.

Revelation 10:9 (ESV)

9 So I went to the angel and told him to give me the little scroll. And he said to me, "Take and eat it; it will make your stomach bitter, but in your mouth it will be sweet as honey."

In Scripture, the healthful properties of honey are likened to gracious words and wisdom for the soul, because it is sweet to the taste, but also because it is good for the health as well. Certainly, we benefit spiritually from the gracious words of our Creator, in the same way, that honey is beneficial for our soul (body).

Scripture also uses honey illustratively for its sweetness and the pleasure of eating it, as we can see from the above Ezekiel 3:2-3 and Revelation 10:9. Honeycomb is frequently talked about because it is thought of as being superior in flavor, sweetness, and richness to honey that has been out in the air for some time. Solomon stresses the goodness and satisfaction of the words spoken by the Shulammite girl; her shepherd lover says, "Your lips drip sweetness like the honeycomb." (Song of Solomon 4:11) 'The rules of Jehovah are true, and righteous altogether ... sweeter also than honey and drippings of the honeycomb.' (Ps 19:9-10) "How sweet are your words to my taste, sweeter than honey to my mouth!"—Ps 119:103.

Fish

Ecclesiastes 9:12

¹² For man does not know his time. Like fish that are taken in an evil net, and like birds that are caught in a snare, so the children of man are snared at an evil time, when it suddenly falls upon them.

Scripture also likens men to fish. Solomon likened men to fish from the perspective of their being "snared at an evil time." Jesus Christ views his disciples as "fishers of men." (Mark 1:17) On another occasion, he likened righteous ones to good fish, and unrighteous ones to bad fish.-- Matthew 13:47-50.

Mealtime

In Bible times, it was an indication of bonding in fellowship, to eat food together. (Gen. 31:54; 2 Sam. 9:7, 10, 11, 13) If someone refused to eat with another, this was an indication of anger or some feeling or attitude against the host. (1 Sam. 20:34; Ac 11:2, 3; Gal. 2:11, 12) In addition, food was used, at times, as a gift, to acquire or make sure of the friendliness of another. For one to accept food as a gift, it then obligated the receiver to remain at peace with the giver.—Gen. 33:8-16; 1 Sam 9:6-8; 25:18, 19; 1 Ki 14:1-3.

Hand Washing

Mark 7:2-5

² they saw that some of his disciples ate with hands that were defiled, that is, unwashed. ³ (For the Pharisees and all the Jews do not eat unless they wash their hands properly, holding to the tradition of the elders, ⁴ and when they come from the marketplace, they do not eat unless they wash. And there are many other traditions that they observe, such as the washing of cups and pots and copper vessels and dining couches.) ⁵ And the Pharisees and the scribes asked him, "Why do your disciples not walk according to the tradition of the elders, but eat with defiled hands?"

Matthew 15:2

² "Why do your disciples break the tradition of the elders? For they do not wash their hands when they eat."

It is not that Jesus' disciples did not wash their hands at all, but rather did not partake of the ceremonial washing that the Scribes and

Pharisees attached great importance. The Scribes and Pharisees were not washing their hands for hygienic reasons, but were following the traditions of former men (elders), washing their hands up to the elbows. The Babylonian Talmud, Sotah 4b, views eating with unwashed hands (the ceremonial way), as being equal to having sexual relations with a harlot, and whoever does not take hand washing serious, will be "uprooted from the world."

RECLINING AT THE TABLE A model of a table, eating utensils, and terracotta pottery typical of the Roman period. Zondervan Illustrated Bible Backgrounds

Eating

John 13:23, 25; 21:20

23 One of his disciples, whom Jesus loved, was reclining at table at Jesus' side, 25 So that disciple, leaning back against Jesus, said to him, "Lord, who is it?" 21:20 Peter turned and saw the disciple whom Jesus loved following them, the one who also had leaned back against him during the supper and had said, "Lord, who is it that is going to betray you?"

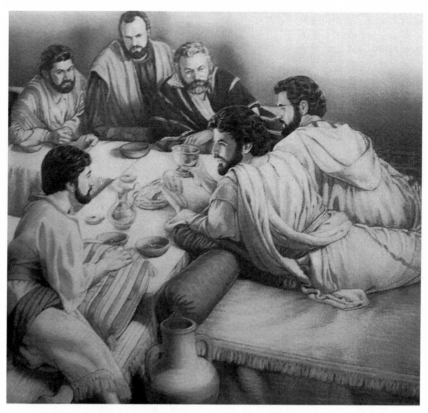

Generally, guests at banquets and feasts reclined on their left side using a pillow to support their elbow. Typically, there would be 3-5 persons occupying each couch. The back of a person's head would be toward the breast, or bosom, of the person behind him. The person who had no one behind him would have been considered the one holding the honorable position at the dinner, with each succeeding person as the next position of honor. As we will notice from the image above, this required persons to be very close to one another, and so the custom was to place friends next to friends. This undoubtedly made conversation much more lively, as well as private comments if preferred. The person who was in the bosom position of the most honored one at a banquet or feast was viewed as one having a favored position with that honored one. In the Gospel of John, we repeatedly see that it is the beloved Apostle John in this favored position with Jesus.

John 13:23-25

23 One of his disciples, whom Jesus loved, was reclining at table at Jesus' side, 24 so Simon Peter motioned to him to ask Jesus of whom he was speaking. 25 So that disciple, leaning back against Jesus, said to him, "Lord, who is it?"

John 21:20

20 Peter turned and saw the disciple whom Jesus loved following them, the one who also had leaned back against him during the supper and had said, "Lord, who is it that is going to betray you?"

Viewpoint, Feelings, Thinking, Expressions

Kneeling

Luke 22:41

41 And he withdrew from them about a stone's throw, and knelt down and prayed

Kneeling was a common position when praying, but not the only position. In addition, while many times a Scripture may have the plural "knees," this does not exclude that it could be the person is on one knee.—1 Kings 8:54; Acts 9:40; 20:36; 21:5; Ephesians 3:14

Bowing

It was a common practice for the Jews to bow before a person in a position of authority to show respect. It was also a common practice within the Persian Empire for people to bow down or do obeisance to the king. Obeisance is not necessarily an act of worship (dependent on the heart of the person), it is more of a gesture of respect or deference shown to another, especially royalty, in which one bows, kneels, or prostrates the body before another. "The Persian scholar P. Briant raises some questions about the exact meaning of proskynesis (Gr., obeisance), and notes that on the Persian monuments the gesture of obeisance is not prostration but a slight inclination of the body and a hand-kiss." King Ahasuerus gave a command that Haman was to be shown this honor. The entire account of Esther hangs on the fact that Mordecai will not bow before Haman. It is not stated why Mordecai refuses to do so, because as was stated above, this is not an act of worship for the Israelites (e.g., 1 Sam 24:8; 2 Sam 14:4; 1 Ki 1:16). However, some history says that that Persians saw the king as being divine.

What is the most likely reason for Mordecai refusing to bow before Haman?

> It is obvious from this, that Mordochai had declared to those who asked him the reason why he did not fall down before Haman, that he could not do so because he was a Jew,—that as a Jew he could not show that honour to man which was due to God alone. Now the custom of falling down to the earth before an exalted personage, and especially before a king, was customary among Israelites; comp. 2 Sam. 14:4, 18:28, 1 Kings 1:16. If, then, Mordochai refused to pay this honour to Haman, the reason of such refusal must be sought in the notions which the Persians were wont to combine with the action, i.e., in the circumstance that they regarded it as an act of homage performed to a king as a divine being, an incarnation of Oromasdes.[195]

While the possibility of Mordecai's failure to bow before Haman might be because the king was viewed as divine, it seems that there is a more likely reason. There had to be occasions for Mordecai to have to do obeisance to King Ahasuerus; otherwise, he would have never received the promotion that comes later in the account. Unquestionably, what motivated Mordecai is the fact that Haman was an Agagite, probably a royal Amalekite, an enemy of the Israelite people in the extreme. Mordecai's Jewish ancestry stands in opposition to Haman's Agagite ancestry. Jehovah had declared the subsequent execution of the Amalekites as they had revealed their hatred of God and his people by attacking the Israelites at Rephidim in the wilderness. (Ex 17:8–16; Deut. 25:17–19; 1 Sam 15:17–20) Therefore, righteous Mordecai faithfully rejected the notion of prostrating himself before Haman. Bowing would symbolize not only respect, but also would have possibly sent the message that there was to be peace and perhaps reverence to the point of a worshipful attitude toward this Amalekite.

Placing Hand Under Thigh

Genesis 24:2-4 Updated American Standard Version (UASV)

2 And Abraham said to his servant, the elder of his house, that ruled over all that he had, "Put, I pray thee, thy hand under my thigh. 3 And I will make thee swear by Jehovah, the God of heaven and the God of the earth, that you will not take a wife for my son of the daughters of the

---

[195] Carl Friedrich Keil and Franz Delitzsch, Commentary on the Old Testament, Es 3:3–4 (Peabody, MA: Hendrickson, 1996).

Canaanites, among whom I dwell. ⁴ But you will go to my country, and to my kindred, and take a wife for my son Isaac.

A method of making an oath was to place one's hand under the other's thigh, as Abraham's servant did in swearing that he would not take a wife for his son of the daughters of the Canaanites, but would go to Abraham's country, and to his relatives, and take a wife for Isaac. (Gen. 24:2, 9).

Throwing Dust on the Head

Joshua 7:6 Updated American Standard Version (UASV)

⁶ And Joshua tore his clothes, and fell to the earth upon his face before the ark of Jehovah until the evening, he and the elders of Israel. And they put dust upon their heads.

There were many signs in ancient Israel that would tell others that one is going through grief. For example, throwing dust on the head, tearing clothes, wearing sackcloth, cutting off or shaving, or pulling out one's hair, and beating one's breast, to name just a few.

In first Corinthians 8:1-13, we will discover that there were those who restricted themselves from eating meat that was sacrificed to idols (leftovers being sold in the meat market), as they were struggling to get over their former idolatrous life, and could not set aside their worshipful attitude. On the other hand, there were ones, who exercised their freedom to partake of this meat and viewed the former as spiritually weak ones. As we will see, those who had the accurate knowledge lacked the wisdom of how to apply that knowledge, because they were puffed up.

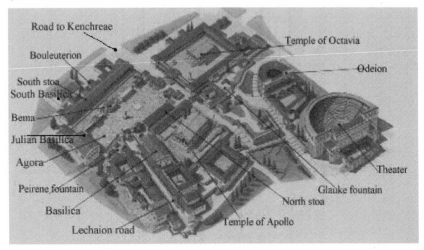

Food Offered to Idols

1 Corinthians 8:1-2

[1] Now concerning food offered to idols: we know that "all of us possess knowledge." This "knowledge" puffs up, but love builds up. [2] If anyone imagines that he knows something, he does not yet know as he ought to know.

In the Greek culture of the first-century C.E., there were families that made sacrificial offerings of meat to idols in the temples. Only certain portions of the meat were used, with the rest being taken home by the family, or sold to the meat market. The question that lies before the Christian: 'is it then permissible to eat the meat at the market.' It is true that "all of us possess knowledge." However, is it accurate knowledge, and do we possess wisdom, the ability to apply the knowledge correctly? Thus, the actual danger for the Corinthian Christians is their belief that they have the accurate knowledge, which has him puffed up when in truth, it is not accurate at all.

1 Corinthians 8:3

[3] But if anyone loves God, he is known by God.

The obvious mark that a Christian has love for God will be evidenced in his or her attitude and actions toward fellow Christians, as "love builds up."

1 Corinthians 8:4-6

[4] Therefore, as to the eating of food offered to idols, we know that "an idol has no real existence," and that "there is no God but one." [5] For although there may be so-called gods in heaven or on earth, as indeed there are many "gods" and many "lords," [6] yet for us there is one God, the Father, from whom are all things and for whom we exist, and one Lord, Jesus Christ, through whom are all things and through whom we exist.

Paul is making the point that *even though* there are so-called gods, their claim is false. The gods "in heaven" would include deities such as Jupiter, the chief of the pagan gods, and Aphrodite, the patron deity of the colony. The gods "on earth" may be an allusion to the way the Roman imperial family was worshiped and considered divine. At Corinth, there was a temple of Octavia, dedicated to the sister of the emperor Augustus. The focus for a provincial imperial cult, based at Corinth, was established about a.d. 54. There was a regular festival celebrating the imperial family; thus a Christian attending a banquet in honor of the deified emperor might be compromised.[196]

The Corinthians Christians knew "there is one God, the Father, from whom are all things and for whom we exist, and one Lord, Jesus Christ, through whom are all things and through whom we exist." (8:6) Living in the pagan city, they were well aware that there were many false, non-existent gods and lords, which were worshiped by the citizens of Corinth. They knew that these idols were simply pieces wood, stone or metal, and were powerless. Based on this knowledge, the Corinthian Christians should have known that meat in the market that had been part of what was offered to idols, had no power over them, being no different from any of the other meat at the market.

However, is this basic knowledge, able to guide them in the wisdom of whether they should eat it or not? While some were spiritually mature enough, to realize that eating such meat meant nothing. However, there were others in the Corinthian congregation, new ones, and older ones, who were spiritually weak, unable to make the connection. Paul goes on,

1 Corinthians 8:7

[7] However, not all possess this knowledge. But some, through former association with idols, eat food as really offered to an idol, and their conscience, being weak, is defiled.

These Christians being referred to in verse 7 were former idolaters, who had been very much involved in the practices of the false gods, and were unable to make the connection. If they ate such meat, even being told this was permissible, they would not be able to set aside the worshipful spirit that they had previously experienced. Therefore, they could not accept that it would be permissible to eat such meat. In addition, in their case, because they still possessed a worshipful spirit, it would have been wrong. Paul touched on this with the Romans, "But whoever has doubts is condemned if he eats, because the eating is not from faith. For whatever does not proceed from faith is sin." (Rom. 14:23)

1 Corinthians 8:8-11

[8] Food will not commend us to God. We are no worse off if we do not eat, and no better off if we do.[9] But take care that this right of yours does not somehow become a stumbling block to the weak.[10] For if

---

[196] Clinton E. Arnold, *Zondervan Illustrated Bible Backgrounds Commentary Volume 3: Romans to Philemon.* (Grand Rapids, MI: Zondervan, 2002), 143.

anyone sees you who have knowledge eating in an idol's temple, will he not be encouraged, if his conscience is weak, to eat food offered to idols? [11] And so by your knowledge this weak person is destroyed, the brother for whom Christ died.

In keeping with the rest of the New Testament, Paul often used the word translated "we are worse" (*hystereo*) to mean "to be lacking" or "to be in need" (cf. 2 Cor. 11:9; Phil. 4:12). The word translated "we are better" (*perisseuo*) appears to carry the meaning "abound, overflow" in every other Pauline usage. In 8:8 these words most probably refer not to moral or spiritual benefit or damage, but to material prosperity. This corresponds well with the idea in the ancient world that sacrifices procured material blessings from the gods. This seems an even more likely reading in light of the famines in Greece at the time of this letter.[197]

This is where insight must come in for the spiritually mature Christian, as he would be sinning if he ate meat in front of such spiritually weak ones, as he may stumble such ones. The spiritually weak one may draw the conclusion that the mature ones in the Corinthian congregation were partaking in false worship to pagan idols. On the other hand, they may think that it is fine to eat the meat, still possessing their worshipful spirit, which remains from former days. Thus, the spiritually mature one would have caused his brother to sin.

1 Corinthians 8:12-13

[12] Thus, sinning against your brothers and wounding their conscience when it is weak, you sin against Christ. [13] Therefore, if food makes my brother stumble, I will never eat meat, lest I make my brother stumble.

Therefore, it was not enough to be aware that they possessed the freedom to eat the meat because the meat was no different from any other, and had no power over them; they needed to have insight into how to apply that knowledge wisely. The alleged mature Christian, who failed to consider those who were spiritually weak, is 'puffed up with knowledge,' when he should be 'building up with love' of his fellow brothers. This one sees the weak as being overly rigid and dogmatic, as opposed to struggling to get over a former way of life. Therefore, while he might possess the accurate knowledge, he fails to use it wisely, and is

---

[197] Richard L. Pratt Jr, *I & II Corinthians*, vol. 7, Holman New Testament Commentary (Nashville, TN: Broadman & Holman Publishers, 2000), 140.

foolish, because, in the end, he has sinned against Christ. He did not allow love to be the guide of that knowledge.

The Whole Armor of God

Ephesians 6:10-19 American Standard Version (ASV)

[10] Finally, be strong in the Lord, and in the strength of his might. [11] Put on the whole armor of God, that you may be able to stand against the wiles of the devil.

[12] For our wrestling is not against flesh and blood, but against the principalities, against the powers, against the world-rulers of this darkness, against the spiritual hosts of wickedness in the heavenly places. [13] Wherefore take up the whole armor of God that you may be able to withstand in the evil day, and, having done all, to stand. [14] Stand therefore, having **girded your loins with truth,** and having put on **the breastplate of righteousness,** [15] and having **shod your feet with the preparation of the gospel of peace;** [16] in all circumstances taking up **the shield of faith,** with which you will be able to quench all the fiery darts of the evil one. [17] And take **the helmet of salvation,** and **the sword of the Spirit,** which is the word of God: [18] with **all prayer and supplication** praying at all seasons in the Spirit, and watching to that end in all perseverance and supplication for all the saints, [19] And on my behalf, that utterance may be given unto me in opening my mouth, to make known with boldness the mystery of the gospel,

We may be thinking that it seems very unlikely that any human can be at odds with a demonic spirit creature, and come out victorious, as they have unimaginable superhuman abilities. It is only possible by our reliance on Christ Jesus. We must have a complete grasp of God's Word, and apply it in a balanced manner in our lives each day. Only by doing so, can we be freed from the bodily, moral, emotional and mental harm that those under demonic or satanic control have gone through.--Ephesians 6:11; James 4:7

Defending the Loins, the Breast, and the Feet

Girding Our Loins with Truth

First-Century Roman Armor

The loins are the area on each side of the backbone of a human between the ribs and hips. At the time that the Apostle Paul wrote this to the Ephesians, soldiers wore a belt or girdle-like we see in the image of Roman soldiers. It was 2 to 6 inches in width. This belt served a double duty: (1) to protect the soldier's loins, (2) but it also serves in supporting his sword. When a soldier girded up his loins, this meant he was getting ready to go into battle. This soldier and his belt served as the perfect analogy, of how a Christian is to put on the belt of biblical truth, to protect his life. The truths of Scripture should be pulled tight around us, helping us to live a life that is reflective of that truth, and so that we can use that Bible truth to defend the faith, contend for the faith, and save those who doubt. (1 Peter 3:15, Jude 3, 21-22) If we are to accomplish these tasks, we will have to study the Bible carefully and consider its contents. Prophetically, it was said of Jesus, "your law is within my heart." (Psalm 40:8) If Jesus came under attack by the enemy of truth, he was able to refer to biblical truth from memory.—Matthew 19:3-6; 22:23-32.

Isaiah 30:20-21

20 And though the Lord give you the bread of adversity and the water of affliction, yet your Teacher will not hide himself anymore, but your eyes shall see your Teacher. 21 And your ears shall hear a word behind you, saying, "This is the way, walk in it," when you turn to the right or when you turn to the left.

Breastplate of Righteousness

The breastplate of the soldier was a piece of armor that covered the chest, protecting one of the most important organs, the heart. As all Christians likely know, we have a figurative heart, which is our inner person, and it needs special protection because it leans toward wrongdoing. (Genesis 8:21) Therefore, we must cultivate a love for God's Word and the standards and values that lie within. (Psalm 119:97, 105) Our love for the Word of God should be to such a depth that we would reject "the desires of the flesh and the desires of the eyes and pride of life." (1 John 2:15-17) In addition, once we have developed such a desire for right over wrong, we will be able to avoid paths that would have otherwise led us to a ruination. (Psalm 119:99-101; Amos 5:15) Our greatest example in everything, Jesus Christ, evidenced this to such an extent that Paul could say, "You have loved righteousness and hated wickedness."—Hebrews 1:9.

Shod Our Feet with the Preparation of the Gospel of Peace

Roman soldiers needed suitable footwear, which (1) kept the soldier's footing sure in battle, and (2) allowed him to march some 20 miles during a campaign while wearing or carrying some 60 pounds of armor and equipment. Thus, Paul's ongoing analogy of the armor of a Roman soldier was right on target, as the appropriate footwear for the readiness of a Christian minister active in spreading the gospel message is even more important. The importance is shown by Paul again in his letters to the Roman congregation when he asks how the people will get to know God if the Christian is not willing and ready to bring it to him, as he preaches and teaches?—Romans 10:13-15.

Once again, we must look to our exemplar Jesus Christ, as he says to the Roman Governor Pontius Pilate, "For this purpose I was born and for this purpose I have come into the world, to bear witness to the truth. Everyone who is of the truth listens to my voice." For three and a half years, Jesus walked throughout the land of Palestine, preaching to all who would listen, giving the ministry a top priority in his life. (John 4:5-34; 18:37) If we, like Jesus, are eager to declare the good news, we will find many opportunities to share it with others. Furthermore, our being absorbed in our ministry will help keep us spiritually strong. Acts 18:5

The Shield of Faith, the Helmet of Salvation, and the Sword of the Spirit

Thureon is the Greek word rendered "shield," which actually refers to a shield that was "large and oblong, protecting every part of the soldier; the word is used metaphorically of faith."[198] This shield of faith would and will protect the Christian from the "the fiery darts of the evil one." In ancient times, the darts[199] of the soldiers were often hollowed out having small iron receptacles, which were filled with a clear colorless flammable mixture of light hydrocarbons that burned. This was one of the most lethal weapons as it caused havoc among the enemy troops unless the soldiers had the large body shields that had been drenched in water and could quench the fiery darts. In fact, the earliest manuscripts repeat the definite article, literally "the darts of the evil one, the fiery (darts)," emphasizing the fact that they were above all destructive. If the soldier's shield caught fire, he would be tempted to throw it down, leaving himself open to the enemy's spear.

What does the highly metaphorical language of the fiery darts depict and how does this weaken or undercut our faith? It may come in the form of minor persecution if we live in the Western world, such as being ridiculed for our Christian faith, even verbally assaulted by Bible critics. Another fiery dart may be the temptation to put money over the ministry. Then, there is the constant temptation from Satan's world to lure us into immorality. We would have to be literally blindfolded not to see sexually explicit images hundreds of times per day, as it is used to sell everything. It is not only the images but also the mindset. Here is one example, and please excuse the graphic nature. The modern day junior high school teens (13 and 14 years old); literally view oral sex as being no different than kissing one another on the lips.

---

[198] W. E. Vine, Merrill F. Unger and William White, Jr., vol. 2, Vine's Complete Expository Dictionary of Old and New Testament Words (Nashville, TN: T. Nelson, 1996), 571.

[199] 6.36 belos, ous n: a missile, including arrows (propelled by a bow) or darts (hurled by hand)—'arrow, dart.' In the NT belos occurs only in a highly figurative context, to bele … peporomena 'flaming arrows (or darts)' Eph 6:16, and refers to temptations by the Devil.—Louw and Nida 6.36.

If we are to protect our Christian family, our congregation of brothers and sisters, and ourselves, we must possess **"the shield of faith."** Faith is not a simple belief in Jesus Christ as some misinformed ones might tell us; rather it is an active faith in Jesus Christ. James tells at 1:19 "You believe that God is one; you do well. Even the demons believe, and shudder!" The demons and Satan believe in the existence of Jesus Christ, and yet this brings them no salvation whatsoever. Faith comes from taking in an active knowledge of the Father and the Son to the point of building a relationship, a friendship based on the deepest love, and the committing of oneself to the point of turning our life over completely. It is regular prayerful communication, understanding and valuing how he protects us.—Joshua 23:14; Luke 17:5; Romans 10:17.

Yet again, we turn to our great exemplar, Jesus Christ, who demonstrated his faith throughout some very trying times. He completely trusted the Father to accomplish his will and purposes. (Matthew 26:42, 53, 54; John 6:38) A great example of this trust can be found when Jesus was in the garden of Gethsemane. He was in great anguish because he knew that he was going to be executed as a blasphemer of his Father, and even then, he fell with his face to the ground and prayed, "My Father, if it is possible, may this cup be taken from me. Yet not as I will, but as you will." (Matthew 26:39) Not that he was backing out of the execution, the ransom that is, but he wanted to be executed for another reason, other than a blasphemer. Jesus was an integrity keeper, which brought great joy to the Father. (Proverbs 27:11) As we face difficult times in the world that is alienated from God, we will do well to imitate Jesus great faith, and not give ours under the pressures of the world that lies in the hands of the evil one. Moreover, our faith will be refined if we trust in God, evidencing our love for him, by applying his Word in our daily walking with him. (Psalm 19:7-11; 1 John 5:3) The immediate gratifications that this world has to offer could never compare with the blessings that lie ahead.—Proverbs 10:22.

Not long ago, those trying to curb the use of drugs within the American youth had the saying, "the mind is a terrible thing to waste." Our next piece of armor of God would be a very useful tool for protecting the Christian mind, **the helmet of salvation.** The Apostle Paul said to the Thessalonians, "we must stay sober and let our faith and love be like a suit of armor. Our firm hope that we will be saved is our helmet," because it protects our Christian mind. (1 Thessalonians 5:8) Even though we may have accepted Christ, and have entered onto the path of salvation, we still suffer from imperfect human weaknesses. Even though our foremost desire is to do good, our thinking can be corrupted by this fleshly world that surrounds us. We need not be like this world but rather openly allow God to alter the way we think, through his Word the Bible, which will help us fully to grasp everything that is good and pleasing to him. (Rom. 7:18; 12:2) We likely recall the test that Jesus faced, where Satan offered him "all the kingdoms of the world and their glory." (Matt. 4:8-10) Jesus response was to refer to Scripture, "Be gone, Satan! For it is written, 'you shall worship the Lord your God and him only shall you serve.'" Paul had this to say about Jesus, "looking to Jesus, the founder and perfecter of our faith, who for the joy that was set before him endured the cross, despising the shame, and is seated at the right hand of the throne of God."—Hebrews 12:2.

We need to understand that the above examples of faith, does not come to us automatically. If we are focusing on what this current system of things has to offer, as opposed to focusing on the hopes that are plainly laid out in Scripture, we will be weak in the face of any difficult trial. After a few stumbles, it may be that we suffer spiritual shipwreck and lose our hope altogether. Then again, if we frequently feed our minds, or concentrate the mind on the promises of God, we will carry on delighting in the hope that has been offered us. Romans 12:12.

If we are to keep our Christian mind on the hope that lies ahead, we need to possess **the Sword of the Spirit**. The loving letter from our heavenly Father, his Word, the Bible is stated to be "living and active, sharper than any two-edged sword, piercing to the division of soul and of spirit, of joints and of marrow, and discerning the thoughts and intentions of the heart." This Word, if understood correctly, applied in a balanced manner, can transform our lives, and help us avoid or minimalize the pitfalls of this imperfect life. We can depend on that Word when we are overwhelmed, or temple to give way to the flesh, and when the Bible critics of this world attempt to do away with our faith. (2 Corinthians 10:4-5) We need to heed the words of the Apostle Paul to his spiritual son, Timothy:

2 Timothy 3:15-17

[14] But as for you **[Timothy]**, continue in what you have learned and have firmly believed, knowing from whom you learned it **[Paul, who Timothy traveled with and studied under for 15 years]** [15] and how from childhood you have been acquainted with the sacred writings **[the whole Old Testament]**, which are able to make you wise for salvation through faith in Christ Jesus. [16] All Scripture is breathed out by God and profitable for teaching, for reproof, for correction, and for training in

righteousness, [17] that the man of God may be complete, equipped for every good work.

Today's Bible student has a plethora of priceless Bible study tools that will allow them easily to gain access to the geographical and historical setting of any Bible person, place, topic, or event. Christian Publishing House is currently working on CPH Old and New Testament Commentary volumes that cover all of the sixty-six books of the Bible. These volumes are a study tool for the pastor, small group biblical studies leader, or the churchgoer. The primary purpose of studying the Bible is to learn about God and his personal revelation, allowing it to change our lives by drawing close to God. These volumes are written in a style that is easy to understand. The Bible can be difficult and complex at times. Their effort is to make it easier to read and understand, while also accurately communicating truth.

CPH Old/New Testament Commentary will convey the meaning of the verses within each Bible book. In addition, they will also cover the Bible background, the custom, and culture of the times, as well as Bible difficulties. Another important feature of CPH Old and New Testament Commentary is its range of information. They have made every effort to supply their readers with important textual information in a simple way. In addition, the reader will be introduced to one of the original languages of the Bible by way of transliteration (English letters), Hebrew / Aramaic / Greek. Moreover, they will be covering all of the Bible difficulties from Genesis to Revelation.

This thorough information should benefit their readers in becoming more in-depth students of the fully inerrant, inspired Word of God, as well as being better qualified to defend to anyone who asks them for a reason for their hope. – 1 Peter 3:15.

CHAPTER 7 Identify the Literary Context

The Bible is a very powerful weapon in the spiritual warfare that is being waged today. Paul called God's word "the sword of the spirit." (Eph. 6:12, 17) If the Bible is used appropriately, it has the power to free people from the bondage of Satan and this world that is under his influence. It is the only weapon on the planet that is saving lives, as opposed to destroying them. Therefore, as Christians, should we not seek to use it skillfully?

A polygamist says, "The number one thing that God hates is sexual sin." This is referring to such things as rape, incest, temple prostitution, King's stealing the wife of soldiers, having said soldier killed in battle, it is not however mentioned as the number one thing God hates. Polygamy is, however, an accepted practice through volumes of the Bible, history, modern day cultures. Quoting a verse or referring to a verse out of context, so as to get it to say what you want is misrepresenting God's Word. When we take words out of context, we distort their meaning; we twist what the Bible author meant by those words. Satan distorted God's Words when he tempted Jesus. Satan said to Jesus, "If you are the Son of God, throw yourself down; for it is written, "'He will command his angels concerning you,' and "'On their hands, they will bear you up, lest you strike your foot against a stone.'" (Matt. 4:1-11) Satan quoted Psalm 91:11-12 out of context. On this verse, Steven Lawson writes, "In part, this sovereign guardianship will be carried out by his **angels** whom the Lord will **command** and commission **to guard you in all your ways**. Satan quoted these verses to Christ in his temptation and shrewdly omitted this last phrase, "in all your ways" (Matt. 4:6; Luke 4:10–11). This divine protection extends only to the place of trusting and obeying God. The **angels will lift you up in their hands so that you will not strike your foot against a stone** (Ps. 34:7).[200]

This is called proof texting or proof-texting, where one uses isolated verses, out of context, to establish his or her doctrinal position. There is nothing with pulling isolated verses from different parts of the Bible, so as to make a biblical point of view but you must take the context of the verses into account, which will help us to convey an accurate meaning of what the author meant by his words. Therefore, when you study a verse, look at what the author said before and after that verse.

---

[200] Lawson, Steven. *Holman Old Testament Commentary - Psalms 76-150* (Kindle Locations 2561-2564). B&H Publishing Group. Kindle Edition.

2 Timothy 2:15 Updated American Standard Version (UASV)

[15] Do your best to present yourself to God as one approved, a workman who does not need to be ashamed, rightly handling[201] the word of truth.

We are in a spiritual warfare within Satan's world. But for a moment think of a soldier in a physical world when swords were common. If the soldier was not proficient with his sword, his life would be lost quite quickly. It is only by practice and learned to use his sword well. The same holds true for us and our spiritual warfare, our spiritual sword, the Bible.

What can help us to "rightly handling the word of truth," as we share the Word of God with others? It is impossible to impart truths from Scripture, if we seldom study the Bible, if we seldom prepare for the Christian meetings if we never dig beneath the surface into the deeper things of God's Word. This means too, as we study we must pay attention to the context of what we study. Context is the parts of God's Word that immediately precede and follow a word or passage and clarify its meaning.

Galatians 5:13 Updated American Standard Version (UASV)

[13] For you were called to freedom, brothers; only do not turn your freedom into an opportunity for the flesh, but through love serve one another.

What **freedom** was Paul speaking about here? Was Paul speaking about our freedom from sin and death, our freedom from false teachings, exactly what freedom was he referring to here? It is the context that unlocks the answer to our question. The context shows us that we were and are 'freed from the curse of the Law.' (Gal. 3:13, 19-24; 4:1-5) This freedom belongs to Christians because "Christ redeemed us from the curse of the law by becoming a curse for us." (Gal. 3:13) If we appreciate that freedom, we will slave for one another out of love. Those in the Galatian congregation that lacked love were busy 'backbiting and devouring one another. – Galatians 5:15.

The word "context" has another meaning. The synonyms for "context" include "background, conditions, . . . situation." If we are going to understand the Scriptures correctly, we need the "background" information, such as who wrote the Bible book, when it was written and what were the circumstances for writing it. We need to understand the "conditions" that existed at the time of its writing, which moved the

---

[201] Or *accurately handling* the word of truth; *correctly teaching* the word of truth

author to pen the book, such as the social, moral, and religious practices of the day. What were the "situations," that is, the set of circumstances in which the person (Timothy, Titus, Philemon) or congregation (Corinth, Galatia, Ephesus, etc.) finds themselves in at the time of the letter being written?

The Background of Second Timothy

Let us take a moment and look at the book of Second Timothy. First, we want to begin with the background of the book. Who wrote the book? When was it written? What were the circumstances that moved its author to pen the book? What was the situation of the Timothy named in the book that moved its author to write it? Why did Timothy need this information? Knowing these things will help us to appreciate the book better and see how we can benefit from the information today.

The author tells us he is "Paul, an apostle of Christ Jesus." (1:1) He tells us that he is writing "to Timothy, my beloved child." Who was this "Timothy"? Timothy was the "personal name meaning "honoring God." Friend and trusted co-worker of Paul. When Timothy was a child, his mother Eunice and his grandmother Lois taught him the Scriptures (2 Tim. 1:5; 3:15). A native of Lystra, he may have been converted on Paul's first missionary journey (Acts 14:6–23). Paul referred to Timothy as his child in the faith (1 Cor. 4:17; 1 Tim. 1:2; 2 Tim. 1:2). This probably means that Paul was instrumental in Timothy's conversion. When Paul came to Lystra on his second journey, Timothy was a disciple who was well respected by the believers (Acts 16:1–2). Paul asked Timothy to accompany him. Timothy's father was a Greek, and Timothy had not been circumcised. Because they would be ministering to many Jews and because Timothy's mother was Jewish, Paul had Timothy circumcised (Acts 16:3). Timothy not only accompanied Paul but also was sent on many crucial missions by Paul (Acts 17:14–15; 18:5; 19:22; 20:4; Rom. 16:21; 1 Cor. 16:10; 2 Cor. 1:19; 1 Thess. 3:2, 6)"[202]

Other verses help us to see when this letter was written to Timothy. We note at internal verses within the book that Paul is being persecuted yet again. He was in chains for his spreading of the Gospel and has been forsaken by many. The apostle Paul felt that the end was near. (2 Tim. 1:15-16; 2:8-10; 4:6-8) Therefore, it is very likely that he wrote the book during his second imprisonment in Rome, which took place about 65

---

[202] Robert J. Dean, "Timothy," ed. Chad Brand et al., *Holman Illustrated Bible Dictionary* (Nashville, TN: Holman Bible Publishers, 2003), 1597–1598.

C.E., immediately before he was martyred under the Roman Emperor, Nero. Timothy was undoubtedly still at Ephesus, where Paul had encouraged him to stay. (1 Tim. 1:3) That is the basic background of Second Timothy.

We notice, even under the shadow of death, Paul was not writing to complain about his difficulties in life. Instead, Paul warned Timothy of the hard times that lay ahead for him and the Christian faith. He encouraged him not to be sidetracked by distractions. Paul encouraged him to "be strong in the grace that is in Christ Jesus; and the things which you have heard from me in the presence of many witnesses, entrust these to faithful men who will be able to teach others also." He went on to say, "Consider what I am saying, for the Lord will grant you understanding in all things." (2 Tim. 2:1-7) Here Paul offers Timothy and by extension us an excellent example of unselfish concern for the faith, even in the face of imminent death!

When Paul first encountered Timothy, he was perhaps in his late teens or early twenties. Now, receiving this letter, it would seem that he was in his mid-30's, still viewed by Paul as being in his youth. (1 Tim. 4:12) Nevertheless, Paul was like a spiritual father looking at his son, as Timothy had already had a very excellent record of faithfulness, as he had slaved with Paul for the true some 15-16-years at this point. (Phil. 2:19-22) Even though Paul saw Timothy as a young man, Paul gave him the responsibility of counseling congregation elders "not to fight about words," who were likely far older than he was, encouraging them to focus on important matters, such as faith and endurance. (2 Tim. 2:14) Paul also gave Timothy the authority to appoint the elders and servants within the Christian congregation. (1 Timothy 5:22) Though, he may have been a little hesitant and shy about exercising this authority.–2 Timothy 1:6-7.

This was no easy task for Timothy, as he needed to "avoid empty speeches that violate what is holy, for they will lead to more and more ungodliness, and their word will spread like gangrene; Hymenaeus and Philetus [were] among them. men who have gone astray from the truth." These two were spreading false teachings, " saying that the resurrection has already taken place, and they upset the faith of some." (2 Tim 2:17-18) Possibly they were twisting Paul's words at Ephesians 2:1-6, taking them out of context. Paul warned Timothy that such apostates would be on the increase. He warned that these ones would not stay with the truth but would turn away from it, listening to false stories and those who twisted the Scriptures. Paul was giving Timothy an advanced warning.

2 Timothy 4:2-4 Updated American Standard Version (UASV)

² preach the word; be ready in season and out of season; reprove, rebuke, exhort, with complete patience and teaching. ³ For there will be a time when they will not put up with sound teaching, but in accordance with their own desires, they will accumulate teachers for themselves to have their ears tickled,[203] ⁴ and will turn away their ears from the truth and will turn aside to myths. ⁵ But you, be sober-minded[204] in all things, endure hardship, do the work of an evangelist, fulfill your ministry.

Applying Second Timothy Today

From what we have learned in the above, we see that Paul penned this epistle to Timothy for at least the following three reasons. (1) Paul knew that his death was coming soon and he wanted to prepare Timothy to move the Christian faith ahead without him. (2) He wanted to help Timothy to protect the Christian congregation from apostasy (standing off from the truth) and any other harmful influences. (3) Paul wanted Timothy not to grow weary but instead say busy in growing the faith and rely on an accurate knowledge (*epignosis*)[205] of the inspired, fully inerrant, authoritative, Scriptures, as opposed to false teachings.

Today, there are 41,000 different congregations, all claiming to be the truth and the way, yet most by far are apostates like Hymenaeus and Philetus who promote their own ideas and twisted biblical views that are not in harmony with the Word of God, which has subverted the faith of tens of millions. Moreover, Paul said that "But realize this, that in the last days difficult times will come." When are these "last days"? (2 Tim. 3:1) On this verse, Knute Larson writes, "The "last days" is not some future event to which we look. It is now, Jesus Christ initiated this epoch, and it will continue uninterrupted until his return. Paul defined this expansive time period as "terrible." God's extravagant grace also characterizes this era, establishing salvation and the church. But these days unleash Satan's wild attempts to destroy and undermine God's redemptive intentions. In

---

[203] Or *to tell them what they want to hear*

[204] **Sober Minded:** (Gr. *nepho*) This denotes being sound in mind, to be in control of one's thought processes and thus not be in danger of irrational thinking, 'to be sober-minded, to be well composed in mind.'–1 Thessalonians 5:6, 8; 2 Timothy 4:5; 1 Peter 1:13; 4:7; 5:8

[205] **Accurate Knowledge:** (Gr. *epignosis*) A strengthened or intensified form of *gnosis* (*epi*, meaning "additional"), meaning, "true," "real," "full," "complete" or "accurate," depending upon the context. Paul and Peter alone use *epignosis*. – Rom. 1:28; Eph. 1:17; Phil. 1:9; Col. 1:9-10; 1 Tim 2:4.

giving us this information, Paul desired that believers maintain a readiness of spirit and life. The battle will rage. What each believer must decide is whether he will prepare for the promised difficulties or given to personal safety and comfort."[206] Many Christians today have experienced the truth of Paul's words, "all who desire to live godly in Christ Jesus will be persecuted." (2 Tim. 3:12) How can we maintain our integrity in these "difficult times"? We can find truly conservative leaders and imitate their faith, as Timothy did with the apostle Paul. In addition, we can be very regular with our personal Bible study, prayer, and Christian meetings. We can also heed Paul's words, "Hold to the pattern of sound[207] words which you heard from me, in the faith and love which are in Christ Jesus." (2 Tim. 1:13) What are the "sound words" of which Paul spoke?

The Pattern of Sound Words

Sound Words: (Gr. *hygiainō logos*) This is in reference to our Christian doctrine. It means that our doctrine must be sound, that is, healthful (Lu 5:31; 7:10; 15:27; 3 John 2; Matt. 8:13), right, correct, or accurate (1 Tim. 1:10; 6:3; 2 Tim. 1:13; 4:3; Tit 1:9, 13; 2:1-2, 8). It means that our biblical teachings will be free from error. On 2 Timothy 1:13, Larson writes, "A sense of urgency filters through Paul's words as he focused on Timothy and pleaded, **what you heard from me, keep as the pattern of sound teaching.** Once again, Paul pressed home a familiar theme. The true gospel is founded upon the prophets, the words of Jesus, and apostolic teaching. Acutely aware of the damage inflicted by false teachers, Paul returned to the need for orthodoxy as revealed through Christ to Paul. It is this pure doctrine which is the pattern of sound teaching."[208] He goes on to say,

> The word translated "sound" comes from the Greek *hugies*, used in the Gospels to describe the healing of the sick by Jesus. Paul used the word to distinguish apostolic doctrine from false doctrine. Truth produces health; it results in right thinking and godly behavior.
>
> Paul did not prescribe intellectualism, the building of theological structures for their own sake. Truth is meant for life, and it is to be

---

[206] Knute Larson, *I & II Thessalonians, I & II Timothy, Titus, Philemon*, vol. 9, Holman New Testament Commentary (Nashville, TN: Broadman & Holman Publishers, 2000), 300.

[207] Or *wholesome; healthful; beneficial*

[208] Knute Larson, *I & II Thessalonians, I & II Timothy, Titus, Philemon*, vol. 9, Holman New Testament Commentary (Nashville, TN: Broadman & Holman Publishers, 2000), 270.

dispensed **with faith and love in Christ Jesus.** What we proclaim must be matched by our lives. If we are to guide people to Christ, we must hold a sincere trust in our Lord. Equally, our lives must be distinguished by love, divine in strength and giving. Both faith and love should be centered in Jesus.

Paul's words reverberate with his awareness that death was drawing closer. He was anxious that Timothy comprehend the importance and urgency of following through with his instructions. He told him to guard the apostolic revelation: **the good deposit that was entrusted to you.**

Each generation is so charged, for the gospel must be presevered in purity. We must protect it from destructive teachings. It is a serious responsibility, for we handle the very words of God. But we must also admit our inability to fulfill so noble a task. This is why Timothy and all Christians must guard Christ's gospel **with the help of the Holy Spirit who lives in us.** Paul again reminded us of this wonderful gift of God, this person of his Spirit who enables us to perform what God calls us to do.

This is a great picture of the Christian life and responsibility. God grants to us his gifts of grace and his Spirit of life—gifts freely given as we trust Jesus Christ as Savior. Our responsibility is to respond with obedient trust, not to gain salvation, but to express love, and to fulfill the calling of God upon our lives (Eph. 4:1).

Paul describes this interaction of giftedness and responsibility in Philippians. There he says to "work out your salvation" (Phil. 2:12) with a sense of respect and fear, not to gain salvation, but to flesh it out, to work out in our life the implications of being saved. Then the promise is given, "it is God who works in you to will and to act according to his good purpose" (Phil. 2:13).

Thus, we have personal responsibility before God but the promise of strength and provision by his Spirit as well. We are not alone.[209]

The basis for our Christian life, for our preaching, and for our teaching is the inspired, fully inerrant, authoritative Word of God. We are to trust the Bible fully. The apostle Paul tells us, "All Scripture is inspired by God and profitable for teaching, for reproof, for correction, for training in righteousness; so that the man of God may be fully competent, equipped for every good work." (2 Tim. 3:16-17) The apostle Peter says

---

[209] Knute Larson, *I & II Thessalonians, I & II Timothy, Titus, Philemon*, vol. 9, Holman New Testament Commentary (Nashville, TN: Broadman & Holman Publishers, 2000), 270–271.

that the Bible authors were "carried along by the Holy Spirit spoke from God."

Using Persuasion In Our Apologetic Evangelism

Acts 19:8 Updated American Standard Version (UASV)

[8] And he entered the synagogue and for three months **spoke boldly, reasoning** and <u>**persuading**</u> them about the kingdom of God.

In some ways, many might think that the word "persuasion" seems like a sneaky or devious kind of word. Some might think of the salesperson that sells cars, who comes across as pushy or those using deceptive language in a contract that someone wants us to sign. Maybe the word "persuasion" hits us as if it is simply manipulation. It is used in a similar vein by the apostle Paul when he writes of Christians in Galatia, "You were running well. Who hindered you from obeying the truth? This **persuasion** is not from him who calls you." (Gal. 5:7-8) The Greek word used here *peismone* has the sense of 'persuasion, i.e., communication intended to induce belief or action.'[210] Paul also told the Colossians, "I say this so that no one will delude you with **persuasive** argument." (Col 2:4) The Greek word use here *pithanologia* has the sense of 'persuasive speech, namely, using language effectively to please or persuade.'[211] When persuasion is used in this way, it does have somewhat of a negative connotation, as it hinges on crafty arguments built on false details. However, the sense of the two words is very similar.

Nevertheless, we have the apostle Paul using the art of persuasion or convincing with a different implication. In his second letter to Timothy Paul writes, "You, however, continue in the things you have learned and were **persuaded** to believe, knowing from whom you have learned them." (2 Tim. 3:14, UASV) The NASB renders the verse this way, "Continue in the things you have learned and become **convinced** of." (The ESV, HCSB and LEB render it similarly.) The Greek word here Pistoo[212] has the sense of 'being convinced, or being persuaded or sure of the truthfulness or validity of something.'[213] When Paul was speaking of what Timothy had been persuaded or convinced to believe, it was used in

---

[210] Bible sense Lexicon by Logos Bible Software

[211] IBID

[212] The Greek word epistothes in the New Testament is identified as a New Testament hapax legomenon, a word of which there is only one recorded use.

[213] Bible sense Lexicon by Logos Bible Software

a different connotation from the above Greek words, while still having the same sense as the other two Greek words. In the above verses to the Galatians and Colossians it was a manipulation of the truth that was being used to persuade, while here Timothy's mother and his grandmother were persuading or convincing Timothy to believe based on the truth itself.– 2 Timothy 1:5.

When Paul was under house arrest in Rome, he effectively witnessed to many. The account reads, "When they had appointed a day for him, they came to him at his lodging in greater numbers; and he expounded to them, testifying about the kingdom of God and trying to **persuade** them concerning Jesus both from the Law of Moses and from the Prophets, from morning till evening." The Greek word *peitho* has the sense persuading, causing someone to adopt a certain position, belief, or course of action.'[214] Was the apostle Paul manipulating truth to deceive those to whom he was witnessing? No, he was persuading them to believe about Jesus Christ based on truth. Therefore, the art of persuasion can be used for good or for bad. Christians use persuasion to help others adopt a certain position, belief about the Father and the Son, and the Word of God. As teachers, evangelists, proclaimers we can use sound logical reasoning, as we explain, persuade and convince, convicting others of Bible truth. (2 Tim. 2:15) Clearly, one of the most skilled persuaders in the history of Christianity was the apostle Paul. Demetrius, the "silversmith in Ephesus who incited a riot directed against Paul because he feared that the apostle's preaching would threaten the sale of silver shrines of Diana, the patron goddess of Ephesus." He said of Paul, "And you see and hear that not only in Ephesus but in almost all of Asia this Paul has persuaded and turned away a great many people, saying that gods made with hands are not gods."–Acts 19:26

Using Persuasion in Our Evangelism

Jesus commanded all Christians, "Go therefore and make disciples of all nations, baptizing them in the name of the Father and of the Son and of the Holy Spirit, teaching them to observe all that I have commanded you. And behold, I am with you always, to the end of the age." Christianity has been sending missionaries for centuries, and it has been very productive in that Christian congregations are now found throughout the entire world. The last forty years or so, many missionaries have come to believe that evangelism is needed to enter a new era of all Christians effective evangelizing in their own communities.

---

[214] IBID

A *Part-Time or Full-Time Evangelist* is one who sees this as their calling and chooses to be very involved as an evangelist in their local church and community. They may work part-time to supplement their work as an evangelist. They may be married with children, but they realize their gift is in the field of evangelism. If it were the wife, the husband would work toward supporting her work as an evangelist and vice-versa. If it were a single person, he or she would supplement their work by being employed part-time, but also the church would help as well. This person is well trained in every aspect of bringing one to Christ. *Congregation Evangelists* should be very involved in evangelizing their communities and helping the church members play their role at the basic levels of evangelism. There is nothing to say that one church could not have many within, who have the calling of an evangelist, which would and should be cultivated. What are some tools that can use in our effort to persuade others of the truth of God's Word?

Listening Carefully will enable us to understand fully what the unbeliever knows about any subject that we may be discussing with him. For example, if he says that he does not believe in the Bible, it may seem natural to launch into a solid explanation as to why he should believe in the Bible. However, we need to know specifically what it is that has him rejecting the Bible. Is it because he thinks it is just a man's book or does he feel it is full of contradictions and errors, or that it is an ancient book and not practical for today. Therefore, we need to listen carefully to the "why" of a stated position and not just assume we know what he means.–Proverbs 18:13.

Asking Questions goes right along with listening. Questions can be used to reiterate, making sure we understand what they meant. Questions can be used to get them to explain exactly what it they meant by a statement or a position. Questions can be used to lead a person to the right answer. We might ask the above person that does not believe in the Bible, "have you always felt that way and what is it that contributed to your not believing in the Bible?" After they give us the specifics of why we can use questions to dig deeper or lead. Suppose they said, 'it is because the Bible is full of contradictions and errors.' We can ask, "Have you ever considered what the difference between errors and contradictions and Bible difficulties is? "Have you ever studied the subject of errors or contradictions within the Scriptures?" After those questions, we might ask, "Do you have a couple examples of those errors and contradictions?" There are literally thousands of Bible difficulties between Genesis 1:1 and Revelation 22:21, which the Bible critic labels as errors and contradictions. Everyone uses common ones as their examples, if we recognize one and know that there is a reasonable explanation, we might offer a brief explanation of what a Bible difficulty is. Then we can demonstrate how that helps us better understand these are not errors and contradictions at all, as we also give him a reasonable explanation of his supposed error or contradiction. Then, we can ask, "would you agree with this explanation?" When we use questions and listen, we involve the unbeliever to join us in a respectful conversation, giving them a chance to be heard, as opposed to him just hearing us go on and on about a subject.

Using Sound Reasoning will help us reach the heart and mind of our listeners. For example, the above listener said he did not believe in the Bible and we asked why, got the specifics that he was hung up on perceived errors and contradictions, and gave him reasonable and logical answers that they were actually Bible difficulties, followed by a reasonable and logical explanation of his specific error or contradiction. Thus, we close out with the following, "The authors of Bible claim that what they wrote was inspired by God and they were moved along by Holy Spirit as they penned God's Words. (2 Tim 3:16-17; 2 Pet. 1:20-21) Those inspired authors tell us of an opportunity at eternal life, if we trust in the Son of God. (John 3:16) Would you not agree that while this is not evidence that it is, in fact, the Word of God and those things are true, but that it would be sensible nonetheless to investigate it objectively and find out if such claims are true or not?

The person above, who claimed he did not believe in the Bible, gave his reason, saying it is full of errors and contradictions. In our listening and asking questions, he gave us an example, when he says, "If God hardened the Pharaoh's heart, what exactly makes Pharaoh responsible for the decisions he makes?" When we look at the verse below, it does seem to say what our listener has claimed. How can God harden the heart of Pharaoh, so that he says no to all requests from Moses and Aaron and then punish him and his people for his saying no?

Exodus 4:21 Updated American Standard Version (UASV)	Exodus 4:21 Revised Standard Version (RSV)
21 Jehovah said to Moses, "When you go and return to Egypt see that you perform before Pharaoh all the wonders which I have put in your hand; but I will harden his heart so that he will not let the people go.	21 And the Lord said to Moses, "When you go back to Egypt, see that you do before Pharaoh all the miracles which I have put in your power; but I will harden his heart so that he will not let the people go.

Answer: This is actually a prophecy. God knew that what he was about to do would contribute to a stubborn and obstinate Pharaoh, who was going to be unwilling to change or give up the Israelites so they could go off to worship their God. Therefore, this is not stating what God is going to do; it is prophesying that Pharaoh's heart will harden because of the actions of God. The fact is, Pharaoh allowed his own heart to harden because he was determined not to agree with Moses' wishes or accept Jehovah's request to let the people go. Moses tells us at Exodus 7:13 that "Pharaoh's heart was hardened,[215] and he would not listen to them, as Jehovah had said." Again, at 8:15, we read, "But when Pharaoh saw that there was a relief, he hardened[216] his heart and would not listen to them, as Jehovah had said."

Dealing With the Emotional Beliefs of Others

Everyone has deeply held beliefs that if jabbed emotions may flare. We may be in a conversation with a devout Catholic, who believes that it is proper to address prayers to Mary as intercessor. Even if we were to show Scriptures and respectfully reason with him, he might come back sternly, "I still believe it proper to address prayers to Mary as intercessor." Whether we are witnessing to a Catholic, an atheist, an agnostic, a Muslim, a Hindus, a Buddhist, A Jehovah's Witness, a Mormon and so on, emotions are involved. In some cases, like the Witnesses, it is against their beliefs to be witnessed to, but they can witness to others. If you are aware of their teachings, their background and begin to question these things, even in a respectful manner, they will abandon the conversation quickly.

Many view their beliefs as absolute truths, even relativism,[217] which claims there is no such thing as absolute truth. When relativist's state there is no such thing as absolute truth, this is self-defeating within itself, as they are defeating the very absolute truth claim that they are trying to make, i.e., "all truth is relative." If there is no absolute truth; then, their belief that there are no absolutes cannot be true.[218] However, they would argue

---

[215] Lit *strong*

[216] Lit *made heavy*

[217] Relativism is the belief that concepts such as right and wrong, goodness and badness, or truth and falsehood are not absolute but change from culture to culture and situation to situation.

[218] "To claim that all moral truths are relative is self-defeating. A statement is self-defeating when what is being affirmed fails to meet its own requirements. An example is the statement, "I can't speak a word in English," to which one might respond, "You just did."

their belief vigorously as though it were absolutely true, even get emotional over it. Our beliefs are our worldview. A worldview is "the sum total of answers that a person gives to the most important questions in life." (Dr. Ronald Nash) Dr. Nash goes on to say, "Many people remain blissfully unaware that they have a worldview, even though the sudden change in their life and thought resulted from their exchanging their old worldview for their new one."[219] If we are going to overturn any false reasoning within one's worldview, say that of an atheist, it will take more than mere logic or even Scriptures that would demonstrate their view is erroneous.

We will have to be empathetic and have compassionate hearts, kindness, humility, meekness, and patience, as we use the art of persuasion. (Rom. 12:15; Col. 3:12) We as a teacher, an evangelist, a proclaimer of God's Word, never water down the truth. Moreover, we have strong convictions in what we hold to be true, i.e., our biblical or Christian worldview. For example, Paul stated it this way, "I am convinced that ..." and "I know and am convinced ..." (Rom. 8:38; 14:14, NASB) Even though we know we possess absolute truth, this does not mean we are free to be dogmatic or self-righteous about it, which can come across in our tone. Moreover, we would never use sarcasm or talk down to another when we are sharing our biblical truths, even if this is the way we are being treated in the conversation. We would never want to cause offense or even insult our listener.–Proverbs 12:18.

The apostle Peter tells us that we are to "sanctify Christ as Lord in your hearts, always being ready to make a defense to everyone who asks you to give an account for the hope that is in you, yet with gentleness and reverence." (1 Pet. 3:15, NASB) We will reach far deeper into their mind and heart if we respect their beliefs acknowledging that they have a right to possess them, even though we do not agree with them. This will require humility on our part, for which Paul makes the point that we should "do nothing from selfish ambition or conceit, but in humility count others more significant than yourselves." (Phil 2:3-4, ESV) Jesus in one of his parables said, "For everyone who exalts himself will be humbled, but the one who humbles himself will be exalted." (Luke 18:9-14, ESV) Yes, if we are to persuade others, it will come through our humility, as we truly

---

The moral relativists' claim commits the same error, since the statement 'All truth is relative' is itself an absolute claim for truth. It is impossible to consistently hold the claims of moral relativism because it denies what it tries to affirm in its very statements."–Hindson, Ed (2008-05-01). The Popular Encyclopedia of Apologetics (p. 354). Harvest House Publishers.

[219] Zondervan (2010-06-19). Life's Ultimate Questions: An Introduction to Philosophy (p. 32). Zondervan.

appreciate God for his helping us to see the truth, and our greatest desire it to share that same truth with others.

Paul wrote to the Corinthians, "For the weapons of our warfare are not of the flesh but have divine power to destroy strongholds. We destroy arguments and every lofty opinion raised against the knowledge of God, and take every thought captive to obey Christ." (2 Cor. 10:4-5) "Paul was certain that he was on a course **to demolish** the **strongholds** or fortifications of **arguments and every pretension** that anyone set up **against the knowledge of God.** As Paul traveled the world proclaiming the gospel of Christ, he encountered pretentious disbelief supported by clever arguments and powerful personalities. But through the "weakness" of preaching Christ, Paul went about taking **captive every thought to make it obedient to Christ."** (Pratt Jr 2000, p. 417) We as Christians seek to use the Word of God, logic,[220] reason,[221] in our art of persuasion to "destroy arguments and every lofty opinion." We must remember that God has shown us much patience in our early walk in coming to know him. We are over joyed that we have the Word of God, this powerful tool (Heb. 4:12), which will enable us to overturn false reasoning, reaching hearts and minds with the art of persuasion.

---

[220] What is logic? And why in the world would anyone want to study it? Isn't it just a bunch of incomprehensible and arbitrary rules that no one really follows anyway? What good does it do? To most people, logic is an unknown language about an unknown realm, where everything is turned upside down and no one with an IQ below 300 is allowed. You can see it in the panic on their faces when you just mention the word-LOGIC!

Despite all the bad press, logic is not so tough. In fact, it is one of the simplest things to use because you use it all the time, though you may not realize it. We don't mean that you put all of your thoughts into logical form and do a formal analysis of each thought. But when you are at the supermarket and one brand of sugar is 3 cents per ounce but another is 39 cents per pound, it doesn't take long for you to pull out your calculator and settle the issue. Why do you do that? Because you recognize that, those ounces and pounds have to be put in the same category to be compared. That's logic. You use logic to do most everything. When you decide to take your shower after you work out instead of before, you don't necessarily go through all the formal steps it takes to reach that conclusion validly, but your decision rests on logic nonetheless. Logic really means putting your thoughts in order.– Ronald M. Brooks; Norman L. Geisler. Come, Let Us Reason: An Introduction to Logical Thinking (p. 11)

[221] "God is rational, and the principles of good reason do flow from his very nature. Consequently, learning the rules of clear and correct reasoning is more than an academic exercise. For the Christian, it is also a means of spiritual service."–IBID p. 7

Exercise

Someone just said to you, "I don't believe the Bible, as it is full of errors and contradictions." How would you persuade him that this is not the case?

Use the Word of God Skillfully

Ephesians 6:17 Updated American Standard Version (UASV)

[17] And take the **helmet of salvation**, and **the sword of the Spirit**, which is the word of God.

Not long ago, those trying to curb the use of drugs within the American youth had the saying, "the mind is a terrible thing to waste." Our next piece of the armor of God would be a very useful tool for protecting the Christian mind, **the helmet of salvation.** The Apostle Paul said to the Thessalonians, "we must stay sober and let our faith and love be like a suit of armor. Our firm hope that we will be saved is our helmet," because it protects our Christian mind. (1 Thessalonians 5:8) Even though we may have accepted Christ, and have entered onto the path of salvation, we still suffer from imperfect human weaknesses. Even though our foremost desire is to do good, our thinking can be corrupted by this fleshly world that surrounds us. We need not be like this world, but rather openly allow God to alter the way we think, through his Word the Bible, which will help us fully to grasp everything that is good and pleasing to him. (Romans 7:18; 12:2) You likely recall the test that Jesus faced, where Satan offered him "all the kingdoms of the world and their glory." (Matthew 4:8-10) Jesus response was to refer to Scripture, "Be gone, Satan! For it is written, 'you shall worship the Lord your God, and him only shall you serve.'" Paul had this to say about Jesus, "looking to Jesus, the founder and perfecter of our faith, who for the joy that was set before him endured the cross, despising the shame and is seated at the right hand of the throne of God."–Hebrews 12:2.

We need to understand that the examples of faith within Scripture do not come to us automatically. If we are focusing on what this current satanic world that caters to the fallen human flesh and what it has to offer, as opposed to focusing on the hopes that are plainly laid out in Scripture, we will be weak in the face of any severe trial. After a few stumbles, it may be that we suffer spiritual shipwreck and lose our hope altogether. Then again, if we frequently feed our minds or concentrate the mind on the promises of God, we will carry on delighting in the hope that has been offered us.–Romans 12:12.

If we are to keep our Christian mind on the hope that lies ahead, we need to possess the **Sword of the Spirit**. The book that reveals heavenly Father, his will and purposes, i.e., the Bible is stated to be "living and active, sharper than any two-edged sword, piercing to the division of soul and of spirit, of joints and of marrow, and discerning the thoughts and intentions of the heart." This Word, if understood correctly, applied in a balanced manner, can transform our lives, and help us avoid or minimalize the pitfalls of this imperfect life. We can depend on that Word when we are overwhelmed, or temple to give way to the flesh, and when the Bible critics of this world attempt to do away with our faith. (2 Corinthians 10:4-5) We need to heed the words of the Apostle Paul to his spiritual son, Timothy:

2 Timothy 3:15-17 Updated American Standard Version (UASV)

[14] You [Timothy], however, continue in the things you have learned and were persuaded to believe, knowing from whom you have learned them **[Paul, who Timothy traveled with and studied under for 15 years]**, [15] and that from infancy[222] you have known the sacred writings **[the whole Old Testament]**, which are able to make you wise for salvation through trust[223] in Christ Jesus. [16] All Scripture is inspired by God and profitable for teaching, for reproof, for correction, for training in righteousness; [17] so that the man of God may be fully competent, equipped for every good work.

The goal of all this instruction, discipline, and training is not to keep us busy. God intends **that the man of God may be thoroughly equipped for every good work**. We study the Bible, we rely upon God's Spirit, his revelation, and the community of the faithful to keep us on track—obedient and maturing in faith. Continuing in this commitment will enable us to do whatever God calls us to do. Timothy could withstand the attacks of false teachers, the abandonment of professing believers, and the persecution that surrounded him because God had equipped him for the task. God never calls us to do something without first enabling us through his Spirit and the power of his truth to accomplish the task.

We neglect the Scriptures at our own peril. Through them we gain the ability to serve God and others. The Scriptures not

---

[222] *Brephos* is "the period of time when one is very young–'childhood (probably implying a time when a child is still nursing), infancy." – GELNTBSD

[223] *Pisteuo* is "to believe to the extent of complete trust and reliance—'to believe in, to have confidence in, to have faith in, to trust, faith, and trust.' – GELNTBSD

only point the way; through the mysterious union of God's Word and faith, they give us the ability to serve. (Larson 2000, 307)

After two years of proclaiming the good news, Jesus entered into another campaign throughout Galilee. "Jesus went throughout all the cities and villages, teaching in their synagogues and proclaiming the gospel of the kingdom and healing every disease and every affliction." Jesus had compassion for the lost sheep of Israel,

Matthew 9:36-38 Updated American Standard Version (UASV)

[36] When he saw the crowds, he had compassion for them, because they were harassed and scattered, like sheep without a shepherd. [37] Then he said to his disciples, "The harvest is plentiful, but the workers are few. [38] Therefore, beg the Master of the harvest to send out workers into his harvest."[224]

After stating the above, Jesus "called to him his twelve disciples" and "sent out after instructing them." (Matt. 9:35-38; 10:1, 5) Later, Jesus "appointed seventy[225] others and sent them on ahead of him, two by two, into every town and place where he himself was about to go. Then he was saying to them: 'The harvest, indeed, is great, but the workers are few; therefore beg the Master of the harvest to send out workers into his harvest.'"–Luke 10:1-2

This was true in Jesus' day when there were but about one hundred million people on the planet, how much more true it is today with over seven billion. Moreover, the need for workers is far graver today, as the churches are not sending workers out into their communities to share the good news.

John 4:34-35 Updated American Standard Version (UASV)

[34] Jesus said to them, "My food is that I do the will of the one who sent me and complete his work. [35] Do you not say, 'There are yet four months and the harvest comes'? Behold, I say to you, lift up your eyes and look at the fields, that they are white for harvest already.

The fields of humankind alienated from God are, indeed, white for harvesting. Therefore, all should pray that God gathers together workers,

---

[224] **9:37-38 LAC:** All Christians are to request prayerfully that the Father "send out workers into his harvest." Therefore, all Christians must act on behalf of their prayers by zealously participating in proclaiming the Word of God, teaching, and making disciples. (Matt. 24:14; 28:19-20; Act 1:8)

[225] Some mss read *seventy-two*

preparing them, to go out into the communities of their churches, to sow the good news. When we pray such things, we need to act in harmony with our prayers. One way we can do this is by reading such books as CONVERSATIONAL EVANGELISM, THE EVANGELISM HANDBOOK, and THE CHRISTIAN APOLOGIST, all by Edward D. Andrews. These books will prepare all Christians to share God's Word effectively in their community, in their family, in the workplace or school, and informally.– Matthew 28:19-20; Mark 13:10.

The Word of God Is Living and Active

Hebrews 4:12 Updated American Standard Version (UASV)

[12] For the word of God is living and active and sharper than any two-edged sword, and piercing as far as the division of soul and spirit, of both joints and marrow, and able to judge the thoughts and intentions of the heart.

What power the message within the Word of God has! It is so powerful that it can change the entire makeup of anyone's inner person if they are receptive to the truth.

Colossians 3:9-10 Updated American Standard Version (UASV)

[9] Do not lie to one another, seeing that you have put off the old man[226] with its practices [10] and have put on the new man[227] who is being renewed through accurate knowledge[228] according to the image of the one who created him,

The Bible contains so much wisdom; it is almost unfathomable to contemplate it. There are endless amounts of life principles, do's and don'ts, commands, counsel, which can help its reader to have far more success in this wicked world than those who refuse to consider its unrivaled wisdom. Psalm 119:105 makes the point perfectly, 'the Word of God is a lamp to my feet [immediate concerns] and a light to my path [what lies ahead].' The Bible will lead us in the way we ought to go in making everyday decisions, or choosing friends, deciding entertainment, employment choices, just how revealing our clothes will be, and so on. (Ps. 37:25; Prov. 13:20; John 15:14; 1 Tim. 2:9) Living by the principles

---

[226] Or *old person*

[227] Or *new person*

[228] *Epignosis* is a strengthened or intensified form of *gnosis* (*epi*, meaning "additional"), meaning, "true," "real," "full," "complete" or "accurate," depending upon the context. Paul and Peter alone use *epignosis*.

and counsel of the Word will help us to have better relationships with others. (Matt. 7:12; Phil. 2:3-4) We can make a decision for the day, but we can also plan a life, based on what the future hold, as we have our roadway lit with the Word. (1 Tim. 6:9) Our objective is to live under the umbrella of God's sovereignty, to live according to his will and purposes. (Matt. 6:33; 1 John 2:17-18) Life need not be meaningless to the one living by the Word of God.

Then, there is the fact that the Bible is also a weapon in spiritual warfare. The apostle Paul referred to the Word of God as "the sword of the Spirit." (Eph. 6:12, 17) **"The sword of the Spirit** pictures the soldier's weapon sheathed to his belt and used both for offensive and defensive purposes. Taking the sword of the Spirit–defined for us as the Word of God–can be understood as using Scripture specifically in life's situations to fend off attacks of the enemy and put him to flight. We see the example of Jesus using the Scripture this way in Matthew 4:1–11."[229] If we are effective in our evangelism, we can be used by God as his ambassador, helping those within Satan's world to be set free from spiritual bondage. Unlike imperfect man sword of carnal warfare, "the sword of the Spirit, which is the word of God," saves lives rather than destroy them. However, this is dependent on just how effective we are at wielding this sword.

Teach the Word of Truth Correctly

Can we imagine the ancient soldier who dared enter into warfare without practicing with his sword? How effective would he be with his weapon? He would likely be killed within minutes. The same holds true with our use of "the sword of the spirit," namely, God's Word, in our spiritual warfare, i.e., we would be beaten down by the critic or opponent in short order. If our faith is genuine, we will be like the prophet Jeremiah. In the beginning, he was hesitant to speak out, saying to God, who had just commissioned him to be his prophet to the nations, "I do not know how to speak, for I am only a youth." However, in time Jeremiah became a force to be reckoned with, so effective a communicator that his enemies viewed him as one that makes gloomy predictions of impending disaster. (Jer. 38:4) After that day of saying, but "I am only a youth," Jeremiah would go on to serve as God's prophet for 65 years, becoming one of the best-known prophets in the history of God's Word. So much so, when Jesus came, the people were discussing

---

[229] (Anders, Holman New Testament Commentary: vol. 8, Galatians, Ephesians, Philippians, Colossians 1999, p. 192)

who the Son of Man might be, and some thought he was Jeremiah the prophet returned. Thus, we must ask, how did the young, she boy overcome his reluctance to proclaim God's Word? Jeremiah tells us,

Jeremiah 20:9 Updated American Standard Version (UASV)

⁹ If I say, "I will not mention him,
  or speak any more in his name,"
then it becomes in my heart like a fire burning
  shut up in my bones,
and I am weary of holding it in,
  and I cannot endure it.

Yes, the truth of God's Word in the heart of man is so very powerful; it will compel, provoke, and encourage him to speak. While we may be shy or reluctant to proclaim God's Word to others, it will become a burning fire within us, to the point we will eventually share it. However, if we have not prepared ourselves to use "the sword of the spirit," namely, God's Word, in our spiritual warfare, we will be beaten down by the critic or opponent quickly. Do not believe that every critic is one with a closed heart and mind. Many are critics because they had begun to doubt and started to read books or listen to talks by Bible critics, which only served to reinforce their doubts, and they have never heard anyone overturn these Bible difficulties floating around in their mind and heart. We may recall that the apostle Paul 'reasoned with the unbelievers from the Scriptures, explaining and proving' the truth to those he came across. We may be thinking, "yes, but I am no Jeremiah the prophet nor the apostle Paul." Well, neither were they at one time, and we cannot know who new are until we allow ourselves to be used by God. Paul told young Timothy, "Do your best to present yourself to God as one approved, a worker who has no need to be ashamed, rightly handling the word of truth." (2 Tim. 2:15, ESV) On this, New Testament Bible scholar Knute Larson writes,

> Timothy, by contrast, must do his best to **present [himself] to God as one approved, a workman who does not need to be ashamed.** Timothy, and all who follow Christ, are to consecrate themselves to God, working diligently for his approval. The teacher whom God approves has no need of shame in his presence.

> God bestows his approval on the one who exhibits truth, love, and godliness in daily living, and who **correctly handles the word of truth.** The false teachers were mishandling God's words, using them for their own benefit. Timothy was

commissioned to handle the words of God correctly. All preaching should present the truth clearly, cutting through erroneous ideas or inaccurate opinions. (Larson 2000, p. 286)

The English Standard Version renders the participial clause of 2:15 "rightly handling the word of truth," while the Holman Christian Standard Bible renders it "correctly teaching the word of truth," and the New American Standard Bible, "accurately handling the word of truth." The Greek word, *orthotomeo*, means "to give accurate instruction—'to teach correctly, to expound rightly.' ... 'do your best ... to teach the word of truth correctly' 2 Tm 2:15."[230] This is all that can be asked of any Christian, that 'we do our best to teach the word of truth correctly.'

What can help us to teach the word of truth correctly? If we are to teach another, we must correctly and clearly understand the Word ourselves. When we clearly understand something, we are able to give reasons as to why it is so. Moreover, we are able to express it in our own words. If we are to understand the Bible correctly, we must read it within the context of the verses that surround it, the chapter it is within, the Bible book it is within, the Testament that it is in, and the Bible as a whole. According to the Merriam-Webster Dictionary, immediate context (i.e., of a word, phrase, clause or sentence) is "the words that are used with a certain word or phrase and that help to explain its meaning."[231] The meaning of a text is what the author meant by the words that he used. On this Robert H. Stein writes,

Great confusion can result if we do not pay careful attention to context. For instance, both Paul (Rom. 4:1–25) and James (2:14–26) use the term "faith" (*pistis*). Yet we will misunderstand both if we assume that by faith they mean "a body of beliefs." We will misunderstand Paul if we assume that he means "a mere mental assent to a fact," and we will misunderstand James if we assume that he means "a wholehearted trust." It is evident from the context that Paul means the latter (cf. Rom. 4:3, 5) and that James means the former (cf. 2:14, 19). (Stein 1994, p. 59)

Stein also wrote, "A context is valuable because it assists the reader in understanding the meaning the author has given the text." Another example would be Paul's statement at Galatians 5:13 (ESV), "For you

---

[230] Louw, Johannes P.; Nida, Eugene A. (**Greek-English Lexicon of the New Testament based on Semantic Domains**)

[231] http://www.merriam-webster.com/dictionary/context

were called to freedom, brothers. Only do not use your freedom as an opportunity for the flesh, but through love serve one another." If we were looking at this verse alone, not considering what is before and after, we would be asking, what does Paul mean by "freedom"? Was he speaking of freedom from sin and death, freedom from being enslaved to false beliefs, freedom from corruption, or was it something entirely different? If we consider the context, we get our answer. The context tells us the "freedom" that Paul spoke of was our being freed from "the curse of the law," as Christ became the curse for us. (Gal. 3:13, 19-24; 4:1-5) If we look at Galatians 3:10, "Paul quotes Deuteronomy 27:26 to prove that, contrary to what the Judaizers claimed, the law cannot justify and save. It can only condemn. The breaking of any aspect of the law brought a curse on the person who broke the law. Since no one can keep the law perfectly, we are all cursed. Paul, with this argument, destroys the Judaizers' belief that a person is saved through the law." [232] Thus, Paul was referring to the freedom that Christians possess. Just because we are not under the Mosaic Law, a law that imperfect man cannot keep perfectly, this is no excuse to use our "freedom as an opportunity for the flesh." Rather, if we truly understand and value our freedom, we will slave for one another because of our love for one another. However, those in the Galatian congregation who lacked that love were engaged in vicious infighting and quarreling.–Galatians 5:15.

There is another meaning of the word "context," i.e., background, conditions, historical setting, and situation. Some call the surrounding text cotext and the historical setting context. Either way, the second meaning here is just as important. The background information that must be considered is, who penned the book, when and where was it written and under what historical setting. Why was the author moved to pen the book, or more realistically, why did God move him to write the book? Within any book on Bible backgrounds, the author will discuss the social, moral, and religious practices of the time Bible book was written. [233]

Correctly handling the word of truth goes deeper than simply explaining a biblical truth accurately. We do not want to use our knowledge of God's Word in an intimidating way. Of course, we want to

---

[232] (Anders, Holman New Testament Commentary: vol. 8, Galatians, Ephesians, Philippians, Colossians 1999, p. 37)

[233] An outstanding study tool in getting background information about the New Testament is:
BIBLE BACKGROUNDS OF THE NEW TESTAMENT
Parables, Metaphors, Similes, Gestures and Attitudes
http://www.christianpublishers.org/apps/webstore/products/show/5904404

defend the truth offensively and defensively, following the example of Jesus, who used Scripture to defeat Satan the Devil when under temptation. Nevertheless, figuratively speaking, we do not use the Bible to club others over the head. (Deut. 6:16; 8:3; 10:20; Matt. 4:4, 7, 10) Rather, we want to follow the counsel Peter gave, "in your hearts honor Christ the Lord as holy, **always being prepared to make a defense** to anyone who asks you for a reason for the hope that is in you; **yet do it with gentleness and respect.**"–1 Peter 3:15.

New Testament Bible scholar Richard L. Pratt Jr. offered the following on 2 Corinthians 10:3-5,

> Paul responded by reminding the Corinthians that his ministry was successful warfare. He had previously described his gospel ministry as a parade of victory in war, and he used similar military analogies elsewhere as well. His apostolic effort was a war he was sure to win.
>
> Paul admitted that he and his company **live[d] in the world**, but insisted that they did not **wage war as the world does**. They did not employ the intimidation, coercion, and violence normally associated with worldly authorities. Instead of employing **the weapons of the world**, Paul relied on **divine power**. These **weapons** appeared weak by worldly standards, but they were actually very powerful. The preaching of the cross brought great displays of God's power in the lives of believers everywhere, including Corinth.
>
> Consequently, Paul was certain that he was on a course **to demolish** the **strongholds** or fortifications of **arguments and every pretension** that anyone set up **against the knowledge of God**. As Paul traveled the world proclaiming the gospel of Christ, he encountered pretentious disbelief supported by clever arguments and powerful personalities. But through the "weakness" of preaching Christ, Paul went about taking **captive every thought to make it obedient to Christ.** (Pratt Jr 2000, p. 417)

2 Corinthians 10:3-5 Updated American Standard Version (UASV)

[3] For though we walk in the flesh, we do not war according to the flesh, [4] for the weapons of our warfare are not of the flesh[234] but powerful

---

[234] That is *merely human*

to God for destroying strongholds.[235] [5]We are destroying speculations and every lofty thing raised up against the knowledge of God, and we are taking every thought captive to the obedience of Christ,

If we have a sound understanding of the Scriptures and are always working toward growing it, we can accomplish much. Our use of God's Word can "destroy strongholds," namely, expose the false or mistaken beliefs of others, any irreligious practices, as well as all worldviews that are not biblical, but rather are fleshly. In Addition, we will be able to remove "every lofty opinion raised against the knowledge of God." Moreover, we can use our knowledge of Scripture to help unbelievers to bring their thinking in line with a biblical worldview, as we make disciples.

We must keep in mind that our obligation is not just toward the unbeliever, but also toward the others who claim to be Christians, who are on a false path. No true conservative, evangelical Christian would consider Catholicism to be the true way to pure worship of God, and the same would hold true of Pentecostalism, among many other so-called Christian denominations. Both the unbeliever and those claiming to be Christian are holding onto unbiblical beliefs that are deeply embedded in their mind and heart. If we are able to use the Scriptures, logic, and reason effectively, we will be able to remove "every lofty opinion raised against the knowledge of God." In the end, then they will understand and find the knowledge of God.

Using Questions Effectively

Why does it matter that we use question effectively when we are witnessing to others about the Word of God? Imagine that you just took your car into the garage because it has been having many different problems. In the first scenario, the mechanic says to throw your keys over on the desk; he can have it fixed as good as new for you, come back Saturday to pick it up. Would you feel comfortable with the mechanic, or would alarms be going off? In a second scenario, you take the car to another garage, and the mechanic stops what he is doing; he comes over and asks you some probing questions, like 'what is it doing, what sounds is it making,' and the like. He has you start it; he revs the engine and listens. He asks if he can take it around the block. After that, he asks you some more leading questions based on what he has thus learned. Now, he gives you a preliminary diagnosis but says it would be best to put it on

---

[235] That is *tearing down false arguments*

the diagnostics machine to verify his findings. He comforts you with the words; we can get such and such parts in here and have it fixed for you by this Saturday. Why does the second scenario give you much more confidence in the competency of the mechanic? In any field, a person must ask probing and leading questions, to discover symptoms or evidence that can lead them to help find the 'why' or the 'what.' If we are to help an unbeliever, find the truth, we must ask effective questions. If we are to help a "Christian" on a false path, find the correct path, we must ask effective questions. Just like the second mechanic, we are trying to discover the cause of what is contributing to the unbelief or the wrong belief. After that, we can use the Word of God to lead them in the way they ought to go.

Jesus was the master teacher, who used questions as he learned more about the student but also allowed the one listening to feel involved in the discussion. For example, when the disciples were in need of a lesson in humility, Jesus started with a question, not a lecture. (Mark 9:33) To teach Peter how to find the principle behind the black and white, Jesus offered him a multiple-choice question. (Matt. 17:24-26) When Jesus sought the disciples understanding of who he was, he asked them viewpoint questions. (Matt 16:13-17) Jesus was about imparting knowledge and understanding, but he did not do this with sermons alone. He also used questions combined with statements, which got down into the hearts of his listeners, moving them to act in harmony with the gospel message he was sent by the Father to deliver to the lost sheep of Israel. We use questions in our ministering to other because we want to help them to act in harmony with the Word of God. We also want to use questions to overcome their objections that are designed to dismiss us. Moreover, we want to find those with receptive hearts.

What would we do as a parent, if our child came to us, saying, 'I am constantly being challenged about my belief in creation as opposed to evolution?' Certainly, we want our children to be able to have faith in the Word of God as absolute truth and to be able to defend that truth with fellow classmates, even teachers. Rather than stressing the importance of defending God's Word, which may come across as being critical, or offering advice, why not show him how effective viewpoint questions can be.

FIRST EXAMPLE

Father: Say you were to ask your science teacher how DNA is packed with the chromosomes, what would she say?

Son: She would go on and on about it, talking about how efficient that it is. She would say something like, "The most striking property of every chromosome within the eukaryotic cell nucleus is the length of each molecule of DNA incorporated and folded into it. The human genome of 3 x 109 bp would extend over a meter if unraveled and straightened, yet it is compacted into a nucleus only 10-5 m in diameter. **It is an astonishing feat of engineering** to organize such a long linear DNA molecule within ordered structures that can reversibly fold and unfold within the chromosome."[236]

Father: What if you were to ask her, "How do we explain that such an astonishing feat of engineering rose by an undirected chance of events; does not a feat of engineering suggest an engineer?

SECOND EXAMPLE

Father: Say you were to ask your science teacher, 'Can you please explain to me about DNA's capacity for stored information,' what would she say?

Son: She would say something like; "The information stored in DNA must by no means be underestimated. So much so, that one human DNA molecule contains enough information to fill a million-page encyclopedia or to fill about 1,000 books. Note this fact well: one million encyclopedia pages, or 1,000 books. This is to say that the nucleus of each cell contains as much information as would fill a one-million-page encyclopedia, which is used to control the functions of the human body. To draw an analogy, we can state that even the 23-volume-Encyclopaedia Britannica, one of the greatest mines of information in the world, has 25,000 pages. Therefore, before us lies an incredible picture. In a molecule found in a nucleus, which is far smaller than the microscopic cell wherein it is located, there exists a data warehouse 40 times bigger than the biggest encyclopedia of the world that includes millions of items of information. This means a massive 1000-volume encyclopedia which is unique and has no equal in the world."

"Computers are currently the most advanced form of technology for storing information. A body of information, which, 30 years ago, was routinely stored in a computer the size of a room, can today be stored in small "discs," yet even the latest technology invented by human intelligence, after centuries of accumulated knowledge and years of hard work, is far from reaching the information storage capacity of a single cell nucleus. The following comparison made by the well-known professor of

---

[236] http://what-when-how.com/molecular-biology/chromosomes-molecular-biology/

microbiology Michael Denton, will probably suffice to highlight the contrast between the tiny size of DNA and the great amount of information it contains:"

The information necessary to specify the design of all the species of organisms which have ever existed on the planet, a number according to G.G. Simpson of approximately one thousand million, could be held in a teaspoon and there would still be room left for all the information in every book ever written. (*Michael Denton. Evolution: A Theory in Crisis. London: Burnett Books, 1985, p. 334*)[237]

Father: What if you were to ask her, "How is it that human computer technicians are unable to accomplish these types of results, yet we are to believe that mindless matter can do so alone?"

From a few more examples like this, the son can begin to see how effective viewpoint questions are. Many great publications out there offer strong apologetic reasoning for intelligent design. Some leading authors would be John C. Lennox, William A. Dembski, Jonathan Witt, Stephen C. Meyer, David Klinghoffer, Michael J. Behe, Michael Denton, among many others. How else can we become more effective in our evangelism of others?

Using God's Word with Persuasion

A confusion that arises over using the Bible effectively when witnessing to others is the belief that it simply boils down to knowing and quoting Scripture. What do we read of the way the apostle Paul went about witnessing to others. It says, "He entered the synagogue and for three months **spoke boldly, reasoning** and **persuading** them." (Ac 19:8-9) On another occasion, "when some became stubborn and continued in unbelief, speaking evil of the Way before the congregation, he withdrew from them and took the disciples with him, **reasoning** daily in the hall of Tyrannus." Persuasion is "attempting to win others over to one's own point of view. It can be either positive, as with preaching the gospel, or it can spring from a malign intent to seduce people from the truth." (Manser 2009) When one is persuaded, he is won over by the ability of the persuader's reasoning, arguments (reasons put forward in support), explaining of the Scriptures, i.e., he is so convinced that he gains confidence in God's Word. When Christians persuade a person to accept the Bible as the inspired, inerrant Word of God, we are winning him

---

[237] http://www.dnarefutesevolution.com/human_celli.html

over, so that he will place his trust in the Bible. If we are to accomplish this in the skeptical, atheistic, agnostic, humanistic, liberal, progressive world that we live in, we must possess the skills to teach our listeners of the truthfulness of our reasons we put forward in support of the biblical worldview, or rather in opposition to the fleshly worldview of today's' hedonistic society.

We do not want to shy away from using God's Word; because that just demonstrates that, we have a lack of respect for it. The modern day critic of the 20th and 21st centuries has taken over in the driving of the conversation, and it is he who decides what evidence is and what is not. The critic's conclusion is that Bible manuscripts that date back 2,300 years are not historical, archaeological evidence, but rather are biased material and if we cannot offer up secular evidence for what we say; well then, we have no evidence at all. The modern day Bible scholar has chosen to play by the critic's rules of engagement, so they actually run around looking for ways to prove things with secular history alone. First, we do not cower before Satan and his people, leaving them to determine whether we can draw attention to God's Word. It is certainly beneficial and appropriated that our great apologetists like Norman L. Geisler, William Lane Craig, or Craig Evans defend the truth against the lies of the great minds of Satan's side. However, our primary commission is winning the hearts and minds of those receptive to the truth, not winning arguments against those who will never accept the truth, regardless of the evidence.[238]

Therefore, we need to be quite familiar with the Word of God and know what the authors meant by the words that they used. Whether we open our Bible to share a Scripture or reference it aloud, draw attention to the importance of what God's thinking is on the subject that we may be discussing. After a very brief introduction and our mission of sharing God's Word, we might open with an open-ended question. We might say, fifty percent of marriages in America fail, and then ask, "Why do you think that is?" [Allow for an answer] How do you think this principle from God's Word would help, Paul said, "Let no one seek his own good, but the good of his neighbor." (1 Cor. 10.24, ESV) If both mates were to seek the good of the other, how might we see that playing out, can you think of any examples? [Allow for an answer] If the person is receptive,

---

[238] Keep in mind that when Geisler, Craig and Evans are debating to on stage against a atheist scientist or the like; they are talking past him, if he is unreceptive to any in the audience that may be receptive. It is evidence that we have answers in the conversation, whether they want to hear them or not, so that unbelievers can see that we do have reasonable, logical answers to the deep questions that plague humanity.

offer a couple more Bible principles that deal with spouses that seem to be growing apart (Phil 1:10), mates that fail to fulfill their responsibilities (Rom 14:12), the husband that seems to not care where the family is heading (Pro. 14:1) habits that annoy one another (Col. 3:13), and so on.

We need to reason from the Scripture where we leave our listeners with no doubt whatsoever that what they are hearing is the truth. Therefore, we need to use genuine, warm, earnest, profound and honest entreaty, with sound logic. As Jesus and Paul, our objective is to reach the heart of those to whom we witness. This is realized in the words of wise King Solomon, "The purpose in a man's heart is like deep water, but a man of understanding will draw it out." (Pro. 20:5) Yes, we need to draw out what is in the heart of our listener, by using kind, loving and respectful questions that evidence we are personally interested in them. We must avoid being too direct and frank. In other words, we do not want to have a cutting edge to our questions, nor do we want to be too frank or straightforward and showing no delicacy or consideration when using questions. When we are making arguments to substantiate a point, make them clear and logical. We want to offer evidence that will satisfy the listener. Moreover, we want to share what the Bible author meant by the use of his words, not what we think he meant. Time is critical and should be used judiciously. Rather than rush through reading three or four verses that make our point, we should choose the clearest one, use it well by explaining, reasoning and illustrating. When we think of using corroborative evidence, again, we turn to Solomon, "From a wise mind comes wise speech; the words of the wise are persuasive." (Pro. 16:23, NLT) If there is a need for more research on our part, say so, by stating that we will look into this further and get back to them another time.

Carry on Using God's Word Skillfully

The world is ever changing toward being more wicked each and every day. In fact, Paul told Timothy, "Evil people and impostors will go on from bad to worse, deceiving and being deceived." (2 Tim. 3:13) Thus, 2,000 years later this is even truer. Therefore, it is highly significant that "we destroy arguments and every lofty opinion raised against the knowledge of God, and take every thought captive to obey Christ." We do this by using "the sword of the Spirit, which is the word of God."– (Eph. 6:17) As the author of Hebrews tells us, "For the word of God is living and active, sharper than any two-edged sword, piercing to the division of soul and of spirit, of joints and of marrow, and discerning the thoughts and intentions of the heart." (Heb. 4:12, ESV) Jesus words ring true, "For what will it profit a man if he gains the whole world and

forfeits his soul? Or what will a man give in exchange for his soul?" –
Matthew 16:26, NASB.

Exercise

Someone just said to you, "I don't believe the Bible, as it is just a
book by men, not the Word of God." How would you persuade him that
this is not the case?

CHAPTER 8 Interpreting Words

A word is a meaningful sound or combination of sounds that is a unit of language or its representation in a text.

Word Meaning: First, I would like to note that the reader of Hebrew, Aramaic, and Greek have a small advantage over the reader that only knows English. The reader of the original languages can ascertain what the writer meant to convey by the words he used, while the English reader can only ascertain what the translator meant by the rendering of his English words. In an attempt to understand any given word within Scripture, one must keep some simple basic points in mind:

- A word can have several meanings. For example, the English word "hand" can mean the thing at the end of our wrist, or a hand of cards, or a worker, and so on. It is the context of a sentence that will establish which meaning was intended.
- A word will only mean what the writer meant to convey by his use of it within the context of how he chose to use it.
- Along with the above point is the fact that the writer is going to use words in such a way that his audience will understand. In other words, "house" is not going to mean a "river." This may sound ridiculous at this point, but it will pay dividends when we begin looking at word meaning.
- The range of meaning will be found in a lexicon, and the context will tell us which one the writer intended.

Word Study Fallacies

Etymological Fallacies: Some of this will be repeated again later in this chapter and other chapters, as repetition for emphasis. A word's meaning must come from its use at the time of the writing. To find the origin of a word and its historical meaning throughout history is not going to add anything to its meaning. Moreover, the form of a word has nothing to do with its meaning. This would also mean that most compound words do not attribute to the meaning of a word by looking at the two separate words that have been combined. For example, the word "pineapple," if broken apart into "pine" and "apple" add nothing to its meaning. Another fallacy would be to look at how a word is used centuries later, but in all likelihood, the word's meaning will have been altered over time. In 1611 the English word "let" meant to "stop" or "restrain." Today it means "to allow." (See 2 Thess 2:7 KJV/ESV) The only time the history of a word may be some help is when there is no possible way of knowing its meaning at the time of use, or with names. (Louw, 1982)[239]

One of the primary fallacies comes from those that only use one specific Bible translation, as the King James Version only Bible students do. If we are only studying or reading on the surface, we will never discover what is behind some of those English words. The other aspect of this is the reader is thinking with his or her modern day mindset.

Philippians 2:5-8 King James Version (KJV)

[5]Let this mind be in you, which was also in Christ Jesus: [6]Who, being in the form of God, thought it not robbery to be equal with God: [7]But **made himself of no reputation**, and took upon him the form of a servant, and was made in the likeness of men: [8]And being found in fashion as a man, he humbled himself, and became obedient unto death, even the death of the cross.

Philippians 2:5-8 Updated American Standard Version (UASV)

[5] Have this mind[240] in yourselves which was also in Christ Jesus, [6] who, though he was in the form of God, did not count equality with God a thing to be grasped, [7] but **emptied himself**, taking the form of a servant, being made in the likeness of men. [8] Being found in appearance as a man, he humbled himself by becoming obedient to the point of death, even death on a cross.

Philippians 2:5-8 New American Standard Bible (NASB)

[5]Have this attitude in yourselves which was also in Christ Jesus, [6]who, although He existed in the form of God, did not regard equality with God a thing to be grasped, [7]but **emptied Himself**, taking the form of a bond-servant, and being made in the likeness of men. [8]Being found in appearance as a man, He humbled Himself by becoming obedient to the point of death, even death on a cross.

Looking at the King James Version, and our English mindset, how are we to understand that Jesus **made himself of no reputation?** It can give us the impression that he was simply attempting to avoid fame, to avoid a reputation. This is certainly not the case, and by exploring more than one translation, it can wake us up to a misunderstanding, or at least a

---

[239] Louw, J. P.: Semantics of the New Testament Greek. Atlanta, Georgia: Scholars Press, 1982, pp. 23-31.

[240] Lit *be thinking, mental attitude*

difference that needs to be investigated. While there seems to be no end to the line of new English translations, it must be said that there will always be a need for new translations. 'Why'? We may be asking. If we were to turn to the many translators in the field of Bible translation, they would offer at least three good reasons: **(1)** the manuscripts that have been discovered over the centuries are always being studied and better understood, and this increased knowledge may mean adjustments in the translation. **(2)** Our knowledge of the Bible languages just keeps improving over the years, and once again this can lead to more accurate translations. **(3)** Languages are living and growing and changing over time, altering the meaning of words, and in some cases, to the opposite. In 1611, "let" in "I let John go to school" meant "stop" or "restrain." However, it is not just the need to have something other than the King James Version.

What I recommend is that for the study of God's Word, use 2-3 very good literal translations, and 2-3 dynamic equivalents as a sort of quick commentary on Scripture. As to the literal translations, we would recommend the English Standard Version, 2001 (ESV), The Updated New American Standard Bible, 1995 (NASB), the American Standard Version, 1901 (ASV), the Christian Standard Bible, 2017 (CSB), especially the Updated American Standard Version (UASV).[241] As to the dynamic equivalent, we recommend the New Living Translation, 2007 (NLT), the Good News Bible, 2001 (GNB), and the Contemporary English Version, 1995 (CEV). However, the dynamic equivalent is not to be used as Bible translations, which they are not, but rather as mini commentaries.

The Root Fallacy

The basis of this fallacy is that I acquire my understanding of the Hebrew or Greek word by its root. The root of a word is the simplest possible form of a word, the smallest meaningful element of speech or writing. An English example for *runners* is *run*. This fallacy assumes that every word has a meaning that is derived from its shape or parts. It is often said that the person who has only learned enough Hebrew or Greek to be dangerous commits this mistake. However, once we read enough commentaries, we will find that the scholars commit this fallacy as well.

A verbal cognate is a noun that functions as the object of a verb that is from the same etymological root, as in "to dream a dream" or "to think a thought." The pastor regularly says that the verbal cognate of apostle

---

[241] http://www.uasvbible.org/

(apostolos) is "I send" (*apostellō*); therefore, the root meaning of "apostle" is "one who is sent", "send forth" or "send off." A leading Bible dictionary, Holman has it this way, "APOSTLE Derivation of the Greek word apostolos, one who is sent."[242] This meaning is established by breaking *apostellō* apart, *apo* + *stellō*. It is likely that 'sent out' is an aspect of apostolos (apostle), it is not the primary meaning. The word *apostolos* primarily means 'a special messenger, a representative,' with the idea of being sent out as an implication from the background. (Louw 1982, 27-28)

This is not how language works. If we turn to an English example, it may clear things up for us. Say 2,000 year from now; a linguist is trying to discover the meaning of our English word "pineapple." He discovers that the document that he is holding was written in a part of the United States that had a lot of pine trees, with many apple tree orchard nearby. The linguist suggests to his colleagues that the scientists back in the 20th and 21st century must have combined the genetics of these two fruits to produce a pineapple tree. The parts of a word do not determine its meaning. Just because an ice cream truck brings us ice cream, are we to expect that a fire truck brings us fire? Does the word "parkway" mean a large parking lot? No. Does a "driveway" infer that it is a place for driving a vehicle? What would linguistic scholars 2,000 years from now think of our English language?

Having made a case for the above, one must say there are no absolutes, as some words carry a meaning based on their parts that make them up. The way we should hold this within our thinking is this way, 'largely, words do not derive their meaning from their parts, their internal structure. However, at times, this can be the case. Yet, the key is what did that word mean to that culture, those people at that time, how was it commonly used, and in what context was it used?' An example of this is the fact that at times a preposition was added in the form of a word for intensification purposes. An example would be *gnosis*, which is the Greek word for "knowledge," with the preposition *epi* (meaning "additional") added to the front, giving us *epignosis*, meaning *complete*, *accurate* or *full* knowledge.

---

[242] Chad Brand, Charles Draper, Archie England et al., *Holman Illustrated Bible Dictionary* (Nashville, TN: Holman Bible Publishers, 2003), 88.

The Time Frame fallacy

This fallacy is the act of taking the meaning of a word hundreds of years before or after the time of the writing and applying that meaning to the word under consideration, to get the meaning we want. For example, the teacher may take the meaning of the Greek word *hades*, as it was understood in classical Greek ("netherworld," hundreds of years before) and apply it to the New Testament meaning of *hades* (grave).

The apostle Paul tells us in Romans 1:16 that the 'gospel is God's **power** for salvation. The Greek word for the English "power" is *dynamis*, which means "power, might, strength, and force." However, the pastor will say that *dynamis* is where we get our English word *dynamite* from. Then he will go on to say that 'the gospel is the *dynamite* of God.' We the reader can obviously see the fallacy in this from a timeframe standpoint. The apostle Paul was not aware of the word dynamite and the meaning it conveys is not what was going through his mind as he penned the word dynamis. What word pictures do us the reader draw at the idea of dynamite? It is used to blow things up, to destroy things, and terrorists use it. There is really nothing about the word that can be read into what Paul meant by dynamis.

> To say that the gospel is "power" is to acknowledge the dynamic quality of the message. In the proclamation of the gospel God is actively at work in reaching out to the hearts of people. The gospel is God telling of his love to wayward people. It is not a lifeless message but a vibrant encounter for everyone who responds in faith. Much religious discourse is little more than words and ideas about religious subjects. Not so the gospel. The gospel is God at work. He lives and breathes through the declaration of his redemptive love for people. To really hear the gospel is to experience the presence of God.[243]

The Overload Fallacy

As we have discussed, every word has more than one meaning, and the context that determines that meaning. Those who are guilty of this fallacy take a word that has multiple meanings and attempts to incorporate all of those meanings into this one word. The word has one meaning in its context, that the author intended by its use in that context

---

[243] Robert H. Mounce, vol. 27, *Romans*, electronic ed., Logos Library System; The New American Commentary (Nashville: Broadman & Holman Publishers, 2001), 70.

he placed it in, at the time and place of the writing. Worse still, the person chooses the meaning that he likes and applies that to the word, regardless of its context.

Concordance: While the lexicon will give us the range of meaning, another approach is how a writer uses a word. We may look up a word that Paul has used and see where he has used it elsewhere. It is best if it is in the subject matter that we are dealing with, or at least in the same book. However, one could go to the book of Romans to consider a word in Galatians, if it is dealing with the same subject matter. One may even consider the New Testament as a whole, or even the Septuagint (The Greek Old Testament). However, a word of caution, the further removed that we get from the writer and the area our word is found in, the more danger we are in, coming away with the wrong meaning. There is no reason to believe that just because Paul and Peter used the same word that they must have intended the same meaning by its use.

The Importance of Context

The immediate context is the words, phrases, or passages that come before and after a particular word or passage in the Bible and help to explain its full meaning. Of course, the larger context would be the section of Scripture that your word or verse is in, as well as the chapter, the book, the Old or New Testament, or the Bible as a whole.

Preunderstanding is all the knowledge and understanding that we possess before we begin a study session. Thus, we will need to allow the important preunderstanding to affect us (e.g., Bible is inerrant). However, we are not to be biased by the other portions. Therefore, we need to take those unimportant portions and place them on a lower priority or give it less prominence. Preunderstanding is everything that we are, and can be broken down into four categories, as discussed by Ferguson, *Biblical Hermeneutics.*

(1) **Information:** This is the information, right or wrong, that we may possess before we begin reading about the subject.

(2) **Attitude:** This is the mindset that we bring to the study: such as prejudice, bias, or predisposition (i.e., a favorable attitude toward somebody or something, or an inclination to do something).

(3) **Idealism:** This is our worldview of everything, our perspective in life, a particular evaluation of a situation or facts, especially from our point of view.

(4) **Methodology**: This is our way of expressing ourselves on a given subject. In other words, we may at times, explain things by way of science, history, or explaining our conclusions based on our observation.

This preunderstanding of things belongs to all of us, and there is no way to dislodge ourselves from it, the best we can hope for is to garner a measure of control over its influence on us, as we go about the task of Biblical interpretation. An example would be point number (3), idealism. If we are a scientific-minded individual, we may start to set aside some of the supernatural acts of God and his human workers that he gave power and authority, as being impossible according to modern science. Therefore, we start to rationalize how it may have come about according to our understanding of science.

A **preconception** is an idea that we have in advance, and can be based on little or no information, reflecting bias. For example, one may approach the study of hellfire, a teaching of eternal torment for the damned, one that he has held from childhood, because of going to church with his grandmother. In his research, he will subconsciously or even willfully accept information that supports his preconception, but reject or ignore other information that does not support it. However, there are presuppositions that a Christian will want to accept as true:

(1) The Word of God is inspired and fully inerrant,

(2) The Bible is authoritative and true,

(3) The Bible is full of diverse material (but unified),

(4) The Bible has one meaning that the reader must discover, and

(5) Those meanings have many implications, and so on.

How can we know if our preunderstanding is at odds with Scripture? It would be advisable for us to pray from this day forward that God may give us understanding, that he helps us to place our preunderstanding on a lower priority or give it less prominence until He helps us to uncover the truth of it or to set it aside as untrue. From then on, work in harmony with that prayer, to establish if that preunderstanding is in harmony with the biblical data.

As we have discussed at length, every word has a range of meaning, and it is the context that will determine what was meant. For example:

2 Timothy 3:17 King James Version (KJV)

The word of God was given so [17] that the man of God may be **perfect**, thoroughly furnished unto all good works.

What is meant by "perfect" in the KJV? Are we to expect that by following the Word of God, we will become sinless? Will we become incapable of erring? While "perfect" is an option in the range of meaning, it a poor choice. Before we visit other translations, let us attempt to work it out by looking at the context.

2 Timothy 3:16-17 King James Version (KJV)

[16]All scripture is given by inspiration of God, and is **profitable for doctrine**, for **reproof**, for **correction**, for **instruction** in righteousness: [17]That the man of God may be perfect, **thoroughly furnished unto all good works.**

By looking at what comes before and after our word "perfect," it is not talking about becoming sinless. It is saying that the Bible is beneficial in helping us live an **equipped, competent, adequate,** or **complete** godly life by establishing true doctrine and teaching others, by evaluating ourselves against Scripture in a reproof or corrective way, which will instruct us in the right way to walk with God. Therefore, as you can see in this case, the context alone, corrected any possible misunderstandings. If we visit other translations, we will discern this as well: "that the man of God may be **competent**" (ESV), "that the servant of God may be **thoroughly equipped**" (NIV), "so that the man of God may be **adequate**" (NASB), or "so that the man of God may be **complete**." (HCSB)

Notice the meaning of our word is easily established by a careful observation of what surrounds it. The entire Bible is open to this form of intensive observation. The context will always disclose the correct meaning.

John was in the backyard working on his car when he yelled at his wife in the house, 'Lisa, can you give me a hand for a second?' While it may seem silly to the English reader, one learning English may ask two questions, (1) 'surely she is not going to cut off her hand and give it to him?' (2) 'Who would need help on something for a second; it is such a short period of time?' Give me a *hand* also means help with something, and a *second* can mean various lengths of time in American English. Actually, it is not that "hand" means "help," or that "second" means longer than a second does. The technical term for this is **metonymy**, which is like an extension of that meaning, a word or phrase used in a figure of speech in which an attribute of something is used to stand for the thing itself. My asking a server at a restaurant for a cup of mud is the same as asking for a cup of coffee and is metonymy.[244]

Again, no two languages are exactly equivalent in grammar, vocabulary, and sentence structure.

Ephesians 4:14 American Standard Version (ASV)

[14] As a result, we are no longer to be children, tossed here and there by waves and carried about by every wind of doctrine, by the trickery [lit., dice playing] of men, by craftiness in deceitful scheming

The Greek word *kybeia* that is usually rendered "craftiness" or "trickery," is literally "dice-playing," which refers to the practice cheating others when playing dice. If it was rendered literally, "carried about by every wind of doctrine, by the trickery dice-playing of men," the meaning would be lost. Therefore, the meaning of what is meant by the 'dice playing' must be the translator's choice.

Romans 12:11 English Standard Version (ESV)

[11] Do not be slothful in zeal, be fervent [lit., boiling] in spirit, serve the Lord.

When Paul wrote the Romans, he used the Greek word *zeontes*, which literally means "boil," "seethe," or "fiery hot." Some very serious Bible students may pick up on the thought of "boiling in spirit," as being "fervent in spirit," or better "aglow with the spirit," or "keep your spiritual fervor." Therefore, for the sake of making sense, it is best to take the literal "boiling in spirit", determine what is meant by those words, "keep your spiritual fervor", and render it thus.

Matthew 5:3 New International Version (NIV)

[3] "Blessed are the poor in spirit, for theirs is the kingdom of heaven.

Matthew 5:3 (GOD'S WORD Translation)

[3]"Blessed are those who [are poor in spirit] recognize they are spiritually helpless. The kingdom of heaven belongs to them.

This one is really a tough call. The phrase "poor in spirit" carries so much history, and has been written as to what it means, for almost 2,000 years that, even the dynamic equivalent translations are unwilling to translate its meaning, not its words. Personally, this writer is in favor of

---

[244] In Australia, we could ask for "bangers and mash", and expect to receive a plate containing two or three sausages, some mashed potato, and some peas and gravy.

the literal translation of "poor in spirit." Those who claim to be literal translators, should not back away because "poor in spirit" is ambiguous, and there are a variety of interpretations. The above dynamic equivalent translation, God's Word, has come closest to what was meant. Actually, "poor" is even somewhat of an interpretation, because the Greek word *ptōchoi* means "beggar." Therefore, "poor in spirit" is an interpretation of "beggar in spirit." The extended interpretation is that the "beggar/poor in spirit" is aware of his or her spiritual needs as if a beggar or the poor would be aware of their physical needs.

2 Samuel 8:3 Christian Standard Bible (CSB)

³ David also defeated Hadadezer son of Rehob, king of Zobah, when he went to restore his control [hand] at the Euphrates River.

The Hebrew (*yāḏ*) literally reads, "as he went to restore his *hand* at the River." (italics mine). **Looking at the literal and semi-literal translations,** the ESV reads "restore his *power,*" the CSB "restore his *control,*" the NASB reads "restore his *rule,*" the UASV reads "restore his *authority,*" the ASV reads "recover his *dominion,*" and the LEB reads "restore his *monument.*" **Looking at the dynamic equivalent,** interpretative translations, the NLT reads, "to strengthen his *control,*" the CEV reads "to build a *monument,*" the ERV reads "to set up a *monument,*" the WYC reads "to recover his *land,*" and the NIRV reads "to repair his monument."

1 Kings 10:13 English Standard Version (ESV)

¹³And King Solomon gave to the queen of Sheba all that she desired, whatever she asked besides what was given her by the bounty [hand] of King Solomon. So she turned and went back to her own land with her servants.

Proverbs 18:21 English Standard Version (ESV)

²¹ Death and life are in the power [hand] of the tongue, and those who love it will eat its fruits.

The English word "hand" has no meaning outside of its context. It could mean, "end of arm," "pointer on a clock," "player's cards," "round in a card game," "part in doing something," "round of applause," "member of a ship's crew," or "worker." The Hebrew word "yad," which means "hand," has many meanings as well, depending on the context, as it can mean "control," "bounty," or "power." This one word is translated in more than forty different ways in some translations. Let us look at some English sentences, to see the literal way of using hand, and then add what it means, as a new sentence.

- Please give a big *hand* to our next contestant. Please give a big *applause* for our next contestant.

- Our future is in our own *hands*. Our future is in our own *power*. Our future is in our own *possession*.

- Attention, all *hands*! Attention, all *ship's crew*!

- She has a good *hand* for gardening. She has a good *ability* or *skill* for gardening.

- Please give me a hand; I need some help.

- The copperplate writing was beautifully written; she has a nice hand.

At times, even a literal translation committee will not render a word the same every time it occurs, because the sense is not the same every time. The only problem we have is that the reader must now be dependent on the judgment of the translator to select the right word(s) that reflect the meaning of the original language word accurately and understandably. Let us look at the above texts from the Hebrew Old Testament again, this time doing what we did with the English word "hand" in the above. It is debatable if any of these verses really needed to be more explicit, by giving the meaning in the translation, as opposed to the word itself.

who went to restore his *hand* at the Euphrates River – who went to restore his control at the Euphrates River

she asked besides what was given her by the *hand* of King Solomon - she asked besides what was given her by the *bounty* of King Solomon

Death and life are in the *hand* of the tongue - Death and life are in the power of the tongue

Examples of What Can Be Learned from Word Study

Accurate Knowledge: (Gr. *Epignosis*) A strengthened or intensified form of *gnosis* (*epi*, meaning "additional"), meaning, "true," "real," "full," "complete" or "accurate," depending upon the context. Paul and Peter alone use *epignosis*.–Rom. 1:28; Eph. 1:17; Php 1:9; Col. 1:9-10; 1 Tim 2:4.

Adoption: (Gr. *huiothesia*) The Greek noun is a legal term that literally means "adoption as son," which means to take or accept a son or daughter who is not naturally such by relationship, including complete inheritance rights. The apostle Paul mentions adoption several times in reference to those with a new status as called and chosen by God. These ones were born as offspring of the imperfect Adam, were formerly in slavery to sin. Through purchase by means of Jesus' life as a ransom, many have received the adoption as sons and daughters becoming heirs with the only-begotten Son of God, Jesus Christ.–Rom. 8:15, 23; 9:4; Gal. 4:5; Eph. 1:5.

Antichrist: (Gr. *antichristos*) The term "Antichrist," occurs in the NT five times. From those five times, we gather this entity is "against" (i.e. denies Christ) or "instead of" (i.e., false Christs) Jesus Christ. There are *many antichrists* that began back in the apostle John's day and will continue up unto Jesus' second coming. (1 John 2:18) The antichrist is referred to as a number of individuals taken together, i.e., collectively. (2 John 1;7) Persons who deny Jesus Christ are the antichrist. (1 John 2:22) All who deny the divinity of Jesus Christ as the One and Only Son of God is the antichrist. (1 John 2:22; John 10:36; Lu 9:35) Some antichrists are apostates, one who left the faith and are now in opposition to the truth. (1 John 2:18-19) Those who oppose the true followers of Jesus are the antichrist. (John 15:20-21) Individuals or nations that oppose Jesus or try to supplant his kingly authority are antichrists.–Ps. 2:2; Matt. 24:24; Rev. 17:3, 12-14; 19:11-21.

Apostasy: (Gr. *apostasia*) The term literally means "to stand away from" and is used to refer to ones who 'stand away from the truth.' It is abandonment, a rebellion, an apostasy, a refusal to accept or acknowledge true worship. In Scripture, this is used primarily concerning the one who rises up in defiance of the only true God and his people, working in opposition to the truth.–Ac 21:21; 2 Thess. 2:3.

Archangel: (Gr. *archangelos*) Michael is the only spirit named as an archangel in the Bible. Nevertheless, some Bible scholars believe that 'it is possible that there are other' archangels. However, the prefix "arch," meaning "chief" or "principal," indicates that there is only one archangel, the chief angel. Yes, Gabriel is very powerful, but no Scripture ever refers to him as an archangel. If there were multiple archangels, how could they even be described as an arch (chief or principal) angel? In the Scriptures, "archangel" is never found in the plural. Clearly, Michael is the only archangel and as the highest-ranking angel, like the highest-ranking general in the army, Michael stands directly under the authority of God, as he commands the other angels, including Gabriel, according to the

Father's will and purposes. Michael, the Archangel, whose name means, "Who is like God?"); he disputed with Satan over Moses body. (Jude 9) Michael with Gabriel stood guard over the sons of Israel and fought for Israel against demons. (Dan. 10:13, 21) He cast Satan and the demons out of heaven. (Rev. 12:7-9) He will defeat the kings of the earth and their armies at Armageddon, and he will be the one given the privilege of abyssing Satan, the archenemy of God.–Rev. 18:1-2; 19:11-21.

Believe, faith, Trust in: (Gr. *pisteuo*) If *pisteuo* is followed by the Greek preposition *eis*, ("into, in, among," accusative case), it is generally rendered "trusting in" or "trust in." (John 3:16, 36; 12:36; 14:1) The grammatical construction of the Greek verb *pisteuo* "believe" followed by the Greek preposition *eis* "into" in the accusative gives us the sense of having faith into Jesus, putting faith in, trusting in Jesus.–Matt. 21:25, 32; 27:42; John 1:7, 12; 2:23–24; 3:15-16, 36; 6:47; 11:25; 12:36; 14:1; 20:31; Acts 16:31; Rom. 4:3.

Blameless: (Heb. *tam, tamim;* Gr. *amomos, amometos*) means, "perfect, blameless, sincerity, entire, whole, complete, and full." Of course, Noah, Jacob, and Job were not literally perfect. When used of imperfect humans, the terms are relative, not absolute. However, if we are *fully* committed to following, a life course based on God's will and purposes, fully living by his laws, repent when we fall short, he will credit us righteousness.–Gen. 6:6; 25:27; Job 9:20-22l Ps. 119:1; Pro. 11:20; Phil 2:15; 1 Thess. 5:23.

Book of Life: (Gr. *biblos tēs zōēs*) In biblical times, cities had a register of names for the citizens living there. (See Ps. 69:28; Isa. 4:3) God, figuratively speaking, has been writing names in the "book of life" "from the foundation of the world." (Rev. 17:8) Jesus Christ talked about Abel as living "from the foundation of the world," this would suggest that we are talking about the world of ransomable humankind after the fall. (Lu 11:48-51) Clearly, Abel was the first person to have his name written in the "book of life." The individuals who have their names written in the "book of Life" do not mean they are predestined to eternal life. This is evident from the fact that they can be 'blotted out' of the "book of life." (Ex 32:32-33; Rev. 3:5) Jesus ransom sacrifice alone gets one written in the "book of life," if they accept the Son of God. However, it is remaining faith to God that keeps them from being 'blotted' out of the "book of life." (Phil. 2:12; Heb. 10:26-27; Jam. 2:14-26) It is only by remaining faithful until the end that one can be retained permanently in the "book of life."–Matt. 214:13; Phil. 4:3; Rev. 20:15.

Born Again, Born of God, Born of the Spirit, Regeneration (Rebirth): (Gr. *gennaō anōthen*; *gennaō theos*; *gennaō pneuma*; *palingenesia*) This regeneration is the Holy Spirit working in his life, giving him a new nature, who repents and accepts Christ, placing him on the path to salvation. By taking in this knowledge of God's Word, we will be altering our way of thinking, which will affect our emotions and behavior, as well as our lives now and for eternity. This Word will influence our minds, making corrections in the way we think. If we are to have the Holy Spirit controlling our lives, we must 'renew our mind' (Rom. 12:2) "which is being renewed in knowledge" (Col. 3:10) of God and his will and purposes. (Matt 7:21-23; See Pro 2:1-6) All of this boils down to each individual Christian digging into the Scriptures in a meditative way, so he can 'discover the knowledge of God, receiving wisdom; from God's mouth, as well as knowledge and understanding.' (Pro. 2:5-6) As he acquires the mind that is inundated with the Word of God, he must also "be doers of the Word."–John 3:3; 6-7; 2 Cor. 5:17; Titus 3:5; Jam. 1:22-25.

Bread of Life: (Gr. *artos zōēs*) It was for "the life of the world," of redeemable humankind that Jesus gave his flesh. And anyone of the world of humankind who eats symbolically of that "bread of life" (spiritual nourishment), by trusting in the redeeming power of Jesus' sacrifice, may "enter through the narrow gate. For the gate is small and the way is narrow that leads to life, and there are few who find it," (Matt 7:13-14) i.e. the path to eternal life.–John 6:35, 48.

Drift Away: (Gr. *pararreō*) The sense of *pararreō* is to disbelieve or drift away gradually or slowly from what one had formerly known to be true. It is like being carried away by water current. These Hebrew Christians because of their daily harassment from the Jews in and around Jerusalem, living in the place where they can see what we now call the eighth wonder of the world, the Jewish temple, were gradually giving up their belief in the truth.–Heb. 2:1.

Fall Away, Forsake, or Turn Away: (Gr. *parapiptō*) The sense of *parapiptō* is to fall away or forsake the truth.–Heb. 6:6.

Feel regret over: (Heb. *nacham*) The Hebrew word *nacham* translated "be sorry," "repent," "regret," "be comforted, "comfort," "reconsider" and "change one's mind" can pertain to a change of attitude or intention. God is perfect and therefore does not make mistakes in his dealings with his creation. However, he can have a change of attitude or intention as regards how humans react to his warnings. God can go from the Creator of humans to that of a destroyer of them because of his unrepentant wickedness and failure to heed his warnings. On the other hand, if they repent and turn from their wicked ways, he can be compassionate and merciful, slow to anger, and abounding in loyal love; and he will "reconsider" the calamity that he may have intended.–Genesis 6:6; Exodus 32:14; Joel 2:13.

Gehenna: (Gr. *geenna*) (Gehenna) occurs 12 times and is the Greek name for the valley of Hinnom, southwest of Jerusalem (Jer. 7:31), where the horrendous worship of Moloch took place, and it was prophetically said that where dead bodies would be thrown. (Jer. 7:32; 19:6) It was an incinerator where trash and dead bodies were destroyed, not a place to be burned alive or tormented. Jesus and his disciples used Gehenna to symbolize eternal destruction, annihilation, or the "second death," an eternal punishment of death.

Hades: (*hades*) Hades is the standard transliteration into English of the corresponding Greek word haides, which occurs ten times in the UASV. (Matt. 11:23; 16:18; Lu 10:15; 16:23; Ac 2:27, 31; Rev. 1:18; 6:8; 20:13, 14.) It has the underlying meaning of 'a place of the dead, where they are conscious of nothing, awaiting a resurrection, for both the righteous and the unrighteous.' (John 5:28-29; Acts 24:15) It corresponds to "Sheol" in the OT. It does not involve torment and punishment.

Hearing, Dull of: (Gr. *nōthros tais akoais*) This is an idiom, which literally means that one has 'lazy ears.' In other words, they are slow to learn, to understand, to react, lacking intellectual perception, with the implication that this is so because they are lazy. Have we become lethargic in the truth, to the point of having lazy ears? Are we slow to learn, to understand, to react, lacking intellectual perception?–Heb. 5:11.

Heart, Evil and Unbelieving: (Gr. *kardia ponēra apistias*) The sense of *kardia* is the inner person, the person's thoughts (mind), volition (decisions, choices, desires), emotions, and knowledge of right and wrong, i.e., the conscience. The sense of *ponēra* is evil, wicked, morally bad or wrong. The sense of *apistias* is unbelief. In the context of the book of Hebrews, it is the trait of not trusting in or relying on God and his Word. Paul warned the Hebrew Christians about developing an evil, unbelieving heart. We cannot remain "pure in heart" if we develop a heart "lacking faith."–Heb. 3:12.

Pay Attention: (Gr. *prosechō*) The sense of *prosechō* is to give heed or the need to pay attention. One must hold more firmly to what they believe, or what they have known to be true. Paul is telling these Hebrew Christians, who no longer have the visual aids like the temple, or the

Jewish high priest, you need to hold more firmly to the things that you have heard.–Heb.2:1.

Perfect; Perfection: (Heb. *tāmîm*; Gr. teleiŌsis; teleios) The terms can be used in an absolute sense (God is perfect); however, they are not always used in such a way when it comes to humans after the fall (Matt. 5:48). In the Scripture "perfect" and "Perfection" are often used in a relative sense. The Hebrew and Greek Bible words translated "perfect" regularly mean "complete," "mature," "full-gown," "adult," or "faultless" according to standards set by the Word of God. Imperfect humans at this time fall short of the perfection of Adam and Eve prior to the fall. However, God makes allowances for this falling short and better still has offered His Son as a Ransom to cover these human weaknesses. Being "perfect" at this time means that we are to remain clean spiritually, morally, mentally, and physically, and if we fall short, we repent and our shortcomings are covered by the ransom sacrifice of Christ.–Matt 5:48; Phil. 3:15; Matt 20:28; Rom. 5:12-21; 1 John 2:1.

Question, Ask Question: (*eperotao*; *erotao*) The Greek word *eperotao*, which means to ask, to question, to demand of, for "questioning" was far more than the Greek word *erotao*, which meant to ask, to request, to entreat, such as a boy's inquisitiveness. *Eperotao* refer to questioning, which one might hear in a judicial hearing, such as a scrutiny, inquiry, counter questioning, even probing question, a sort of interrogation.

Recreation: (Gr., *palingenesiai*) (*palin*, "again," plus *genao*, "to give birth") This is a period in which the already existing world (earth) and soul (person) begins anew, starting over, being refashioned into God's originally intended purpose. This is a renewal of the world during the second coming of Christ, after abyssing Satan and the demons, bringing in a new age that will restore the earth to its original purpose.–Dan. 7:13-14; Rev. 3:21; 20:1-6.

Regeneration (Rebirth), Born Again, Born of God, Born of the Spirit: (Gr. palingenesiai; gennaō *anōthen*; *gennaō theos*; *gennaō pneuma*) This regeneration is the Holy Spirit working in his life, giving him a new nature, who repents and accepts Christ, placing him on the path to salvation. By taking in this knowledge of God's Word, we will be altering our way of thinking, which will affect our emotions and behavior, as well as our lives now and for eternity. This Word will influence our minds, making corrections in the way we think. If we are to have the Holy Spirit controlling our lives, we must 'renew our mind' (Rom. 12:2) "which is being renewed in knowledge" (Col. 3:10) of God and his will and purposes. (Matt 7:21-23; See Pro 2:1-6) All of this boils down to each individual Christian digging into the Scriptures in a meditative way, so he can 'discover the knowledge of God, receiving wisdom; from God's mouth, as well as knowledge and understanding.' (Pro. 2:5-6) As he acquires the mind that is inundated with the Word of God, he must also "be doers of the Word."–John 3:3; 6-7; 2 Corinthians 5:17; Titus 3:5; James 1:22-25.

Sheol: (Heb. *sheol*) Sheol occurs sixty-six times in the UASV. The Greek Septuagint renders Sheol as Hades. It has the underlying meaning of 'a place of the dead, where they are conscious of nothing, awaiting a resurrection, for both the righteous and the unrighteous.' (Gen. 37:35; Psa. 16:10; Ac 2:31; John 5:28-29; Acts 24:15) It corresponds to "Hades" in the NT. It does not involve torment and punishment.

Sin: (Heb. *chattath*; Gr. *hamartia*) Any spoken word (Job 2:10; Ps 39:1), wrong action (Lev. 20:20; 2 Cor. 12:21) or failing to act when one should have (Num. 9:13; Jam. 4:17), in mind and heart (Prov. 21:4; Rom. 3:9-18; 2 Pet 2:12-15) that is contrary to God's personality, ways, will and purposes, standards, as set out in the Scriptures. It is also a major sin to lack faith in God, doubting in mind and heart, even subtly in our actions, that he has the ability to carry out his will and purposes. (Heb. 3:12-13, 18-19). It is commonly referred to as missing the mark of perfection.

- **Error:** (Heb., *'āwōn*; Gr. *anomia, paranomia*) The Hebrew word *awon* essentially relates to erring, acting illegally or wrongly. This aspect of sin refers to committing a perverseness, wrongness, lawlessness, law breaking, which can also include the rejection of the sovereignty of God. It also focuses on the liability or guilt of one's wicked, wrongful act. This error may be deliberate or accidental; either willful deviation of what is right or unknowingly making a mistake. (Lev. 4:13-35; 5:1-6, 14-19; Num. 15:22-29; Ps 19:12, 13) Of course, if it is intentional; then, the consequence is far more serious. (Num. 15:30-31) Error is in opposition to the truth, and those willfully sinning corrupt the truth, a course that only brings forth flagrant sin. (Isa 5:18-23) We can be hardened by the deceitfulness of sin.–Ex 9:27, 34-35; Heb. 3:13-15.

- **Transgression:** (Heb. *'avar*; Gr. *parabasis*) Sin can take the form of a "transgression." This is an overstepping, namely, to exceed a moral limit or boundary. Biblically speaking, this would be crossing the line and saying, feeling, thinking or doing something that is contrary to God's personality, standards, ways, will and purposes, as set out in the Scriptures. It is breaking God's moral law.–Num. 14:41; Deut. 17:2, 3; Josh. 7:11, 15; 1 Sam 15:24; Isa 24:5; Jer. 34:18; Rom. 2:23; 4:15; 5:14; Gal. 3:19; 1 Tim. 2:14; Heb. 2:2; 9:15+.

- **Trespass:** (Gr. *paraptōma*) This is a sin that can come in the way of some desire (lusting), some thinking (entertaining a wrongdoing) or some action (carrying out one's desires or thoughts that he or she has been entertaining) that is beyond or overstepping God's righteous standards, as set out in the Scriptures. It is falling or making a false step as opposed to standing or walking upright in harmony with the righteous requirements of God.–Matt. 6:14; Mark 11:25; Rom. 4:25; 5:15-20; 11:11; 2 Cor. 5:19; Gal. 6:1; Eph. 1:7; 2:1, 5; Col 2:13.

- **Sinner:** (Gr. *hamartōlos*) In the Scriptures "sinners" is generally used in a more specific way, that is, referring to those willfully living in sin, practicing sin, or have a reputation of sinning.–Matt. 9:10; Mark 2:15; Luke 5:30; 7:37-39; John 9:16; Rom. 3:7; Gal. 2:15; 1 Tim. 1:15; Heb. 7:26; Jam. 4:8; 1 Pet 4:18; Jude 1:15.

- **Sensuality, Debauchery, Promiscuity, Licentiousness, Lewdness:** (Gr. *aselgeia*) This is behavior that is completely lacking in moral restraint, indulgence in sensual pleasure, driven by aggressive and selfish desires, unchecked by morality, especially in sexual matters.–Mark 7:22; Rom. 13:13; 2 Cor. 12:21; Gal. 5:19; Eph. 4:19; 1 Pet. 4:3; 2 Pet. 2:2, 7, 18; Jude 4+.

- **Sexual Immorality:** (Heb. *zanah*; Gr. *porneia*) A general term for immoral sexual acts of any kind: such as adultery, prostitution, sexual relations between people not married to each other, homosexuality, and bestiality.–Num. 25:1; Deut. 22:21; Matt. 5:32; 1 Cor. 5:1.

- **Shameful Behavior:** (*zimmā(h)*) This is wickedness, shameful behavior or conduct that is lewd, shameless regarding sexual behavior. (Lev. 18:17; 19:29; 20:14; Judges 20:6; Job 31:11; Jer. 13:27; Eze. 16:27) It can also refer to the evil thought process that one goes through in plotting their wickedness. (Ps 26:10; 119:150; Pro. 10:23; 21:27; 24:9; Isa 32:7; Hos

6:9+) Finally, it can be the plans that results from thinking person's evil desires.–Job 17:11.

Sin, Hardened by Deceitfulness of: (Gr. *sklērynthē apatē hamartias*) The sense of *sklērynthē* is stubborn or to be hardened. One is being stubborn and obstinate when it comes to the truth. The sense of *apatē* is deception. A person causes another to believe something that is not true by misleading or deceptive views. The sense of *hamartias* is sin, failure or falling short. *Hamartia* is anything that is not in harmony with or contrary to God's personality, standards, ways, and will. This can be in word, deed, or failing to do what should be done, or in mind or heart attitude.–Heb. 3:13.

Sober Minded: (Gr. *nepho*) This denotes being sound in mind, to be in control of one's thought processes and thus not be in danger of irrational thinking, 'to be sober-minded, to be well composed in mind.'–1 Thessalonians 5:6, 8; 2 Timothy 4:5; 1 Peter 1:13; 4:7; 5:8.

Sound in Mind: (Gr. *sophroneo*) This means to be of sound mind or in one's right mind, i.e., to have understanding about practical matters and thus be able to act sensibly, 'to have sound judgment, to be sensible, to use good sense, sound judgment.'–Acts 26:25; Romans 12:3; 2 Timothy 1:7; Titus 2:6; 1 Peter 4:7.

Stumble, fall away, to be offended: (Gr. *skandalizomai*) In Greek, "stumbling block" (*skandalon*) was originally a device or trap, which contained bait, to ensnare or catch something alive. (1 John 2:10) It is used in the Scriptures as a trap, obstacle, or snare that stumbles one into sinning. (Rom. 11:9; Matt. 13:41) It can also be used as an obstacle that causes offense, resulting in opposition. (1 Cor. 1:23; Gal. 5:11) The Greek, (*skandalizomai*) refers to one who ceases to believe because of tribulation. (Matt. 13:21) It can also refer to one who is spiritually weak, immature in the faith, resulting in their falling into sin. (2 Cor. 11:29) In addition, it can refer to one who takes offense to some action. (Matt. 15:12) It can refer to one who causes another no longer to believe (John 6:61) It can also refer to something or someone that causes another to sin because they are spiritually weak or immature in the faith. (Matt. 5:29; Rom. 14:21) It can refer to another who is angered or shocked by something or someone, which could result in their sinning.–Matt. 17:27; John 6:61.

Thinking Ability: (Heb. *mezimmah*) In the evil sense, this can mean wicked plans, evil ideas, schemes, and devices. In the favorable sense, it can mean shrewdness, perceptiveness, discretion, and prudence. In the favorable sense, it is the ability to judge wisely and objectively. *Mezimmah*, therefore, the human mind and thoughts can be used for an admirable and upright end, or for evil purposes.–Ps 10:2; Pro. 1:4; 2:10-12; 5:1-2.

Studying The Bible One Phrase at a Time

A phrase is a string of words that form a grammatical unit, usually within a clause or sentence. A phrase is a small group of words that adds meaning to a sentence. A phrase is not a sentence because it is not a complete idea with a subject, verb and a predicate. This is a brief string of words that encapsulates an aspect of the whole of the author meant to convey. Look at the phrases within just one small verse (Matt 24:14): "And this gospel of the kingdom will be proclaimed in all the inhabited earth as a testimony to all the nations, and then the end will come."

- This gospel

- Of the Kingdom

- Will be proclaimed

- In all the inhabited earth

- As a testimony

- To all nations

- Then the end

- Will come

Let work through just one verse in the NT in the book of James by Jesus' half-brother. We will not go into the great detail that could be possible but will offer enough so the reader can see how to study the Bible word-by-word and phrase-by-phrase. So that the reader can see the importance of deeper Bible study.

Deeper study is no guarantee that mature faith will result, but shallow study guarantees that immaturity continues.—Dr. Lee M. Fields.

James 1:22 Updated American Standard Version (UASV)

[22] But be doers of the word, and not hearers only, deceiving yourselves.

be doers of the word

Clearly, the "word" here is the Word of God. However, what does James mean by "doers"? The Greek (*poiētēs*) behind our English word "doers" has the sense of one who is an obeyer of something or someone. The apostle Paul writes to the Christians in Rome, "For it is not the hearers of the law who are righteous before God, but the doers (*poiētēs*) of the law who will be justified." (Rom. 2:13) So, James expects all Christians to hear what the word says, to then study that word, meditating on it, pondering what the author meant, and then fully applying it in his or her lives.

It should be made plain that neither Paul nor James are against the hearing of the word or the law, for both know, and Paul said, "How then will they call on him in whom they have not believed? And how are they to believe in him of whom they **have never heard**? And **how will they hear** without someone to preach?"–Romans 10:14.

As Christians, we need to *be doers of the word* (applying it) in our daily lives, which evidences that we, in fact, believe it to be *the* true *word* of God. We need to have a deeper knowledge of *the word* so that we have a biblical mindset, which will guide us in the way that we need to go. Jesus said, "happy are those **hearing** the word of God and **keeping** it!"–Luke 11:28.

not hearers only

By talking about "doers" we have had to discuss "hearers" as well. Nevertheless, let us look up the original language word (*akroatēs*), which has the sense of one who listens attentively, an active listener. For James, you have to hear the word, correctly understand the word before you can be a "doer" or an obeyer of the word. What James and Paul **do not want** is "hearers only." One who hears the word but then never moves on to study, meditate, and ponder, to get a correct understanding, let alone obeying the word.

Let us keep in mind, one who listens to God's Word with intent to follow through are righteous in God's eyes, and most certainly the ones who follow through to become doers are righteous in the eyes of God. However, the "hears only" are not declared righteous by God. Many Jewish people had gone to the synagogue in the decades leading up to the Messiah and had heard the Scriptures read again and again but they still ended up rejecting the Messiah when he arrived.

If we are going to be genuine hearers, we need to have faith in what we hear, which means that we study the word, meditate and ponder its meaning, to the point where our faith moves us to act on it, becoming a doer of the word. The apostle Paul said, "So faith comes from hearing." (Rom. 10:17) We must first hear what the word says. Then, we must study that word, meditate on it, ponder its meaning, if it is going to convict our hearts because we believe it to be reliable, moving us to become doers of the word.

Listen to the words of the apostle Paul about the Beroeans. "The brothers immediately sent Paul and Silas away by night to Berea, and when they arrived, they went into the synagogue of the Jews. Now, these were more noble-minded than those in Thessalonica, who **received the word with all eagerness,** examining the Scriptures daily to see whether these things were so." (Ac 17:10-11) Note that the Beroeans "received the word with all eagerness." In other words, with all *readiness of mind.* The Greek word *prothumias* means that one is eager, ready, mentally prepared to engage in the study or examination of God's Word. What evidenced the Beroeans eagerness? They examined the Word of God daily. The Greek (*anakrinō*) means to **examine closely.** It has the sense of doing **detailed research** so as to get at **what the author meant** by the words that he used. It means that the Beroeans studied the Scriptures thoroughly each day, so as to learn the truth through a careful and detailed examination, which convinced them of the reliability of what Paul said. Yes, "many of them believed" the apostle Paul. (Ac 17;12) Why is being a hearer only deceiving yourselves?

deceiving yourselves

The Greek (*paralogizomai*) behind the English rendering "deceiving" means literally to "deceive" or "delude" oneself in this case. It has the sense of deceiving oneself with subtle and often false, inaccurate, baseless or erroneous reasoning. In other words, the hearer deceives themselves into believing that God does not really want us to do deeper Bible study. They say things to themselves like, "you do not have to have a seminary degree to find favor in God's eyes." Or, "it isn't about head knowledge, it is about heart knowledge, knowing in your heart that God loves you." The first deceptive statement is a strawman argument, for no one said that one had to have a seminary degree to have a righteous standing before God. However, this ignores the dozens of Scriptures that encourage even commands us to carry out a regular deeper study of God's Word. (Deut. 11:18-23; Josh. 1:8; Pro. 2:1-6; 3:1-2; Matt. 4:4; John 8:32; Ac 17:11; 2 Tim. 2:2, 15; 3:14-17; 1 Pet 3:15, and dozens more could be listed) The second is the either or fallacy when it actually takes both. It is from both the head to the heart (seat of motivation) that we gain a righteous standing before God. It is going from head knowledge to heart application.

Remember, Jesus, said, "'Not everyone who says to me, 'Lord, Lord,' will enter the kingdom of heaven, but the one who does the will of my Father who is in heaven.'" (Matt. 7:21) You can hear that verse all you want to but if you do not have an accurate knowledge of what the will of the Father is, you will be saying things that were your will to Jesus on Judgment day. 'On that day you will say to Jesus, 'Lord, Lord, did we not attend Christian meetings, listening respectfully to what is said, and engage in a daily Bible reading?' (Matt. 7:22) And then Jesus will declare to you, "'I never knew you; depart from me, you who practice lawlessness.'" (Matt. 7:23) You may have thought that meeting attendance, personal Bible reading, reading Christian books, saying emotional prayers, listening respectfully at the meetings, giving money to the church, even helping the poor were the will of the Father but you will have been sadly mistaken. These are all fine and good but they are not the primary thing that makes up the will of the Father.

The Importance of Observation

While this may seem like a given in Bible study, it is important that we understand the importance of observation, as we study our Bible and the tools that are out there, for there is no way we are going to arrive at a correct interpretation if we are missing key elements. There are times that we may be looking for something, like our car keys, and spend 30 minutes of desperately searching for them, to find that they have been laying there right before our eyes the whole time. If we were to take one small book, like the book of Jude and read it 50 times, meticulously, over the next month, taking notes, we would discover that we missed many things after we opened a few commentaries. Therefore, our message for this chapter is observation, observation, and even more observation.

This is about slowing down, looking deeper, and pondering the Word of God. The world around us is all about immediate gratification. This is why in Appendix C; it is recommended that we commit to a Bible reading plan that runs for 4 – 5 years, not just 1 year. Once we are a few months into that careful Bible reading plan, we will fully appreciate how much we have been missing. It is like taking a train through the most beautiful countryside in England, observing the beauty of God's handiwork. Now imagine that same train ride on a bullet train, at 130 mph. The same is true with those who are speed-reading through the Bible, while they are covering much ground, do they really remember what they have read, let alone understand what they have read, and more importantly, can they explain what they have read, or defend what they have read?

Observation: This is paying close attention to the text, so that we can see what Jehovah God has laid out for us, becoming aware, for ascertaining all the details.

Joshua 1:8

8This Book of the Law shall not depart from your mouth, but you shall meditate on it day and night so that you may be careful to do according to all that is written in it. For then you will make your way prosperous, and then you will have good success.

Let us test just how much we can pull from a verse that is informing us of what was said in the opening paragraphs. First, we see that we need to **meditate** on it **day and night** (Psalm 1). The day and night are really hyperbole for reading it every day. The Hebrew word behind meditate (*haghah*) can be rendered "mutter." In other words, as we read, we are to read in an undertone, slightly out load, like muttering to oneself. The process of hearing the words increases our retention of the material dramatically. As Bible students, we read to understand and remember what we read, and we are obligated to share this good news with others. Gesenius' Hebrew and Chaldee Lexicon (translated by S. Tregelles, 1901, p. 215) say of haghah: "Prop[erly] to speak with oneself, murmuring and in a low voice, as is often done by those who are musing."—See also Ps 35:28; 37:30; 71:24; Isa 8:19; 33:18.

The last phrase in verse 8, "you will have good success" can be rendered to "act with insight." How was Joshua to acquire this ability "to act with insight"? He was to meditate on God's Word day and night. What is the equation of Joshua 1:8? If Joshua were to read meditatively (in an undertone) from God's Word daily, applying it in his life, he would be able to act with insight, resulting in his prospering. Of course, the prospering is not financial gain. It is a life of joy and happiness in an age of difficult times. It is avoiding the pitfalls that those in the world around us suffer daily.

The Precision of Observation

The eminent physician, Sir William Osler, made it a point to stress the importance of observation to his medical students. One day he took a bottle off his desk, saying, 'This bottle contains a sample for analysis. It's possible by testing it to determine the disease from which the patient suffers.' Bringing this object lesson home, he dipped his finger into the fluid in the jar and then into his mouth. 'Now, I am going to pass the bottle around. Each of you tastes the contents *as I did* and see if you can diagnose the case.' Thereafter, the bottle was passed from student to student, with each student nervously sticking their finger in the liquid of the jar, and bravely sticking their finger in their mouth, tasting a sample. After Osler had retrieved the bottle, he announced, 'Now you will understand what I mean when I speak about details. Had you been observant you would have seen that I put my index finger into the bottle but my middle finger in my mouth.' Let me ask, did you the reader notice that I italicized Osler's words to do "*as I did*"? A later chapter will cover this in greater detail.

Active Reading

Reading is active, not a passive activity. This means that our mind is not wondering about, it is actively involved in the material in front of us. As we are reading a given chapter, see if we are in agreement with the things being said. What is it that the writer is trying to get across? How does what he is saying support his theme? Is this information to be applied in our life (prescriptive), or is it simply historical information to move the story along (descriptive)? If it is prescribed for us, in what way are we to apply it in our life?

As we are reading, let our mind capture the moment, placing us in the midst of the events. Smell the flowers, see the mountains, wade through the rivers, listen to the children as they play, catch the scent of freshly baked bread, take note of the way people are dressed, and be distraught over the injustices.

Reading can be an adventure if we allow it. However, there are deep reasons for active reading, i.e., meditative reading. There are at least five reasons:

(1) We want to develop a relationship with our heavenly Father,
(2) we want to recall what we have read,
(3) we want to apply these principles in our lives,
(4) we want to share the truths we discover with others,
(5) and we want to be able to overturn false reasoning and save those who doubt.

Live by the Rules

The Rule is to Remember Context

As we know by now, the context is the surrounding verses and chapters, to the text under consideration, as well as the book, and the entire Word of God. Is the interpretation we have come away with, in harmony with the context? Does this interpretation fit the **pattern of meaning,** of the historical setting? For example, Psalm 1:1-3 tells us that if we do not walk in the counsel of the wicked, or stand in the path of sinner, nor sit in the seat with scoffers, but delight in the Word of God, 'whatever he does, he will prosper.' Is that how we are to understand this, **whatever** we do, we will prosper? No. In psalms, proverbs and other genre, there is an invisible "generally" before these absolute statements. In other words, 'generally speaking, whatever we do, we will prosper.'

The Rule is Know the Whole of the Word of God

One needs to be familiar with the whole of the Word of God, to not be misled when someone presents us with Scriptures that are out of context. Too many people take a verse by what it says, without looking at what comes before or after it. For example, Jesus said at John 15:7, "ask whatever you wish, and it will be done for you." This raises the immediate questions: (1) can we simply ask for anything and God will give it to us, (2) and even if it is according to His will and purposes, are we guaranteed of getting it? First, the context of the first part of that verse qualifies what is being talked about here, as Jesus said, "If you abide in me, and my words abide in you . . ." Thus, we must be doing **A** to get **B**. However, as we have already learned, this is not an absolute, as it has the invisible "generally speaking" before it. In other words, "generally speaking," if we are abiding in Jesus and his words, the Father will answer our prayer if it is in harmony with his will and purposes.

Scripture Will Never Contradict Itself

If something is ever said in one place in Scripture that is at odds with another text in Scripture, it is being misinterpreted, or the context is being violated or misunderstood. There are verses that say the earth will be here forever, and then 2 Peter 3:7 says "the heavens and earth that now exist are stored up for fire." This would seem like a contradiction to the many other verses that say the earth will be here forever. However, if we look at the second half of that verse, it lets us know who is going to be destroyed, namely, "destruction of the ungodly."

We are Not to Hang Our Doctrinal Beliefs on Texts that are Hard to Understand

Do not be ashamed of struggling with passages that are hard to understand, because the apostle Peter even felt this way about some of the Apostle Paul's letters. ". . . our beloved brother Paul also wrote to you according to the wisdom given him, as he does in all his letters when he speaks in them of these matters. There are some things in them that are hard to understand, which the ignorant and unstable twist to their own destruction, as they do the other Scriptures."--2 Peter 3:15-16

Always Literal Interpretation

The Bible is to be interpreted literally, in accordance with what it meant to the original audience at the time of its being written. We are to seek the obvious meaning of the words that the author used, and in the context, he used them, as well as the language he used. This rule does not mean that we are to be ignorant regarding idiomatic,[245] hyperbolic,[246] symbolic[247] or figurative[248] language, where Jesus says he is a door, and Jehovah says he is a rock. Herein, we still take it literally, as to what the figurative language means. In other words, we get a correct understanding of the idiomatic, hyperbolic, symbolic or figurative words, and this is what we take literally. For example, if Jesus meant that he is the way , it is through him that we receive life, we take that message literally, not that we actually believe he is literally some movable barrier used to open and close the entrance to a building, room, closet.

There is but One Meaning, which is What the Author Meant by the Words He Used

This rule has been stressed all throughout this book. The meaning is what the author meant by the words that he used, as should have been understood by his readers, at the time of writing. We must understand that descriptive history to move the text along is not necessarily prescribing what we should do. For example, in Judges Chapter 6, Gideon, desiring evidence that God was with him, requested that a fleece

---

[245] "Flowing with milk and honey" (Exodus 3:8)

[246] "You blind guides, who strain out a gnat and swallow a camel!" (Matt. 23:24)

[247] "... Israel committed adultery ..." (Jer 3:8-9) How does a nation commit adultery? Adultery is symbolic of idolatry.

[248] Jesus said to his disciples, "You are the light of the world." (Matt. 5:14)

be exposed at night on the threshing floor and be wet with dew the next morning but that the floor be dry. This does not mean that we follow this as an example, to see if God wants us to do something. This was descriptive, not prescriptive.

Not All Commentaries are Created Equal

Sadly, not all commentaries are equal. Sadly, theological bias affects us all, some more than others do. Therefore, it is good to find a few dependable commentary sets (e.g., Holman, New American, and the forthcoming CPH Old and New Testament Commentary volumes) and rely on them, until we discover others just as dependable.

CHAPTER 9 Reading, Studying and Applying God's Word

1 Timothy 4:13 Updated American Standard Version (UASV)

¹³ Until I come, devote yourself to the public reading of Scripture, to exhortation, to teaching.

Our taking in and applying accurate knowledge of God's Word can lead to eternal life. (John 17:3) Therefore, all Christian should realize just how important it is to read, study, and apply the Holy Scriptures, as well as Bible study literature. In fact, hundreds of millions of Christians today are blessed with Bible study tools, unlike any previous generation. From the moment we accept Christ as our Lord and Savior, we are also accepting the command to proclaim, exhort, to teach the Scriptures, so as to make disciples. (Matthew 24:14; 28:19-20; Acts 1:8) On 1 Timothy 4:13 Thomas D. Lea and Hayne P. Griffin write,

> **4:13** A second emphasis Paul wanted Timothy to make involves proclaiming God's message. Until Paul arrived back on the scene, Timothy was to apply himself to reading, preaching, and teaching. The very brevity of these instructions indicates their genuineness. If these words had come from the second century, the list would have been longer and would have included some reference to the ordinances. Some interpreters see these instructions as a model for public worship patterned after the synagogue. Fee points out that public worship also included prayers (2:1–7), singing (cf. the hymn in 1 Tim 3:16), words of testimony (1 Cor 14:26), and the Lord's Supper (1 Cor. 11:17–34). Public worship was much more than reading, praying, and teaching. These instructions are not merely a pattern for worship, but they present a positive method of opposing false teaching.
>
> "Reading" refers to the public reading of Scripture. Scripture included at least the Old Testament, but it may have referred also to the rapidly growing collection of New Testament writings (see 2 Pet 3:16). The command to read would presuppose a wise selection of passages for reading and an alertness to guard against the reading of suspicious or erroneous words. At a time when believers lacked personal copies of God's Word, such a practice was essential to promote knowledge of the divine message. "Preaching" includes moral instruction that appeals to the will (e.g., Acts 13:15). "Teaching" makes an appeal to the intellect and informs listeners about the truths of the Christian faith. (See Rom 12:7–8,

266

where Paul mentioned teaching and encouraging together.)[249]

There is a pleasure, genuine happiness, contentment, and joy, which come from reading, studying, and applying God's Word. This is true because the Scriptures offer us guidance and direction that aids us in living a life that coincides with our existence as a creation of Almighty God. For example, we have a moral law that was written on our heart. (Rom. 2:14-15) However, at the same time, we have a warring against the law of our mind and taking us captive in the law of sin which is in our members. (Rom. 7:21-25) When we live by the moral law, it brings us joy, when we live by the law of sin; it brings about distress, anxiety, regret to both mind and heart, creating a conflict between our two natures. Listen to the apostle Paul,

The Conflict of Two Natures

Romans 7:14-25 Updated American Standard Version (UASV)

[14] For we know that the law is spiritual, but I am of the flesh, sold under sin. [15] For what I am doing, I do not understand; for I am not practicing what I would like to do, but I am doing the very thing I hate. [16] But if what I am not willing to do, this I am doing, I agree that the law is good. [17] So now I am no longer the one doing it, but sin that dwells in me. [18] For I know that nothing good dwells in me, that is, in my flesh; for the desire is present in me, but the doing of the good is not. [19] For the good that I want, I do not do, but I practice the very evil that I do not want. [20] But if what I do not want to do, this I am doing, I am no longer the one doing it, but sin which dwells in me.

[21] I find then the law in me that when I want to do right, that evil is present in me. [22] For I delight in the law of God according to the inner man, [23] but I see a different law in my members, warring against the law of my mind and taking me captive in the law of sin which is in my members. [24] Wretched man that I am! Who will deliver me from this body of death? [25] Thanks be to God through Jesus Christ our Lord! So then, I myself serve the law of God with my mind, but with my flesh, I serve the law of sin.

7:14–17. Paul begins his shift in emphasis from the past tense to the present tense in this verse. In this entire section (7:14–25), he says the

---

[249] Thomas D. Lea and Hayne P. Griffin, *1, 2 Timothy, Titus*, vol. 34, The New American Commentary (Nashville: Broadman & Holman Publishers, 1992), 138.

same thing in several different ways (**it is sin living in me**, v. 17; "it is sin living in me," v. 20; "the law of sin at work within my members," v. 23). Like a prism, he splits a ray of truth into its component parts, allowing the whole to be seen in light of its parts. If Paul's point in this section were to be summarized in one verse, Galatians 5:17 would likely be it: "For the sinful nature desires what is contrary to the Spirit, and the Spirit what is contrary to the sinful nature. They are in conflict with each other, so that you do not do what you want." As we have already seen, the Spirit is absent from this discussion save for the reference in verse 6 where Paul contrasts the era of the written code with the new way of the Spirit. That conflict continues to be his theme in the remainder of Romans 7.

At the outset, it must be noted that, just as the debate was joined in 7:7–13 concerning the identity of the "I" in those verses, so the debate rages on here. The primary thorn in the flesh of interpreters is verse 14 itself, where Paul says he is **unspiritual, sold as a slave to sin.** After all, was not the point of Romans 6 to say that the believers "used to be slaves to sin" but were now "slaves to righteousness" (Rom. 6:17–18)? Verse 14, along with verses 18 and 24, make it difficult for many to believe that Paul is describing his experience as normative for the Christian life.

Some interpreters (e.g., Stott, pp. 209–211) see Paul writing as a believer, but as an Old Testament, or pre-Pentecost, believer who does not have the benefit of the Holy Spirit's presence and power. Still others reject the notion that Paul is writing from the perspective of spiritual regeneration; that 7:14–25 describes the experience of an unregenerate person (e.g., Moo, pp. 445–451).

Appealing once again to the plainness of Scripture, it is entirely credible to take Paul's words at face value in describing his present Christian experience (and thus what is likely to be the experience of all believers). The key to understanding Paul's perspective is the ability to hold in tension seemingly conflicting points of view in the present eschatological age in which we live. What is true *positionally* for the believer may not always be true *practically* in his or her experience. Seemingly, if we are no longer slaves to sin, we would never sin again; perfectionism would be achieved.

But in all the times when Paul chastised sinning believers such as the Corinthians and the Galatians, he never accused them of not being Christians. He called them weak, immature, childish, but not unregenerate. Paul understood the tension between positional truth and practical expression. Thus, in his own life, he could bemoan the intense realization of the pull of sin and its constant assault on the members of his body and its use of the law to provoke him to sin, while at the same time confess that "in my inner being I delight in God's law" (v. 22). No unbeliever delights in God's law. According to Paul, unbelievers view God's truth as foolishness, not a source of delight (1 Cor. 1:18–27; 2:14).

Consistent with Jewish thought, Christian eschatology recognizes that the present age is not the age to come; there is a difference between the two (2 Cor. 1:22; 5:5; Eph. 1:21; 1 Tim. 4:8; Titus 2:12). One does not begin when the other ends; rather, they overlap. George E. Ladd's writings on the kingdom of God best illuminate the "tension" in which we now live (see, e.g., his *The Gospel of the Kingdom*, 1959, esp. ch. 2). The inclusion of the kingdom of God into the kingdom of Satan vis-à-vis the ministry of Jesus has created conflicting kingdoms for a period of time until the kingdom of God is consummated and fills the earth. It is the conflicting period of time that accounts for the tension between the desire to do right and the temptation to do wrong. *We do not achieve on earth the perfection we will enjoy in heaven.*

Romans 6, 7, and 8 should not be viewed in a linear fashion, as if the believer moves from one to the other.

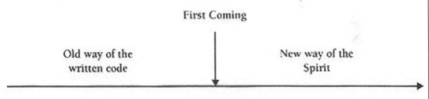

Rather, all are true for the believer, all the time (except for Rom. 7:7–13, which pictures the preconversion person's relationship with the law). And they take place in the tense period of overlap illustrated below:

During this period of overlap, the believer occupies a position described by C. K. Barrett:

It is of the essence of Christian life that men are *simul justi, simul peccatores*, at the same time righteous and sinners. They are righteous in Christ, sinners in themselves (or, in Adam). Because Christ is now hidden from men's eyes in heaven until his *parousia* [presence, second coming], the holiness and righteousness of Christians, which are not their own but his, are hidden, and the body of sin is all too clearly visible.... [The believer] is, and he is not, free from sin; he lives, and he does not live, for God; he is at the same time a righteous man and a sinner. This ambiguous personal position reflects the eschatological situation. The Age to Come has dawned, in the life, death, and resurrection of Jesus; but the present age has not passed. The two exist uneasily side by side, and Christians still look earnestly for the redemption of the body (8:23), knowing that they have been saved in hope (8:24). (Barrett, pp. 120–121, 142–143)

Paul had been a Christian approximately twenty-five years when he wrote the letter to the Romans. Why do we think that Paul should have walked in perfection, or even in victory, every moment of his own spiritual experience? Remember, he had no one to lean on and learn from. How long would it have taken him to make the radical transformation from living life under the law to living life under grace (Rom. 6:14)?

Throughout his apostolic ministry, Paul was painting a picture of the dawning of a new age while trying to sit back and enjoy the sunrise himself. Who does not know mature believers today who continue to wrestle with sin and identify with Paul's experience, while at the same time remaining submitted to the Holy Spirit in their life? Rather than being a picture of an unbeliever, Romans 7:14–25, together with Romans 8, pictures the believer who has been positionally delivered from the law but who, experientially, lives in the tension of the "now but not yet."

It probably is true that in the lives of most earnest Christians the two conditions Paul described [the struggle of Romans 7 and the victory of Romans 8] exist in a sort of cyclical advance. Recognition of our inability to live up to our deepest spiritual longings (ch. 7) leads us to cast ourselves upon God's Spirit for power and victory (ch. 8). Failure to continue in reliance upon the power of the Spirit places us once again in a position inviting defeat. Sanctification is a gradual process that repeatedly takes the believer through this recurring sequence of failure through dependency upon self to triumph through the indwelling Spirit. (Mounce, pp. 167–168)

And it is not just with regard to the law that we find this tension. Anders Nygren has noted the consistency of tension in describing sanctification all the way through chapters 6 through 8 of Romans (noted by Mounce, p. 168). We can illustrate it this way:

	We are ...	Yet we ...
Romans 6	free from sin	must battle against sin
Romans 7	free from the law	are not free from its criteria for righteousness
Romans 8	free from death	long for the redemption of the body

Seeing the tension that exists in all realms of our sanctification makes the second half of Romans 7 easier to understand. The first contrast Paul draws between himself and the law is that the law is **spiritual** (good, holy, righteous) but that he is **unspiritual**. When he looks at the law and sees that it contains what he should do, and then looks at himself doing what he does not do, he does not **understand**. That is more a statement of consternation than confusion, for Paul clearly understands: **it is no longer I myself who [does the opposite of the law], but it is sin living in me.** Does Paul *have* to commit the sin that the law sets before him vis-à-vis its commands? No—he has been rescued from the obligation to obey sin and disobey the law, as he will testify in verses 24–25. But the conflict is there, and it presents itself in two ways.

7:18–20. First, Paul does what is not desired, "those things which [he] ought not to have done" in the words of the Anglican confession. When Paul says, **What I do is not the good I want to do; no, the evil I do not want to do—this I keep on doing,** his words must be measured against his life for interpretation. Had Paul not done much that he desired to do in obedience to Jesus Christ? Had he not suffered greatly for the sake of the spread of the gospel, nearly losing his life on more than one occasion? Certainly there is evidence that Paul did much of what he wanted to do. What then of his words?

He is speaking of the sinful capacity that lives in him still. If it were up to Paul (or to us), we would do only what the law wants us to do. Yet we **keep on doing** the opposite. Paul does not mean that he does only evil, or that he does more evil than good, but that the conflict with evil is one that keeps on (present active indicative of *prasso*). The lure of sin is not dead though we have died to it. It will not die during "this present age" until we die physically. Only in "the age to come" will we be free from doing those things which we ought not to do.

Not only does Paul do what is not desired; he does not do what is desired.

7:21–23. Here Paul uses the law motif to illustrate from another angle the conflict he experiences. Two laws are mentioned: **the law of my mind** (his desire to obey God's law), and **the law of sin** (that which wars against the law of his mind). He states a principle by which these two laws conflict with one another: **when I want to do good, evil is right there with me.** All of us can identify with the apostle's succinct summary of the spiritual experience.

Not only Paul, but all believers, have "left undone those things which we ought to have done." And as the Anglican confession rightly concludes ("there is no health in us"), Paul is about to explode with his own spiritual diagnosis.

One of the results of the gospel is that it delivers us from the condemnation of the law. "Of what use then is the Law? To lead us to Christ, the Truth, to waken in our minds a sense of what our deepest nature, the presence, namely, of God *in* us, requires of us—to let us know, in part by failure, that the purest efforts of will of which we are capable cannot lift us up even to the abstaining from wrong to our neighbor" (George MacDonald, in Lewis, p. 20).

The law did its perfect work in the apostle Paul, reviving his soul (Ps. 19:7a). It convicted him of his sin and showed him that the only deliverance for him was Jesus Christ. No wonder Paul could call the law a "tutor to lead us to Christ, that we may be justified by faith" (Gal. 3:24, NASB). That is exactly what the law did for him. Once delivered from the law, Paul was able to serve the ends of the law—righteousness—in the power of the Holy Spirit (Rom. 7:6).

Paul summarizes the entire chapter—the conflict of the believer that causes him or her to remain dependent upon the Spirit—in the final verse. When it is Paul the believer talking, he makes himself a **slave to God's law.** But when his sinful capacity speaks out, he is **a slave to the law of sin.** As mentioned in this chapter earlier, it is a shame that chapter divisions in our Bibles cause us to "stop" at certain points in the consideration of the text. While this is a logical point in the flow of Paul's thought for a pause, Romans 7 and 8 should be read together. Immediately, Paul moves from wretchedness to victory in declaring that

> the law of the Spirit of life in Christ Jesus has set him "free from the law of sin and death" (Rom. 8:2). The gospel is indeed good news, delivering the believer from death by law to life by grace through the Spirit.[250]

The apostle John informs Christians just how blessed they are if they are reading, studying and applying God's Word. He writes, "Blessed is the one who reads and those who hear the words of the prophecy, and who keep what is written in it, for the time is near." (Rev. 1:3) There is a "special blessing to the reader and to the ones hearing and complying with the moral and ethical standards to be advocated in the following chapters' words."[251] Yes, we need to read, study, and apply the words of all forty plus Bible authors in their sixty-six books that reveal the will and purposes of the Father. (Matt. 7:21-23; 1 John 2:15-17) Listen to the words of the Psalmist,

The Way of the Righteous and the Wicked

1 Blessed is the man
   who walks not in the counsel of the wicked,
nor stands in the way of sinners,
   nor sits in the seat of scoffers;
2 but his delight is in the law of Jehovah,
   and on his law he meditates day and night.

3 He is like a tree
   planted by streams of water
that yields its fruit in its season,
   and its leaf does not wither.
In all that he does, he prospers.

> 1:1 The commendation is expressed in the opening words, **blessed is the man.** The term "blessed" does not imply that God has bestowed some particular favor; a different Hebrew term is used to indicate that. Rather, it means that the person has so conducted himself that a condition of blessedness has resulted. "Oh, the happiness *that man* experiences," the psalmist is saying. And it is a happiness that is very definitely related to conduct. The good life is attractive and brings real, not superficial,

---

[250] Kenneth Boa and William Kruidenier, *Romans*, vol. 6, Holman New Testament Commentary (Nashville, TN: Broadman & Holman Publishers, 2000), 227–232.

[251] Robert L. Thomas, *Revelation 1-7: An Exegetical Commentary* (Chicago: Moody Publishers, 1992), 59–60.

happiness.

The source of this happiness is twofold. First, it lies in the avoidance of all of the ways of the wicked. There are some things that a righteous man, a wise man, will not do. (He) **does not walk in the counsel of the wicked**, refusing to adopt their hedonistic philosophy or to be taken in by their devious casuistry.

The wicked are the godless. Isaiah says that they "are like the tossing sea, which cannot rest, whose waves cast up mire and mud," adding, " 'there is no peace,' says my God, 'for the wicked' " (Isa 57:20–21). **Or stand in the way of sinners.** Note the progression—"walks, stands, sits." That is the nature of involvement in sin. One begins by tuning in on evil counsel. He next ventures an occasional indulgence, in the presence of bad company, even if it means a violation of his conscience. Then, before he realizes it, his life is cast in the new mold; and the change has been so complete that he has become one of that circle who take delight in sneering at goodness and ridiculing religion. The righteous man habitually shunned all of this. The verbs, in the Hebrew, are *perfect* (completed action), indicating with the negatives what, all the while, he has never done, i.e., "who has never walked."

1:2 The state of blessedness or happiness in life finds its source more in what a person does than in what he refrains from doing. The wise man refuses to walk in the way of evil, not because he is bound by an oversensitive conscience but because he has chosen to walk a better way. When it is a matter of choice between the counsel of the wicked and the way of the Lord, for him it is no contest. He chooses the latter. To him **the law of the Lord** is not a burden to be borne, nor even an obligation to be met, but a **delight** to be enjoyed. It is a gift from the Creator of life providing instruction on how best to live in such a way as to find fullness of life and, consequently, happiness. In a word, happiness is not found by searching for it, not an achievement of the will; happiness is doing what is right. And God has revealed what right is. Any of us who ignores God's direction does so at great peril, for the law of the Lord alone gives meaning and direction to human existence. To abandon the Scriptures is to be left adrift on the sea of life without chart or compass.

On his law he meditates. The purpose of such concern for God's law is indicated in Josh 1:8—"that you may be careful to do everything written in it." The delight lies in doing the will of God, not just in knowing it. Thus Jesus would say: "Blessed rather are [Oh, the happiness to them!] those who hear the word of God and obey it" (Luke 11:28).

1:3 To indicate what it is like to walk in the way of God, the psalmist uses the figure of a luxurious tree **planted by streams of water.** The tree, thus situated, is enabled to do what is natural to it; **which yields its fruit in season.** Just so, vitality and fruitfulness are characteristics of the life of righteousness, not as a reward or enticement, but as a natural consequence of such a life. In bearing fruit, the tree is fulfilling the purpose for which it was created. The man of wisdom is doing the same, finding his purpose in life and life's fulfillment in doing the will of God.

Whatever he does prospers. This statement appears to be a categorical assertion to the effect that the righteous man will never experience any reverses. However, human experience says the contrary (consider Job, for example), and elsewhere the Psalms deal with the suffering of the righteous. Dahood proposes an alternate translation: "Whatever it (the tree) produces is good." On the basis of the Hebrew text, this is possible. Charles A. Briggs and others translate: "So all that he doeth, he carries through successfully"[7]—or to a successful outcome—meaning that whatever he does will result in good. A righteous man, like a good tree, will bear good fruit. God's law of the harvest is immutable.[252]

Active Thinking and Meditation

How can we get the most out of our reading of God's Word and the overabundance of Bible study tools available today? First, not all Bible study tools are created equal. Second, each Bible verse has but one meaning, which is what the author meant by the words that he used. It is best if we have at least a fundamental understanding of how to interpret the Scriptures ourselves.[253] This way, we are able to see if a Bible scholar is going beyond what the Biblical author intended, or worse still, concealing what the Bible author meant to convey. It is also imperative that we trust only literal translations to be the Word of God (ASV, ESV, NASB, and the UASV). An interpretive translation (CEV, NLT, NIV, NRSV and the like), is nothing more than what the translator or committee believe the Bible author meant by the words that he used. On the other hand, the literal translation is what the Bible author said in our modern day languages.

---

[252] S. Edward Tesh and Walter D. Zorn, *Psalms*, The College Press NIV Commentary (Joplin, MO: College Press, 1999), 87–89.

[253] INTERPRETING THE BIBLE: Introduction to Biblical Hermeneutics by Edward D. Andrews

Moreover, not all Bible commentaries and encyclopedias are to be absolutely trusted either. We have over 40,000 different Christian denominations that believe that they are the truth and the way. Is the "truth" important? Yes, very much so, the Father describes himself as "the God of truth." (Psa. 31:5) He judges according to truth. (Rom. 2:2; compare John 7:24) In his Word, the Father has given just ordinances and true laws, good statutes and commandments. (Neh. 9:13; Psa. 19:9; 119:142, 151, 160) God's Word is truth and only one absolute truth. (John 17:17; compare James 1:18) It is our job to ascertain that truth. Those who desire to have a righteous standing before God should walk in his truth and serve him in truth. (Josh. 24:14; 1 Sam. 12:24; Psa. 25:4, 5; 26:3-6; 43:3; 86:11; Isa. 38:3) Just know that there are multiple views on every Bible doctrine.

DIVERSITY OF BIBLICAL INTERPRETATION
DIVERSITY OF CHRISTIAN BELIEFS

In his forward to R. C. Sproul's Knowing Scripture, J. I. Packer observes that Protestant theologians are in conflict about biblical interpretation. To illustrate the diversity of biblical interpretations, William Yarchin pictures a shelf full of religious books saying different things, but all claiming to be faithful interpretations of the Bible. Bernard Ramm observed that such diverse interpretations underlie the "doctrinal variations in Christendom." A mid-19th century book on biblical interpretation observed that even those who believe the Bible to be "the word of God" hold "the most discordant views" about fundamental doctrines." Below are just a few examples.

Four Views of Hell	Four Views of Salvation	Two Views of Inspiration	Three Views of Atonement
Four Views of creation	Four Views of Eternal Security	Four Views of Inspiration	Four Views of Works in Final Judgment
Four Views of Inerrancy	Four Views of Sanctification	Two Views of Fasting	Four Views of the Book of Revelation
Two Views of Christology	Three Views of Image of God	Three Views of Grace	Three Views of Human Constitution
Four Views of Providence	Two Views of Lord's Supper	Four Views of Free Will	Two Views of Charismatic Gifts
Two Views of Baptism	Three Views of Jesus' Return	Two Views of Sabbath	Four Views of Predestination
Three Views of Purgatory	Four Views of the Church	Four Views of End Times	Four Views of Christian Spirituality
Four Views of Antichrist	Three Views of Neutrality	Three Views of Heaven	Two Views of Foreknowledge

While God will not miraculously implant biblical truths within our minds, he will guide us if we are receptive to what is true. Let us follow in the footsteps of Joshua, who lead the Israelites after their trek through the wilderness. He was told, "Only be strong and very courageous, being careful to do according to all the law that Moses my servant commanded you; do not turn from it to the right or to the left, so that you may have success wherever you go. This Book of the Law shall not depart from your mouth, but you shall meditate on it day and night, so that you may be careful to do according to all that is written in it; for then you will make your way prosperous, and then you will have good success." (Josh. 1:7-8) On these verses Max Anders and Kenneth Gangel writes,

1:7-8. At the center of Joshua's faith would be the Word of God, **this Book of the Law.** The word **meditate** could be rendered "mutter." As Madvig puts it, "When one continually mutters God's Word to himself, he is constantly thinking about it. Knowledge of God's law is not enough; one must also 'be careful to do' what it commands" (Madvig, 257). Most scholars believe this refers to some portion of the Levitical law already held by the priests. Certainly the Ten Commandments would be a part of it, but the reference would spread far beyond those boundaries. Joshua would receive direct revelation and was in that exact mode while God talked to him, but that didn't change the importance of the written word.

I like the way Francis Schaeffer puts it:

> But though Joshua was going to have this special leading from the Lord, this was not to detract from the central reference point and chief control: the written book. The Word of God written in the book set the limitations. Thus, Joshua was already functioning in the way Bible-believing Christians function. Sometimes God does lead in other ways, but such leading must always be within the circle of his external, propositional commands in Scripture. Even if a person had an Urim and a Thummin as well as a priest to guide him, this would not change his basic authority. The primary leading would come from the written, propositional revelation of God, from the Bible (Schaeffer, 32).

Much has been made of the word **successful** that appears in verses 7 and 8, and also the word **prosperous** to which it attaches at the end of verse 8. It should be obvious to any serious Bible student that financial achievement is not in view here. The so-called "prosperity gospel" cannot be argued from any portion of God's Word and certainly not from these verses in the first chapter of Joshua. Success and prosperity come when a person follows God's will, obeys God's Word, and achieves God's goal, not when the offerings are greater this year than they were last year at this time.

God never forces us to live a victorious Christian life. He teaches and promises and provides principles. But if we fail to cross the river and possess the land, we will remain in a spiritual desert. God is not looking for people with self-confidence but people with God-confidence.

Joshua understood how important the principles of the law are to God. The Lord didn't just airmail the stone tablets to Israel on a windstorm; he met personally with their leader. Exodus 24 tells us that

Joshua was the only other person on that mountain with Moses that day. We don't know how close he was to the glory cloud, but it must have been an awesome experience. What looked like consuming fire on top of the mountain engulfed Moses for forty days and nights while he met with God. Joshua was the first to see the glow of God's glory on Moses' face and the first to see the stones etched by the finger of God.

My son Jeff coaches a recreational department boy's basketball team. Half the boys who play have never participated in organized basketball before, so Jeff works hard to build their confidence. He does that by reminding them to remember what they learn and do in practice when they get into a game. If they follow the basic rules and remember the basic skills, they can play well.

In simple terms, this is what God said to Joshua and what he says to us: "Get back to the basics. Remember the rules. Learn the law. Practice the principles."

The problem is that sometimes we become like those little boys. We get out on the basketball court of life where referees blow whistles and people in different colored shirts try to take the ball away, and we lose our confidence and composure. Then we discover that every time we forget God's promises and principles we end up in chaos.[254]

An important note to keep in mind is; we are not interested in speed, i.e., seeing how fast we can cover God's Word. If we have set a period of time to read and study the Bible, do not fret over covering a lot of material, but rather we will want to take our time. Keep in mind that we are studying so as to draw close to God as we make changes in our lives, to help us affect changes in our family and congregation life, to evangelize and help save the lives of other, and finally, to help save some who may have begun to doubt. At times, we may become bogged down in a verse that is difficult and complex, and it may require extra attention, to get at what the author meant. As we work our way through this publication, take note of the commentaries that are used throughout and how they offer us depth in understanding. As we read and study, consider things actively. Analyze what the Bible or person in the Bible is saying, 'what is there point,' or how can I use this in my life or share this information with another? As the author of the book of proverbs says, "The heart of the righteous ponders how to answer." (Proverbs 15:28)

---

[254] Anders, Max; Gangel, Kenneth. Holman Old Testament Commentary - Joshua (pp. 13-15). B&H Publishing. Kindle Edition.

CHAPTER 10 Holy Spirit and Biblical Interpretation

2 Corinthians 4:3-4 Updated American Standard Version (UASV)

³ And even if our gospel is **veiled**, it is veiled to those who are perishing. ⁴ In their case the god of this world has **blinded the minds of the unbelievers**,²⁵⁵ to keep them from seeing the light of the gospel of the glory of Christ, who is the image of God.

2 Corinthians 3:12-18 Updated American Standard Version (UASV)

¹² Therefore having such a hope, we use great boldness in our speech, ¹³ and are not like Moses, who used to put a veil over his face so that the sons of Israel would not look intently at the end of what was fading away. ¹⁴ But their **minds were <u>hardened</u>**; for until this very day at the reading of the old covenant the same veil remains unlifted, because **it is taken away only by means of Christ**. ¹⁵ But to this day whenever Moses is read, a veil lies over their hearts; ¹⁶ but whenever one **turns to the Lord, the veil is taken away**. ¹⁷ Now the Lord is the Spirit, and where the Spirit of the Lord is, there is freedom. ¹⁸ But we all, with unveiled face, beholding as in a mirror the glory of the Lord, are being transformed into the same image from glory to glory, just as from the Lord, the Spirit.

Let us start by looking at an example of blind minds within Scripture. This was not a case of physical blindness, but mental blindness. There was a Syrian military force coming after Elisha, and God **blinded them <u>mentally</u>**. If it had been physical blindness, then each of them would have to have been led by the hand. However, what does the account say?

---

²⁵⁵ By **unbelievers** Paul has in view non-Christians (1 Cor. 6:6; 7:12–15; 10:27; 14:22–24). First, the unbelievers of verse 4 are a subset of those who are perishing in verse 3. In other words, the two are the same. Second, the unbelievers are not persons, who have never heard the truth. No, rather, they are persons who have heard the truth, and have rejected it as foolish rubble. This is how this writer is using the term "unbeliever" as well. Technically, how could one ever truly be an unbeliever if they had never heard and understood the truth, to say they did not believe the truth? Therefore, to be an unbeliever, one needs to hear the truth, understand the truth, and reject that truth (i.e., not believing the truth is just that, the truth).

2 Kings 6:18-20 Updated American Standard Version (UASV)

[18] And when the Syrians came down against him, Elisha prayed to Jehovah and said, "Please strike this nation[256] with blindness." So he struck them with blindness in accordance with the prayer of Elisha. [19] Then Elisha said to them, "This is not the way, nor is this the city; follow me and I will bring you to the man whom you seek." And he brought them to Samaria.

[20] When they had come into Samaria, Elisha said, "O Jehovah, open the eyes of these men, that they may see." So Jehovah opened their eyes and they saw; and behold, they were in the midst of Samaria.

Are we to believe that one man led the entire Syrian military force to Samaria? If they were physically blind, they would have to have all held hands. Were the Syrian military forces not able physically to see the images that were before them? No, rather, it was more of an inability to understand them. This must have been some form of mental blindness, where we see everything that everyone else sees, but something just does not register. Another example can be found in the account about the men of Sodom. When they were blinded, they did not become distressed, running into each other.

Definitely, Paul is speaking of people, who are not receptive to truth, because their heart is hardened to it, callused, unfeeling. They are not responding because their figurative heart is opposed. It is as though, God handed them over to Satan, to be mentally blinded from the truth, not because he disliked them per se, but because they had closed their hearts and minds to the Gospel. Thus, no manner of argumentation is likely to bring them back to their senses.

However, at one time Saul (Paul) was one of these. Until he met the risen Jesus on the road to Damascus, he was mentally blind to the truth. He was well aware of what the coming Messiah was to do, but Jesus did none of these things because it was not time. Thus, Paul was blinded by his love for the Law, Jewish tradition, and history. So much so, he was unable to grasp the Gospel. Not to mention, he lived during the days of Jesus ministry, studied under Gamaliel, who was likely there in the area. He could have even been there when Jesus impressed the Jewish religious leaders, at the age of twelve. Therefore, Saul (Paul) needed a real wake-up call, to get through the veil that blinded him.

---

[256] Or *people*

Hence, a mentally blind person sees the same information as another, but the truth cannot or will not get down into their heart. I have had the privilege of talking to dozens of small groups of unbelievers, ranging from four people to ten people in my life. I saw this in action. As I spoke to these groups, inevitably, I would see the light going off in the eyes of some (they would be shaking their heads in agreement as I spoke). However, others having a cynical look, a doubting look (they would be shaking their heads in disgust or disapproval), and they eventually walked away. This is not saying that the unbeliever cannot understand the Bible; it is simply that they see no significance in it, as it is foolishness to them.

1 Corinthians 2:14 Updated American Standard Version (UASV)

14 But the natural man <u>does not accept</u> the things of the Spirit of God, for <u>they are foolishness</u> to him, and <u>he is</u> **not able to** <u>understand</u>[257] <u>them, because they are examined spiritually.</u>

Hundreds of millions of Christians use this verse as support that without the "Holy Spirit," we can fully understand God's Word. They would argue that without the "Spirit" the Bible is nothing more than foolish nonsense to the reader. What we need to do before, arriving at the correct meaning of what Paul meant, is grasp what he meant by his use of the word "understand," as to what is 'foolish.' In short, "the things of the Spirit of God" are the "Spirit" inspired Word of God. The natural man sees the inspired Word of God as foolish, and "he is not able to understand them."

Paul wrote, "But the natural man does not accept the things of the Spirit of God, for they are foolishness to him." What did Paul mean by this statement? Did he mean that if the Bible reader did not have the "Spirit" helping him, he would not be able to grasp the correct meaning of the text? Are we to understand Paul as saying that without the "Spirit," the Bible and its teachings are beyond our understanding?

We can gain a measure of understanding as to what Paul meant, by observing how he uses the term "foolishness" elsewhere in the very same letter. At 1 Corinthians 3:19, it is used in the following way, "For the wisdom of this world is foolishness with God." This verse helps us to arrive at the use in two stages: (1) the verse states that human wisdom is foolishness with God, (2) and we know that the use of foolishness here

---

257 "The Greek word *ginosko* ("to understand") does not mean comprehend intellectually; it means know by experience. The unsaved obviously do not experience God's Word because they do not welcome it. Only the regenerate have the capacity to welcome and experience the Scriptures, by means of the Holy Spirit."— (Zuck 1991, 23)

does not mean that God cannot understand (or grasp) human wisdom. The use is that He sees human wisdom as 'foolish' and rejects it as such.

Therefore, the term "foolishness" of 1 Corinthians 3:19 is not in reference to not "understanding," but as to one's view of the text, its significance, or better yet, lack of significance, or lack of value. We certainly know that God can understand the wisdom of the world, but condemns it as being 'foolish.' The same holds true of 1 Corinthians 1:20, where the verbal form of foolishness is used, "Has not God made foolish the wisdom of the world?" Thus, we have the term "foolishness" being used before and after 1 Corinthians 2:14, (1:20; 3:19). In all three cases, we are dealing with the significance, the value being attributed to something.

Thus, it seems obvious that we should attribute the same meaning to our text in question, 1 Corinthians 2:14. In other words, the Apostle Paul, by his use of the term "foolishness," is not saying that the unbeliever is unable to understand, to grasp the Word of God. If this were the case, why would we ever share the Word of God, the gospel message with an unbeliever? Unbelievers can understand the Word of God; however, unbelievers see it as foolish, having no value or significance. The resultant meaning of chapters 1-3 of 1 Corinthians is that unbelieving world of mankind can understand the Word of God. However, they view it as foolish (missing value or significance). God, on the other hand, understands the wisdom of the world of mankind but views it foolish (missing value or significance). Therefore, in both cases, the information is understood or grasped; however, it is rejected because to the party considering it, believes it lacks value or significance.

We pray for the guidance of the Holy Spirit, and our spirit, or mental disposition, needs to be attuned to God and His Spirit through study and application. Now, if our mental disposition is not in tune with the Spirit, we will not come away with the right answer. As Ephesians shows, we can grieve the Spirit.

Ephesians 4:30 Updated American Standard Version (UASV)

[30] And do not **grieve the Holy Spirit** of God, by[258] whom you were sealed for the day of redemption.

---

[258] Lit *in*

How do we grieve the Holy Spirit? We do that by acting contrary to its leading through deception, human weaknesses, imperfections, setting our figurative heart on something other than the leading.

Ephesians 1:18 Updated American Standard Version (UASV)

[18] having the **eyes of your heart** enlightened, that you may know what is the hope to which he has called you, what are the riches of the glory of his inheritance in the holy ones,

"Eyes of your heart" is a Hebrew Scripture expression, meaning spiritual insight, to grasp the truth of God's Word. So we could pray for the guidance of God's Spirit, and at the same time, we can explain why there are so many different understandings (many wrong answers), some of which contradict each other. This is because of human imperfection that is diluting some of those interpreters, causing them to lose the Spirit's guidance.

A person sits down to study and prays earnestly for the guidance of Holy Spirit, that his mental disposition be in harmony with God's Word [or simply that his heart be in harmony with . . .], and sets out to study a chapter, an article, something biblical. In the process of that study, he allows himself to be moved, not by a mental disposition in harmony with the Spirit, but by human imperfection, by way of his wrong worldview, his biases, his preunderstanding.[259] A fundamental of grammatical-historical interpretation is that that we are to look for the simple meaning, the essential meaning, the obvious meaning. However, when this one comes to a text that does not say what he wants it to say, he rationalizes until he has the text in harmony with his preunderstanding. In other words, he reads his presuppositions into the text,[260] as opposed to discovering the meaning that was in the text. Even though his Christian conscience was tweaked at the correct meaning, he ignored it, as well as his mental disposition that could have been in harmony with the Spirit, to get the outcome he wanted.

In another example, it may be that the text does mean what he wants, but this is only because the translation he is using is full of theological bias, which is **violating** grammar and syntax, or maybe textual criticism rules and principles that arrive at the correct reading. Therefore, when this student takes a deeper look, he discovers that it could very well

---

[259] Preunderstanding is all of the knowledge and understanding that we possess before we begin the study of the text.

[260] Presupposition is to believe that a particular thing is so before there is any proof of it

read another way, and likely should because of the context. He buries that evidence beneath his conscience, and never mentions it when this text comes up in a Bible discussion. In other words, he is grieving the Holy Spirit and loses it on this particular occasion.

Human imperfection, human weakness, theological bias, preunderstanding, and many other things could dilute the Spirit, or even grieve the Spirit. So that while one may be praying for assistance, he is not getting it or has lost it, because one, some, or all of these things he is doing has grieved the Spirit.

Again, it is not that an unbeliever cannot understand what the Bible means; otherwise, there would be no need to witness to him. Rather, he does not have the spiritual awareness to see the significance of studying Scripture. An unbeliever can look at "the setting in which the Bible books were written and the circumstances involved in the writing," as well as "studying the words and sentences of Scripture in their normal, plain sense," to arrive the meaning of a text. However, without having any spiritual awareness about themselves, they would not see the significance of applying it in their lives. 1 Corinthians 2:14 says, "The natural person does not **accept** [Gr., dechomai] the things of the Spirit of God." Dechomai means, "to welcome, accept or receive." Thus, the unbeliever may very well understand the meaning of a text, but just does not *accept, receive* or *welcome* it as truth.

Acts 17:10-11 Updated American Standard Version (UASV)

[10] The brothers immediately sent Paul and Silas away by night to Berea, and when they arrived, they went into the synagogue of the Jews. [11] Now these were more noble-minded than those in Thessalonica, who received the word with all readiness of mind,[261] examining the Scriptures daily to see whether these things were so.

Unlike the natural person, the Bereans accepted, received, or welcomed the Word of God eagerly. Paul said the Thessalonians "received [*dechomai*] the word in much affliction, with the joy of the Holy Spirit." (1 Thess. 1:6) At the beginning of a person's introduction to the good news, he will take in the knowledge of the Scriptures (1 Tim. 2:3-4), which if his heart is receptive, he will begin to apply them in his life, taking off the old person and putting on the new person. (Eph. 4:22-24) Seeing how the Scriptures have begun to alter his life, he will start to have a genuine faith in the things he has learned (Heb. 11:6), repenting of

---

[261] Or with all *eager readiness of mind.* The Greek word *prothumias* means that one is eager, ready, mentally prepared to engage in some activity.

his sins. (Acts 17:30-31) He will turn around his life, and his sins will be blotted out. (Acts 3:19) At some point, he will go to God in prayer, telling the Father that he is dedicating his life to him, to carry out his will and purposes. (Matt. 16:24; 22:37) This regeneration is the Holy Spirit working in his life, giving him a new nature, placing him on the path to salvation.—2 Corinthians 5:17.

A new believer will become "acquainted with the sacred writings, which are able to make [him] wise for salvation through faith in Christ Jesus." (2 Tim. 3:15) As the Bible informs us, the Scriptures are holy and are to be viewed as such. If we are to acquire an accurate or full knowledge, to have the correct mental grasp of the things that we carried out an exegetical analysis on, it must be done with a prayerful and humble heart. It is as Dr. Norman L. Geisler said, "the role of the Holy Spirit, at least in His special work on believers related to Scripture, is in illuminating our understanding of the significance (not the meaning) of the text. The meaning is clear apart from any special work of the Holy Spirit." What level of understanding that we are able to acquire is based on the degree to which we are **not** grieving the Holy Spirit with our worldview, our preunderstanding, our presuppositions, our theological biases? In addition, anyone living in sin will struggle to grasp God's Word as well.

No interpreter is infallible. The only infallibility or inerrancy belonged to the original manuscripts. Each Christian has the right to interpret God's Word, to discover what it means, but this does not guarantee that they will come away with the correct meaning. The Holy Spirit will guide us into and through the truth, by way of our working on behalf of our prayers to have the correct understanding. Our working in harmony with the Holy Spirit means that we buy out the time for a personal study program, not to mention the time to prepare properly and carefully for our Christian meetings. In these studies, do not expect that the Holy Spirit is going to give us miraculously some flash of understanding, but rather understanding will come to us as we set aside our personal biases, worldviews, human imperfections, presuppositions, preunderstanding, opening our mental disposition to the Spirit's leading as we study.

The Work of the Holy Spirit

The following is adopted and adapted from Douglas A. Foster of Abilene Christian University.

Christian Publishing House's understanding of the Holy Spirit is **not** that of the Charismatic groups (the ecstatic and irrational), but rather the calm and rational. The work of the Holy Spirit is inseparably and uniquely linked to the words and ideas of God's inspired and inerrant Word. We see the indwelling of the Holy Spirit as Christians taking the words and ideas of Scripture into our mind and drawing spiritual strength from them. The Spirit moves persons toward salvation, but the Spirit does that, in the same way, any person moves another—by persuasion with words and ideas:

Now we cannot separate the Spirit and the Word of God, and ascribe so much power to the one and so much to the other; for so did not the Apostles. Whatever the word does, the Spirit does, and whatever the Spirit does in the work of converting, the word does. We neither believe nor teach abstract Spirit nor abstract word, but word and Spirit, Spirit and word. But the Spirit is not promised to any persons outside of Christ. It is promised only to them who believe and obey him.[262]

The Holy Spirit works only through the word in the conversion of sinners. In other words, the Spirit acting through the Word of God can accomplish everything claimed to be affected by a personal indwelling of the Spirit.

Longtime preacher Z. T. (Zachary Taylor) Sweeney, in His book *The Spirit and the Word: A Treatise on the Holy Spirit in the Light of a Rational Interpretation of the Word of God*, writes after examining every Scripture that might be used by advocates of a literal personal indwelling of the Holy Spirit,

In the above cases, we have covered all the conceivable things a direct indwelling Spirit could do for one, and have also shown that all these things the Spirit does through the word of God. It is not claimed that a direct indwelling of the Spirit makes any new revelations, adds any new reasons or offers any new motives than are found in the word of God. Of what use, then, would a direct indwelling Spirit be? God makes nothing in vain. We are necessarily, therefore, led to the conclusion that, in dealing with his children today, God deals with them in the same psychological way that he deals with men in inducing them to become children. This conclusion is strengthened by the utter absence of

---

[262] Alexander Campbell, The Christian System (6th ed.; Cincinnati: Standard, 1850), 64.

any test by which we could know the Spirit dwells in us, if such were the case.[263]

This author and Christian Publishing House is defined by our rejection of Holiness and Pentecostal understandings of the Holy Spirit. The Holy Spirit transforms a person, empowering him through the Word of God, to put on the "new person" required of true Christians, "So, as those who have been chosen of God, holy and beloved, put on a heart of compassion, kindness, humility, gentleness and patience." – Colossians 3:12.

Ephesians 4:20-24 Updated American Standard Version (UASV)

[20] But you did not learn Christ in this way, [21] if indeed you have heard him and have been taught in him, just as truth is in Jesus, [22] that you take off, according to your former way of life, the old man, who is being destroyed according to deceitful desires, [23] and to be renewed in the spirit of your minds, [24] and put on the new man,[264] the one created according to the likeness of God in righteousness and loyalty of the truth.

Colossians 3:9-10 Updated American Standard Version (UASV)

[9] Do not lie to one another, seeing that you have put off the old man[265] with its practices [10] and have put on the new man[266] who is being renewed through accurate knowledge[267] according to the image of the one who created him,

How Are We to Understand the Indwelling of the Holy Spirit?

1 Corinthians 3:16 Updated American Standard Version (UASV)

[16] Do you not know that you are a temple of God and that the Spirit of God dwells in you?

---

[263] Z. T. Sweeney, The Spirit and the Word (Nashville: Gospel Advocate, n.d.), 121–26.

[264] An interpretive translation would have, "put on the new person," because it does mean male or female.

[265] Or old person

[266] Or new person

[267] See Romans 3:20 ftn.

Before delving into the phrase, "indwelling of the Holy Spirit, let us consider the **mistaken view** of New Testament scholars Simon J. Kistemaker and William Hendriksen, who wrote,

The Spirit of God lives within you." The church is holy because God's Spirit dwells in the hearts and lives of the believers. In 6:19 Paul indicates that the Holy Spirit lives in the physical bodies of the believers. But now he tells the Corinthians that the presence of the Spirit is within them, and they are the temple of God.

The Corinthians should know that they have received the gift of God's Spirit. Paul had already called attention to the fact that they had not received the spirit of the world but the Spirit of God (2:12). He teaches that Christians are controlled not by sinful human nature but by the Spirit of God, who is dwelling within them (Rom. 8:9).

The behavior—strife, jealousy, immorality, and permissiveness—of the Christians in Corinth was reprehensible. By their conduct the Corinthians were desecrating God's temple and, as Paul writes in another epistle, were grieving the Holy Spirit (Eph. 4:30; compare 1 Thess. 5:19).[268]

First, it must be told that I am almost amazed at how so many Bible scholars say nonsensical things, contradictory things when it comes to the Holy Spirit. Bible Commentators use many verses to say that the Holy Spirit literally,

(1) **dwells in** the individual Christian believers,

(2) having **control over** them,

(3) **enabling them** to live a righteous and faithful life,[269]

(4) with the believer **still being able to sin**, even to the point of grieving the Holy Spirit (Eph. 4:30).

Let us walk through this again, and please take it slow, ponder whether it makes sense, is reasonable, logical, even Scriptural. The Holy Spirit literally dwells in individual believers, controlling them so they can live a righteous and faithful life, yet they can still freely sin, even to the point of grieving the Holy Spirit. Does this mean that the Holy Spirit is

---

[268] Simon J. Kistemaker and William Hendriksen, *Exposition of the First Epistle to the Corinthians*, vol. 18, New Testament Commentary (Grand Rapids: Baker Book House, 1953–2001), 117

[269] Millard J. Erickson, *Introducing Christian Doctrine* (Grand Rapids: Baker Book House, 1992), 265–270

not powerful enough to prevent their sinful nature from affecting them? The commentators say the Holy Spirit now controls the Christian, not their sinful nature. If that were true, it must mean the Holy Spirit is ineffectual and less powerful than their sinful nature of the Christian, because the Christian can still reject the Holy Spirit and sin to the point of grieving the Holy Spirit. If the Holy Spirit is controlling the individual Christian, how is it possible that he still possesses free will?

Let us return to the phrase of "indwelling of the Holy Spirit." Just how often do we find "indwelling" in the Bible? I have looked at over fifty English translations and found it once in the King James Version ad two in an earlier version of the New American Standard Bible. One reference is to sin dwelling within us, and the other reference is to the Holy Spirit dwelling within us.

The Updated American Standard Version removed such usage. We may be asking ourselves since "indwelling" is almost nonexistent in the Scriptures, why the commentaries, Bible encyclopedias, Hebrew and Greek word dictionaries, Bible dictionaries, pastors and Christians using it to such an extent, especially in reference to the Holy Spirit? I say in reference to the Holy Spirit because some scholars refer to the indwelling of Christ and the Word of God.

Before addressing those questions, we must take a look at the Greek word behind 1 Corinthians 3:16 "the Spirit of God dwells [οἰκέω] in you." The transliteration of our Greek word is *oikeo*. It means "'to dwell' (from *oikos*, 'a house'), 'to inhabit as one's abode,' is derived from the Sanskrit, *vic*, 'a dwelling place' (the Eng. termination —'wick' is connected). It is used (a) of God as 'dwelling' in light, 1 Tim. 6:16; (b) of the 'indwelling' of the Spirit of God in the believer, Rom. 8:9, 11, or in a church, 1 Cor. 3:16; (c) of the 'indwelling' of sin, Rom. 7:20; (d) of the absence of any good thing in the flesh of the believer, Rom. 7:18; (e) of the 'dwelling' together of those who are married, 1 Cor. 7:12-13."[270]

Thus, for our text, means the Holy Spirit dwelling in true Christians. The TDNT tells us, "Jn.'s μένειν [*menein*] corresponds to Paul's οἰκεῖν [oikein], cf. Jn. 1:33: καταβαῖνον καὶ μένον ἐπ᾽ αὐτόν [descending and remaining upon him]. The new possession of the Spirit is more than ecstatic."[271] What does TDNT mean? It means that John is using *meno*

---

[270] W. E. Vine, Merrill F. Unger, and William White Jr., *Vine's Complete Expository Dictionary of Old and New Testament Words* (Nashville, TN: T. Nelson, 1996), 180.

[271] Gerhard Kittel, Geoffrey W. Bromiley, and Gerhard Friedrich, eds., *Theological Dictionary of the New Testament* (Grand Rapids, MI: Eerdmans, 1964–)

("to remain," "to stay" or "to abide") in the same way that Paul is using *oikeo* ('to dwell').

When we are considering the Father or the Son alone, and even the Father and the Son together, we are able to have a straightforward conversation. However, when we get to the Holy Spirit we tend to get off into mysterious and mystical thinking. When we think of humans and the words *dwell* and *abide*, both have the sense of where we 'live or reside in a place.'

However, there is another sense of 'where we might stand on something,' 'our position on something.' Thus, in English dwell and abide can be used interchangeably, similarly, just as Paul and John use *meno* "abide" or "remain" and *oikeo* "dwell" similarly. Let us look at the apostle John's use of meno,

1 John 4:16 Updated American Standard Version (UASV)

¹⁶ We have come to know and have believed the love which God has for us. God is love, and the one who remains [*meno*] in love remains in God, and God remains [*meno*] in him.

Here we notice that God is the embodiment of "love" and if we **abide in** or **remain in** that love, God then **abides in** or **remain in** us. We do not attach any mysterious or mystical sense to this verse, such as God literally being in us and us being in God. If we suggest that this verse, i.e., God being in us, means his taking control of our lives, does our being in God, also mean we control his life? We would think to suggest such a thing is unreasonable, illogical, nonsensical, and such. Commentator Max Anders in the *Holman New Testament Commentary* says, "This is the test of true Christianity in the letters of John. We must recognize the basic character of God, rooted in love. We must experience that love in our own relationship with God. Others must experience this God kind of love in their relationships with us." (Walls and Anders 1999, 211) Our love for God and man is the motivating factor in what we do and not do as Christians. John is saying that we need to remain in that love if we are to remain in God and God is to remain in us. We may be thinking, well, is it not true that God guides and direct us? Yes, however, this is because we have given our lives over to him.

1 John 2:14 Updated American Standard Version (UASV)

¹⁴ I have written to you, fathers, because you know Him who has been from the beginning. I have written to you, young men, because you are strong, and the word of God remains [*meno*] in you, and you have overcome the evil one.

Here we see that the Word of God abides or remains in us. Does this mean that the Word of God is literally within our body, controlling us? No, this means that our love for God and our love for his Word is a motivating factor in our walk with God. We are one with the Father as Jesus was and is one with the Father and he is one with us. Listen to the words of Paul in the book of Hebrews,

Hebrews 4:12 Updated American Standard Version (UASV)

¹² For the word of God is living and active and sharper than any two-edged sword, and piercing as far as the division of soul and spirit, of both joints and marrow, and able to judge the thoughts and intentions of the heart.

Is the Word of God literally living, and an animate thing? No, it is an inanimate object. Is our Bible literally sharper than a two-edged sword? No, if we decide to stab someone with it, it would look quite silly. Is the Word of God literally able to pierce our joints and marrow? No, again, this would seem ridiculous. If we literally hold the Bible up to our head, is it able to discern our thinking, what we intend to do? What did Paul mean? The Word of God does these things by our being able to evaluate ourselves by looking into the light of the Scriptures, which helps us to identify the intentions of our heart, i.e., inner person. When we meditatively read God's Word daily and ponder what the author meant, we are taking into our mind, God's thoughts and intentions. When we accept the Bible as the inspired, inerrant Word of God, take its counsel and apply its principles in our lives, it will have an impact on our conscience. The conscience is the moral code that God gave Adam and Eve, our mental power or ability that enables us to reason between what is good and what is bad. (Rom. 9:1) Then, the inner voice within us is not entirely ours, but is also God's Word, empowering us to avoid choosing the wrong path.

1 John 2:24 Updated American Standard Version (UASV)

²⁴ As for you, let that remain [*meno*] in you which you heard from the beginning. If what you heard from the beginning remains [*meno*] in you, you also will remain [*meno*] in the Son and in the Father.

Those who had followed Jesus **from the beginning** of his three and half ministry cleaved to what they had heard about the Father and the Son. Therefore, if the same truths are within our heart, inner person, our mental power or ability, we too can **abide** or **remain [*meno*]** in the Son and the Father. (John 17:3) It is as James said, if we draw close to God, through his Word the Bible, he will draw close to us. (Jam. 4:8) In other words, God becomes a part of us and we a part of him through the Word of God that is "living and active, sharper than any two-edged sword, piercing to the division of soul and of spirit, of joints and of marrow, and discerning the thoughts and intentions of the heart."

In John chapter 14, we see this two-way relationship more closely. Jesus said, "Believe me that I am in the Father and the Father is in me, or else believe on account of the works themselves." **(14:11)** He also said, "In that day you will know that I am in my Father, and you in me, and I in you." **(14:20)** We see that the Father and Son have a close relationship, a relationship that we are invited to join.

All through the above discussion of the Father and the Son, we likely had no problem following the line of thought. However, once we interject the Holy Spirit, it is as though our common sense is thrown out. Christians know that the Father and the Son reside in heaven. They also understand that when we speak of the Word of God, the Father and the Son dwelling in us, it is in reference to our being one with them, our unified relationship, by way of the Word of God. However, when we contemplate the Holy Spirit, it is as though our mental powers shut down, and we enter the realms of the mysterious and mysticism. However, we just understood John **14:11** and **14:20**, i.e., how Jesus is in the Father, the Father in Jesus, and their being in us. So, let us now consider the verses that lie between verse **11** and **20**.

Jesus Promises the Holy Spirit

John 14:16-17 English Standard Version (ESV)

[16] And I will ask the Father, and he will give you another Helper, to be with you forever, [17] even the Spirit of truth, whom the world cannot receive, because it neither sees him nor knows him. You know him, for he dwells [*meno*] with you and will be in you.

John 14:16-17 Updated American Standard Version (UASV)

[16] And I will ask the Father, and he will give you another Helper, that he may be with you forever; [17] the Spirit of truth, whom the world cannot receive, because it does not see him or know him, but you know him because he remains [*meno*] with you and will be in you.

Do we not find it a bit disconcerting that, all along when looking at John's writings as to the Son and the Father abiding [*meno*] in one another, in us, and us in them. In those places, the translation rendered *meno* as abiding, but now that the Holy Spirit is mentioned, they render *meno* as "dwell."

Do these verses call for us to drive off the path of reason, into the realms of mysteriousness and mysticism talk? No, these verses are very similar to our 1 John 2:24 that we dealt with above, but will quote again, "Let what you heard from the beginning **abide [meno]** in you. If what you heard from the beginning **abides [meno]** in you, then you too will **abide [meno]** in the Son and in the Father." In 1 John 2:24, we are told that if the Word of God that we heard from the beginning of being a Christian, **abides [meno]** in us, we will **abide [meno]** in the Son and the Father. In John 14:15-17, if we keep Jesus' commands, the Holy Spirit will **dwell**, actually **abide [meno]** in us. In all of this, the common denominator has been the spirit inspired, fully inerrant Word of God. It is what we are to take into our mind and heart, which will affect change in our person, and enable us to abide or remain in the Father and the Son, and they in us, as well as the Holy Spirit, abiding or remaining in us.

The Holy Spirit, through the Spirit-inspired, inerrant Word of God is the motivating factor for our taking off the old person and putting on the new person. (Eph. 4:20-24; Col. 3:8-9) It is also the tool used by God so that we can "be transformed by the renewal of your mind so that you may approve what is the good and well-pleasing and perfect will of God." (Rom. 12:2; See 8:9) *The Theological Dictionary of the New Testament* compares this line of thinking with Paul's reference, at Romans 7:20, to the "sin that dwells within me."

The dwelling of sin in man denotes its dominion over him, its lasting connection with his flesh, and yet also a certain distinction from it. The sin which dwells in me (ἡ οἰκοῦσα ἐν ἐμοὶ ἁμαρτία) is no passing guest, but by its continuous presence becomes the master of the house (cf. Str.-B., III, 239).[272] Paul can speak in just the same way, however, of the lordship of the Spirit. The community knows (οὐκ οἴδατε, a reference to catechetical instruction, 1 C. 3:16) that the Spirit of God dwells in the new man (ἐν ὑμῖν οἰκεῖ, 1 C. 3:16; R. 8:9, 11). This "dwelling" is more than ecstatic rapture or impulsion by a superior power.[273]

How does the Holy Spirit control a Christian? Certainly, some mysterious or mystical feeling does not control him.

---

[272] Str.-B. H. L. Strack and P. Billerbeck, *Kommentar zum NT aus Talmud und Midrasch*, 1922 ff.

[273] Gerhard Kittel, Geoffrey W. Bromiley, and Gerhard Friedrich, eds., *Theological Dictionary of the New Testament* (Grand Rapids, MI: Eerdmans, 1964–), 135

Paul told the Christians in Rome,

Romans 12:2 Updated American Standard Version (UASV)

² And do not be conformed to this world, but be transformed by the **renewing of your mind**, so that you may prove what the will of God is, that which is good and acceptable and perfect.

Just how do we **renew our mind**? This is done by taking in an accurate knowledge of Biblical truth, which enables us to meet God's current standards of righteousness. (Titus 1:1) This Bible knowledge, if applied, will allow us to move our mind in a different direction, by filling the void, after having removed our former sinful practices, with the principles of God's Word, principles that guide our actions, especially ones that guide moral behavior.

Psalm 119:105 Updated American Standard Version (UASV)

¹⁰⁵ Your word is a lamp to my feet
and a light to my path.

The Biblical truths that lay in between Genesis 1:1 and Revelation 22:21 will transform our way of thinking, which will in return affect our mood and actions and our inner person. It will be as the apostle Paul said to the Ephesians. We need to "to put off your old self, which belongs to your former manner of life and is corrupt through deceitful desires, and to be renewed in the spirit of your minds, and to put on the new self, created after the likeness of God in true righteousness and holiness ..." (Eph. 4:22-24) This force that contributes to our acting or behaving in a certain way, for our best interest is internal.

Paul told the Christians in Colossae,

Colossians 3:9-11 Updated American Standard Version (UASV)

⁹ Do not lie to one another, seeing that you have put off the old man²⁷⁴ with its practices ¹⁰ and have put on the new man²⁷⁵ who is being **renewed through accurate knowledge**²⁷⁶ according to the image of the one who created him, ¹¹ where there is not Greek and Jew, circumcised and uncircumcised, barbarian, Scythian, slave, free; but Christ is all, and in all.

---

²⁷⁴ Or *old person*

²⁷⁵ Or *new person*

²⁷⁶ See Romans 3:20 ftn.

Science has indeed taken us a long way in our understanding of how the mind works, but it is only a grain of sand on the beach of sand in comparison to what we do not know. We have enough in these basics to understand some fundamental processes. When we open our eyes to the light of a new morning, it is altered into and electrical charge by the time it arrives at the gray matter of our brain's cerebral cortex. As the sound of the morning birds reaches our gray matter, it comes as electrical impulses. The rest of our senses (smell, taste, and touch) arrive as electrical currents in the brain's cortex as well. The white matter of our brain lies within the cortex of gray matter, used as a tool to send electrical messages to other cells in other parts of the gray matter. Thus, when anyone of our five senses detects danger, at the speed of light, a message is sent to the motor section, to prepare us for the needed action of either fight or flight.

Here lies the key to altering our way of thinking. Every single thought, whether it is conscious or subconscious makes an electrical path through the white matter of our brain, with a record of the thought and event. This holds true with our actions as well. If it is a repeated way of thinking or acting, it has no need to form a new path; it only digs a deeper, ingrained, established path.

This would explain how a factory worker who has been on the job for some time, gives little thought as he performs his repetitive functions each day; it becomes unthinking, automatic, mechanical. These repeated actions become habitual. There is yet another facet to be considered; the habits, repeated thoughts, and actions become simple and effortless to repeat. Any new thoughts and actions are harder to perform, as there need to be new pathways opened up.

The human baby starts with a blank slate, with a minimal amount of stable paths built in to survive those first few crucial years. As the boy grows into childhood, there is a flood of pathways established, more than all of the internet connections worldwide.

Our five senses are continuously adding to the maze. Ps. 139:14: "I will give thanks to you, for I am fearfully and wonderfully made. . . ." (NASB) So, it could never be overstated as to the importance of the foundational thinking and behavior that should be established in our children from infancy forward.

Paul told the Christians in Ephesus,

Ephesians 4:20-24 Updated American Standard Version (UASV)

²⁰ But you did not learn Christ in this way, ²¹ if indeed you have heard him and have been taught in him, just as truth is in Jesus, ²² that you take off, according to your former way of life, the old man, who is being destroyed according to deceitful desires, ²³ and to be **renewed in the spirit of your minds,** ²⁴ and put on the new man,²⁷⁷ the one created according to the likeness of God in righteousness and loyalty of the truth.

How are we to understand being **renewed in the spirit of our minds?** Christian living is carried out through the study and application of God's Word, in which, our spirit (mental disposition), is in harmony with God's Spirit. Our day-to-day decisions are made with a biblical mind, a biblically guided conscience, and a heart that is motivated by love of God and neighbor. Because we have,

- Received the Word of God,

- treasured up the Word of God,

- have been attentive to the Word of God,

- inclining our heart to understand the Word of God,

- calling out for insight into the Word of God,

- raising our voice for an understanding of the Word of God,

- sought the Word of God like silver,

- have searched for the Word of God like gold,

- we have come to understand the fear of God and have

- found the very knowledge of God, which now

- leads and directs us daily in our Christian walk.

Proverbs 23:7 New King James Version (NKJV)

⁷ For as he thinks in his heart, so is he. "Eat and drink!" he says to you, But his heart is not with you. [Our thinking affects our emotions, which in turn affects our behavior.]

---

²⁷⁷ An interpretive translation would have, "put on the new person," because it does mean male or female.

Irrational thinking produces irrational feelings, which will produce wrong moods, leading to wrong behavior. It may be difficult for each of us to wrap our mind around it, but we are very good at telling ourselves outright lies and half-truths, repeatedly throughout each day. In fact, some of us are so good at it that it has become our reality and leads to mental distress and bad behaviors.

When we couple our leaning toward wrongdoing with the fact that Satan the devil, who is "the god of this world," (2 Co 4:4) has worked to entice these leanings, the desires of the fallen flesh; we are even further removed from our relationship with our loving heavenly Father. During these 'last days, grievous times' has fallen on us as Satan is working all the more to prevent God's once perfect creation to achieve a righteous standing with God and entertaining the hope of eternal life. – 2 Timothy 3:1-5.

When we enter the pathway of walking with our God, we will certainly come across resistance from three different areas (Our sinful nature, Satan and demons, and the world that caters to our flesh). **Our greatest obstacle** is **ourselves** because we have inherited imperfection from our first parents Adam and Eve. The Scriptures make it quite clear that we are **mentally bent toward bad**, not good. (Gen 6:5; 8:21, AT) In other words, our natural desire is toward wrong. Prior to sinning, Adam and Eve were perfect, and they had the natural desire of doing good, and to go against that was to go against the grain of their inner person. Scripture also tells us of our inner person, our heart.

Jeremiah 17:9 Updated American Standard Version (UASV)

⁹ The **heart is more deceitful** than all else,
and desperately sick;
who can understand it?

Jeremiah's words should serve as a wake-up call, if we are to be pleasing in the eyes of our heavenly Father, we must focus on our inner person. Maybe we have been a Christian for many years; maybe we have a deep knowledge of Scripture, perhaps we feel that we are spiritually strong, and nothing will stumble us. Nevertheless, our heart can be enticed by secret desires, where he fails to dismiss them; he eventually commits a serious sin.

Our conscious thinking (aware) and subconscious thinking (present in our mind without our being aware of it) originates in the mind. For good, or for bad, our mind follows certain rules of action, which if entertained one will move even further in that direction until they are eventually consumed for good or for bad. In our imperfect state, our bent thinking will lean toward wrong, especially with Satan using his world, with so many forms of entertainment that simply feeds the flesh.

James 1:14-15 Updated American Standard Version (UASV)

[14] But each one is tempted when he is carried away and enticed by his own desire.[278] [15] Then the desire when it has conceived gives birth to sin, and sin when it is fully grown brings forth death.

1 John 2:16 Updated American Standard Version (UASV)

[16] For all that is in the world, the lust of the flesh and the lust of the eyes and the boastful pride of life, is not from the Father, but is from the world.

Matthew 5:28 Updated American Standard Version (UASV)

[28] but I say to you that everyone who looks at a woman with lust[279] for her has already committed adultery with her in his heart.

1 Peter 1:14 Updated American Standard Version (UASV)

[14] As children of obedience,[280] do not be conformed according to the desires you formerly had in your ignorance,

If we do not want to be affected by the world of humankind around us, which is alienated from God, we must again consider the words of the Apostle Paul's. He writes (Rom 12:2) "Do not be conformed to this world, but be transformed by the renewal of your mind that by testing you may discern what is the will of God, what is good and acceptable and perfect." Just how do we do that? This is done by taking in an accurate knowledge of the Biblical truth, which enables us to meet God's current standards of righteousness. (Titus 1:1) This Bible knowledge, if applied, will enable us to move our mind in a different direction, by filling the void with the principles of God's Word, principles that guide our actions, especially ones that guide moral behavior.

---

[278] Or "own *lust*"

[279] ἐπιθυμία [*Epithumia*] to strongly desire to have what belongs to someone else and/or to engage in an activity which is morally wrong–'to covet, to lust, evil desires, lust, desire.'– GELNTBSD

[280] I.e., *obedient children*

Psalm 119:105 Updated American Standard Version (UASV)

¹⁰⁵ Your word is a lamp to my feet
and a light to my path.

We have said this before but it bears repeating. The Biblical truths that lay in between Genesis 1:1 and Revelation 22:21 will transform our way of thinking, which will in return affect our mood and actions and our inner person. It will be as the apostle Paul set it out to the Ephesians. We need to "to put off your old self, which belongs to your former manner of life and is corrupt through deceitful desires, and to be renewed in the spirit of your minds, and to put on the new self, created after the likeness of God in true righteousness and holiness ..." (Eph. 4:22-24) This force that contributes to our acting or behaving in a certain way, for our best interest is internal.

Bringing This Transformation About

The mind is the mental ability that we use in a conscious way to garner information and to consider ideas and come to conclusions. Therefore, if we perceive our realities based on the information, which surrounds us, generally speaking, most are inundated in a world that reeks of Satan's influence. This means that our perception, our attitude, thoughts, speech, and conduct are in opposition to God and his Word. Most are in true ignorance to the changing power of God's Word. The apostle Paul helps us to appreciate the depths of those who reflect this world's disposition. He writes,

Ephesians 4:17-19 Updated American Standard Version (UASV)

¹⁷ This, therefore, I say and bear witness to in the Lord, that you no longer walk as the Gentiles [unbelievers] also walk, in the futility of their mind [emptiness, idleness, sluggishness, vanity, foolishness, purposelessness], ¹⁸ being darkened in their understanding [mind being the center of human perception], alienated from the life of God, because of the ignorance that is in them, because of the hardness of their heart [hardening as if by calluses, unfeeling]; ¹⁹ who being past feeling gave themselves up to shameless conduct,²⁸¹ for the practice of every uncleanness with greediness.

---

²⁸¹ Or "loose conduct," "sensuality," "licentiousness" "promiscuity" Greek, *aselgeia*. This phrase refers to acts of conduct that are serious sins. It reveals a shameless condescending arrogance; i.e., disregard or even disdain for authority, laws, and standards.

Hebrews 4:12 Updated American Standard Version (UASV)

[12] For the word of God is living and active and sharper than any two-edged sword, and piercing as far as the division of soul and spirit, of both joints and marrow, and able to judge the thoughts and intentions of the heart.

By taking in this knowledge of God's Word, we will be altering our way of thinking, which will affect our emotions and behavior, as well as our lives now and for eternity. This Word will influence our minds, making corrections in the way we think. If we are to have the Holy Spirit controlling our lives, we must 'renew our mind' (Rom. 12:2) "which is being renewed in knowledge" (Col. 3:10) of God and his will and purposes. (Matt 7:21-23; See Pro 2:1-6) All of this boils down to each individual Christian digging into the Scriptures in a meditative way, so he can 'discover the knowledge of God, receiving wisdom; from God's mouth, as well as knowledge and understanding.' (Pro. 2:5-6) As he acquires the mind that is inundated with the Word of God, he must also,

James 1:22-25 Updated American Standard Version (UASV)

[22] But be doers of the word, and not hearers only, deceiving yourselves. [23] For if anyone is a hearer of the word and not a doer, he is like a man who looks intently at his natural face[282] in a mirror.

[24] for he looks at himself and goes away, and immediately forgets what sort of man he was. [25] But he that looks into the perfect law, the law of liberty, and abides by it, being no hearer who forgets but a doer of a work, he will be blessed in his doing.

---

[282] Lit *the face of his birth*

Bibliography

Aland, Kurt, and Barbara Aland. *The Text of the New Testament.* Grand Rapids: Eerdmans, 1995.

Anders, Max. *Holman New Testament Commentary: vol. 8, Galatians, Ephesians, Philippians, Colossians.* Nashville, TN: Broadman & Holman Publishers, 1999.

—. *Holman Old Testament Commentary - Proverbs .* Nashville: B&H Publishing, 2005.

Anders, Max, and Doug McIntosh. *Holman Old Testament Commentary - Deuteronomy.* Nashville: B&H Publishing, 2009.

Anders, Max, and Steven Lawson. *Holman Old Testament Commentary - Psalms: 11.* Grand Rapids: B&H Publishing, 2004.

Anders, Max, and Trent Butler. *Holman Old Testament Commentary: Isaiah.* Nashiville, TN: B&H Publishing, 2002.

Andrews, Stephen J, and Robert D Bergen. *Holman Old Testament Commentary: 1-2 Samuel.* Nashville: Broadman & Holman, 2009.

Archer, Gleason L. *A Survey of Old Testament Introduction.* Chicago: Moody, 1994.

—. *Encyclopedia of Bible Difficulties.* Grand Rapids: Zondervan, 1982.

Baer, Daniel. *The Unquenchable Fire.* Maitland, FL: Xulon Press, 2007.

Barnett, Paul. *The Birth of Christianity: The First Twenty Years (After Jesus, Vol. 1) .* Grand Rapids, MI: Wm. B. Eerdmans , 2005.

Boa, Kenneth, and William Kruidenier. *Holman New Testament Commentary: Romans.* Nashville: Broadman & Holman, 2000.

Borgen, Peder. *Philo of Alexandria: An Exegete for His Time.* Leiden, Boston: Brill, 1997.

Brand, Chad, Charles Draper, and England Archie. *Holman Illustrated Bible Dictionary: Revised, Updated and Expanded.* Nashville, TN: Holman, 2003.

Bromiley, Geoffrey W. *The International Standard Bible Encyclopedia (Vol. 1-4).* Grand Rapids, MI: William B. Eerdmans Publishing Co., 1986.

Butler, Trent C. *Holman New Testament Commentary: Luke.* Nashville, TN: Broadman & Holman Publishers, 2000.

Butler, Trent C. *Holman Old Testament Commentary - Hosea, Joel, Amos, Obadiah, Jonah, Micah .* Nashville: Broadman & Holman Publishers, 2005.

Carson, D. A. *The Gospel According to John, The Pillar New Testament Commentary.* Leicester, England; Grand Rapids, MI: Inter-Varsity Press; W.B. Eerdmans, 1991.

Comfort, Philip. *Encounterring the Manuscripts: An Introduction to New Testament Paleography and Textual Criticism.* Nashville: Broadman & Holman, 2005.

Comfort, Philip W. *New Testament Text and Translation Commentary.* Carol Stream: Tyndale House Publishers, 2008.

Comfort, Philip Wesley. *The Quest for the Original Text of the New Testament.* Eugene: Wipf and Stock, 1992.

Cooper, Rodney. *Holman New Testament Commentary: Mark.* Nashville: Broadman & Holman Publishers, 2000.

Cruse, C. F. *Eusebius' Eccliatical History.* Peabody, MA: Hendrickson, 1998.

Davids, Peter H. *The Letters of 2 Peter and Jude, The Pillar New Testament Commentary.* Grand Rapids, MI: William B. Eerdmans Pub. Co., 2006.

Deissmann, Adolf. *LIGHT FROM THE ANCIENT EAST: The New Testament Illustrated by Recently Discovered Texts of the Graeco-Roman World.* New York and London: Hodder and Stoughton, 1910.

Easley, Kendell H. *Holman New Testament Commentary, vol. 12, Revelation.* (Nashville, TN: Broadman & Holman Publishers, 1998.

Edwards, James R. *The Pillar New Testament Commentary: The Gospel according to Mark.* Grand Rapids: Wm. B. Eerdmans Publishing Co., 2002.

Ehrman, Bart D. *Misquoting Jesus: The Story Behind Who Changed the Bible and Why.* New York: Harper One, 2005.

Ehrman, Bart D. Holmes, Michael W. *The Text of the New Testament in Contemporary Research: Essays on the Status Quaestionis* . Grand Rapids, MI: Eerdmans, 1995.

Ehrman, Bart D. *Lost Christianities: The Battles for Scripture and the Faiths We Never Knew* . New York: Oxford University Press, 2003.

Elwell, Walter A. *Baker Encyclopedia of the Bible.* Grand Rapids: Baker Book House, 1988.

F. Garcia Martinez, Julio Barrera, Trebolle, Florentino Garcia Martinez, and J. Trebolle Barrera. *The People of the Dead Sea Scrolls: Their Writings, Beliefs and Practices.* Leiden: Brill Academic, 1995.

Ferguson, Everett. *Backgrounds of Early Christianity.* Grand Rapids, MI: Wm. B. Eerdmans, 2003.

Gamble, Henry Y. *Books and Readers in the Early Church: A History of Early Christian Texts.* New Haven: New Haven University Press, 1995.

Gangel, Kenneth O. *Holman New Testament Commentary: Acts.* Nashville, TN: Broadman & Holman Publishers, 1998.

Gangel, Kenneth O. *Holman New Testament Commentary, vol. 4, John* . Nashville, TN: Broadman & Holman Publishers, 2000.

—. *Holman Old Testament Commentary: Daniel.* Nashville: Broadman & Holman Publishers, 2001.

Geisler, Norman L. *Baker Encyclopedia of Christian Apologetics.* Grand Rapids: Baker Books, 1999.

Greenlee, J Harold. *Introduction to New Testament Textual Criticism.* Peabody: Hendrickson, 1995.

Grudem, Wayne, Leland Ryken, John C Collins, Vern S Poythress, and Bruce Winter. *Translating Truth: The Case for Essentially Literal Bible Translation.* Wheaton: Crossway Books, 2005.

Hill, Charles E., and Michael J. Kruger. *The Early Text of the New Testament.* Oxford: Oxford University Press, 2012.

Hindson, Ed, and Ergun Caner. *The Popular Encyclopedia of Apologetics: Surveying the Evidence for the Truth of Christianity.* Eugene: Harvest House, 2008.

Holmes, Michael W. *The Apostolic Fathers: Greek Texts and English Translations.* Grand Rapids: Baker Academics, 2007.

Johnson, William A, and Holt N Parker. *Ancient Literacies: The Culture of Reading in Greece and Rome.* Oxford: Oxford University Press, 2011.

Komoszewski, J. Ed, James M. Sawyer, and Daniel Wallace. *Reinventing Jesus .* Grand Rapids, MI: Kregel Publications, 2006.

Larson, Knute. *Holman New Testament Commentary, vol. 9, I & II Thessalonians, I & II Timothy, Titus, Philemon.* Nashville, TN: Broadman & Holman Publishers, 2000.

Lea, Thomas D. *Holman New Testament Commentary: Vol. 10, Hebrews, James.* Nashville, TN: Broadman & Holman Publishers, 1999.

Manser, Martin H. (Managing Editor) McGrath, Alister E. (General Editor) Packer, J. I. (Consultant Editor). *DICTIONARY OF BIBLE THEMES: The Accessible and Comprehenssive Tool for Topical Studies.* Grand Rapids: Zondervan Publishing Company, 2009.

Martin, Glen S. *Holman Old Testament Commentary: Numbers.* Nashville: Broadman & Holman Publishers, 2002.

McKenzie, John L. *Light on the Epistles: A Reader's Guide.* Chicago, IL: Thomas More Press, 1975.

Metzger, Bruce M. *The Text of the New Testament: Its Transmission, Corruption, and Transmission.* New York: Oxford University Press, 1964, 1968, 1992.

Metzger, Bruce M. *A Textual Commentary on the Greek New Testament.* New York: United Bible Society, 1994.

Metzger, Bruce M., and Bart D. Ehrman. *The Text of the New Testament: Its Transmission, Corruption, and Restoration (4th Edition).* New York: Oxford University Press, 2005.

Moo, Douglas. *The Letter of James: Pillar New Testament Commentary.* Grand Rapids: William B. Eerdman's Publishing Company, 2000.

Mounce, William D. *Mounce's Complete Expository Dictionary of Old & New Testament Words.* Grand Rapids, MI: Zondervan, 2006.

Myers, Allen C. *The Eerdmans Bible Dictionary .* Grand Rapids, Mich: Eerdmans, 1987.

O'Brien, Peter Thomas. *The Pillar New Testament commentary: The Letter to the Ephesians .* Grand Rapids, MI : Eerdmans Publishing Co, 1999.

Orchard, Bernard. *J. J. Griesbach: Synoptic and Text - Critical Studies* . Cambridge: Cambridge University Press, 1776-1976, 2005.

Parker, David C. *The living Text of the Gospels.* Cambridge: Cambridge University Press, 1997.

Pratt Jr, Richard L. *Holman New Testament Commentary: I & II Corinthians, vol. 7.* Nashville: Broadman & Holman Publishers, 2000.

Ramm, Bernard. *Protestant Biblical Interpretation: A Textbook of Hermeneutics, 3rd rev. ed.* Grand Rapids, MI: Baker, 1999.

Ray, Vernon. "The Formal vs Dynamic Equivalent Principle in New Testament Translation." *Restoration Quarterly 25*, 1982: 46-56.

Richards, E. Randolph. *The Secretary in the Letters of Paul.* Tübingen: J.C.B. Mohr, 1990.

Robertson, A. T. *An Introduction to the Textual Criticism of the New Testament.* London: Hodder & Stoughton, 1925.

Rooker, Mark F. *Holman Old Testament Commentary: Ezekiel.* Nashville: Broadman & Holman Publishers, 2005.

Royse, James R. *Scribal Habits in Early Greek New Testament Papyri (New Testament Tools and Studies) (New Testament Tools, Studies and Documents).* Leiden & Boston: Brill Academic Pub, 2008.

Schurer, Emil. *A HISTORY OF THE JEWISH PEOPLE IN THE TIME OF JESUS CHRIST (Volume II).* Edinburgh: T. & T. Clark, 1890.

Scott, Julius J. Jr. *Jewish Backgrounds of the New Testament.* Grand Rapids, MI: Baker Academic, 1995.

Sproul, R. C. *KOWING SCRIPTURE (Expanded ed.).* Downers Groves: InterVarsity Press, 2016.

Stein, Robert H. *A Basic Guide to Interpreting the Bible: Playing by the Rules.* Grand Rapids: Baker Books, 1994.

Terry, Milton S. *Biblical Hermeneutics: A Treatise on the Interpretation of the Old and New Testaments.* Grand Rapids: Zondervan, 1974.

Thomas, Robert L. *Evangelical Hermeneutics.* Grand Rapids: Kregel Publications, 2002.

Thomas, Robert L. ""Current Hermeneutical Trends: Toward Explanation or Obfuscation?" *JETS 39*, June 1996: 241-256.

Vine, W E. *Vine's Expository Dictionary of Old and New Testament Words.* Nashville: Thomas Nelson, 1996.

Virkler, Henry A, and Karelynne Gerber Ayayo. *Hermeneutics: Principles and Processes of Biblical Interpretation.* Grand Rapids, MI: Baker Academic, 1981, 2007.

Walls, David, and Max Anders. *Holman New Testament Commentary: I & II Peter, I, II & III John, Jude.* Nashville: Broadman & Holman Publishers, 1996.

Walton, John H., Victor H. Matthews, and Mark W Chavalas. *The IVP Bible Background Commentary: Old Testament.* Downers Grove: IVP Academic, 2000.

Weber, Stuart K. *Holman New Testament Commentary, vol. 1, Matthew.* Nashville, TN: Broadman & Holman Publishers, 2000.

Wegner, Paul D. *A Student's Guide to Textual Criticism of the Bible: Its History Methods & Results.* Downers Grove: InterVarsity Press, 2006.

Westcott, B. F., and Hort F. J. A. *The New Testament in the Original Greek, Vol. 2: Introduction, Appendix.* London: Macmillan and Co., 1882.

Whiston, William. *The Works of Josephus.* Peabody, MA: Hendrickson, 1987.

Wood, D R W. *New Bible Dictionary (Third Edition).* Downers Grove: InterVarsity Press, 1996.

Made in the USA
Middletown, DE
19 January 2023

22588649R00187